ReadyGEN®

W9-BIG-437

GRADE **4**

Scaffolded Strategies
HANDBOOK

PEARSON

Glenview, Illinois • Boston, Massachusetts • Chandler, Arizona • Upper Saddle River, New Jersey

Acknowledgments of third-party content appear on page 461, which constitutes an extension of this copyright page.

ISBN-13: 978-0-328-85173-7
ISBN-10:   0-328-85173-6
6 7 8 9 10   19 18 17 16

Table of Contents

Part 1 Unlock the Text

Unit 1 Becoming Researchers 4

MODULE A
Cognate Chart 6
Anchor Text Porpoises in Peril 8
Supporting Text Mary Anning: The Girl Who Cracked Open the World 14
Supporting Text The Frog Scientist 20

MODULE B
Cognate Chart 26
Anchor Text Skeletons Inside and Out 28
Supporting Text Movers and Shapers 34
Supporting Text King of the Parking Lot 40

Unit 2 Interactions in Nature and Culture 46

MODULE A
Cognate Chart 48
Anchor Text Why the Sea Is Salty 50
Supporting Text How the Stars Fell into the Sky 56
Supporting Text Pecos Bill and John Henry 62

MODULE B
Cognate Chart 68
Anchor Text The Longest Night 70
Supporting Text Northwest Coast Peoples 76
Supporting Text Three Native Nations: Of the Woodlands, Plains, and Desert 82

Unit 3 Exploring Impact and Effect 88

MODULE A

Cognate Chart 90
Anchor Text Earthquakes. 92
Supporting Text Quake!. 98
Supporting Text Earthshaker's Bad Day; The Monster Beneath the Sea 104

MODULE B

Cognate Chart 110
Anchor Text Anatomy of a Volcanic Eruption. 112
Supporting Text Escape from Pompeii 118
Supporting Text A Tsunami Unfolds 124

Unit 4 Creating Innovative Solutions. 130

MODULE A

Cognate Chart 132
Anchor Text Lunch Money. 134
Supporting Text Max Malone Makes a Million. 140
Supporting Text Coyote School News. 146

MODULE B

Cognate Chart 152
Anchor Text Using Money 154
Supporting Text A Tale of Two Poggles. 160
Supporting Text The Boy Who Invented TV. 166

Table of Contents

Part 2 Unlock the Writing

Scaffolded Lessons for the Performance-Based Assessments

Unit 1, Module A: Informative/Explanatory 175

Unit 1, Module B: Informative/Explanatory 181

Unit 2, Module A: Narrative 187

Unit 2, Module B: Opinion 193

Unit 3, Module A: Opinion 199

Unit 3, Module B: Informative/Explanatory 205

Unit 4, Module A: Narrative 211

Unit 4, Module B: Opinion 217

Scaffolded Lessons for the Writing Types

Unlock Opinion Writing 224

Unlock Informative/Explanatory Writing 234

Unlock Narrative Writing 244

Part 3 Routines and Activities

Reading Routines

Quick Write and Share. 258

Ask and Answer Questions. 259

Three-Column Chart with Graphic Organizer 261

Venn Diagram with Graphic Organizer. 263

Web with Graphic Organizer. 265

Story Map with Graphic Organizer. 267

Story Prediction with Graphic Organizer. 269

Story Comparison with Graphic Organizer 271

KWLH with Graphic Organizer 273

Main Idea and Details with Graphic Organizer 275

Problem and Solution with Graphic Organizer 277

Cause and Effect with Graphic Organizer. 279

Steps in a Process with Graphic Organizer. 281

Sequence of Events with Graphic Organizer. 283

Time Line with Graphic Organizer 285

Draw Conclusions with Graphic Organizer 287

Writing Routines

Narrative Paragraph Writing with Graphic Organizer. 289

Narrative Essay Writing with Graphic Organizer. 291

Informative/Explanatory Writing with Graphic Organizer 293

Opinion Writing with Graphic Organizer 295

Description: Sensory Details with Graphic Organizer 297

Table of Contents

Listening and Speaking Routines

Retell or Summarize with Graphic Organizer 299

Monitor Understanding: Listening Skills Log 301

Express Opinions 303

Prepare for Discussions 304

Understanding Media 306

Language Routines and Activities: Vocabulary and Conventions

Preview and Review Vocabulary 307

Act Out or Draw Meaning 308

Analyze Cognates 310

Word Knowledge Strategy 313

Multisyllabic Word Strategy 314

Analyze Idioms and Expressions 315

Analyze Multiple-Meaning Words 316

Noun Activities 317

Pronoun Activities 321

Verb Activities 324

Articles and Adjective Activities 330

Adverb Activities 332

Preposition and Conjunction Activities 333

Sentence Activities 334

Punctuation Activities 340

Word Study Activities 342

Vocabulary Activities and Games 360

Part 4 Unlock Language Learning

Anchor Text, Supporting Text, and Writing

Unit 1 Module A Anchor Text and Supporting Text 367

Module B Anchor Text and Supporting Text 374

Module A and B Writing 381

Unit 2 Module A Anchor Text and Supporting Text 384

Module B Anchor Text and Supporting Text 393

Module A and B Writing 400

Unit 3 Module A Anchor Text and Supporting Text 403

Module B Anchor Text and Supporting Text 412

Module A and B Writing 419

Unit 4 Module A Anchor Text and Supporting Text 422

Module B Anchor Text and Supporting Text 429

Module A and B Writing 436

Language Routines and Resources

Language Routines 439

Language Resources 453

Acknowledgments

Acknowledgments 461

About This Book

What is the Scaffolded Strategies Handbook?

The *Scaffolded Strategies Handbook* is a valuable resource that provides support at the module level for all learners. As part of an integrated reading and writing program, this handbook works in tandem with each unit of the *ReadyGEN™ Teacher's Guide* to help you guide students as they read and write about the texts within each module. It provides models of scaffolded instruction, useful strategies, and practical routines that you can employ during reading and writing to support

- English language learners
- struggling readers
- students with disabilities
- accelerated learners

It is intended that these lessons be used during small-group time with students that you determine need additional scaffolded instruction for any of the ReadyGEN texts or writing activities. Refer to this handbook during planning to determine which lessons will provide the most focused scaffolds for your students. You may use any or all of the lessons or lesson parts as dictated by the needs of your students. Keep in mind that this handbook is meant not only for the classroom teacher, but can be used by any support person working with the diverse student population in your school.

Using the Scaffolded Strategies Handbook

Part 1 Unlock the Text

Within Part 1 of this handbook, titled Unlock the Text, every anchor and supporting text in the ReadyGEN program is supported by research-proven scaffolds and strategies. Each lesson is divided into three parts:

- **Prepare to Read** This portion of the lesson provides more intensive readiness before reading. Students preview the text, activate background knowledge, and are introduced to troublesome vocabulary.

- **Interact with Text** Here, students do close reading and focus on stumbling blocks in the text.

- **Express and Extend** This section allows students to react to the text by discussing and writing about their ideas.

With every student text, qualitative measures of text complexity, such as those determined by the Common Core Learning Standards, are identified:

- Levels of Meaning
- Structure
- Language Conventionality and Clarity
- Knowledge Demands

Each of the three lesson parts is divided to address all of these qualitative measures. These become customized access points for your specific student populations, allowing all students to access and make sense of complex texts.

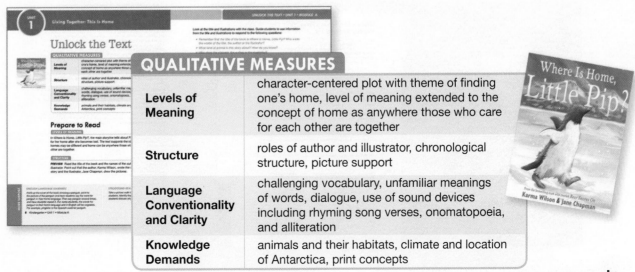

QUALITATIVE MEASURES	
Levels of Meaning	character-centered plot with theme of finding one's home, level of meaning extended to the concept of home as anywhere those who care for each other are together
Structure	roles of author and illustrator, chronological structure, picture support
Language Conventionality and Clarity	challenging vocabulary, unfamiliar meanings of words, dialogue, use of sound devices including rhyming song verses, onomatopoeia, and alliteration
Knowledge Demands	animals and their habitats, climate and location of Antarctica, print concepts

Part 2 Unlock the Writing

Part 2 of this handbook, titled Unlock the Writing, features two types of scaffolded writing lessons.

First, there are scaffolded lessons for each of the module-level Performance-Based Assessments in the core Teacher's Guide. Each lesson in the handbook walks students through the Performance-Based Assessment for that module, providing guidance with unlocking the task, breaking it apart, thinking through the process, and then evaluating their writing.

Next, there are scaffolded writing lessons that provide grade-appropriate support and guidelines for teaching each of the writing types required by the Common Core Learning Standards:

- Opinion Writing
- Informative/Explanatory Writing
- Narrative Writing

Each of these three lessons is divided into the tasks specific to the writing type. Instructional support is provided to help you introduce and model each task so that students will better understand the writing type and how to become proficient writers of each. There are ample opportunities for practice, including robust Deeper Practice activities.

As in Part 1, Unlock the Text lessons, the Unlock the Writing lessons provide specific scaffolded "notes" to support English language learners as well as both struggling and accelerated writers.

Part 3 Routines and Activities

Part 3 of the *Scaffolded Strategies Handbook* is a collection of routines and reproducible graphic organizers as well as engaging activities that you can use for support as you teach English Language Arts skills and address the Common Core Learning Standards. When appropriate, specific routines and activities are suggested and referred to in the lessons in Part 1 of this handbook.

You will find routines, many with accompanying graphic organizers, for teaching skills in

- Reading
- Writing
- Listening and Speaking
- Language, including Vocabulary and Conventions

Part 3 also contains a variety of activities that provide extra scaffolded practice and instruction for language skills and vocabulary development, such as

- Noun and Pronoun Activities
- Verb Activities
- Adjective and Adverb Activities
- Sentence Activities
- Punctuation Activities
- Word Study Activities
- Vocabulary Activities and Games

This section of the handbook will be useful at any time during your teaching day. As you become familiar with the routines, graphic organizers, and activities, feel free to use them whenever they fit the needs of your students. Think of this section as a toolbox of ideas and suggestions to use with your struggling readers and writers. Turn to it often.

Using the Scaffolded Strategies Handbook

Part 4 Unlock Language Learning

Part 4 of the *Scaffolded Strategies Handbook* provides additional instruction for each Anchor Text selection and for each Supporting Text selection in the ReadyGEN program. Use these lessons to help English language learners construct meaning in the selections and explore vocabulary in order to develop mastery of reading, writing, and speaking.

Part 4 scaffolded support includes:

- **Build Background** Students explore important information needed to comprehend and enjoy each selection. Student pages provide practice and stimulate conversation.

- **Talk About Sentences** Students discover how good sentences are constructed. They learn to access key ideas by understanding the relationships between words and phrases in sentences.

- **Speak and Write About the Text** Students build academic language skills by asking and answering critical questions. Writing frames support students' development as they express ideas in specific writing modes.

- **Expand Understanding of Vocabulary** Students discover the generative nature of vocabulary and develop a curiosity about language as they gain an understanding of how words function in sentences.

- **Writing** Students benefit from extra scaffolding, including a student model, as they work toward addressing the Performance-Based Assessment writing prompt.

The following **Part 4** Routines provide English language learners with additional scaffolded instruction in reading, speaking, and listening.

- Dig Deeper Vocabulary
- Sentence Talk
- Clarifying Key Details
- Clarifying Information
- Have a Discussion
- Reach a Consensus
- Text-Based Writing

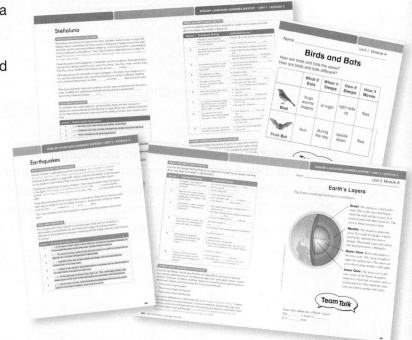

PART 1

Unlock the Text

Becoming Researchers

MODULE A **Cognate Chart**.. **6**

Anchor Text Science Squad: Porpoises in Peril......................... **8**

Supporting Text Mary Anning: The Girl Who Cracked
Open the World **14**

Supporting Text Fragile Frogs *from* The Frog Scientist **20**

TEXT SET

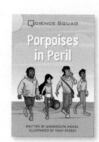

ANCHOR TEXT
Porpoises in Peril

SUPPORTING TEXT
Mary Anning: The Girl Who
Cracked Open the World

SUPPORTING TEXT
Fragile Frogs *from*
The Frog Scientist

MODULE B **Cognate Chart**.. **26**

Anchor Text Skeletons Inside and Out.................................. **28**

Supporting Text Movers and Shapers **34**

Supporting Text King of the Parking Lot............................... **40**

TEXT SET

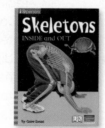

ANCHOR TEXT
Skeletons Inside and Out

SUPPORTING TEXT
Movers and Shapers

SUPPORTING TEXT
King of the Parking Lot

Cognates

Cognates are words that have similar spellings and meanings in two or more languages. Many words in English and Spanish share Greek or Latin roots, and many words in English came from French, which is closely connected to Spanish (and to Portuguese, Italian, and Romanian). Because of this, many literary, content, and academic process words in English (e.g., *gracious/ gracioso; volcano/volcán; compare/comparar*) have recognizable Spanish cognates.

Making the connection to cognates permits students who are native Spanish speakers to understand the strong foundation they have in academic and literary English. These links between English and Spanish are also useful for native speakers of English and other languages because they help uncover basic underlying features of our language.

ANCHOR TEXT **Science Squad: Porpoises in Peril**

ENGLISH	SPANISH	ENGLISH	SPANISH
agency	agencia	initials	iniciales
algae	algas	interrupted	interrumpió
arrest	arrestar	lenses	lentes
botanist	botánico	member	miembro
cedar	cedro	mining	minería
citrus	cítrico	ocean	océano
coast	costa	opals	ópalos
colleagues	colegas	particles	partículas
company	compañía	population	población
concentration	concentración	precious	precioso
connection	conexión	prove	probar
contaminated	contaminado	recently	recientemente
disappeared	desapareció	recognize	reconocer
disastrous	desastroso	satellite	satélite
dismantle	desmantelar	sediment	sedimento
ecological	ecológico	signal	señal
effects	efectos	stable	estable
emergencies	emergencias	station	estación
engineering	ingeniería	strange	extraño
equipment	equipamiento	terrace	terraza
eventually	eventualmente	thermometer	termómetro
executive	ejecutivo	tourists	turistas
formulate	formular	transportation	transporte
hypothesis	hipótesis	triumph	triunfo
illegal	ilegal	tunnel	túnel
importance	importancia	unusual	inusual

SUPPORTING TEXT Mary Anning: The Girl Who Cracked Open the World

ENGLISH	SPANISH	ENGLISH	SPANISH
collectors	coleccionistas	fossils	fósiles
completely	completamente	geology	geología
convinced	convencido	independent	independiente
creatures	criaturas	magnificent	magnífico
curiosities	curiosidades	monster	monstruo
detailed	detallado	mystery	misterio
dinosaur	dinosaurio	paleontology	paleontología
discoveries	descubrimientos	rock	roca
enormous	enorme	skeleton	esqueleto
experts	expertos	south	sur
exposed	expuesto	survive	sobrevivir
extinct	extinto	treasure	tesoro

SUPPORTING TEXT Fragile Frogs *from* The Frog Scientist

ENGLISH	SPANISH	ENGLISH	SPANISH
amphibian	anfibio	native	nativo
animal	animal	ozone	ozono
area	área	parasite	parásito
combine	combinar	park	parque
conference	conferencia	populations	poblaciones
deformity	deformidad	prevent	prevenir
difficult	difícil	problem	problema
extinction	extinción	scientists	científicos
global	global	similar	similar
habitat	hábitat	species	especie
imagine	imaginar	stomach	estómago
international	internacional	surprise	sorpresa
national	nacional	temperature	temperatura
		vulnerable	vulnerable

These lists contain many, but not all, Spanish cognates from these selections.

Unlock the Text

QUALITATIVE MEASURES

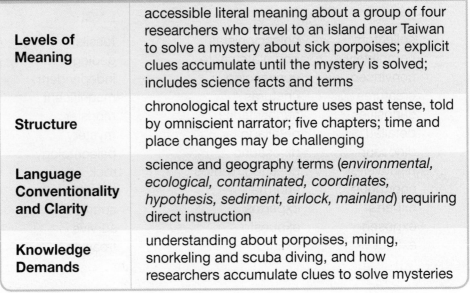

Levels of Meaning	accessible literal meaning about a group of four researchers who travel to an island near Taiwan to solve a mystery about sick porpoises; explicit clues accumulate until the mystery is solved; includes science facts and terms
Structure	chronological text structure uses past tense, told by omniscient narrator; five chapters; time and place changes may be challenging
Language Conventionality and Clarity	science and geography terms (*environmental, ecological, contaminated, coordinates, hypothesis, sediment, airlock, mainland*) requiring direct instruction
Knowledge Demands	understanding about porpoises, mining, snorkeling and scuba diving, and how researchers accumulate clues to solve mysteries

SCIENCE SQUAD

Porpoises in Peril

WRITTEN BY GWENDOLYN HOOKS
ILLUSTRATED BY TONY FORBES

Prepare to Read

LEVELS OF MEANING

Porpoises in Peril is the story of four researchers (Jada, Kate, Cam, and Reggie) led by Professor Q, who travel to an island near Taiwan to find out why the local porpoises are losing weight and acting strangely. By interviewing people and making intelligent observations, they work together to solve the mystery and bring a criminal to justice.

STRUCTURE

PREVIEW Have students read the title of the story. Explain that this is a fictional narrative that includes many scientific facts. Make sure

ENGLISH LANGUAGE LEARNERS

Pair students at different reading levels together to serve as buddies to partner read. Prior to reading, allow partners to preview the text together to locate unfamiliar words. Use the Word Knowledge Strategy Routine in Part 3 to help students define as many words as possible prior to reading.

STRUGGLING READERS

Use a world map to point out Los Angeles, Taipei, Taiwan, and Japan. Explain that the four main characters in this story will travel by airplane to a tiny island between Taiwan and Japan. Point out the illustrations on pages 9, 11, 14, 21, and 28 that show what the island looks like.

that students understand what a porpoise is. Refer them to the illustrations of porpoises on pages 7, 26, and 40. Introduce and define the word *predicament* (a difficult or challenging situation). Ask: What kind of predicaments might a porpoise experience? (They might not have enough to eat. They might be chased by a larger fish. They might get sick or injured.)

LANGUAGE CONVENTIONALITY AND CLARITY

PREVIEW VOCABULARY Use the Preview and Review Vocabulary Routine in Part 3 to assess what students know about the following words: *contaminated, population, formulate, snorkeling, dredged, depths, scrutinize, evidence,* and *dismantle.*

COGNATES Use the list of Spanish cognates at the beginning of this module to guide your Spanish-speaking students as they read the selection.

DOMAIN-SPECIFIC VOCABULARY Use the Vocabulary Activities in Part 3 to pre-teach the following domain-specific vocabulary: *environmental, ecological, algae, coordinates, hypothesis, coral reefs, pods, barge, current, sediment, airlock,* and *opal.* Explain that these words are all associated with ocean science or mining.

KNOWLEDGE DEMANDS

ACTIVATE BACKGROUND KNOWLEDGE Explain that the main characters in *Porpoises in Peril* work together to solve a mystery. Ask students to share what they already know about solving mysteries. Use the Quick Write and Share Routine in Part 3. Ask: How do detectives and scientists find out about mysteries? What ways do they gather information? How do they see connections between clues? What allows or leads them to solve the mysteries?

STRUGGLING READERS

Many students with reading difficulties will rely on the illustrations to understand what is happening in the text. Consider having students write captions for each illustration that uses details from the story. For example, the caption of the illustration on page 3 might be "Jada walked into the agency to meet the other members of the Science Squad."

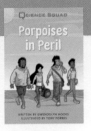

Interact with Text

As you read *Porpoises in Peril*, assess students' understanding of how researchers observe and record clues that add up to solutions. For example on page 12, Jada says "Let's start with what we know." Then, beginning with the man with the briefcase on page 16, they begin to observe and keep track of clues. Have students list all of the clues that lead to solving the mystery.

If . . . students have difficulty identifying the clues and how they "add up,"

then . . . use the Cause and Effect Routine and Graphic Organizer in Part 3 to support understanding.

Suggest to students that a clue is like a cause. It connects to an understanding that is like an effect. For example, the letters "DD" are a clue. They lead the researchers to realize that Drake Darkly Jewels is part of the solution to the mystery.

STRUCTURE

Point out that the story is told in chronological order beginning with the meeting of the Science Squad and Professor Q and ending with them going surfing. The narrative happens in five chapters. Have students summarize each chapter after they read it. Each chapter's summary should include a beginning, middle, and end. Help students understand how much time passes between chapters. Also, make sure they understand where each chapter takes place.

If . . . students have difficulty summarizing each chapter, including time and place,

then . . . use the Story Sequence Routine and Graphic Organizer in Part 3 to support understanding.

Have students complete a Story Sequence graphic organizer for each of the five chapters, using specific details from the text.

MORE SUPPORT

ENGLISH LANGUAGE LEARNERS

Have small groups of students at various reading levels work together to write a list of questions they have about key events in the story. Then have students switch papers and respond to another group's questions. Share some questions and responses as a class.

STRUGGLING READERS

To help students sequence the major events of each chapter, create a time line using the words *first, next, then,* and *finally*. Help students understand that they can use their chapter summaries to write a summary of the entire story using these same transition words.

LANGUAGE CONVENTIONALITY AND CLARITY

While much of the language will be clear and accessible to students, they may need extra support with terms about science and geography.

If . . . students have difficulty understanding science and geography terms and other domain-specific language,

then . . . make a list of the terms and their definitions to display in the classroom.

In addition, remind students that context can help them define unfamiliar words. For example, when Kate asks "What about any unusual algae?" on page 19, the context in the next sentence can help them understand that algae is a plant that lives in coastal waters.

Have students use context clues to understand other scientific terms that may be unfamiliar. Remind students that the illustrations can also help them with unfamiliar science words. For example, the illustration on page 43 will help them understand what an *opal* looks like. The illustration on pages 44-45 can help them understand *airlock*.

KNOWLEDGE DEMANDS

Some students may not be familiar with the actions of snorkeling and diving. They also may be unfamiliar with underwater mining equipment. Show students images of these activities and the equipment they use and require from nonfiction texts or from the Internet and have them compare and contrast the images with the illustrations in the story. Make sure they understand that the underwater playground is not a playground at all. The mining equipment includes parts that look like a ladder, a slide, and a jungle gym that allows a person to enter and exit the mine.

ENGLISH LANGUAGE LEARNERS

Have students work in pairs to read parts of the story aloud, taking turns with each new paragraph. Both reading aloud and hearing text read aloud make it significantly easier for students to process information and picture what it happening. After students read an entire chapter, have them recall and list the most important words and what they mean.

MORE SUPPORT

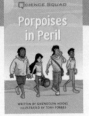

Express and Extend

EXPRESS Explain that this story shows that researchers use clues to solve mysteries and problems and to make new discoveries. Say: When Dr. Vloodman described the mining barge that wandered close to the island and then disappeared, the Science Squad knew it was an important clue. Reggie took notes so they would not lose any of the details. Kate decides to find out the barge's location, its route, and its final destination. This information, added to other clues, leads directly to solving the mystery and saving the porpoises.

If . . . students have difficulty seeing the cause-and-effect relationship between the clues and the solutions,

then . . . have students work in small groups to analyze other clues such as the girl on the beach who describes the hungry porpoise on page 22. Help them understand that this clue suggests that the porpoises were not eating normally. This is because the fish that they usually eat have fled from the area because of the illegal mine.

EXTEND Have students research opals, where they are mined, and why they are considered precious. Challenge them to find out why an opal mine would harm an underwater habitat and the creatures that live there.

STRUCTURE

EXPRESS Point out that sometimes the writer describes two events that happen at the same time. For example, while Jada and Cam are interviewing the fisherman and having a snack on pages 25-28, Kate and Reggie are collecting water samples on pages 29-31. The writer can do this because the narrator is omniscient. This means that the narrator "sees everything" and is not limited to the point of view of only one character. Ask students why they think a writer might choose to use an omniscient point of view. Model by saying: If the story were written from only one character's point of view, then we wouldn't be able to learn what happens when the four characters split up. The writer lets us picture things happening in different places at the same time. We learn a lot more that way. Then have students discuss how the story would have been different if it had been told by one of the team members or Professor Q. How would it be different if it were told by Drake Darkly?

EXTEND Have students write a summary of the story's action using the voice of Jada or Professor Q. Remind students to use the first-person pronoun "I" to refer to themselves as if they are the character. Tell students to include details from the text in their writing.

ENGLISH LANGUAGE LEARNERS

Suggest that students make webs for each of the four characters, including details about their appearance, their actions, their words, their special talents, and which clues in the story they help discover.

STRUGGLING READERS

Suggest that students create a word web to keep track of words and phrases that describe the underwater mine beginning with Kate's first photographs on page 30, continuing through her second dive on pages 40-44. These concrete details will help them picture where the exciting climax of the story took place.

LANGUAGE CONVENTIONALITY AND CLARITY

EXPRESS Talk about Sentences and Words

Display and read aloud the following sentences from *Porpoises in Peril.*

> "But that barge that came out of nowhere sure dredged up a mess, scaring our fish so bad that all of us headed home with empty coolers." The other fishermen grumbled in agreement.

Point out that the writer uses context to help the reader understand the meaning of the science term *dredged*. The words "a mess" and "scared our fish" help the reader picture murky seawater as a result of something happening on the ocean floor. To dredge means "to stir up the ocean floor."

TEAM TALK Have partners use context clues to write definitions for the following technology related terms from the story: *credit card, tablet, satellite receiver, wireless connection, laptop*, and *upload*.

EXTEND Have students explore the word *hypothesis* as it is used on page 23. First, have them guess at the word's meaning from its context. Then, have them look up the word in a dictionary. Suggest that they look up its etymology as well as its definition. Next, have them explain why the word is important in the story. Have them explain why the word is important to the field of science, especially in research.

KNOWLEDGE DEMANDS

EXPRESS Have students compare and contrast Scientists and Detectives. Suggest that they think about the jobs that they do and how they do them. Encourage them to consider the goals of each. How does a person become a successful scientist or a good detective? Challenge them to identify one research scientist and one detective from a current news article and to summarize how each one is successful.

If . . . students have difficulty discerning between similarities and differences,

then . . . have them use the Venn Diagram Graphic Organizer to record details and ideas.

EXTEND Divide the class into four groups to write and perform skits based on each of the four chapters. Encourage each group to use costumes, scenery, and props to act out the action of their chapter. Have the groups present their skits in order. Then discuss how each chapter contributes to solving the mystery and what science facts they, as readers, learned in each one.

ACCELERATED LEARNERS

Have students learn more about porpoises, their behaviors, and their habitats. Ask them to discover the differences between these animals and their close relatives, dolphins. Have them write and present short reports about these fascinating sea creatures. Encourage them to include photographs, drawings, or even videos.

Unlock the Text

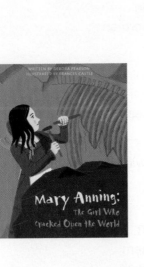

QUALITATIVE MEASURES

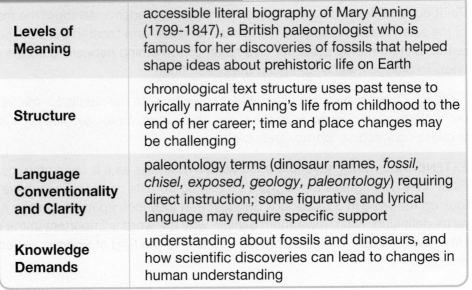

Levels of Meaning	accessible literal biography of Mary Anning (1799-1847), a British paleontologist who is famous for her discoveries of fossils that helped shape ideas about prehistoric life on Earth
Structure	chronological text structure uses past tense to lyrically narrate Anning's life from childhood to the end of her career; time and place changes may be challenging
Language Conventionality and Clarity	paleontology terms (dinosaur names, *fossil, chisel, exposed, geology, paleontology*) requiring direct instruction; some figurative and lyrical language may require specific support
Knowledge Demands	understanding about fossils and dinosaurs, and how scientific discoveries can lead to changes in human understanding

Prepare to Read

LEVELS OF MEANING

Mary Anning: The Girl Who Cracked Open the World is the biography of a real woman in England during the 1800s whose father taught her to collect fossils. After her father's death, she continued the work and discovered three new ancient species based on their bones. Mary Anning overcame both prejudices against women in science and a lack of formal education to continue her research throughout her lifetime. Her work led to advances in human understanding of the prehistoric world.

ENGLISH LANGUAGE LEARNERS

Make sure students understand the meaning of the word *fossil*, which is key to understanding this narrative. Use the Word Knowledge Strategy Routine in Part 3 to help students define the word for themselves. List the way the word is expressed in other languages.

STRUGGLING READERS

Preview all of the illustrations with struggling readers before they read the text. Ask them to describe what they see in each one and to locate Mary Anning in the ones that include her. Point out that the illustrations show Anning at various ages.

STRUCTURE

PREVIEW Have students read the title of the story. Explain that this is a true narrative, a biography, about one important woman who "cracked open the world" in more ways than one. She literally cracked open rocks to find fossils. She figuratively cracked open existing ideas to let new knowledge emerge. Show the class an egg. Crack it open. Ask: How is being a researcher like cracking open an egg? (You don't know what is inside. You lose the shell to get to the egg. It requires work. You can use it to make or cook other things.)

LANGUAGE CONVENTIONALITY AND CLARITY

PREVIEW VOCABULARY Use the Preview and Review Vocabulary Routine in Part 3 to assess what students know about the following words: *exposed, lurked, encased, magnificent, ancient, plaster,* and *accomplish*.

COGNATES Use the list of Spanish cognates at the beginning of this module to guide your Spanish-speaking students as they read the selection.

DOMAIN-SPECIFIC VOCABULARY Use the Vocabulary Activities in Part 3 to pre-teach the following domain-specific vocabulary: *fossils, chisel, ichthyosaur, Plesiosaurus, Pterosaur, geology,* and *paleontology*. Explain that these words are all associated with the research of fossils and dinosaurs.

KNOWLEDGE DEMANDS

ACTIVATE PRIOR KNOWLEDGE Explain that the subject of Mary Anning: *The Girl Who Cracked Open the World* studies and collects fossils of ancient creatures. Ask students to share what they already know about dinosaurs or other ancient creatures that lived during the same time as dinosaurs. Use the Web with Graphic Organizer Routine in Part 3 to record facts and ideas with "Dinosaurs" as the central concept. Ask questions such as: What are dinosaurs? When did they live? Where did they live? Why are there no living dinosaurs? What are some other kinds of ancient creatures that you know about already? What animals today are the most like dinosaurs?

STRUGGLING READERS

This biography begins in a lyrical way, with language that describes Mary going "down to the sea." Invite students to listen and follow along as you read the text on page 4 aloud, slowly. Point to the words *curiosities* and *curios*. Suggest that the writer uses this opening paragraph to make the reader curious about Mary. Ask: What questions or subjects do these paragraphs make you curious about?

MORE SUPPORT

Interact with Text

As you read *Mary Anning: The Girl Who Cracked Open the World,* assess students' understanding of how childhood experiences can have an effect on work and career choices adults make. Point out that until page 9 Mary has experience with and learns skills from her father, who was actually a carpenter. Have students make lists of those experiences and skills. Ask students why they think the townspeople whispered about her (page 8). Contrast the whispers with what visitors and other scientists say about her on page 23.

> If . . . students have difficulty identifying how Mary's father influenced her childhood,
>
> then . . . use the Main Idea and Details Routine and Graphic Organizer in Part 3 to support understanding.

Suggest to students that the ellipses between pages 9 and 10 are an important turning point for Mary. Ask: What happens to Mary during the time indicated by the ellipses? Why did the author use this form of punctuation to show this? Is it effective? Why or why not? Have students analyze the other use of ellipses on page 12 (to show that Mary was thinking).

STRUCTURE

Point out that the biography is told in chronological order beginning with Mary's childhood and ending with "After Mary died" and the legacy she left behind. Mostly, the writer tells the reader what happens in a literal way. Sometimes, however, the language becomes lyrical and even figurative. For example, on page 9, "Sadness hung in the air, it lurked in the shadows . . ." is the personification of an emotion. The sentence moves the narrative forward, but not in a literal way.

> If . . . students have difficulty understanding the sequence of events in Mary's life,
>
> then . . . use the Sequence of Events Routine and Graphic Organizer in Part 3 to support understanding.

Have students find other examples in which the writer uses lyrical or figurative language to move the narrative forward (i.e. the repetition of "digging and searching" on page 11, the onomatopoeia of "chip-chipped" on page 12, the instances when the writer describes Mary's thoughts, all of the questions that pepper the narrative).

MORE SUPPORT

ENGLISH LANGUAGE LEARNERS

Mary Anning was the inspiration for this famous 1908 tongue twister: *"She sells seashells by the seashore. So if she sells seashells on the seashore then I'm sure she sells seashore shells."* Challenge students to recite this short rhyme. Would the sentences lose their tongue-twisterly nature if they translated it into students' native languages?

STRUGGLING READERS

Make sure students understand the geography of this biography. On a map of England, point out that Mary Anning and her father worked along Lyme Bay of the English Channel at Lyme Regis, a town in the extreme southwest of the county of Dorset.

LANGUAGE CONVENTIONALITY AND CLARITY

While much of the language will be clear and accessible to students, they may need extra support to understand and pronounce the paleontological terms and names.

If . . . students have difficulty understanding domain-specific words,

then . . . have them make a web for each using the Web with Graphic Organizer Routine.

In addition, remind students that they can see images of skeletons and illustrations of dinosaurs and other ancient creatures on the Internet. Suggest that they can easily compare and contrast Ichthyosaurs, Plesiosaurs, and Pterosaurs using online information and images.

Make sure students understand the relationship of paleontology to geology, as they are defined on page 25. Paleontology lies in the intersection between biology and geology. Use the Venn Diagram with Graphic Organizer Routine in Part 3 to illustrate this relationship. Suggest that Mary's work as it is described on pages 26 and 27 shows some of the things that paleontologists do.

KNOWLEDGE DEMANDS

Some students may not be familiar with the relationship between fossilized bones and the illustrations people have made of dinosaurs and other ancient creatures that lived during the same time period. Show them other illustrations from books or the Internet based on skeletons. Explain that no one really knows what prehistoric life looked like, but that for hundreds of years, artists have combined their imaginations with paleontological findings to create drawings and paintings such as the one on page 20. Challenge students to create their own drawings based on the skulls and other bones illustrated in this biography.

ENGLISH LANGUAGE LEARNERS

Have students locate the many questions that are asked in the narrative. Ask them to decide if each question is answered or not. If it is answered, what is the answer? If a question is not answered, why not?

Express and Extend

EXPRESS Explain that this story shows that women researchers have often encountered prejudice in fields of science that are dominated by men. Say: Mary Anning went through a lifetime process of overcoming negative feelings about her. Other scientists didn't give her credit for two reasons: she was not educated at a university, and she was a woman. Anning overcame these prejudices through hard work, perseverance, and communication. She wrote letters to other scientists and answered their letters when she received them. She shared her work with others throughout her life. She changed people's ideas about both prehistoric life and about how women can make important scientific discoveries.

If . . . students have difficulty recognizing Mary Anning's perseverance,

then . . . have students list all the examples of when her work was questioned or doubted in the narrative. They can use the Main Ideas and Details Graphic Organizer and Routine from Part 3 to record their observations.

EXTEND Have students research another female paleontologist such as Karen Chin, Sue Hendrickson, Ruth Mason, Elizabeth Nicholls, Patricia Vickers-Rich, or Joan Wiffin. Have them compare and contrast one of these women with Mary Anning.

STRUCTURE

EXPRESS Point out that it is unusual to read a biography that contains no dates, as this one does. However, the events in the narrative are arranged chronologically. Model by saying: If this biography were full of dates, it would have a different tone. The writer chose not to focus on dates, but rather on the connections between the events and how one led to the next. She wanted readers to think more about the story and how it unfolds than about exactly when the events occurred. Then have students discuss how the story would have been different if it had included dates. Ask: Was it strange or difficult for you to read a biography that contains no dates? Why or why not?

EXTEND Based on the information in this biography, have students write the speech referred to on page 30 that Henry De la Beche delivered in London. Have them include information about Anning's life in the speech. More importantly, have them summarize her contributions to the field of paleontology in their own words.

ENGLISH LANGUAGE LEARNERS

Help students make a list of other *-ologies*, fields of scientific study named for their subjects. Remind them that such words combine Greek and Latin roots with the suffix *–ology* that means "study of."

STRUGGLING READERS

Make sure students understand the meaning of the word *prehistoric*. The writer refers to "ancient times" on page 19, but does not use any dates or years to make the time frame explicit. *Prehistoric* refers to the time before there were any written records.

MORE SUPPORT

LANGUAGE CONVENTIONALITY AND CLARITY

EXPRESS Talk about Sentences and Words

Display and read aloud the following sentence from *Mary Anning: The Girl Who Cracked Open the World.*

> Mary didn't know at the time, but she was doing the same work that all scientists did: she was asking questions, gathering information, and making drawings and notes of everything she studied.

Point out that the three verbs *asking, gathering,* and *making* are the three most important activities of all scientists. Have students use the Three-Column Chart with Graphic Organizer Routine in Part 3 to list specific examples of all three activities from the biography. Have them include references to the pages on which the examples occur.

TEAM TALK Have partners analyze and summarize Mary's interactions with Henry De la Beche as described on pages 18-20. They can use the Web with Graphic Organizer Routine from Part 3 to record their observations.

EXTEND Have students dive deeply into the sentence on page 22 that says, "Mary was furious when she heard what people were saying about her skeleton." Ask: Why was she furious? (The reasons are noted on page 21.) Encourage them to share times in their own lives when they have been furious when someone didn't believe something they said or did. Have them write paragraphs in which they compare and contrast their own experiences with Mary Anning's.

KNOWLEDGE DEMANDS

EXPRESS Challenge students to imagine what it was like to collect fossils along the rocky cliffs with Mary Anning. Have them write descriptive paragraphs using the first-person "I" as if they were present in 1809, collecting fossils and shells with ten-year-old Mary. Have them use details from the biography as a starting point.

If . . . students have difficulty imagining sensory details,

then . . . have them use the Sensory Details with Graphic Organizer to imagine what it might have been like to collect fossils along the rocky cliffs.

EXTEND Challenge students to use the biographical information in the text to write "The Ballad of Mary Anning" as a poem or a song. Have them include a repeating chorus that describes Anning's most important qualities, deeds, or contributions. Suggest that they use a rhyming dictionary to find words that rhyme.

ACCELERATED LEARNERS

On page 27, the writer notes that Louis Agassiz named two fossil fish after Mary Anning. They are *Acrodus anningiae* and *Belenostomus anningiae.* Challenge students to find more information about Louis Agassiz (1807-1873) and his work. For example, he was the first scientist to propose that the Earth had gone through an Ice Age. Swiss-born, Agassiz came to the United States in 1847 and became a professor of geology and zoology at Harvard University.

Unlock the Text

QUALITATIVE MEASURES

Levels of Meaning	describes the work of scientists who study amphibian decline; explains ecological relationships
Structure	conventional structure with photographs and captions; parentheses
Language Conventionality and Clarity	academic and domain-specific vocabulary; idioms
Knowledge Demands	specialized science content: amphibians; ecology

Fragile Frogs *from* The Frog Scientist, pp. 5–11

Prepare to Read

LEVELS OF MEANING

One purpose of "Fragile Frogs" is to describe how scientists discovered the decline of the amphibian population and tell the reasons why this is occurring. Another purpose is to explain ecological relationships.

STRUCTURE

PREVIEW Have students read the title and the first sentence. Ask students to look at the illustrations, read the caption on p. 5, and try to predict the topic of the article. Ask questions, such as:

- How does the caption on page 5 help you understand the first sentence? (It tells the meaning of the word *amphibian*.)
- Why would the author explain the meaning of this word? (to inform readers about the topic of the article)

ENGLISH LANGUAGE LEARNERS

Encourage students to ask questions about words and concepts they do not understand. Display sentence frames, such as: One question I have is: ___? I understand this paragraph, but I have a question about ___. What does ___ mean?

STRUGGLING READERS

Use picture cards or illustrations for students to refer to so that they are able to visualize the meaning of the words as they read. For example, cards could be made for words such as *amphibian* and *pesticides,* which may be difficult for students to understand.

LANGUAGE CONVENTIONALITY AND CLARITY

PREVIEW VOCABULARY Use the Preview and Review Vocabulary Routine in Part 3 to assess what students know about the following words: *amphibian, habitat, pesticides, disappear, fungus, threatened, deformed, non-native, decline,* and *ozone.*

Use the Vocabulary Activities in Part 3 before, during, and after reading to provide more practice with domain-specific vocabulary.

COGNATES Use the list of Spanish cognates at the beginning of this module to guide your Spanish-speaking students as they read the selection.

PRONUNCIATION OF MULTISYLLABIC WORDS This selection has many multisyllabic scientific words. Use the Multisyllabic Word Strategy Routine in Part 3 to review how to decode and pronounce these words. Remind students to look for clues about pronunciation that the author may provide in the text, such as for the word *chytrid* (KIT-rid).

KNOWLEDGE DEMANDS

ACTIVATE BACKGROUND KNOWLEDGE Use the Quick Write and Share Routine in Part 3 to activate students' background knowledge. Place students in pairs and have them share what they already know about amphibians. Have students look at the photos of amphibians on p. 5. Ask: What can you tell about similarities and differences between amphibians by studying these photos? These photos show one type of amphibian. Based on the title of this selection, what is this type of amphibian called? What do you already know about this type of amphibian?

Interact with Text

Name a frog from the text, and have students name the location where that frog is found in the world.

If . . . students have difficulty following the geographic locations mentioned in the article,

then . . . have students use a globe or map to locate the states, countries, and continents mentioned. Ask them to describe what scientists have learned about frogs in each region.

Point out that the United States is made up of 50 states, including Minnesota, and that continents are divided into countries. For example, the country of Costa Rica is situated in North America, which is a continent.

STRUCTURE

Have students look for ways that the author uses text features, such as parentheses, as they read this selection.

If . . . students have difficulty remembering ways that parentheses can be used,

then . . . point out an example from "Fragile Frogs," and ask what type of information that example provides.

Use a think aloud to give students additional support. Say: Let's find the parentheses on page 6. The text in parentheses reads *chopped into smaller pieces,* and it follows the word *fragmented.* The text in parentheses must be telling the meaning of the word *fragmented.* Find the parentheses on page 8. See if you can tell what type of information the text in parentheses provides on this page.

ENGLISH LANGUAGE LEARNERS

Use the Act Out or Draw Meaning Activity in Part 3 to provide more practice with new vocabulary and expressions, such as *have a taste for, gobble up, gulp down,* and *munch.*

STRUGGLING READERS

Using context clues to infer the meaning of new words is one practice that can be helpful, particularly with informational text. Provide sentences using scientific vocabulary. Give students context clues, and have them draw pictures of what they think the vocabulary word means, based on the context clue.

LANGUAGE CONVENTIONALITY AND CLARITY

While the language of the article is direct and informative, there are some expressions that students might need explained. Periodically stop to assess students' understanding of figurative language.

If . . . students need support to understand idioms or other expressions in the selection,

then . . . have students identify context clues that might help explain the expression.

For example, display the following sentence on p. 9: "The non-native fish usually have a taste for the native tadpoles." Ask students to think about what the word *taste* means. Explain that the word *taste* can be a clue to understand the phrase *to have a taste for,* which means "to like to eat something."

Use the Analyze Idioms and Expressions Routine in Part 3 to explain other phrases that mean "to eat," such as *gobble up, gulp down,* and *munch*.

KNOWLEDGE DEMANDS

At the end of each page, assess whether students understand words related to specialized science content.

If . . . students have difficulty understanding the specialized vocabulary that the author uses,

then . . . model how to determine meaning by finding the definition in the text.

Use a think aloud to give an example of how authors sometimes define words after using them in a sentence. Say: Let's look at these two sentences from the text. "Amphibians are also threatened by introduced species. An introduced species is a creature that shows up somewhere it isn't normally found." Look at the words *introduced species* in the first sentence. Notice that these words also appear in the next sentence. The second sentence gives a definition. By defining scientific vocabulary, the author helps the reader better understand the meaning of the text.

Provide more practice. Guide students to find the definition or context clue in the following example: "Sometimes amphibian habitat is fragmented (chopped in smaller pieces) when roads, houses, or shopping centers are built." Explain that sometimes authors put definitions in parentheses.

Express and Extend

EXPRESS One theory the author suggests is that human interaction caused the population of certain frog species to decline. Other theories point to natural occurrences. Have students work in pairs to list each theory and use details from the text to decide if it involves human interaction or not.

If . . . students have difficulty determining causes of amphibian decline,

then . . . use the Web Routine and Graphic Organizer from Part 3 to organize the information.

Model how to use the web graphic organizer. Write *Causes of Decline* in the middle circle of the web. Have students list causes, such as pesticides, fungus, new species, and habitat loss, in the circles around it. Have pairs reread the text to find details to explain each cause. Use a think aloud to model an example. Say: In the paragraph about habitat loss, the author includes details about building roads, houses, and shopping centers. Building these things are human activities. Therefore, this cause involves human interaction.

EXTEND Form small groups. Have students use the text to select one cause of frog deformities or population decline. Ask them to use logic and creative thinking to propose a solution. Use the Problem and Solution Routine and Graphic Organizer for additional support.

EXPRESS Have partners prepare a poster that informs the public about the locations of amphibian decline around the world, and have them include captions or labels or explain the cause of the problem for each location.

If . . . students have difficulty identifying locations or causes of amphibian decline,

then . . . have students reread the text to look for proper nouns that indicate place names. Students can also use a detailed world map to match place names in the text with place names on the map.

EXTEND Have students research a location that is not mentioned in the text where amphibian decline exists, and write a paragraph describing the causes of the problem in that location.

MORE SUPPORT

ENGLISH LANGUAGE LEARNERS

Guide group discussion with sentence frames such as: One theory is___. A detail I used was ___. This shows that___.

STRUGGLING READERS

Students may need help identifying cause-and-effect relationships. Use the Cause and Effect Routine with Graphic Organizer in Part 3 for more support.

LANGUAGE CONVENTIONALITY AND CLARITY

EXPRESS Talk about Sentences and Words

Display the following paragraph from "Fragile Frogs" and read it aloud.

> Some species of frogs living at high altitudes are threatened by ultraviolet (UV) radiation. Man-made chemicals have thinned the ozone layer in our atmosphere. . . . At high altitudes the air is thinner, and if thin air is combined with a thin ozone area, even more UV radiation can kill the delicate, shell-less eggs of amphibians that live in mountain areas.

Ask: What words does the author use to describe the eggs? (*delicate, shell-less*) Why do you think the author chooses these words? (to show that the eggs are delicate and threatened) What does the abbreviation *UV* stand for? (*ultraviolet*)

Explain that the word *shell-less* is a compound word made up of two smaller words, *shell* and *less,* and a compound word sometimes has a hyphen to separate the two words. Another example from this paragraph is the compound word *man-made,* which is made up of the words *man* and *made.*

TEAM TALK Have partners use the following sentence frame to rewrite the sentence using different words with the same meaning: ___ have thinned the ozone layer in our atmosphere.

EXTEND Have students reread the article and make a list of other hyphenated compound words within the text, identify the two words that make up the compound word, and then define the word based on the meanings of the two smaller words. Some examples are *web-footed, cold-blooded,* and *red-legged.*

KNOWLEDGE DEMANDS

EXPRESS Have small groups use details from the text to explain issues that affect amphibians, such as habitat loss, ozone depletion, or deformation.

If . . . students have difficulty explaining scientific concepts,

then . . . help them to identify the main idea of relevant paragraphs and find details that help explain the topic. Use the Main Idea and Details Routine and Graphic Organizer from Part 3 to organize the information.

EXTEND Provide students with other sources about habitat loss, ozone depletion, or deformation. Have them write a sentence from their research that includes information not found in "Fragile Frogs."

ACCELERATED LEARNERS

Have students research another species that is threatened by extinction. Have them map out the causes and effects that have created this problem.

Cognates

Cognates are words that have similar spellings and meanings in two or more languages. Many words in English and Spanish share Greek or Latin roots, and many words in English came from French, which is closely connected to Spanish (and to Portuguese, Italian, and Romanian). Because of this, many literary, content, and academic process words in English (e.g., *gracious/gracioso; volcano/volcán; compare/comparar*) have recognizable Spanish cognates.

Making the connection to cognates permits students who are native Spanish speakers to understand the strong foundation they have in academic and literary English. These links between English and Spanish are also useful for native speakers of English and other languages because they help uncover basic underlying features of our language.

ANCHOR TEXT Skeletons Inside and Out

ENGLISH	SPANISH	ENGLISH	SPANISH
amphibian	anfibio	gradually	gradualmente
arachnid	arácnido	gymnasts	gimnastas
armor	armadura	horizontal	horizontal
attack	atacar	insect	insecto
calcium	calcio	kangaroo	canguro
cartilage	cartílago	metamorphosis	metamorfosis
chimpanzee	chimpancé	muscles	músculos
creature	criatura	organs	órganos
crustaceans	crustáceos	pincers	pinzas
defend	defender	possible	posible
delicate	delicado	rays	rayos
elephant	elefante	reptiles	reptiles
endoskeleton	endoesqueleto	salamander	salamandra
escape	escapar	scorpion	escorpión
exercise	ejercicio	sensations	sensaciones
exoskeleton	exoesqueleto	simple	simple
expand	expandir	skeleton	esqueleto
extinct	extinto	spine	espina
flexible	flexible	sternum	esternón
fortunately	afortunadamente	suction	succión
fossils	fósiles	vertebrae	vértebras
giraffe	jirafa	vertical	vertical

SUPPORTING TEXT Movers and Shapers

ENGLISH	SPANISH	ENGLISH	SPANISH
action	acción	movement	movimiento
artificial	artificial	nerves	nervios
base	base	parts	partes
central	central	pelvis	pelvis
connect	conectar	positions	posiciones
contain	contener	pressure	presión
control	controlar	prevent	prevenir
cranium	cráneo	rigid	rígido
direction	dirección	scientists	científicos
examined	examinado	special	especial
flexibility	flexibilidad	system	sistema
imagine	imaginar	tendon	tendón
impossible	imposible	x-ray	rayos X
ligament	ligamento		

SUPPORTING TEXT King of the Parking Lot

ENGLISH	SPANISH	ENGLISH	SPANISH
adult	adulto	include	incluir
archaeologist	arqueólogo	locate	localizar
deformed	deformado	modern	moderno
evidence	evidencia	monastery	monasterio
example	ejemplo	monk	monje
excavation	excavación	personality	personalidad
expert	experto	possible	posible
favorite	favorito	respect	respeto
fragile	frágil	reveal	revelar
history	historia	sign	signo
human	humano	tradition	tradición
important	importante		

These lists contain many, but not all, Spanish cognates from these selections.

Unlock the Text

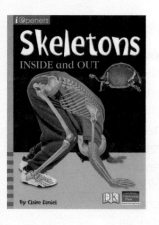

QUALITATIVE MEASURES

Levels of Meaning	understand informational text; main idea and supporting details
Structure	compare-and-contrast structure; table of contents; introduction; chapters; sidebars; pictures; glossary; index
Language Conventionality and Clarity	domain-specific vocabulary
Knowledge Demands	describing skeletons; similarities and differences between human and animal skeletons; classifying animals

Prepare to Read

LEVELS OF MEANING

Skeletons Inside and Out teaches readers about the skeletons of humans and various groups of mammals and insects. Skeletal features are explained, pictured and labeled, and compared and contrasted. Information is presented through animal classification.

STRUCTURE

PREVIEW Form small groups, and have students look at the text features—the title page, table of contents, headings, captions, labels, and sidebars—and discuss their purposes. Ask:

* Why are there different-colored boxes on the pages? (to draw the reader's attention to additional information)

ENGLISH LANGUAGE LEARNERS

Help students expand their understanding of scientific terminology by stating the relationships between pairs of related words. For example: *exoskeleton* and *endoskeleton* (opposites), *horizontal* and *vertical* (opposites), and *vertebrae* and *spine* (part-whole).

STRUGGLING READERS

Demonstrate how the glossary can be used to help students define unfamiliar words. Point to a glossary term in the text, and have students find the word in the glossary. Tell students they can also use a classroom dictionary when they encounter challenging words that do not appear in the glossary.

- What does the table of contents show? (chapter titles and page numbers) Why do the chapter titles and headings have different sizes? (The chapter titles show the main topic of the chapter, and the headings show a topic within a chapter that is related to the main topic.)
- Why does the author use labels and captions? (to give more information about the pictures on each page)
- What information does the glossary give readers? (It defines scientific terms in the text.)

LANGUAGE CONVENTIONALITY AND CLARITY

PREVIEW VOCABULARY Use the Preview and Review Vocabulary Routine in Part 3 to assess what students know about following words: *reptiles, amphibians, crustaceans, arachnids, metamorphosis, endoskeleton, exoskeleton, vertebrae, sternum.*

COGNATES Use the list of Spanish cognates at the beginning of this module to guide your Spanish-speaking students as they read the selection.

KNOWLEDGE DEMANDS

ACTIVATE BACKGROUND KNOWLEDGE Place students into groups. Assign each group a chapter, and have them complete the first two columns of a KWLH chart. Use the KWLH Routine and Graphic Organizer in Part 3. Afterward, display a poster-sized KWLH chart, and have groups share and record on the poster the information from their group's charts.

Keep the poster on display in the classroom. After finishing each chapter, return to the chart, and have students work in pairs or as a class to fill out the *What Did I Learn?* and *How Did I Learn It?* columns.

Continue to assess students' background knowledge by creating a True-or-False questionnaire for students to complete prior to reading the text. As they read, have students record whether their predictions were correct. Example statements might be: All mammals have skeletons made of bones. All living things have skeletons inside their bodies.

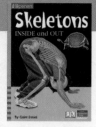

Interact with Text

LEVELS OF MEANING

As you read, assess whether students understand the differences and similarities between skeletons.

If . . . students have trouble understanding differences and similarities between skeletons,

then . . . use the Venn Diagram Routine and Graphic Organizer in Part 3. Have students select two animals and record facts about the animals' skeletons in the Venn diagram.

Use a think aloud to give students additional support. Say: Let's look at the two skeletons shown on page 14—a horse skeleton and a kangaroo skeleton. The text states that a horse's skeleton is made for running, while a kangaroo's skeleton is made for jumping. This is one difference. What are other differences you can see by looking at the pictures? Now let's look for similarities. I see that both skeletons have skulls. Can you see other ways the skeletons are alike?

STRUCTURE

As students read, periodically stop to assess their understanding of the text's structure, especially pictures, sidebars, and captions.

If . . . students have difficulty understanding how pictures, sidebars, and captions relate to the main text,

then . . . use Three-Column Chart Routine and Graphic Organizer in Part 3 to help students organize information about pictures, sidebars, and captions.

For example, read aloud pp. 18–19, and help students summarize the pages. Then, in pairs, have students use the three-column chart to categorize the information conveyed by the pictures, sidebars, and captions. As a class, discuss how that information enhances information from the main text.

MORE SUPPORT

ENGLISH LANGUAGE LEARNERS

Give students facts from the text about skeletons. As you give each fact, have students point to pictures in the book that relate to that fact.

STRUGGLING READERS

If students have difficulty understanding how captions relate to pictures, show them a picture from the text and have them use their own words to tell about the picture in one sentence. Tell them that their sentence can be written as a caption that describes the picture.

LANGUAGE CONVENTIONALITY AND CLARITY

The text contains a number of science terms that may be new to students. At the end of each section, assess whether students understand academic or domain-specific vocabulary.

If . . . students have difficulty understanding new science terms,

then . . . discuss the prefixes and suffixes that will help students determine word meanings.

For example, the prefixes *endo-* and *exo-* mean "inside" and "outside," respectively. Therefore, an endoskeleton is a skeleton inside the body, and an exoskeleton is a skeleton outside of the body.

Discuss with students the use of dark print for some words in the text. For example, on p. 11, *Mammal and Bird Skeletons, killer whale,* and *mammals* appear in dark print. *Mammal and Bird Skeletons* is in dark print because it's a chapter title, *killer whale* because it's a label, and *mammals* because it's a glossary word.

KNOWLEDGE DEMANDS

Lead a discussion about human skeletons and animal skeletons. Pose questions that students can answer using information from the text.

If . . . students have difficulty finding answers in the text,

then . . . use the Ask and Answer Questions Routine in Part 3 to provide additional support.

Instead of having students write on the worksheet provided questions they have about the text, help them use facts in the text to create questions. For example, the caption on p. 15 reads, "Bats are the only flying mammals." Students can use this fact to write the question, "What is the only flying mammal?" Being able to use facts to write questions is a skill that will also help students identify facts in the text in order to answer questions that are posed to them.

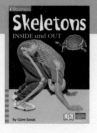

Express and Extend

EXPRESS Have students demonstrate their understanding of a main idea and details. Have pairs choose a chapter in *Skeletons Inside and Out* and identify the main idea as well as some details that support it. Then ask students to explain how headings and graphics help them understand the main idea.

If . . . students have difficulty identifying main ideas or supporting details,

then . . . use the Main Idea and Details Routine and Graphic Organizer in Part 3 to provide support. As students fill in the graphic organizer, remind them that a main idea of a section of text is the most important idea, while supporting details include important information that relates to the main idea.

EXTEND Have students create their own sidebar for one of the pages in the chapter they read. Remind them that the sidebar should contain additional information that will help the reader understand the main idea. Encourage students to use classroom resources when creating their sidebar.

STRUCTURE

EXPRESS In pairs, discuss why a table of contents, glossary, and index are included in the book. Students should write a two-sentence response for the following questions: What is in each section? How do these sections add value to the book? Why do you think it is more important to include these sections in informational texts?

If . . . students have difficulty determining the purpose and relevance of the table of contents, glossary, and index,

then . . . give small groups one section to focus on. Afterward, have students share their answers as well as how they reached them.

EXTEND Gather a variety of informational texts from the classroom or school library. Have students choose one to examine and compare with *Skeletons Inside and Out*. Have them write a paragraph comparing the structures and sections of the two books.

ENGLISH LANGUAGE LEARNERS

This selection has some compound words, such as *wavelike, backbone,* and *lightweight.* Have students tell the two words in each compound word and explain how the two smaller words help them determine the meaning of the compound word.

STRUGGLING READERS

Choose pairs of words or phrases from the text that have similar meanings, and write each word or phrase on an index card. For example, *guards* and *protects* (p. 7), *leap* and *jump* (p. 19). Mix up all of the cards, and ask students to match the terms that mean the same thing.

LANGUAGE CONVENTIONALITY AND CLARITY

EXPRESS Talk about Sentences and Words

Display the following sentence from *Skeletons Inside and Out*, and read it aloud to students.

> Some kinds of young insects, such as young damselflies, dragonflies, and grasshoppers, change shape gradually each time they molt, or shed their exoskeleton.

Ask: What compound words do you see? *(damselflies, dragonflies, grasshoppers)* What does each compound word tell us about the insects? (what the insect looks like or does) What does the word *molt* mean? ("to shed") How do you know the meaning of this word? (The author gives a definition after using the word.)

TEAM TALK Have students turn to a partner and discuss why the author chose to use both *molt* and *shed* to describe what the insect does when it changes.

If . . . students need more support to understand domain-specific language,

then . . . have them create a vocabulary card for both words before discussing in pairs. Use classroom resources to look up other words with similar meanings.

EXTEND Have students rewrite sentences from the text, replacing certain words in the text with other words that have similar meanings. Provide this sentence frame from p. 13 as an example, and have students fill in the blanks with words that have similar meanings to those found in the text: Elephants have ___, ___ leg bones and ___ toe bones that hold up their ___ bodies.

KNOWLEDGE DEMANDS

EXPRESS Assign small groups one animal classification each, such as mammal, bird, amphibian, or insect. Have each group give detailed descriptions of the skeletons in their animal group. Make sure students are given one classification as opposed to one chapter.

If . . . students have difficulty describing skeleton features,

then . . . have them use the diagrams and photos in the text as a guide.

EXTEND Have students use the Venn Diagram Graphic Organizer in Part 3 to compare and contrast the skeletons of two classes of animals.

ACCELERATED LEARNERS

Have students use evidence from the text to write two paragraphs comparing and contrasting the skeletons of a bat and a bird. They should explain how the skeletons meet the common needs of both animals.

Unlock the Text

QUALITATIVE MEASURES

Levels of Meaning	informational text divided into sections by subject; main idea and details
Structure	section headings; text boxes; diagrams with labels; photographs with captions
Language Conventionality and Clarity	varied sentence structures; complex sentences; domain-specific words
Knowledge Demands	specialized science content; exploring the relationships between and functions of bones, joints, muscles, and tendons

Movers and Shapers, pp. 13–31

Prepare to Read

LEVELS OF MEANING

In *Movers and Shapers*, readers learn about the relationships between and functions of bones, muscles, tendons, and joints. Photographs and diagrams enhance the meaning of informational text, while text boxes supply additional fun facts.

STRUCTURE

PREVIEW Have students preview the selection and look at the photos, diagrams, text boxes, and captions. Ask:

- Why does the author include pictures and diagrams? (The author wants to show and give examples of various body parts and functions.)

ENGLISH LANGUAGE LEARNERS

When discussing new vocabulary, include practice with pronunciation. Writing words on the board with stress marks will reinforce students' understanding of correct pronunciation. Allow students to pronounce words on their own before you demonstrate pronunciation.

STRUGGLING READERS

Display pp. 16–17. Review with students the text features related to visuals. Have students tell how they know which part of an image each label refers to. (There are leader lines.) Have students tell how they know which pictures are associated with captions. (Arrows point to the corresponding picture.)

- What is the purpose of the captions and labels—the text next to the pictures and graphics? (They explain how the pictures relate to the text. They describe what is being demonstrated.)

- Why does the author include "Info lab" text boxes? (They give readers additional interesting information about bones, muscles, joints, and tendons.)

- Look at the title, photos, and captions in the first section. What do you think this section will be about? (how our bodies support themselves and how they are able to move)

LANGUAGE CONVENTIONALITY AND CLARITY

PREVIEW VOCABULARY Use the Preview and Review Vocabulary Routine in Part 3 to assess what students know about the following words: *marrow, cartilage, spine, vertebrae, ligaments, septum, larynx, tendons, cranium, mandible, femur, pelvis, fontanel, dislocation.*

Display a large diagram of a human skeleton in the classroom, and create a "Body of Vocabulary" using words from the list above and words students learned from *Skeletons Inside and Out*. After defining the words above, have students mark where each word belongs on the body. Add to the diagram as you continue to read.

COGNATES Use the list of Spanish cognates at the beginning of this module to guide your Spanish-speaking students as they read the selection.

KNOWLEDGE DEMANDS

ACTIVATE BACKGROUND KNOWLEDGE Ask students to recall information they've learned about skeletons from *Skeletons Inside and Out*. Have them focus specifically on what they know about the human skeleton.

Divide students into groups, and give each group a word web with a different word in the center—*bones, muscles, joints, tendons.* Have students work together and fill in the web with what they know about that word. Have each group share their completed web with the class.

Interact with Text

As you read *Movers and Shapers,* stop at the end of each section to assess students' ability to identify main ideas and key details.

> **If . . .** students have difficulty identifying the main idea and key details,
>
> **then . . .** have students use the Main Idea and Details Graphic Organizer in Part 3 to organize ideas in the text.

Before reading, have students write the main title of a spread in the Main Idea box of the graphic organizer. Use a think aloud to provide additional support. Say: Let's look at page 20 as an example. I can write *How joints move* in the Main Idea box. Then, I'll fill in information from that section in the Details boxes. For my details, I will write complete sentences. One of my details for this section could be: *Ball and socket joints help you move your shoulders or hips.* I will write one piece of information in each Details box. After students fill in the graphic organizer using another spread, have them share their details as a class and discuss how each detail supports the main idea.

STRUCTURE

Periodically stop to assess how thoroughly students understand the text's structure. Have students point out text features that are not part of the main body of text.

> **If . . .** students have difficulty understanding how graphics and photographs contribute to the meaning of the text,
>
> **then . . .** have pairs use a two-column chart to explain how each graphic or photograph supports a section of text.

For example, display a two-column chart with the headings *Section* and *Connection to Text*. Use the photograph of the boy's face on p. 22 as an example. Under *Section,* write the section title *On the nose.* Under *Connection to Text,* write: *This picture shows how the cartilage in your nose gives your nostrils their shape. It also shows how cartilage allows your nose to bend and go back to the same shape.* If students need more guidance, work as a class to analyze the remaining pictures on a spread before having them work in pairs.

ENGLISH LANGUAGE LEARNERS

Use visuals to aid understanding of scientific language. Point to various graphics and photos in the book, and ask students to describe what is shown.

STRUGGLING READERS

To help students pronounce difficult words from the selection, such as *reproductive, mandible,* and *fontanels,* have them repeat the words two or three times after you say them.

LANGUAGE CONVENTIONALITY AND CLARITY

Much of the text in *Movers and Shapers* contains scientific and specialized language that students may find difficult to interpret. At the end of each spread, have students list all of the scientific words and definitions from that section.

If . . . students have difficulty with the scientific or specialized language,

then . . . work with students to break down words based on their Greek and Latin prefixes, suffixes, or roots and explore other words with the same parts.

Use a think aloud to provide support. Say: Look at the last section of page 14. The text states that muscles contract. The word *contract* contains the Latin root *tract,* meaning "to drag or pull." In the middle bubble of a word web, I will write the word *contract* and the root *tract* with its definition. I will define the word based on its root and context clues. In surrounding bubbles, have students write other words with the same root and their definitions. Afterward, have students explain how the root *tract* helped them understand the meaning of the word *contract* and the other words in the web. Create a list of Greek and Latin roots with their meanings and display it in a prominent place in the classroom. If additional support is needed, use the Words with Greek Roots Activity or the Words with Latin Roots Activity—both in Part 3.

KNOWLEDGE DEMANDS

Since the text is dense with information, it may be difficult for students to digest all of the facts and ideas. Periodically stop to assess students' ability to remember the information they have read.

If . . . students have difficulty understanding information about bones, muscles, joints, and tendons,

then . . . use a four-column chart to help students understand the functions of the bones, muscles, joints, and tendons in a particular part of the body.

For example, give small groups a four-column chart with the headings *Bones, Muscles, Joints,* and *Tendons.* Assign each group a body part, such as the leg, head, arm, or chest. Students should reread sections of the text and then write facts about their given body part in the appropriate columns.

Express and Extend

EXPRESS Place students into small groups. Have group members take turns reading a section of the book. Then, have each group write and present summaries of what they read to the class.

If . . . students have difficulty summarizing text,

then . . . use the Retell or Summarize Routine and Graphic Organizer in Part 3 to help students collect important information from the text.

EXTEND Have students work in pairs and use the Venn Diagram Graphic Organizer in Part 3 to compare and contrast two different sections of the book. Each group should compare a unique pair of sections.

EXPRESS Have students look at the section headings on one two-page spread and discuss how the headings relate to the content of the text. For example, have students look at p. 31 and tell how the heading "All in a name" relates to the text that discusses the sartorius muscle.

If . . . students have difficulty relating text to its section heading,

then . . . have students reread the section to identify the main idea. Use the Main Idea and Details Routine and Graphic Organizer in Part 3. Then discuss whether the heading relates to main idea of the section.

EXTEND Select a page from the text, and have students read a section, summarize it, and create a new section heading based on information in the text.

MORE SUPPORT

ENGLISH LANGUAGE LEARNERS

To help students summarize certain concepts, such as how various types of joints differ, point to specific pictures in the text that help convey the meaning of the concept, and have students describe what they see in one sentence.

STRUGGLING READERS

To help students with difficult vocabulary, scan a section to identify any unfamiliar words. Relate those words to terms previously discussed in other sections so that students can see how words in a text interact.

LANGUAGE CONVENTIONALITY AND CLARITY

EXPRESS Talk about Sentences and Words

Display and read aloud the following sentences.

> In small babies the bones of the skull have not yet knitted together. Instead the bones are connected by a stretchy material.

Ask: What does the phrase *knitted together* mean? (that two things are joined together) Why is the word *instead* used in the second sentence? (It signals an alternative statement. It tells us we will find out what actually happens to a baby's skull bones.) What word is used instead of *knitted together* to tell that the bones of the skull are joined? *(connected)*

TEAM TALK Have students focus on the phrase *knitted together*. Say: Discuss with a partner how the phrase adequately describes the joining of skull bones.

EXTEND Have students suggest other creative phrases to describe the joining together of two objects. If necessary, provide other examples or phrases from the text for students to reword, such as *work together as a team* (p. 14), *shield the heart* (p. 15), or *forms a shell* (p. 16).

KNOWLEDGE DEMANDS

EXPRESS Have small groups use a T-chart to record what they learned and how they learned it, using the headings *What Did I Learn?* and *How Did I Learn It?* In the *How* column, students should provide a direct quote from the text. For example, if the *What* column says, "I learned babies have soft spots in their skulls," the *How* column might say, "In small babies the bones of the skull have not yet knitted together. Instead the bones are connected by a stretchy material." You may wish to narrow the scope of the activity by selecting a particular spread to focus on.

EXTEND Have partners choose an item from their T-chart that they would like to know more about. Provide grade-appropriate texts for them to read. Have them present four new facts they learned and an interesting picture to demonstrate one of their new facts.

ACCELERATED LEARNERS

Have students do research and give a brief presentation on a bone, muscle, joint, or tendon. The presentation should include pictures and facts that were not discussed in the text. Provide grade-appropriate sources for students to use.

MORE SUPPORT

Unlock the Text

King of the Parking Lot,
pp. 33–44

QUALITATIVE MEASURES

Levels of Meaning	informational text showing the scientific process of discovery; main idea and supporting details
Structure	chronological order; pictures and map to enhance text
Language Conventionality and Clarity	domain-specific language; scientific vocabulary
Knowledge Demands	scientific method and inquiry; roles of scientists

Prepare to Read

LEVELS OF MEANING

In *King of the Parking Lot*, readers learn about Philippa Langley's search to understand King Richard III's true personality. In her search, she uses the scientific method and involves scientists from other fields of study.

STRUCTURE

PREVIEW In pairs, have students read the title and section headings and view the illustrations. Afterward, ask the following questions:

- Look at the cover page. Who might this person be, and how do you know? (The person might be a king. He has a royal cloak and crown, and he is holding a scepter.)

MORE SUPPORT

ENGLISH LANGUAGE LEARNERS

The text includes words from a variety of different categories. After defining each word on its own, enhance understanding of new vocabulary by helping students categorize and draw connections between words.

STRUGGLING READERS

Have students record unfamiliar words, such as *legendary* or *tyrant,* while reading. Allow them to share their words and clarify meaning as a class. Encourage students to use these words in discussion and writing.

- On page 34, it says, "Philippa Langley is a woman on a mission." Based on the illustrations, title, and headings, what do you think her mission is? (to find the lost bones of a past king, perhaps buried under a parking lot)

- How might the map on page 36 be important? What's in the map? (The map shows a highlighted area in the country of England. Perhaps the story will take place there, or perhaps this is where the king ruled long ago.)

- Look at the title. Based on your preview, can you predict what the story will be about? (The story is about Philippa Langley's search for King Richard III.)

LANGUAGE CONVENTIONALITY AND CLARITY

PREVIEW VOCABULARY Use the Preview and Review Vocabulary Routine in Part 3 to preteach the following words: *trenches, evidence, deformed, excavation, archaeologist, laboratory, genealogist, remains, scoliosis, forensic.* It may also be helpful to discuss related domain-specific vocabulary that students have been introduced to earlier in the unit, such as *spine, skeleton, vertebrae,* and *skull.*

COGNATES Use the list of Spanish cognates at the beginning of this module as a reference to guide your Spanish-speaking students as they read the selection.

KNOWLEDGE DEMANDS

ACTIVATE BACKGROUND KNOWLEDGE Complete the Quick Write and Share Routine in Part 3 to activate students' background knowledge. As a whole group, have students share what they already know about archaeology. Ask guiding questions, such as: What does an archaeologist do? How does an archaeologist go about finding something or someone? What other kinds of scientists might an archaeologist ask for help when solving a problem? Have students look at the photos on p. 37 and p. 41 for additional support.

Interact with Text

LEVELS OF MEANING

As you read *King of the Parking Lot*, periodically assess students' ability to identify main ideas and supporting details.

If . . . students have trouble understanding the main idea and supporting details in each paragraph,

then . . . have students use the Main Idea and Details Graphic Organizer in Part 3.

For example, using the first paragraph on p. 34, explain that the first sentence of a paragraph is usually the main idea. Write the first sentence in the Main Idea box. As you read the paragraph, have students tell how the other sentences support the main idea, and fill in the remaining boxes with the help of students.

STRUCTURE

As students read, periodically stop to assess their understanding of the chronological sequence of events in the text regarding the search for and discovery of Richard III's skeleton.

If . . . students have difficulty determining the order of events,

then . . . use the Time Line Routine and Graphic Organizer in Part 3 to help students place events in sequential order.

In the section "What They Found," have students pay close attention to sequence words and phrases, such as *immediately, first, next,* and *after.* Remind students that identifying these words and phrases will help them keep track of the order of events.

MORE SUPPORT

ENGLISH LANGUAGE LEARNERS

Although both King Richard III's death and Philippa's search happened in the past, Philippa's search occurred in the 21st century, while the king's death is a 15th-century historical event. Help students use a T-chart to distinguish events from each time period.

STRUGGLING READERS

Stop after a paragraph that is dense with information, and have students work by themselves or in pairs to summarize what occurred. Have students write their summaries, in their own words, on sticky notes they can put in their book. This will allow them to easily recall key events and ideas later on.

LANGUAGE CONVENTIONALITLY AND CLARITY

Students may have difficulty understanding some of the scientific and academic vocabulary words. Encourage students to use context clues as an aid to understanding the meanings of new words.

If . . . students have trouble identifying or using context clues,

then . . . read aloud a passage and discuss how context clues can be used to help readers determine word meanings.

As an example, read aloud the first paragraph on p. 38 to provide support. Then think aloud. Say: It says here that the archaeologists *dug two long trenches.* So I know an archaeologist must dig into the ground. They found a monastery when they were digging. I am not sure what that is, but it is in the ground so it was probably built a long time ago. So an archaeologist is probably someone who digs into the ground to find things that are from a long time ago.

KNOWLEDGE DEMANDS

As you read, make sure students can identify and understand the roles of the various scientists who helped discover and analyze King Richard III's skeleton.

If . . . students have difficulty understanding the scientists' roles,

then . . . have them make a chart of the experts involved in the excavation.

For example, have students fill out a four-column chart with the following headings: *Archaeologist, Genealogist, Forensic Scientist, Facial Reconstructionist.* Students should list the roles or tasks of each scientist in the appropriate column. Afterward, they should work in pairs to compare and contrast information about each type of scientist.

Express and Extend

EXPRESS After reading "If Bones Could Speak," work as a class to decide what problem the scientists are trying to solve in this section. In pairs, have students write a paragraph explaining the steps the scientists took to find the solution.

> **If . . .** students have trouble identifying the problem or the steps taken to reach a solution,
>
> **then . . .** use the Problem and Solution Routine and Graphic Organizer in Part 3 to help them distinguish between the problem and the solution.

If students need additional support, write words, such as *carbon dating, spine, skull, arm bones,* and *DNA,* and ask students to write a sentence to explain how each word contributed to the scientists' solution.

EXTEND Read aloud the following problem: You're in charge of a bake sale to raise money for a local food pantry. Once you are set up, you realize you forgot to advertise your bake sale. Because of this, no one knows where or when your bake sale will take place, so they can't come and buy the baked goods. If no one comes to your bake sale, then you won't be able to donate any money to the charity. How can you solve this problem?

Have students write the steps they would take to solve the problem. Make sure they include whom they will ask for help.

EXPRESS Have students look at the picture on p. 40. Ask students what, if anything, the picture adds to the information in the selection. Have them share with the class their rationales for including (or not including) the picture.

EXTEND Have students work in pairs to suggest other pictures to put on that page, based on the information presented in the text. If possible, have them search the Internet for other interesting photos that would add information to the topic discussed in the paragraph of text on that page.

MORE SUPPORT

ENGLISH LANGUAGE LEARNERS

When giving students examples of problems to solve, make them culturally appropriate. Students should be able to solve the problem or understand the example regardless of cultural background.

STRUGGLING READERS

Students may have difficulty organizing their thoughts before writing. Whenever possible, use graphic organizers as a way to aid brainstorming and planning. A web can help students list possible answers to a question or list possible solutions to a problem.

LANGUAGE CONVENTIONALITY AND CLARITY

EXPRESS Talk about Sentences and Words

Display and read aloud the following sentence from *King of the Parking Lot.*

> From the moment the skeleton was found, it began providing clues about the man it belonged to.

Ask: What does the pronoun *it* refer to? (the skeleton) How can a skeleton provide clues? (Scientists will get the answers they need when they analyze the skeleton.) Does the phrase *the man it belonged to* mean that someone else owned the skeleton? (No, this phrase is referring to the once-living man who had that skeleton in his body.)

TEAM TALK Have students work in pairs to discuss the meaning of the following sentences in which nonliving things have human qualities: The leaves danced through the air as they fell. The wind howled through the tree branches. The tide swallowed the shore of the beach.

If students need additional support, use the Analyze Idioms and Expressions Routine in Part 3.

EXTEND Have students work in pairs or alone to write their own sentences in which nonliving things have human qualities. Afterward, they can draw a picture of the literal interpretation and compare it to the figurative meaning.

KNOWLEDGE DEMANDS

EXPRESS Have students reread the last paragraph of the selection, and lead a discussion about why the facial reconstruction of King Richard III does not answer Philippa's initial question. First, help students identify Philippa's initial question. ("Had King Richard III really been the bad guy everyone said?") Then, put the initial question in the center of the Web Graphic Organizer from Part 3. In the surrounding circles, write the scientific facts the scientists discovered. Add circles as needed. Have students cross out the facts that don't answer the initial question.

EXTEND As a class, write a summary of the scientists' findings, and include at least one suggestion of something Philippa might do in the future to reach an answer to her initial question.

ACCELERATED LEARNERS

Have students think of a science question they would like answered. Have them write the steps they would take to gain the information they need to answer the question.

Interactions in Nature and Culture

MODULE A **Cognate Chart**.. 48

Anchor Text Why the Sea Is Salty 50

Supporting Text How the Stars Fell into the Sky 56

Supporting Text Pecos Bill *and* John Henry *from*
American Tall Tales 62

TEXT SET

ANCHOR TEXT
Why the Sea Is Salty

SUPPORTING TEXT
How the Stars Fell
into the Sky

SUPPORTING TEXT
Pecos Bill *and* John
Henry *from* American
Tall Tales

MODULE B **Cognate Chart**.. 68

Anchor Text The Longest Night 70

Supporting Text Northwest Coast Peoples 76

Supporting Text Three Native Nations: Of the Woodlands,
Plains, and Desert 82

TEXT SET

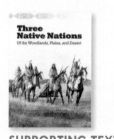

ANCHOR TEXT
The Longest Night

SUPPORTING TEXT
Northwest Coast
Peoples

SUPPORTING TEXT
Three Native Nations: Of
the Woodlands, Plains,
and Desert

Cognates

Cognates are words that have similar spellings and meanings in two or more languages. Many words in English and Spanish share Greek or Latin roots, and many words in English came from French, which is closely connected to Spanish (and to Portuguese, Italian, and Romanian). Because of this, many literary, content, and academic process words in English (e.g., *gracious/gracioso; volcano/volcán; compare/comparar*) have recognizable Spanish cognates.

Making the connection to cognates permits students who are native Spanish speakers to understand the strong foundation they have in academic and literary English. These links between English and Spanish are also useful for native speakers of English and other languages because they help uncover basic underlying features of our language.

ANCHOR TEXT Why the Sea Is Salty

ENGLISH	SPANISH	ENGLISH	SPANISH
adults	adultos	jungle	jungla
bamboo	bambú	markets	mercados
cave	cueva	nervously	nerviosamente
creatures	criaturas	patiently	pacientemente
enormous	enorme	salt	sal
generous	generoso	sauce	salsa
germs	gérmenes	stories	historias
giant	gigante	vegetables	vegetales
horizon	horizonte		
interested	interesado		

SUPPORTING TEXT How the Stars Fell into the Sky

ENGLISH	SPANISH	ENGLISH	SPANISH
animal	animal	important	importante
confusion	confusión	legend	leyenda
coyote	coyote	mosaic	mosaico
design	diseñar	patience	paciencia
disappear	desaparecer	pattern	patrón
dome	domo	pulse	pulso
impatiently	impacientemente		

SUPPORTING TEXT Pecos Bill; John Henry

Pecos Bill		John Henry	
ENGLISH	SPANISH	ENGLISH	SPANISH
appreciate	apreciar	arc	arco
author	autor	breeze	brisa
baby	bebé	cabin	cabaña
coincidence	coincidencia	collapsed	colapsado
combine	combinar	company	compañía
continue	continuar	dignity	dignidad
coyote	coyote	dozen	docena
desert	desierto	impossible	imposible
disaster	desastre	incredible	increíble
heroes	héroes	invention	invención
human	humano	machine	máquina
ignorant	ignorante	mountain	montaña
imagine	imaginar	muscles	músculos
miles	millas	mythical	mítico
naturally	naturalmente	north	norte
plate	plato	protect	proteger
similar	similar	silence	silencio
spirit	espíritu	solid	sólido
terrible	terrible	special	especial

These lists contain many, but not all, Spanish cognates from these selections.

Unlock the Text

QUALITATIVE MEASURES

Why the Sea Is Salty

By Dot Meharry
Illustrated by Paolo Lim

Levels of Meaning	accessible legend set in the Philippines "long ago" that explains that the ocean is salty because of a village's interaction with a friendly giant
Structure	chronological text structure uses past tense to narrate an eight-chapter legend; setting changes may be challenging; narrator is omniscient
Language Conventionality and Clarity	action verbs (i.e. *mined, crouching, measuring, puzzled, wriggled, plucked*) requiring direct instruction; some figurative language and dialogue may require specific support
Knowledge Demands	understanding about salt and its uses, storms, mythological giants, and ants

Prepare to Read

LEVELS OF MEANING

Why the Sea Is Salty is a story that explains a natural phenomenon: the ocean's salinity. It begins by explaining why salt is so important to the people on a Filipino island and how they retrieve it from a giant's cave. When a storm prevents them from going to the giant's island, a boy devises a plan to use the giant's legs as a bridge. The plan works; however, when thousands of ants bite the giant's feet, the salt spills into the ocean. Now, the sea is salty.

STRUCTURE

PREVIEW Explain that this story tells why ocean water is salty. It begins in a time "long ago" when the sea was not salty. However, make sure

ENGLISH LANGUAGE LEARNERS

Make sure students understand the similarities and differences between seawater (saltwater) and freshwater. Suggest that there are some animals that live in freshwater (i.e. trout, frogs) and others that live in seawater (i.e. whales, shrimp).

STRUGGLING READERS

Preview the illustrations on pages 4 and 6. Explain to students that the story takes place on two islands in a nation called the Philippines. Point out its location on a world map. Help students understand that this country is made of 7,107 separate islands!

students understand that this is fictional and that the oceans have always been salty. Ask: Why do people use salt? Do you like the way salt tastes? Why or why not? (People use salt to season foods and to preserve foods. Salt is necessary for human health, but eating too much salt can cause high blood pressure. Some people use salt to melt ice on roads and sidewalks. Salt can also kill germs. Some students will like salt; others will not.)

LANGUAGE CONVENTIONALITY AND CLARITY

PREVIEW VOCABULARY Use the Preview and Review Vocabulary Routine in Part 3 to assess what students know about the following words: *preserve, mined, chamber, crouching, measuring, puzzled, wriggled, plucked*.

COGNATES Use the list of Spanish cognates at the beginning of this module to guide your Spanish-speaking students as they read the selection.

DOMAIN-SPECIFIC VOCABULARY Use the Vocabulary Activities in Part 3 to pre-teach the following domain-specific vocabulary: *Philippines, prawns, bamboo, seasick, squid, horizon, seabed*. Explain that these words are all associated with the culture and geography of islands in the South Pacific.

KNOWLEDGE DEMANDS

ACTIVATE BACKGROUND KNOWLEDGE Explain that one of the main characters in this legend is a giant. Use the Web with Graphic Organizer Routine in Part 3 to record facts and *ideas* with "giant" as the central concept (as a noun, not an adjective). Ask questions such as: What makes someone a giant? What other giants do you know about? Many students will know about the giant in Jack and the Beanstalk. Explain that giants appear in stories from many world cultures. Giants are usually big and strong and live close to nature. The word comes from Greek mythology. It is also used as the name of many sports teams.

STRUGGLING READERS

Have students make lists of words that are related to the word *giant* (large, massive). Then, ask them to list words that are the opposite of *giant* (tiny, little, miniature). Point out that the two main characters in the story are a giant and a child. Ask: Why did the author make the two main characters so different in size? It may be a good time to introduce the concept of exaggeration, common in legends and tall tales.

MORE SUPPORT

Interact with Text

As you read *Why the Sea Is Salty*, assess students' understanding of how cultures use stories to explain natural conditions such as the salinity of ocean water. Point out that this story is a long series of many events that happen over eight chapters. Something happens in each chapter that leads to the events of the next chapter, like a chain. In most cases, the last line of one chapter leads directly to the next chapter. For example, ask students why the author ends Chapter 1 with the sentence, "There was only one place they could get the salt they needed" (page 8).

> **If . . .** students have difficulty seeing how one event leads to the next in the story,
>
> **then . . .** use the Sequence of Events Routine with Graphic Organizer in Part 3 to support understanding.

Suggest to students that they analyze the last sentences in the other chapters. Ask: How does this sentence lead you to what happens in the next chapter? Is this a good way to tell a story? Why or why not? (It creates cohesion. It creates suspense. It gives the reader a purpose for reading the next chapter.)

STRUCTURE

Point out that the story is told in chronological order, but that the action of the story does not begin until Chapter 3 with the words "One day . . ." The first two chapters give the reader background information about the islanders and the giant. In Chapter 1, readers learn how the people used water and how they used salt. In Chapter 2, they learn about the giant, his cave, and his relationship with the people who bring him food in exchange for salt. Chapter 3 introduces a problem (stormy weather prevents people from going to the island to gather salt). Finding its solution is what this story is about.

> **If . . .** students have difficulty understanding what the problem is in Chapter 3,
>
> **then . . .** use the Problem and Solution Routine and Graphic Organizer in Part 3 to support understanding.

Have students describe other events in the story in terms of problems and solutions. For example, vines and twisted tree roots grew across the path to the giant's cave (page 11). They posed a problem. The solution was that the people walked very slowly and carefully to avoid tripping and falling. Another problem was that the smell of the salt made it hard to breathe in the cave (page 12). The solution was that the people filled their baskets as quickly as they could.

ENGLISH LANGUAGE LEARNERS

Discuss the word *bridge* and its multiple meanings (a structure that carries a road over an obstacle, part of a ship, the bony part of the nose). Ask: What do these meanings have in common? (the quality of connecting two things from above)

STRUGGLING READERS

Make sure students understand that tropical fire ants sting humans by injecting a toxic venom when they bite. For humans, this feels like a burn, which is how these ants got their name. The bites often cause nasty red rashes that itch and sting.

LANGUAGE CONVENTIONALITY AND CLARITY

While much of the language will be clear and accessible to students, they may need extra support to understand some of the action verbs.

If . . . students have difficulty understanding some of the action verbs,

then . . . have them make a word web for the action verbs using the Web Graphic Organizer in Part 3.

Students can have fun acting out some of the action verbs from the story. First, have them list the verbs that show actions. Then, create a game of charades with words such as *fill, drank, boiled, bubbled, dried, mined, stored, tripped, crouched, puzzled, wriggled, chuckled, plucked, gasped,* and *wobbled*. Explain that action verbs propel the action of the story forward to its conclusion.

Help students distinguish between the paragraphs that describe what is happening and the paragraphs of dialogue. The characters are not named; they are referred to only as "the boy," "his father" or "the man," "the giant," and "the villagers." Point out that the first two expository chapters have only one line of dialogue. The other chapters have many. Remind them that new paragraphs begin when a new character speaks. The exchange between the boy and several villagers on page 31 is a good example of this.

KNOWLEDGE DEMANDS

Some students may not be familiar with the concept of stories that are passed along from generation to generation to explain facts of nature. Point out that this story is not "Written by Dot Meharry" on the first page, but rather "Retold by Dot Meharry." This means that the writer is simply telling a story that has been told many times before; she has not created the story from her own imagination. Remind them of American folktales and legends such as ones about Paul Bunyan, Brer Rabbit, Casey Jones, John Henry, and Pecos Bill. These stories, too, were not written by one person but passed from storyteller to storyteller. Like *Why the Sea Is Salty*, they are written and owned by an entire culture, not by a single writer.

ENGLISH LANGUAGE LEARNERS

Have students or pairs of students write a caption for each illustration in the story. They can use a sentence from the text or write captions in their own words. For example, the caption for the illustration on page 4 might be, "The people filled their pots with water from the sea." Then, ask them to create one more illustration that is *not* included and write a caption for it.

Express and Extend

EXPRESS Explain that legends not only tell fun stories, they also give readers or listeners information about the people and places they come from. Say: Not only does this legend tell us a story that explains why the sea is salty, it also gives us information about the Philippines, the people who live there, and the foods they eat. In Chapter 1, for example, we learn that the people ate rice, raised pigs and chickens, grew vegetables, dried fish, and made a delicious sauce with prawns.

> If . . . students have difficulty recognizing details about the islands, the people, and their food,
>
> then . . . have students use Three-Column Chart Graphic Organizer in Part 3 to list details from the story. Have students label the columns People, Island, and Food.

EXTEND Have students learn about the Philippines today using online sources. Have them study a map of the Philippines to see the many islands and provinces. Have them find the country's flag, and locate the capital, Manila. If possible, have them use an online translator to translate simple sentences or phrases into Filipino, such as "why the sea is salty."

STRUCTURE

EXPRESS Point out that although the boy is the main character in this narrative, he is not the person who tells the story. The story, like many legends, is told by an omniscient narrator. Model by saying: The "person" who tells this story sees things that happen at the same time in different places. It's like the narrator can "see everything," which is what the word *omniscient* means ("all seeing"). For example, the narrator can see the villagers working on their island and the giant waiting for them on his island at the same time. Then have students discuss how the story would have been different if it had been told by one character.

EXTEND Challenge students to find and share other legends or folktales that use omniscient points of view and the structure of this narrative. For example, the African tales, "Why the Sky is Far Away" "Why the Tortoise Has a Cracked Shell," and "Why the Cheetah's Cheeks Are Stained" are available online. Have students share these stories by retelling them for the whole class.

ENGLISH LANGUAGE LEARNERS

This legend uses sensory language that suggests and describes sights, sounds, smells, tastes, and textures. Have students skim the text and the illustrations to look for these details. Ask: Which sense does the writer appeal to most often?

STRUGGLING READERS

It will help students to be able to hear some of the dialogue of the story read aloud by different voices. Chapter 5, "A Good Idea" contains dialogue between the boy, his father, and the giant. Assign three readers to "play" the three parts while you act as the narrator.

LANGUAGE CONVENTIONALITY AND CLARITY

EXPRESS Talk about Sentences and Words

Display and read aloud the following sentences from *Why the Sea Is Salty.*

> The giant listened carefully as the boy explained how they could make a bridge. The boy's father waited patiently in his boat. The other villagers were strangely silent as they got ready to sail home.

Point out that the three words that end in *–ly, carefully, patiently,* and *strangely,* are examples of adverbs. Adverbs are words that describe verbs, adjectives, or other adverbs. Ask: What words do these three adverbs describe? (*carefully* tells how the giant listened; *patiently* tells how the boy's father waited; *strangely* describes how the people were silent). Point out that in these three examples, the adverbs help explain the characters' feelings or emotions. Use Adverbs for the *When, Where,* and *How* Activity in Part 3 to support student understanding.

TEAM TALK Have partners scan the rest of the story to locate more examples of adverbs that end in *–ly.* Have them determine which words the adverbs describe and discuss what kind of impact the adverbs have on the reader.

EXTEND Have students dive deeply into the climax of the story on pages 38 and 39. Ask: Why were the villagers thrown screaming into the water? (The giant shook them off his legs because of the ant bites.) Encourage them to share times in their own lives when they have been "taken by surprise" and lost their footing.

KNOWLEDGE DEMANDS

EXPRESS Challenge students to imagine what it was like to be one of the villagers who was collecting salt and heading home across the giant's legs. Have them write paragraphs using the first-person "I" in which they include as many sensory details as they can. Ask them to share their paragraphs by reading them aloud.

> **If . . .** students have difficulty imagining sensory details,
>
> **then . . .** use the Description: Sensory Details Routine and Graphic Organizer in Part 3. Guide students to imagine what it might have been like to drop their baskets, tumble into the sea, and be "plucked out of the water" by the friendly giant.

EXTEND Have students use this legend as a model to write one of their own that explains something in nature in your own community. They may write "Why the Pine Trees Grow So Tall," "Why the Moon Changes Shape." Encourage them to use exaggeration as they tell their tales.

ACCELERATED LEARNERS

This narrative is perfect for turning into a drama. Encourage students to rewrite the story as a play, using one, several, or all of the chapters 3 through 8. They can perform the play for the class, for younger children, or in front of a video camera. Another adaptation might be to retell the story as a ballad, a rhyming poem with several stanzas and a chorus about the salty sea. Similarly, have them share their ballads with an appropriate audience.

MORE SUPPORT

Unlock the Text

QUALITATIVE MEASURES

Levels of Meaning	implicit themes of how aspects of the world can be interpreted and how humans are connected to animals and nature
Structure	legend told in third person; illustrations; Native American settings; dialogue
Language Conventionality and Clarity	varied sentence structures, including some lengthy complex sentences; Native American phrases
Knowledge Demands	legend language patterns and sentence structures; Native American imagery and cultural references

How the Stars Fell into the Sky, pp. 74–101

Prepare to Read

LEVELS OF MEANING

How the Stars Fell into the Sky is a retelling of a Navajo legend. It is a legend told to explain one of the mysteries of the world. The theme of the story is not explicitly stated.

STRUCTURE

PREVIEW Form small groups, and have students read the title, look at the illustrations, and scan the text. Ask:

- How is the story formatted? (The story is heavily illustrated. There are no section headings.)

MORE SUPPORT

ENGLISH LANGUAGE LEARNERS

Encourage students to ask clarifying questions when they encounter stumbling blocks. Provide support by providing question starters, such as: What does it mean when ___? Why did the main character ___?

STRUGGLING READERS

Through read alouds, students can be introduced to vocabulary they might not otherwise be able to understand. As you read aloud, stop and guide students to explain the words, phrases, and sentences that may cause confusion.

- How is the story told? (It's a legend told in the third person, and there is a lot of dialogue.)
- What information about the story do the title and illustrations give you? (It will explain how the stars came to exist in the night sky.)

LANGUAGE CONVENTIONALITY AND CLARITY

PREVIEW VOCABULARY Use the Preview and Review Vocabulary Routine in Part 3 to assess what students know about the following words: *pulse, rim, impatiently, dome, mosaic, deliberately, hogan, disarray,* and *haste.*

COGNATES Use the list of Spanish cognates at the beginning of this module to guide your Spanish-speaking students as they read the selection.

KNOWLEDGE DEMANDS

ACTIVATE BACKGROUND KNOWLEDGE Ask students to share what they know about Native American legends. Use the Ask and Answer Questions Routine in Part 3. Ask guiding questions, such as: What is a legend? (A legend is a traditional story sometimes popularly regarded as historical but not authentic.) What legends do you know? (Responses will vary.)

Have students look through the illustrations in the book. Ask: Do you think the events in this legend could really happen? (no) How do you know? Use evidence from the illustrations to support your answer. (Stars cannot be on the ground. People and animals cannot throw stars into the sky. A coyote cannot stand on two legs and talk to a person.)

Interact with Text

LEVELS OF MEANING

Work with students to determine the main theme of the story. Remind them that this text is a legend that details one of the mysteries of the world.

> **If . . .** students have difficulty understanding what theme is,
> **then . . .** explain that theme is the big idea or author's message.

For example, talk with students about how at one time, modern technology didn't exist to examine or analyze objects in space, so people had to create legends to explain mysteries, such as how objects appear in the sky.

STRUCTURE

As students read, periodically stop to assess their understanding of the relationship between the text and the illustrations.

> **If . . .** students have difficulty understanding the connections between the events of the story and the illustrations,
> **then . . .** help students identify where each illustration reflects specific descriptions in the text.

To provide additional support, use a think aloud. Say: Let's look at the text on page 88. Coyote asks if he can help First Woman, and First Woman hands Coyote a star. Now let's look at the illustration on page 89. This picture shows First Woman handing Coyote a star so that he can help her. The picture matches what is stated in the text. Ask students if they can match each sentence on p. 94 to the corresponding illustration.

ENGLISH LANGUAGE LEARNERS

The language in the book often uses nontraditional word order and sentence structure. Encourage students to rewrite sentences, such as "The young mother will sing of them to her child," replacing *of* with *about* to make the sentence, "The young mother will sing about them to her child."

STRUGGLING READERS

Ask students to use visualization to understand imagery. Discuss why the author would use the words *on the blackberry cloth of night*. (A cloth can be the backdrop on which to create a mosaic; blackberry describes the color of the night sky.)

LANGUAGE CONVENTIONALITY AND CLARITY

The sentence structures in this legend can often be confusing. Stop when necessary to explain any sentences that students might find difficult.

If . . . students have difficulty understanding complex sentence structures,

then . . . review the types of sentence structures, and help students break apart each sentence in a way that helps them understand its overall meaning.

Model simplifying sentences by using a think aloud. Say: Let's analyze this sentence from page 80: "First Man turned back impatiently and looked at her squatting there on the rim of the night, a blanket of stars at her feet." I can break this sentence into four smaller sentences to help understand its meaning: "First Man turned back impatiently. He looked at her. She was squatting at the edge of night. A blanket of stars was at her feet." **Show students the complex sentence on p. 82. Have them break this sentence into four or five simpler sentences.**

KNOWLEDGE DEMANDS

How the Stars Fell into the Sky is a Native American legend. Have students find examples of Native American imagery or language patterns that are used to tell the story.

If . . . students have difficulty with the Native American cultural references,

then . . . have students work together to compare the text with the many illustrations that accompany each page.

For example, point out that for each page of text, there is a detailed illustration that helps readers understand the meanings of the words. The word *hogan* is probably an unfamiliar word to most. However, the author includes an illustration of a hogan, so readers can understand it is a type of tent or living structure.

Express and Extend

EXPRESS Have students use appropriate details from the text to summarize the legend. Use the Retell or Summarize Routine and Graphic Organizer in Part 3 for support.

> **If . . .** students have difficulty using their own words to summarize the text,
>
> **then . . .** have them begin by summarizing individual pages of text. Have students give one sentence that tells what is happening on each page.

For example, have students look at p. 98 and summarize the text by writing one sentence that describes what is taking place in all three sentences on the page.

EXTEND Ask students to write one-sentence captions for illustrations in the text. Explain that captions can serve as summaries that describe what is shown in pictures.

EXPRESS Have students discuss who their favorite character is—First Woman, First Man, or Coyote. Students should provide text evidence from the dialogue and events in the text to support their opinions.

> **If . . .** students have trouble keeping track of who is speaking in the dialogue exchanges,
>
> **then . . .** review the words preceding or following quoted text to show students how to identify the speaker.

Use a think aloud to model an example. Say: Let's look at the dialogue on page 78. Two characters are speaking. Each time a different character speaks, the words appear in a new paragraph. What other clues tell me that two characters are speaking? After the first quote, the words *he told her* appear. This tells me First Man is speaking. After the second quote, the words *she answered* appear. This tells me First Woman is speaking. Have students look at the dialogue on p. 92, and use clues in the text to tell when a new character is speaking and identify who the speaker is.

EXTEND Have pairs write a dialogue in which each partner has at least two speaking lines. Students should use what they learned about dialogue to show when a new person is speaking, and they should write text before or after the quotes to indicate who the speaker is.

ENGLISH LANGUAGE LEARNERS

Have students work in groups of four. Have each person choose a section of dialogue and retell that section in his or her own words. Encourage the other students to ask clarifying questions, such as: "Who is speaking now?"

STRUGGLING READERS

Model simplifying one of the sentences. Have partners work together to rewrite another sentence. Have them share their new sentence with other pairs who will then locate the original sentence in the text.

EXPRESS Talk about Sentences and Words

Display the following sentences from *How the Stars Fell into the Sky.* Read them aloud with students.

"Write them on the water then," he said and turned to go, having more important matters on his mind.
"But they will disappear the moment I write them on the water," First Woman called out.
First Man turned back impatiently. . . .

Ask: What is First Man's opinion about writing the laws? (He doesn't think explaining the laws is important.) What words help you understand First Man's point of view? (*having more important matters on his mind; impatiently*)

TEAM TALK Have students work in pairs to rewrite this section of text in their own words.

If . . . students struggle with rewriting the text,

then . . . have them use their own words to describe one page of text to a partner.

EXTEND Place students in pairs. Have one student describe something he or she did earlier that day, and have the other student write the description in his or her own words. Then, have students switch roles and repeat the activity.

EXPRESS Have groups find examples from the story that indicate this is a legend.

If . . . students have difficulty identifying characteristics of a legend,

then . . . explain that a legend uses elements of fantasy to show early man's oneness with nature.

Have students find elements of fantasy on p. 88. (The Coyote is speaking. First Woman's hands are warm from touching stars.) Ask students why the author chose to include these elements of fantasy. (to show that humans are connected to both animals and nature; to help explain how stars got into the sky)

EXTEND Use the Venn Diagram Routine and Graphic Organizer in Part 3 to help students compare and contrast characteristics of *How the Stars Fell into the Sky* with characteristics of *Why the Sea Is Salty.*

ACCELERATED LEARNERS

Have students create a legend about some element of the classroom or their community. Have them write on poster board and include illustrations. Display the finished products around the room.

MORE SUPPORT

Unlock the Text

Pecos Bill, pp. 51–64
John Henry, pp. 65–73

QUALITATIVE MEASURES

Levels of Meaning	themes of folktales and supporting details
Structure	chronological narrative told in the third person; dialogue; pictures
Language Conventionality and Clarity	figurative language, such as simile and hyperbole
Knowledge Demands	folktales and tall-tale traditions; job of a steel driver; cowboy lifestyle

Prepare to Read

LEVELS OF MEANING

In this lesson, students will examine two popular American folktales. "John Henry" is a folktale about a man known as the best steel driver in the country, who lived and worked in the South during the Reconstruction Era after the Civil War. "Pecos Bill" is a tall tale about a legendary cowboy hero who is larger than life.

STRUCTURE

PREVIEW Form small groups, and have students read the titles and scan the author's notes and the first few pages of text. Ask:

- Why do you think the author chose to include notes at the beginning of these stories? (The author probably wanted to help readers understand the setting of the stories better.)

ENGLISH LANGUAGE LEARNERS

Some students might not be familiar with American folktales and tall tales, but they might be familiar with ones from other cultures. Encourage these students to share with the class any folktale or tall tale they know from a different culture.

STRUGGLING READERS

For students who are unfamiliar with folktales or tall tales, provide a dictionary definition of each term. Then share with students a condensed version of a folktale or tall tale so they have a point of reference before reading.

- What can you tell about how the stories are told? (They are both narratives told in the third person. They both contain a lot of dialogue.)
- Which illustrations in the stories show things that may not be true? (In "Pecos Bill," a baby is playing with a bear, and a man is interacting with wild animals, imitating their behavior. In "John Henry," a baby is holding a heavy hammer, and a man is swinging two large hammers at the same time.)

LANGUAGE CONVENTIONALITY AND CLARITY

PREVIEW VOCABULARY Use the Preview and Review Vocabulary Routine in Part 3 to assess what students know about vocabulary words in these stories. For "John Henry," introduce students to the following words: *preacher, lantern, stovepipes, steel driver, tunnel, spikes, ham hocks, molasses, steam drill.* For "Pecos Bill," introduce students to these words: *holler, wallop, tooth and nail, catfish bait, kerplop,* and *kinfolk.*

COGNATES Use the list of Spanish cognates at the beginning of this module to guide your Spanish-speaking students as they read the selection.

KNOWLEDGE DEMANDS

ACTIVATE BACKGROUND KNOWLEDGE Ask students to share what they know about folktales and tall-tale traditions. Use the Ask and Answer Questions Routine in Part 3. Ask: What is a tall tale? (A tall tale is a wildly imaginative story that includes exaggerated adventures of a folk hero in a realistic setting.) What tall tales do you know? (Answers may vary.) What is a folktale? (A folktale is a tale or legend originating among a people and typically becoming part of an oral tradition.) What folktales do you know? (Answers may vary.)

Interact with Text

Work with students to determine the main theme of "John Henry" by looking for details. Remind students that John Henry is a hard-working steel driver. Ask them what the author wants them to learn from this sentence: "A man ain't nothing but a man."

If . . . students have trouble finding other clues in the story about the main theme,

then . . . ask them to look for descriptions in the story that show how hard John Henry works and how good he is to his family and friends.

If students need additional support to determine the theme, ask guiding questions, such as: What made John Henry different from other characters? What is the significance of John Henry competing with a machine? Why do you think railroad workers sang songs about John Henry?

STRUCTURE

Stop periodically to assess whether students understand the chronology of the stories.

If . . . students have difficulty determining sequence of events,

then . . . help them identify words that signal chronology, such as *before, after,* and *finally.*

Model an example by using a think aloud. Say: Let's look at page 63 of "Pecos Bill." The text states, "But after a lovely ceremony, a terrible catastrophe occurred." How do I know which event happened first—the ceremony or the catastrophe? The word *after* tells me that the catastrophe happened later in time. The ceremony happened first. Have students look at the third paragraph on p. 71 of "John Henry" to determine which event happened first—the steam drill working faster than John Henry or John Henry grabbing a second hammer. Have students identify the specific words that provide clues to the sequence of events *(at first, then).*

Use the Sequence of Events Routine and Graphic Organizer in Part 3 if students need additional practice with determining sequence.

ENGLISH LANGUAGE LEARNERS

Students may not have much background knowledge about steel workers or cowboys. Share photographs of actual steel workers and cowboys from books, magazines, or the Internet, and provide some details about what the careers or lifestyles entail.

STRUGGLING READERS

To help students with figurative language, use similes or hyperbole to describe several pictures. Ask students to tell what the figurative language means. For example, *clean as a whistle* describes something neat and tidy.

LANGUAGE CONVENTIONALITY AND CLARITY

Both stories contain examples of figurative language. Explain to students that a simile is a type of figurative language the author uses a lot in "John Henry," while "Pecos Bill" contains hyperbole. Introduce similes and hyperbole to students. A simile is used to compare things or people by using the connecting words *as* or *like*. Hyperbole is an exaggeration, or overstatement, the author uses to entertain readers.

Help students understand similes by presenting them with some examples from the story. For example, "The sky was as black as coal." "His hammer moved like lightning." Ask: What two things are being compared? Can you find other examples of similes in the story? Then help students understand hyperbole by presenting them with some examples from the story. For example, "he teethed on horse shoes" and "he played with grizzly bears." Have students find examples of similes or hyperbole in both stories.

> **If . . .** students have difficulty identifying figurative language,
>
> **then . . .** use the Analyze Idioms and Expressions Routine in Part 3 to help students find expressions that use exaggeration or language that is not meant to be interpreted literally.

KNOWLEDGE DEMANDS

To understand the setting of each story better, have students point out illustrations or words in the text that give clues about each main character's surroundings.

> **If . . .** students have trouble identifying the settings in each text,
>
> **then . . .** use the Story Comparison Routine and Graphic Organizer in Part 3 to help students distinguish between the settings in each story.

For additional support, ask guiding questions, such as: How are the characters of Pecos Bill and John Henry different? What are their jobs? Where do they go to do their jobs? What events show that they are great at their jobs? Where do these events take place?

Express and Extend

EXPRESS Display the following passage from "John Henry." Read it aloud with students, and discuss the theme of the passage.

> …a man ain't nothing but a man. But a man's always got to do his best. And tomorrow I'm going to take my hammer and drive that steel faster than any machine!

Ask: How does this passage support the main theme of the story—that people must strive for excellence? (John Henry says, "a man's always got to do his best.")

Display the following passage from "Pecos Bill."

> Well, call any mountain lion a mangy bobtailed fleabag, and he'll jump on your back for sure. After this one leaped onto Bill, so much fur began to fly that it darkened the sky. Bill wrestled that mountain lion into a headlock, then squeezed him so tight that the big cat had to cry uncle.

Ask: How does this passage support the main theme of the story—that Pecos Bill was one of the greatest cowboys who ever lived? (It shows he was strong and brave.) Students should refer to specific details from the passage during their discussion.

EXTEND Form small groups. Use the Main Idea and Details Routine and Graphic Organizer in Part 3 to help students record and discuss additional supporting details that relate to the theme.

EXPRESS Have small groups summarize the stories of "John Henry" and "Pecos Bill," using dialogue and description to tell the main events of the stories in their own words.

EXTEND Have small groups share and compare their summaries, using evidence from the text to support their decision to include certain pieces of information. After all groups have shared their reasoning, allow each group to revise their summaries based on what they learned from the other groups.

ENGLISH LANGUAGE LEARNERS

If students need additional support to summarize text, provide sentence frames to help them paraphrase ideas using their own words: The main idea of this page is ___. In the dialogue, the characters talk about ___.

STRUGGLING READERS

Have students who are struggling to understand the historical context use the Internet to find and listen to songs about John Henry and Pecos Bill. Ask them to compare the song lyrics to the story to determine what they have in common.

MORE SUPPORT

EXPRESS Talk about Sentences and Words

Read aloud the following sentence from "John Henry."

> It flashed up through the air, making a wide arc more than nineteen feet, then crashed down, driving a steel spike six inches into solid rock.

Have small groups discuss words or ideas in this sentence that make the content of the sentence seem unbelievable or unreal. Some students may have difficulty distinguishing between realistic and unrealistic events in the stories. Have them make a list of expressions that seem to convey something imaginary or unrealistic. Review students' lists with them to clarify any misunderstandings.

TEAM TALK Have students work with a partner to give examples of when the author used exaggeration in the passage. Have them take turns reading them.

EXTEND Have students write two sentences that incorporate exaggeration. Have students trade sentences with a partner. Partners should underline the words in the sentences that show exaggeration.

KNOWLEDGE DEMANDS

EXPRESS Have small groups choose either "John Henry" or "Pecos Bill" and analyze the story to find descriptions that show it is a folktale.

> If . . . students have difficulty identifying the themes of a folktale,
>
> then . . . use a T-chart graphic organizer to help students list realistic elements of the story and unrealistic elements of the story.

EXTEND Have students develop a folktale character based on someone they know. Have them draw an illustration of their character, and include a caption that has the name of their character, along with a description of the character's larger-than-life skills or qualities.

ACCELERATED LEARNERS

Using "John Henry" or "Pecos Bill" as a model for techniques and structure, have students research an actual person and write a legend about him or her, including elements of truth and fantasy.

Cognates

Cognates are words that have similar spellings and meanings in two or more languages. Many words in English and Spanish share Greek or Latin roots, and many words in English came from French, which is closely connected to Spanish (and to Portuguese, Italian, and Romanian). Because of this, many literary, content, and academic process words in English (e.g., *gracious/gracioso; volcano/volcán; compare/comparar*) have recognizable Spanish cognates.

Making the connection to cognates permits students who are native Spanish speakers to understand the strong foundation they have in academic and literary English. These links between English and Spanish are also useful for native speakers of English and other languages because they help uncover basic underlying features of our language.

ANCHOR TEXT The Longest Night

ENGLISH	SPANISH	ENGLISH	SPANISH
arrogant	arrogante	particularly	particularmente
brilliant	brillante	patient	paciente
buffalo	búfalo	prepare	preparar
center	centro	protect	proteger
ceremony	ceremonia	rays	rayos
circle	círculo	recognize	reconocer
continued	continuó	respect	respeto
convinced	convencido	ritual	ritual
coward	cobarde	sacred	sagrado
curve	curva	serious	serio
devour	devorar	strange	extraño
disappeared	desapareció	symbolizes	simboliza
exactly	exactamente	totem	tótem
exhausted	exhausto	tribute	tributo
extinguishing	extinguiendo	triumph	triunfo
humiliating	humillante	venom	veneno
immediately	inmediatamente	vigil	vigilia
incident	incidente	vision	visión
incredibly	increíblemente		
monster	monstruo		
muscles	músculos		
odor	olor		

SUPPORTING TEXT Northwest Coast Peoples

ENGLISH	SPANISH	ENGLISH	SPANISH
adopt	adoptar	movement	movimiento
agriculture	agricultura	nobles	nobles
artists	artistas	ocean	océano
ceremonies	ceremonias	origins	orígenes
clans	clanes	Russians	rusos
climate	clima	symbols	símbolos
disastrous	desastroso	traditional	tradicional
materials	materiales	transportation	transporte

SUPPORTING TEXT Three Native Nations: Of the Woodlands, Plains, and Desert

ENGLISH	SPANISH	ENGLISH	SPANISH
alliance	alianza	legend	leyenda
clan	clan	mask	máscara
colonists	colonos	platform	plataforma
confederacy	confederación	reservation	reserva
descendants	descendientes	silently	silenciosamente
dialects	dialectos	society	sociedad
explorers	exploradores	treaty	tratado
heritage	herencia	tribes	tribus
irrigation	irrigación	tributaries	tributarios
leader	líder	turquoise	turquesa

These lists contain many, but not all, Spanish cognates from these selections.

Unlock the Text

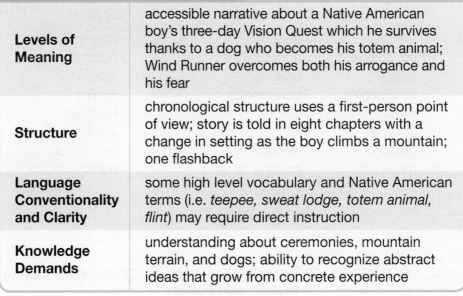

QUALITATIVE MEASURES

Levels of Meaning	accessible narrative about a Native American boy's three-day Vision Quest which he survives thanks to a dog who becomes his totem animal; Wind Runner overcomes both his arrogance and his fear
Structure	chronological structure uses a first-person point of view; story is told in eight chapters with a change in setting as the boy climbs a mountain; one flashback
Language Conventionality and Clarity	some high level vocabulary and Native American terms (i.e. *teepee, sweat lodge, totem animal, flint*) may require direct instruction
Knowledge Demands	understanding about ceremonies, mountain terrain, and dogs; ability to recognize abstract ideas that grow from concrete experience

WRITTEN BY JACQUELINE GUEST
ILLUSTRATED BY ALAN MARKS

The Longest Night

Prepare to Read

LEVELS OF MEANING

The Longest Night is a story of a boy, Wind Runner, who completes a three-day coming-of-age ritual common to his tribe that lives near Hudson Bay. It begins with a dancing ceremony and a sweat lodge with the Elders of his village. During the Vision Quest that follows, a mangy dog leads him to water and teaches him to outsmart and survive a poisonous snake, a hungry wolf, and a black bear. In the process, Wind Runner learns humility and gratitude for the dog as his animal totem. He also learns to accept and overcome his own fear.

ENGLISH LANGUAGE LEARNERS

Have students preview the illustrations in the story. Ask: What are different things the boy does? (He climbs a tree, p. 12; he climbs a mountain, p. 17; he builds a fire, p. 31; he follows the dog, pp. 32-33.) What feelings do the different illustrations suggest? (fear, happiness, relief)

STRUGGLING READERS

Explain to students that in this story Wind Runner performs many actions and other actions happen to him. The writer also describes Wind Runner's thoughts and feelings. Encourage students to look for both actions and feelings in the story.

STRUCTURE

PREVIEW Introduce and explore the word *ceremony*. Explain that a ceremony is an important event performed on a special occasion. Ceremonies follow patterns that often include building a fire, dance performances, and speeches by the elders of the community. Ask: What are some ceremonies in our culture? Record students' responses, using the Web Routine with Graphic Organizer in Part 3 with "ceremony" as the central concept. (ribbon cuttings, groundbreakings, dedications, opening ceremonies of the Olympics, presidential inaugurations, opening days) Explain that this story describes in chronological order a Native American ceremony that happens when boys are fourteen years old.

LANGUAGE CONVENTIONALITY AND CLARITY

PREVIEW VOCABULARY Use the Preview and Review Vocabulary Routine in Part 3 to assess what students know about the following words: *Quest, sacred, warrior, ritual, tribute, ancestors, serpent, obstacle, prey.*

COGNATES Use the list of Spanish cognates at the beginning of this module to guide your Spanish-speaking students as they read the selection.

DOMAIN-SPECIFIC VOCABULARY Use the Vocabulary Activities in Part 3 to pre-teach the following domain-specific vocabulary: *ceremonial, regalia, sweat lodge, Shaman, Elder, teepees, parfleche carrier, totem animal, flint, outcrop.* Explain that these words are all associated with a Native American culture in what is now Canada.

KNOWLEDGE DEMANDS

ACTIVATE BACKGROUND KNOWLEDGE Explain that one of the main characters in this story is a "mangy dog." Explain that mange is a skin disease but that the adjective means "in poor condition, shabby." Invite students to share their own experiences with dogs. Encourage them to share stories about and examples of pets, service dogs, and working dogs. Ask: What roles do dogs play in the lives of humans? Can a dog teach a human a lesson? If so, what kind of lesson would it teach? Record students' responses and return to them after everyone reads the story to see if and how their answers to these questions have changed.

STRUGGLING READERS

Have students locate the illustrations that show the dog. For each illustration, ask: What is the dog doing here? Make a list of their responses, underlining the verbs in phrases such as "climbing a mountain" or "looks at the boy." Make sure they understand the difference between dogs (friendly, comfortable around humans) and wolves (wild, dangerous, predatory). The illustration on page 36 shows a wolf. Ask: How does the illustrator make the wolf look different than the dog? (bared teeth, frightening eyes)

Interact with Text

On page 46, Wind Runner admits, "I see now that I was arrogant." As you read *The Longest Night*, assess students' understanding of *arrogance* and how this abstract concept applies to the events of the story. Explain: Arrogant people have very high opinions of themselves. They think their ideas are right and the ideas of others are wrong. Ask them to give examples of Wind Runner's arrogance throughout the story. Record the list of examples, in chronological order, beginning with his demand for the red glass beads, for everyone to see.

STRUCTURE

Remind students that each chapter title suggests the central event of each chapter, and that all of the chapters are linked together like a chain. However, each chapter also has its own beginning, middle, and end. Each chapter takes place in a certain amount of time, such as one evening, one day, or one night. Challenge students to summarize the events of each chapter as if it were separate from the others.

If . . . students have difficulty describing the sequence of events in each chapter,

then . . . use the Sequence of Events with Graphic Organizer in Part 3 to support understanding.

All of the events in *The Longest Night* happen chronologically, with one important exception. Explain: On page 12, one paragraph happens in an earlier time. The paragraph begins with "When I was twelve . . ." The event described in this paragraph happened two years earlier than the rest of the story. When a narrator describes an earlier event, it is called a flashback. The story of the grizzly bear is a flashback in this story. Ask students why they think the writer considered it important to "go back" and describe this event from the past. (because it foreshadows the bear in chapter 6; because it explains why Wind Runner is so afraid in Chapter 6).

MORE SUPPORT

ENGLISH LANGUAGE LEARNERS

Have students look at the words "*Who's there?*" on p. 17. Make sure they understand that the contraction *Who's* means "Who is." Help them look for other contractions in the story.

STRUGGLING READERS

Help students understand the time frame in this story. It may seem that the story takes place over a long period of time. Emphasize that the story begins in the evening of one day and moves through three more days and nights after that.

LANGUAGE CONVENTIONALITY AND CLARITY

While much of the language will be clear and accessible to students, they may need extra support to understand the Native American proper nouns: Vision Quest, Creator, Shaman, Elder, Spirit Helper, and Medicine Man.

> **If . . .** students have difficulty understanding some of the Native American terms,
>
> **then . . .** use the Web Routine and Graphic Organizer in Part 3 to guide students in creating a word web for challenging terms.

Also, direct students' attention to the antonyms *Worthless* and *Worthy*, both used by Wind Runner to name the dog. Use the words to reinforce their knowledge of the suffixes *–less* (lacking or without) and *–y* (having or holding). Ask: Is it the dog that changes in the story or is it Wind Runner who changes? What evidence supports your answer? (It is Wind Runner who changes. He learns that the dog is not worthless at all. In fact, the dog saves his Vision Quest, and even his life, four different times. He is worthy all along, but Wind Runner is too arrogant to recognize it.)

In addition, call attention to the many adjectives in this text. For example, the paragraph on page 6 that begins "Caught up in the excitement," the writer uses *mangy, angry, foolish, flea-bitten,* and *unafraid.* Emphasize that some adjectives are concrete and sensory (*mangy, flea-bitten*) and others, more abstract, describe feelings and emotions (*angry, foolish, unafraid*). Encourage them to use both kinds of adjectives in their own writing.

KNOWLEDGE DEMANDS

Some students may not be familiar with the concept of spaces or places that hold or contain rituals or ceremonies. In this story, there are three: the dance arena in Chapter 1, the sweat lodge in Chapter 2, and the circle of stones in Chapters 4 through 6. Ask: What are some places that hold ceremonies in our culture? (i.e. gymnasiums, government buildings, pavilions, outdoor arenas, places of worship) Emphasize that sometimes, these places are considered sacred, a word introduced in the first sentence of this text. Usually these places are designed to hold the many people who are present to witness the ceremony. If possible, share photographs of such places, such as St. Peter's Square in the Vatican, the Capital Mall in Washington, D.C., or the space where your high school holds its graduation ceremonies.

ENGLISH LANGUAGE LEARNERS

Invite students to read aloud the words of thanks that Wind Runner speaks to the dog and to the Creator on page 46 as a choral reading. Have them read the words three times together, increasing the volume each time. Make sure they understand the meaning of *symbolizes.* A symbol is a concrete thing (in this case, the dog) that represents an abstract idea (in this case, guidance and loyalty). Ask them to name other symbols, such as a country's flag or national emblem.

Express and Extend

EXPRESS Explain that stories such as *The Longest Night* offer readers or listeners insight into what Native people consider their "wisdom." Say: Listen to a part of the story. The Elders of the tribe are wise. Before his Vision Quest, Wind Runner is not wise. One of the Elders, Many Horses, speaks to Wind Runner as if "he were talking to a small child." Thanks to the dog and a series of challenges, Wind Runner gains wisdom during his Vision Quest. Challenge students to give examples of the wisdom that Wind Runner achieves during his Quest. Suggest that in this story, *wise* might be the opposite of *arrogant*.

If . . . students have difficulty defining wisdom as it applies to this story,

then . . . provide students with the Web Graphic Organizer in Part 3 to record their notes. They can include concrete examples such as "stay still in the presence of a bear" and also more abstract examples such as "being grateful for help."

EXTEND Challenge students to use details from the story to write a paragraph called "The Wisdom of the Raven People." They can use the words and actions of the Elders as a source. They can also interpret the rituals and ceremonies as indicators of the tribe's wisdom.

STRUCTURE

EXPRESS Point out that this story is told using the first person pronoun "I," from Wind Runner's point of view. This choice, made by the writer, limits what the reader discovers. Model by saying: The reader experiences this story as though we are looking through Wind Runner's eyes. You see what he sees. You feel what he feels. However, you also get to know his thoughts as he thinks them. You get to be inside his head. The choice to write a story in the first-person voice allows a writer to share a character's innermost feelings with the reader. Then have students discuss how the story would have been different if it had been told by Many Horses or by Wind Runner's mother.

EXTEND Invite students to write personal narratives about a time when they witnessed or experienced a ritual that symbolized a transition in their lives or in someone else's life. Encourage them to use as many sensory details as possible. Ask them to include a drawing or photograph with a caption. Give students the opportunity to share their narratives with each other, either in pairs, small groups, or with the entire class.

ENGLISH LANGUAGE LEARNERS

This text has many compound words, such as *overlooked, rattlesnake,* and *horsehair.* Have students explain what each smaller word means, and then explain how these two meanings help them understand the meaning of the compound word.

STRUGGLING READERS

Repeated readings and read alouds make it significantly easier for students to recall important passages and process information. Read aloud a section from *The Longest Night.* Then have students tell about the section, using their own words.

MORE SUPPORT

LANGUAGE CONVENTIONALITY AND CLARITY

EXPRESS Talk about Sentences and Words

Display and read aloud the following sentences from *The Longest Night*.

> That bear had made me afraid, made me want to run, made me want to quit, but I had not given into the terror. I had welcomed that fear and made it my own. It had come and gone, just as the bear had come and gone.

Point out that these sentences describe what it happening inside Wind Runner's mind. Words and phrases such as *afraid, want to run, want to quit,* and *terror* describe emotions and feelings that only the narrator could know. Have students locate other paragraphs in the story that describe what is inside the narrator's mind. Remind them that without the first-person point of view, they, as readers, would not know these innermost feelings and thoughts.

TEAM TALK Encourage pairs of students to choose one of the introspective paragraphs from the story to analyze in greater depth. First, have them read the paragraph aloud twice to the other. Then, have them identify the words in the paragraph that show feelings.

EXTEND Have students write paragraphs about fear using the first-person pronoun "I." Have them choose a snake, a wolf, or a bear as their topic. Then, have them imagine an encounter with this wild animal and how they might react based on the "wisdom" they gained from reading *The Longest Night*.

KNOWLEDGE DEMANDS

EXPRESS Challenge students to extend the narrative in *The Longest Night* by writing about what happened when Wind Runner returned to his village. Have them use the first-person "I" to write using Wind Runner's voice and point of view. Pose these questions: What will you say to your mother? To Many Horses? What will your relationship be with the dog? How will your life be different after your Vision Quest?

> **If . . .** students have difficulty imagining these narrative details,
>
> **then . . .** use the Narrative Paragraph Writing Routine with Graphic Organizer in Part 3 to guide students to brainstorm details in a logical way.

EXTEND Ask students to choose an animal totem for themselves based on what they learned by reading *The Longest Night.* Have them bring in photographs or drawings of their totems and share their choices, and the reasons behind them, with the entire group.

ACCELERATED LEARNERS

If a person finds himself or herself in the wilderness without water, there are ways to locate it—even without a dog. Challenge students to research ways to find water in the wilderness and to design and write a short flyer or brochure to impart this "wisdom" to others. Have them document their sources and share their brochures with each other.

MORE SUPPORT

Unlock the Text

QUALITATIVE MEASURES

Northwest Coast
Peoples, pp. 103–117

Levels of Meaning	description of the coastal Northwest Native Americans' culture
Structure	magazine format with columns, two-page spreads; art and photos with captions; sections with headings
Language Conventionality and Clarity	multiple-meaning words; some complex sentences; some domain-specific vocabulary
Knowledge Demands	Northwest Native American history and culture

Prepare to Read

LEVELS OF MEANING

"Northwest Coast Peoples" has two main purposes: to give information about the coastal Northwest Native Americans' culture and to describe their world.

STRUCTURE

PREVIEW Form small groups and have students take a close look at the article's first section. Ask:

• What information does the text box on p. 104 give you? (It lists eleven Native American groups that lived along the Northwest Coast. The map shows you where they lived.)

ENGLISH LANGUAGE LEARNERS

Have students draw pictures of multiple-meaning words. For example, explain that the word *spring* can refer to the season, a coiled piece of metal, or the act of leaping. Have students draw pictures to illustrate these meanings and then use the word in sentences.

STRUGGLING READERS

It may be challenging to decipher where one caption begins and another ends. Model how to read the captions on p. 107. Point out the captions that appear in two columns. Have students use the arrows in each caption to find the picture it describes.

- What do the section headings tell you about the article? (We will learn about the Native Americans' natural resources, village and family life, arts and crafts, and celebrations; the arrival of European settlers to their area; and what the Native Americans are like today.)

LANGUAGE CONVENTIONALITY AND CLARITY

PREVIEW VOCABULARY Use the Preview and Review Vocabulary Routine in Part 3 to assess what students know about the following words: *inland, clan, heritage, traditional, culture, communal, ceremonies, heirlooms,* and *convert*.

Some of the words in this selection have more than one meaning and can be used as nouns or verbs. Use the Analyze Multiple-Meaning Words Routine in Part 3 with the following multiple-meaning words from this selection: *figure, land, spring, rest, spoke, frame,* and *post*.

COGNATES Use the list of Spanish cognates at the beginning of this module to guide your Spanish-speaking students as they read the selection.

KNOWLEDGE DEMANDS

ACTIVATE BACKGROUND KNOWLEDGE Ask students to share what they know about Native Americans from the Northwest. Use the Quick Write and Share Routine in Part 3 to assess students' prior knowledge. As a whole group, have students share what they know about this topic. Have students look through the selection's pictures to get more background information. Ask:

- Where is the coastal Northwest area? (the Pacific Coast from Alaska to Oregon)
- What is culture? (the beliefs, social practices, and characteristics of a group of people based on racial, religious, or social circumstances)
- What do the selection's illustrations tell you about the culture of Native Americans in the Northwest? (Answers may include information about houses, clothes, food, or art. Answers may refer to illustrations that reference the past culture or to photos that reference the present-day culture.)

Interact with Text

Assign pairs a unique spread of the text, and have them determine the main topic of each caption and give details from the caption that relate to the topic.

If . . . students have difficulty determining the main topics and related details in captions,

then . . . use the Web Routine and Graphic Organizer in Part 3 to help them organize information.

Provide additional support by modeling an example for students to use. Use a think aloud. Say: Let's look at the caption on page 104 that is pointing to the map. The first sentence tells the topic of the map and caption—major groups of Northwest Coast Native Americans. I'll write that topic in the center circle of the web. The other sentences in the caption give details that relate to this topic—the groups speaking different languages; having different lifestyles; and being divided into tribes, clans, and family groups. I'll write each of these three details in a different outer circle of the web.

STRUCTURE

Ask students to identify the format of this selection. Ask guiding questions, such as: Is the article more like a book or more like a magazine? (magazine) What features led you to this conclusion? (multiple columns, two-page spreads, lots of four-color illustrations and photos)

If . . . students have difficulty specifying a format,

then . . . have them analyze one spread of the selection and name text features on the pages, such as illustrations and captions.

Discuss how the illustrations are important to the format of the text. Have students examine the illustrations and analyze how they tie into the text and further their understanding of the article.

ENGLISH LANGUAGE LEARNERS

Illustrations can be used to help students interpret the meaning of challenging words. Help students understand the meaning of *totems, candlefish,* and *cradleboard* by pointing to specific pictures in the text that help convey the meaning.

STRUGGLING READERS

Repeated readings make it significantly easier for students to recall important passages and process information. Have students work in pairs. Have one student read a section, and have the other student reread the same section. Then have students explain what they read in their own words.

MORE SUPPORT

LANGUAGE CONVENTIONALITY AND CLARITY

Some of the complex sentences in the article may be difficult for students to understand. Provide practice with analyzing complex sentences. Read these sentences aloud:

> The boiling water made the wood soft, so cross-pieces of wood could be added to push out the sides. After the water was removed, the wood dried and became stiff.

Explain how to break the sentence into smaller parts. Point out how the author uses the connecting words *so* and *after*. Use the Complex Sentences and Independent and Dependent Clauses Activities in Part 3 to provide more practice with complex sentences.

KNOWLEDGE DEMANDS

Some students may have difficulty understanding the specialized words used to describe the Northwest Coast Native American society. Show students how authors sometimes use description to give clues to word meanings. Read aloud the following example from p. 108:

> People of the Northwest Coast often lived in villages that were divided into two groups, called *moieties*. Each moiety was composed of clans. . . . The members of a clan considered themselves related because they shared the same spirit ancestor.

Explain to students that the author defines the term *moieties* in the sentence where the word first appears. In specialized texts, authors often do this to help readers understand the concepts that are being discussed. Have students read the caption on p. 105 and use context clues to determine what a totem pole is.

ENGLISH LANGUAGE LEARNERS

Using context clues can help students infer the meaning of unknown words. Provide sentences using new vocabulary from the selection. Give students context clues, and have them draw pictures of what they think the word means.

Express and Extend

LEVELS OF MEANING

EXPRESS Have pairs of students choose one of the sections in "Northwest Coast Peoples." Have them identify and discuss the main idea and provide key details that support that idea.

> If . . . students have difficulty using text evidence to support the main idea,
>
> then . . . have them use the Main Idea and Details Graphic Organizer in Part 3 to organize the information.

EXTEND Have pairs join other pairs who chose the same section of the article to discuss. Have the sets of partners compare and contrast the main idea and details that they found. Provide groups with the Venn Diagram Graphic Organizer from Part 3 to help them organize information as they compare and contrast. Each group should share its comparison with the class.

STRUCTURE

EXPRESS Have small groups select a section and write a summary paragraph about what they have learned.

> If . . . students have difficulty using their own words to summarize,
>
> then . . . have them reread the section, and help them to list the important details.

To provide additional support, use the Retell or Summarize Routine and Graphic Organizer in Part 3.

EXTEND Have small groups prepare a poster about coastal Northwest Native American culture. Their posters should include illustrations about the culture. Have students write one-sentence captions for each illustration on their poster. Explain that captions can serve as summaries that describe what is shown in a picture.

ENGLISH LANGUAGE LEARNERS

Have students choose a multi-sentence caption and summarize it in a single sentence. Tell students to use their own words and include the most important information.

STRUGGLING READERS

If students have difficulty distinguishing between past and present, provide sentence frames that relate to their own lives: Yesterday, I wore ___. Today, I am wearing ___.

EXPRESS Talk about Sentences and Words

Display the following sentence from p. 110 of "Northwest Coast Peoples." Read it aloud with students.

> The women excelled at weaving baskets and textiles.

Ask: What does the word *excelled* tell you about the women's weaving abilities? (The women were good at weaving different things.) What can you determine about what textiles are? (Textiles are materials that can be woven.) Explain to students that textiles are fabrics used to make clothing or household goods, such as rugs. Show pictures from the text to clarify the meaning.

TEAM TALK Have students work in pairs to replace the word *textiles* in the sentence without changing its meaning.

EXTEND Have students make a list of the natural materials and animal products mentioned in the text that were used to make items other than baskets and textiles, such as canoes, harpoons, and ropes. Ask students to tell why they think the Native Americans in the Northwest made these items themselves.

KNOWLEDGE DEMANDS

EXPRESS Have small groups use evidence from the text to discuss how coastal Northwest Native American culture has changed over the years, and what it is like today.

> If . . . students have difficulty explaining how the culture has changed over the years,
>
> then . . . have students use a graphic organizer to organize the information from the selection.

Explain to students that they can use a two-column chart graphic organizer to sort information about the past and present. Have them use the headings *Past* and *Present* for the columns in their charts.

EXTEND Have students write two to three paragraphs describing two or three interesting traditions from the coastal Northwest Native American culture.

ACCELERATED LEARNERS

Have students choose another Native American tribe to read about. Students can write a brief report, include drawings, and use the same format as the article.

Unlock the Text

QUALITATIVE MEASURES

Three Native Nations
Of the Woodlands, Plains, and Desert

Levels of Meaning	accessible information about three Native nations, including main ideas and details about history, clothing, food, customs, shelter, and community life
Structure	information organized into three sections, each one covering one nation; ten sidebars offer specific information; maps show territories; TOC, glossary and index support text
Language Conventionality and Clarity	some high level vocabulary, including Native American and sociological terms (i.e. *buckskin, wampum, alliance, reservation, dialect, custom*) may require direct instruction
Knowledge Demands	understanding about North American geography and the meaning of "Native American"; ability to recognize broad sociological changes over long periods of history

Prepare to Read

LEVELS OF MEANING

Three Native Nations: Of the Woodlands, Plains, and Desert is an informative text about the Haudenosaunee in what is now New York state, the Sioux in the Northern Plains, and the Pueblo people in deserts of the southwest. Historical facts explain the names of the nations, their various parts, and how each tribe changed when Europeans arrived. Descriptions of food, clothing, shelter, customs, and daily life bring each culture to life. More in-depth information in the sidebars focuses readers on various aspects in greater specificity.

ENGLISH LANGUAGE LEARNERS

Use the list of proper names in the Index to introduce students to the pronunciation of Native names. Add *Haudenosaunee, Sioux,* and *Pueblo* to the list. Say each name, and have students repeat after you.

STRUGGLING READERS

Since the three parts of this passage are completely independent of each other, you may want to address them as three separate texts. Have three groups of students read each of the three parts and then share information with the other groups in oral presentations.

STRUCTURE

PREVIEW Show students a map of the continental United States. Point to New York state and the area near the Great Lakes. Point to the Northern Plains and the location of the Bad Lands (North Dakota). Point to New Mexico and Arizona in the southwest. Ask: How are these three places different from each other? Record students' responses, using the Three-Column Chart Routine in Part 3. Say: You are going to read information about Native people who lived in these three areas. The differences in the three places made their lives different. Their food was different. Their homes were different. Their customs were different. However, despite their differences, they also were alike in some ways. As you read, notice both the similarities and differences, and think about what makes each nation unique and proud.

LANGUAGE CONVENTIONALITY AND CLARITY

PREVIEW VOCABULARY Use the Preview and Review Vocabulary Routine in Part 3 to assess what students know about the following words: *legend, festivals, clan, descendants, reservation, quill, custom, fashion.*

COGNATES Use the list of Spanish cognates at the beginning of this module to guide your Spanish-speaking students as they read the selection.

DOMAIN-SPECIFIC VOCABULARY Use the Vocabulary Activities in Part 3 to pre-teach the following domain-specific vocabulary: *buckskin, wampum, colonists, treaty, sinew, dialect, travois, pueblo, tributary.* Explain that these words are all associated with a Native American culture in different parts of what is now the United States.

KNOWLEDGE DEMANDS

ACTIVATE BACKGROUND KNOWLEDGE Explain that the idea of culture is based on specific details about a group of people. Guide students to complete the Web Graphic Organizer with "culture" as the central idea. Ask: What kinds of information show us something about a culture? Get them started with categories such as *food, clothing, homes,* and *language.* Through discussion and brainstorming, help students understand that *culture* is an abstract idea supported by details that are specific and concrete. After students have filled in the web (and added other ovals to it) with as many examples as possible, let them describe culture in your town, city, or state by giving examples from each category they've defined.

STRUGGLING READERS

Spend time discussing the multiple meanings of *reservation*. In this passage, the word refers to separate pieces of land onto which Native nations have been relocated. Students may also be familiar with another meaning that refers to an arrangement to have something held (such as a room or a seat) for use at a later time. They also may know about "having reservations" about something, that is, feeling doubt or uncertainty. You can find a map and a list of all Native reservations in the United States online.

Interact with Text

LEVELS OF MEANING

As you read *Three Native Nations*, assess not only students' understanding of the facts and details, but also their opinions about what they read. Specifically, solicit two opinions: What detail(s) about this nation do you find the most interesting or unique? Why? Do you think this nation was treated fairly by the United States government? Why or why not? Ask students to cite specific examples that support their opinions. Remind them that any opinion they express, whether in writing or speaking, must be supportable with concrete evidence.

STRUCTURE

Suggest to students that each heading in the text can be the subject of a sentence that expresses a main idea. For example, "The Birth of An Alliance" can be turned into, "Five native nations formed an alliance called The People of the Longhouse." These main ideas, in turn, are supported by the many details the writer has chosen to include. For example, this first main idea is supported by details about Hiawatha and Deganawida, the meaning of wampum, the names of the five nations, the two names, and the map that shows where each nation lived. Invite students to turn each heading into a sentence that expresses the main idea of the section and then list details that support each one.

> **If . . .** students have difficulty recognizing the relationship between main ideas and details,
>
> **then . . .** use the Main Idea and Details Routine with Graphic Organizer in Part 3 to support understanding. They can complete one of these organizers for each section of the text.

Point out the three parts of the text that do not include main ideas and details: the Table of Contents on page 3 and the Glossary and Index on pages 47-48. Ask: What are the purposes of these three text features? (to show the three parts and the page locations, to define unfamiliar words, to show on what pages certain names appear) How are these features different from the rest of the passage? (They support the rest of the passage and help readers understand it better. They are not written in complete sentences. They are not meant to be read from beginning to end. They are not much fun to read by themselves.)

MORE SUPPORT

ENGLISH LANGUAGE LEARNERS

Many words in this passage name collections of people: *nation, clan, village, family, government, society,* and *reservation*. Make a list of these collective nouns and have students locate them in the text. Ask: How are these words alike? (They name groups of people.) How are they different? (The groups have different reasons or purposes.)

STRUGGLING READERS

Make sure students understand the difference between *ancestors* (relatives who came *before* someone) and *descendants* (relatives who are born *after* someone). Have students pronounce each word and use each one in a sentence.

LANGUAGE CONVENTIONALITY AND CLARITY

While much of the language will be clear and accessible to students, they may need extra support to understand the Native American terms and names.

If . . . students have difficulty understanding some of the Native American terms,

then . . . have them refer to the Glossary or add words and definitions to the Glossary that are unfamiliar to them. Also, encourage them to find additional photographs and illustrations online.

Since the author uses both in this text, take the opportunity to teach or reinforce the distinction between concrete nouns and abstract nouns. Say: Concrete nouns name things you can touch, smell, taste, see, or hear. Abstract nouns name ideas that you cannot observe with your senses. For example, on pages 4-6, *birds, belts,* and *trapper* are concrete nouns. On the other hand, *harm, peace,* and *plenty* are abstract. Challenge students to find examples of both kinds of nouns throughout the text.

In addition, call attention to the many examples of compound nouns in the text, such as *woodlands, longhouses, Peacemaker, deerskin*, and *cornstalk*. Challenge students to find other examples. Remind students that compound nouns can be one word (*sunshine*), two words (*New York*), or hyphenated (*modern-day*).

KNOWLEDGE DEMANDS

Some students may not be familiar with the broad historical concept that Native people lived in North America for many centuries before Europeans invaded and took their land. Say: Long, long ago, an ice age froze so much water that humans crossed a land bridge from Asia to North America. New civilizations began in North and South America. They lived in harmony with the land and nature until the Europeans began to arrive in the 1500s. A timeline of the various centuries might help students understand these eras. Explain that there is no way to know how many Natives lived in North America before the Europeans invaded, but that historians estimate that nearly 90% were killed by disease or war by 1800.

ENGLISH LANGUAGE LEARNERS

Invite students to make models of one or several of the structures described in the text: a longhouse, a teepee, The Three Sisters growing, a travois, a False Face, a Husk Face, a pueblo village, or a kachina doll. You might also bring in, if possible, examples of a porcupine quill, dried buffalo, deerskin moccasins, or a beaded belt for students to see and experience.

MORE SUPPORT

Express and Extend

EXPRESS Remind students that one quality of life among all three cultures is that women played important roles in community structure and life. Say: In the Haudenosaunee society, a group was connected by a single woman who was its leader. These women made the important decisions for the whole group. In Sioux communities, men and women were equal but had different roles. In Pueblo society, women headed the clans and owned the property. Men married into the clans of their wives. How is this role of women different from that of other cultures you know about? How is it different from culture in the United States today?

> **If . . .** students have difficulty making generalizations about the role of women in different cultures,
>
> **then . . .** use the Draw Conclusions Routine and Graphic Organizer in Part 3 to guide students in recording their notes and reaching a conclusion.

EXTEND Ask students to write opinion paragraphs about the role of women in one of the nations described in this text. Do they think the role is more powerful or less powerful than in our own culture? Remind them to give specific and concrete reasons and examples to support their opinions.

EXPRESS Point out that each of the three parts of this text begins with a description of representative people. Model by saying: The writer wants to engage your imagination by describing a person from each nation before he begins to give you facts and details. For example, on page 4, he begins by describing two men in the woods, waiting for others to join them. He describes the sounds and the silence. He describes the sight of the wampum. These descriptive details are the writer's way of introducing each nation and hooking the reader into reading more. Then have students examine the introductions to the other two parts. Ask: What senses does the writer appeal to here? Is this introduction effective? Why or why not?

EXTEND Invite students to write their own descriptive paragraphs about one particular place or situation from the text. For example, they might imagine being inside a longhouse or teepee, being on a Lakota buffalo hunt, or planting seeds in a Hopi farm.

ENGLISH LANGUAGE LEARNERS

Have students choose one photograph from the text that they are particularly interested in. First, have them write a caption for the photograph. Then, have them write at least three descriptive words or phrases about what they see.

STRUGGLING READERS

Explain to students that a treaty is an agreement that is negotiated or worked out between two parties (usually whole countries). Usually, in a treaty, each party gives up something and gains something.

LANGUAGE CONVENTIONALITY AND CLARITY

EXPRESS Talk about Sentences and Words

Display and read aloud the following sentences from *Three Native Nations*.

> The Dakota now have more than 245,000 acres of land. Wildlife, including buffalo, have been reintroduced. Children in Spirit Lake learn the Dakota language and the traditional customs and beliefs of the people.

Explain that the main idea of the last paragraph on page 31 is stated in the second sentence: "The people there are trying to recover their traditional ways of life." Say: The writer supports this idea with three specific details in the sentences I just read. First, the Nation has been buying land. Second, they have introduced wildlife such as the buffalo. Third, they teach their children the Dakota language and customs. Remind students that supporting a main idea with at least three strong, solid, and specific details is good informative writing.

TEAM TALK Encourage pairs of students to discuss the effects that the Europeans had on the three nations. In their opinion, which nation suffered most? Encourage them to cite strong, solid, and specific details to support their opinion.

EXTEND Have students write opinion paragraphs about another way that a Native nation might recover, celebrate, or share its traditional ways of life. Suggest that they find an idea in the text.

KNOWLEDGE DEMANDS

EXPRESS Challenge students to find out more information about the American buffalo, also known as the American bison. Ask: What do buffalo eat? Where do buffalo live? How long do they live? Have them combine what they learn with information from the sidebar on pages 20-21 to write either short reports about buffalo or poems that praise Tantanka.

> **If . . .** students have difficulty using details to write a paragraph or poem,
>
> **then . . .** use the Informative/Explanatory Writing Routine and Graphic Organizer in Part 3 to guide students in their writing.

EXTEND Ask students to choose one of the clan animals on page 9 for the subject of a research report. Based on their research, ask: What human qualities would a clan based on this animal value most? Encourage them to make drawings or even masks of their animals to display in the classroom.

ACCELERATED LEARNERS

On page 30, the writer suggests that people who live on reservations "suffer social problems." He cites poverty and low high school graduation rates as two details that support this main idea. He also suggests that employment is a problem, too. Have students find out more about the problems of Native Americans who live on reservations. Encourage them to find out if there is a local reservation, and, if so, to find more information about it.

Exploring Impact and Effect

MODULE A **Cognate Chart** **90**

Anchor Text Earthquakes **92**

Supporting Text Quake! **98**

Supporting Text Earthshaker's Bad Day/The Monster
Beneath the Sea **104**

TEXT SET

ANCHOR TEXT
Earthquakes

SUPPORTING TEXT
Quake!

SUPPORTING TEXT
Earthshaker's Bad Day/
The Monster Beneath
the Sea

MODULE B **Cognate Chart** **110**

Anchor Text Anatomy of a Volcanic Eruption **112**

Supporting Text Escape from Pompeii **118**

Supporting Text A Tsunami Unfolds **124**

TEXT SET

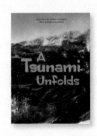

ANCHOR TEXT
Anatomy of a Volcanic
Eruption

SUPPORTING TEXT
Escape from Pompeii

SUPPORTING TEXT
A Tsunami Unfolds

Cognates

Cognates are words that have similar spellings and meanings in two or more languages. Many words in English and Spanish share Greek or Latin roots, and many words in English came from French, which is closely connected to Spanish (and to Portuguese, Italian, and Romanian). Because of this, many literary, content, and academic process words in English (e.g., *gracious/ gracioso; volcano/volcán; compare/comparar*) have recognizable Spanish cognates.

Making the connection to cognates permits students who are native Spanish speakers to understand the strong foundation they have in academic and literary English. These links between English and Spanish are also useful for native speakers of English and other languages because they help uncover basic underlying features of our language.

ANCHOR TEXT Earthquakes

ENGLISH	SPANISH	ENGLISH	SPANISH
apartment	apartamento	international	internacional
area	área	latitude	latitud
arts	artes	longitude	longitud
center	centro	magnitude	magnitud
compare	comparar	million	millón
construction	construcción	miniature	miniatura
continental	continental	moderate	moderado
culture	cultura	modern	moderno
curiosity	curiosidad	movement	movimiento
desert	desierto	museum	museo
destruction	destrucción	natural	natural
digital	digital	observations	observaciones
education	educación	occur	occurir
effect	efecto	ocean	océano
energy	energía	planet	planeta
enormous	enorme	scale	escala
experience	experiencia	sections	secciones
exploration	exploración	seismograph	sismógrafo
future	futuro	solid	sólido
garage	garaje	stresses	estreses
history	historia	suffer	sufrir
immense	inmenso	vertical	vertical
important	importante	violent	violento
indicate	indicar	volcanos	volcanes
intensity	intensidad	zone	zona

SUPPORTING TEXT Quake!

ENGLISH	SPANISH	ENGLISH	SPANISH
agitate	agitar	impossible	imposible
apartments	apartamentos	lamps	lámparas
balconies	balcones	moment	momento
collapse	colapsar	possessions	posesiones
complete	completar	probably	probablemente
continue	continuar	protection	protección
conversation	conversación	recite	recitar
decide	decidir	separate	separado
decorations	decoraciones	silence	silencio
description	descripción	utensils	utensilios
destruction	destrucción	visible	visible
imagine	imaginar	vivid	vívido

SUPPORTING TEXT The Monster Beneath the Sea; Earthshaker's Bad Day

Monster

ENGLISH	SPANISH
alarm	alarma
artist	artista
ceremony	ceremonia
control	controlar
expert	experto
garden	jardín
Japan	Japón
nation	nación
ocean	océano
representation	representación
solid	sólido
system	sistema
trap	atrapar

Earthshaker

ENGLISH	SPANISH
cause	causar
celebrate	celebrar
competition	competición
human	humano
palace	palacio
pearls	perlas
perfect	perfecto
problems	problemas
product	producto
temple	templo
transport	transportar

These lists contain many, but not all, Spanish cognates from these selections.

Unlock the Text

QUALITATIVE MEASURES

Levels of Meaning	learning about the causes and impacts of earthquakes and where they occur
Structure	no headings; heavily illustrated with photos, maps, and diagrams
Language Conventionality and Clarity	informational narrative; scientific terms clearly defined; illustrations and photos aid word meaning; multiple-meaning words
Knowledge Demands	geology of earthquakes; geography; scientific terminology

✦ Smithsonian

Seymour Simon

EARTHQUAKES

Prepare to Read

LEVELS OF MEANING

The main purpose of *Earthquakes* is to inform about the causes and impacts of earthquakes and to show the areas of the world where they usually occur.

STRUCTURE

PREVIEW Have students preview the text, focusing on how the text and illustrations interact. Ask these guiding questions: Which images did the author include captions for? (maps and diagrams) Why do you think this is? (to give the reader detailed information about what is shown in the maps and diagrams) Look at the maps included in the selection. What do the maps show? (They show areas of the United States and the world where earthquakes occur.) What information does the glossary provide? (definitions for scientific terms in the text) What information does the

ENGLISH LANGUAGE LEARNERS

To give students guidance with multiple-meaning words, display the sentence, "Faults run through the Earth's crust." Have students read the text that defines the words *fault* and *crust* and find pictures of both in the selection. Then have partners use both words in sentences.

STRUGGLING READERS

Have students begin creating a glossary to use throughout this unit. As students encounter new words, have them record the word, the definition (or definitions in the case of multiple-meaning words), and a small illustration.

index provide? (the page numbers where certain topics, photos, and illustrations can be found)

LANGUAGE CONVENTIONALITY AND CLARITY

PREVIEW VOCABULARY Use the Preview and Review Vocabulary Routine in Part 3 to assess what students know about the following words: *earthquake, destruction, tsunami,* and *observation*.

CRITICAL VOCABULARY Use the Vocabulary Activities and Games in Part 3 to teach critical, domain-specific vocabulary words, such as *shockwave, aftershock, seismograph, tremor,* and *magnitude*.

MULTIPLE-MEANING WORDS Help students expand their understanding of words with multiple meanings by using the Act Out or Draw Meaning Routine in Part 3. For example, contrast *wave* as a verb, meaning "to move one's hand back and forth as a greeting," with *wave* as a noun, meaning "a moving ridge on the water's surface." Create an illustration for each use. Then, have students do the same with other multiple-meaning words in the text, such as *shock, crust, fault, mantle, plate, floor, coast, rim,* and *record*.

COGNATES Use the list of Spanish cognates at the beginning of this module to guide your Spanish-speaking students as they read the selection.

KNOWLEDGE DEMANDS

ACTIVATE BACKGROUND KNOWLEDGE Tell students that in this unit, they will be reading four texts about earthquakes. Use the Quick Write and Share Routine in Part 3 and have students share what they already know about earthquakes. Ask: What is an earthquake? What do you think an earthquake feels like? What might cause an earthquake? How do people deal with earthquakes?

Model a response, such as: I know that earthquakes are natural disasters and that they can cause damage to buildings and roads. I remember hearing about an earthquake in California. The news said it was very bad and destroyed the baseball stadium in San Francisco! I don't know what causes earthquakes to happen, but I know they are powerful enough to destroy large things.

Smithsonian

EARTHQUAKES

Seymour Simon

Interact with Text

As students read *Earthquakes*, periodically assess their ability to identify the main ideas and supporting details. Have students choose one of the following topics and identify the main idea about the topic and details in the text that support the main idea: the destructive forces of earthquakes, causes of earthquakes, places where earthquakes happen, measuring the size of earthquakes, or protection from earthquakes.

If . . . students have difficulty identifying the main idea and supporting details for their chosen topic,

then . . . use the Main Idea and Details Routine and Graphic Organizer in Part 3 for additional support. After writing a main idea in the box at the top of the graphic organizer, help students identify and record supporting details in the remaining boxes. Provide students with the following sentence frames as needed: The most important idea is ___. One detail about this idea is ___.

STRUCTURE

Since the text is not divided into chapters and does not contain headings, students may need additional guidance to follow the writer's flow of ideas. Have students work in groups to summarize the information on each spread.

If . . . students have difficulty summarizing information,

then . . . use the Retell or Summarize Routine and Graphic Organizer in Part 3 for additional guidance.

Remind students that summaries should include the most important information from the text, stated in their own words.

ENGLISH LANGUAGE LEARNERS

Illustrations can be used to help students understand challenging words. Give students extra support by pointing to specific pictures in the text that help convey the meanings of certain words, such as *collapsed, fault, immense,* and *magnitude.*

STRUGGLING READERS

If students need additional guidance to summarize text, provide the following sentence frames to help them put important information into their own words: The main idea of this page is ___. One important idea in the text is ___.

LANGUAGE CONVENTIONALITY AND CLARITY

The writer uses clear explanations and helps convey word meanings with useful illustrations. For example, read aloud and display the following passage from p. 9:

> Sections of the crust have slipped past each other along the two strike-slip faults and offset this ridge in Wyoming (left). Sometimes one side of a fault will slip up over the other. This is what happened along this highway in the Mojave Desert in California (right). This kind of upward movement is called a thrust fault.

Ask pairs of students to describe the words *strike-slip faults, ridge,* and *thrust fault* in their own words, based on the passage, the photos, and the arrows in the photos. Tell students that, since every spread has an image, they can use this strategy for other geological terms in the text.

KNOWLEDGE DEMANDS

After reading, divide students into small groups. Have each group find and choose one main topic from the text; examples include how earthquakes are formed, where earthquakes occur, or how earthquakes are studied and measured. After choosing a topic, have students create a script for either an informative presentation or a skit about their topic. The scripts should include vocabulary and specific details from the text. Allow students the time and materials necessary to make props or visual aids, as needed.

Give students time to practice their performance, and then have students present to the class. Remind students to actively listen when they are not performing and to generate questions for the class after each presentation to reinforce the themes. Use the Monitor Understanding: Listening Skills Log Routine in Part 3 if students need additional practice as active listeners.

Express and Extend

LEVELS OF MEANING

EXPRESS Point out to students that this text has many cause-and-effect relationships. Explain that sometimes it is easier to identify the effect and then revisit the text to find the cause or causes. In pairs, have students use text evidence to find and discuss the cause of sand boils.

If . . . students have difficulty identifying causes,

then . . . use the Cause and Effect Routine and Graphic Organizer in Part 3 to provide additional support.

Demonstrate how to fill in the graphic organizer, using the causes of an earthquake on the top of p. 8. After writing the effect, "Blocks (tectonic plates) at rest," have students help you fill in the rest.

EXTEND Have students write a letter to a friend or family member about the importance of earthquake safety, and have them reference an example of an earthquake from the text. Tell them to include where the earthquake was, what caused it, and what happened afterward. This exercise will help students synthesize and critically analyze the information from the text.

STRUCTURE

EXPRESS Initiate a discussion about the importance of the illustrations, photographs, and diagrams in the text. Have students explain how the text would be different without the illustrations, photographs, and diagrams. Ask: How do these features help you better understand the text?

EXTEND Have students choose five photographs from the text and write captions for those photographs. Remind them that captions tell more about photographs. Have students share their captions with a partner.

MORE SUPPORT

ENGLISH LANGUAGE LEARNERS

Use sentence frames to support students' speaking and writing tasks. As an example, have them look at the photo on p. 18 and fill in these sentence frames: The man is a ___. He is studying a ___ to measure earthquake ___.

STRUGGLING READERS

Help students distinguish between causes and effects by explaining that causes happen before effects. Provide a demonstration by dropping a pencil on the floor. Ask students to identify the cause (dropping pencil) and the effect (pencil falling to floor).

LANGUAGE CONVENTIONALITY AND CLARITY

EXPRESS Talk about Sentences and Words

Display the following passage from *Earthquakes*, and read it aloud with students:

> Scientists have learned much about earthquakes and their effects. They can measure the slightest movements along faults. But we need to know much more about earthquakes before we can predict weeks and even days in advance when a big one will hit.

Ask: What does the author mean by a *big one will hit?* (A big earthquake will happen.) Why do you think the author chose to use these words? (to convey excitement or drama) What does *fault* mean in this passage? What is another meaning? ("the line where two plates come together"; "a failing")

TEAM TALK Have students turn to a partner and use *fault* in sentences to show both meanings.

EXTEND Have students apply concepts from the text to write a letter to a friend who is moving to California. In their letter, students should explain to their friend the importance of understanding earthquakes. Students should use and define scientific terms from the text correctly in context. Have students share their letter with a partner.

KNOWLEDGE DEMANDS

EXPRESS Have pairs or small groups write a brief description of what a seismologist does. Tell students to include an explanation telling why studying earthquakes is important.

If . . . students have difficulty explaining the importance of studying earthquakes,

then . . . lead a discussion about how the information in this book might be useful to people.

EXTEND Have students use the Venn Diagram Graphic Organizer in Part 3 to compare the Richter Scale and the Mercali Intensity Scale. Include their uses, numerical scales, and when they are used. Discuss student's diagrams as a class.

ACCELERATED LEARNERS

Using the text for guidance, have students create a brochure for people in southern California detailing what to do before, during, and after an earthquake to stay safe. Students should include illustrations alongside the text. Allow time for research, if needed.

MORE SUPPORT

Unlock the Text

Quake! pp. 5–24

QUALITATIVE MEASURES

Levels of Meaning	historical fiction about the 1906 San Francisco earthquake; emotional account of bravery as told by a witness who lives through the earthquake
Structure	three sections of a longer book; section titles; two illustrations with captions; italicized text
Language Conventionality and Clarity	vivid figurative language; dialogue; dialect; phrasal verbs
Knowledge Demands	earthquakes; immigrants; animal senses; life in the early 1900s

Prepare to Read

LEVELS OF MEANING

The author's main purpose in *Quake!* is to describe what happens to Jacob, his family, and his dog during and after the 1906 earthquake in San Francisco. An underlying purpose is to give a vivid description of the destruction, shock, fear, and disorientation the people experienced in the aftermath.

STRUCTURE

PREVIEW Have students preview the text, focusing on how the structure is different from the structure of *Earthquakes*. Ask: How is the structure different? (There are chapters with chapter titles, two illustrations, and no photographs or maps.) Look at the illustrations. How are they different from those in *Earthquakes*? What else do you notice? (They are drawings of characters and settings. The pictures show the effects earthquakes have on people—not just the effects they have on the land. There are captions

ENGLISH LANGUAGE LEARNERS

Students may have difficulty understanding the meanings of the verbs in the phrasal verbs. For example, they may not know what *hustled* means. Have students look up the definition of unknown words to help them determine the meaning of the phrasal verbs.

STRUGGLING READERS

Research shows that it takes many repetitions for new words to be recalled and acquired. Use the Vocabulary Activities and Games in Part 3 to provide more practice with new words that students are having difficulty with.

to explain the drawings.) What clues does the cover of the book give you about the story? (The title and subtitle tell us that the story is about an earthquake in San Francisco in 1906. The illustration shows a boy and his dog, who are probably main characters.)

LANGUAGE CONVENTIONALITY AND CLARITY

PREVIEW VOCABULARY Use the Preview and Review Vocabulary Routine in Part 3 to assess what students know about the following words: *disaster, frantic, terror, agitated, collapse, tremble, debris, calamity, rubble*.

COGNATES Use the list of Spanish cognates at the beginning of this module to guide your Spanish-speaking students as they read the selection.

PHRASAL VERBS Explain that sometimes when a verb appears before a preposition, the meaning of the two words together can be difficult to understand. This is because the meaning of the two words together is not based on the meaning of each individual word. Use a think aloud. Start by displaying and reading aloud the following sentence: We are going to hang around until our ride shows up. Say: In this sentence, the phrase *hang around* means "stay," and the phrase *shows up* means "arrives." I can say, "We are going to stay until our ride arrives," and it means the same thing. Write on the board the following phrasal verbs from the selection. Help guide students to determine what each phrasal verb means.

doze off	weigh in	catch up	take off
bear with	make up	keep up	tag along

Have students write a sentence using each phrasal verb. Ask them to share their sentences with a partner. Tell students to record other phrasal verbs they encounter as they read.

KNOWLEDGE DEMANDS

ACTIVATE BACKGROUND KNOWLEDGE After reading *Earthquakes*, students should understand the damage an earthquake can inflict on people and places. Refer students back to the photo of the San Francisco earthquake. As a whole group, have students share what they know about earthquakes. Use the Quick Write and Share Routine in Part 3, and ask: What kind of destruction can earthquakes cause? (They can make buildings collapse and injure people.) What state in the United States has the highest threat of earthquakes? (California) What else do you know about earthquakes? (Responses will vary.)

Interact with Text

LEVELS OF MEANING

Most students will have difficulty understanding what it feels like to live through a life-threatening earthquake. Students can experience the drama of the San Francisco earthquake of 1906, its aftermath, and Jacob's courage by reading the text. Read aloud this passage from the text.

> Buildings began weaving in and out, and the street pitched like a stormy sea. . . . The ground shook with such violence that Jacob thought the world was coming to an end.

Have partners discuss how a person would feel if he or she experienced an earthquake. Students should answer the following questions: What would that person think or worry about? What descriptive words and sensory details could you use to tell what that person would think, feel, taste, touch, and smell? Have students refer back to the text for clues.

STRUCTURE

Have students discuss why the author uses italics throughout the selection.

If . . . students have difficulty understanding why italics are used,

then . . . provide an example that uses a context clue.

Use a think aloud to analyze an example from the text. Say: On page 14, I read, *"Why is the dog running toward me?* Jacob wondered." The phrase "Jacob wondered" is not in italics, but it tells me that the rest of the sentence is something that Jacob is thinking—not saying out loud.

Point out that the italicized words indicate Jacob's thoughts, which gives insight into his feelings. Have students look through the selection and find other examples of italicized text.

MORE SUPPORT

ENGLISH LANGUAGE LEARNERS

Students may have trouble reading the colloquial dialect passages. To aid students, read the dialect aloud and have them tell you what they think happened. Then have students read aloud a section with dialect and help them decipher the meaning.

STRUGGLING READERS

If students need additional practice using descriptive words that relate to the senses, use the Description: Sensory Details Routine and Graphic Organizer in Part 3. Have students name things they see, hear, taste, smell, and touch during their school day.

LANGUAGE CONVENTIONALITY AND CLARITY

Some of the language the author uses in the characters' dialogue is dialect. Read aloud this example of dialect in the story.

> Look, kid. There ain't no point in breakin' yer neck tryin' to dig through all this. If yer family was trapped in this here building, they're goners, and that's the truth of it. If somebody was still alive, here, we would've heard 'em screamin' by now.

Explain that dialect is a variation of language distinguished by features of vocabulary, grammar, and pronunciation. It is not the standard language of a country, but it is usually a more regional, informal, and familiar way of talking to people.

Discuss with students the features of dialect in this passage. Ask: What do the apostrophes replace? (missing letters) Based on the context, what does the idiom *breakin' yer neck* mean? (trying very hard) Can you find an example of a nonstandard English word? (*Ain't* is incorrect English for *isn't*.) Based on the context of the paragraph, what do you think a goner is? (a person who is doomed or cannot be saved)

Use the Contractions Activity in Part 3. Ask student pairs to take turns reading the passage and then interpreting how it would be written in standard English. Encourage them to find other examples of dialect in the story and perform the same activity.

KNOWLEDGE DEMANDS

Point out that Jacob's family and many other people in his neighborhood are immigrants. Clarify that an immigrant is a citizen of one country who has moved to a different country. Jacob's family lives in a boardinghouse, which is a place where paying guests are provided meals and lodging. Give students a brief description of life in the 1900s—what technology was available, how people got around, and what jobs people held. Use the Quick Write and Share Routine from Part 3 to guide students to think about what life may have been like as an immigrant during that time. After they finish writing, have students pair up to share their opinions.

Express and Extend

LEVELS OF MEANING

EXPRESS Ask pairs of students to use evidence from the text to describe Jacob's reactions as he witnessed the earthquake and its aftermath. Have students use this evidence to describe Jacob's personality.

> **If . . .** students have difficulty identifying Jacob's reactions,
>
> **then . . .** display a list of personality traits, such as terrified, courageous, determined, agitated, caring, and worried, for students to choose from. Explain the meaning of each trait and give examples to clarify meaning.

EXTEND Form small groups of 3–4 to act out key parts of the selection. Tell students to use the descriptive words for Jacob's emotions and actual quotes to help them act out how he must have felt.

STRUCTURE

EXPRESS Remind students that the selection consists of only three sections from the book. We don't know what happens at the end. Ask students to predict what will happen. Have small groups present brief summaries of their predictions.

> **If . . .** students have difficulty making predictions,
>
> **then . . .** use the Story Prediction Routine and Graphic Organizer in Part 3 to provide additional support.

EXTEND Have students write a conclusion to *Quake!* that follows from the events in the story. The conclusion can be in the form of a short narrative, a short dialogue, or a combination of both. Encourage curious readers to check the book out of the library to find out what really happens and compare their prediction with the author's ending.

MORE SUPPORT

ENGLISH LANGUAGE LEARNERS

To help students with figurative language, use figurative language to describe several pictures. Ask students to tell what the figurative language means in the descriptions. For example, to be "on cloud nine" describes a happy person.

STRUGGLING READERS

Have students discuss how the dog is an important character in the story, even though the dog doesn't have a name or speak any words. Provide sentence frames to begin the discussion: One important thing the dog does is ___. The author uses other terms for the word *dog*, such as ___.

LANGUAGE CONVENTIONALITY AND CLARITY

EXPRESS Talk about Sentences and Words

The author uses vivid figurative language throughout the story. Have students find expressions in the story that use words in a nonliteral way.

If . . . students need more practice with figurative language,

then . . . use the Analyze Idioms and Expressions Routine in Part 3.

Display and read aloud the following passage from *Quake!*

> The ground started to sway. Bending his knees, Jacob tried to ride the movement. The street heaved and rolled, like the ocean during a storm. It was as though a giant sleeping below the cobblestones had suddenly decided to get up.

Ask: What does the author compare the street to? (an ocean during a storm) What verbs convey movement? (*sway, heaved, rolled*) What image does the last sentence express? (There is a giant sleeping under the pavement who suddenly awakes and wants to get out of bed.) Do you think the author's descriptions are accurate? Why or why not? (Responses will vary.)

TEAM TALK Have students turn to a partner and explain how these images convey the movement caused by the earthquake.

If . . . students need more support to understand the imagery in the passage,

then . . . have them illustrate the literal meaning of the sentences, and then guide them to understand the descriptive meaning.

EXTEND Have students write a critique of the author's use of figurative language, stating their opinion and supporting their views with examples from the text. Have students share their writing with a partner.

KNOWLEDGE DEMANDS

EXPRESS The dog seems to detect things Jacob doesn't. For example, the dog senses when something dangerous is about to happen. Jacob notes that other animals are also acting strangely. Have students discuss with a partner their opinions about the animals' abilities to sense weather events before people do. Tell them to use examples from the text.

EXTEND Have students conduct research, either in print media or online, about animal senses, answering the question of whether animals can sense things their owners cannot. Have students write a report, providing examples to support their point of view.

ACCELERATED LEARNERS

Have students plan a disaster-relief program for a city that has a strong likelihood of being struck by an earthquake. They can do research online or in print media to gather ideas for their plan. Then, have them write a letter to the mayor of that city detailing what should be done to prepare.

Unlock the Text

ReadyGEN
Text Collection 4

Earthshaker's Bad Day &
The Monster Beneath the
Sea, pp. 25–36

QUALITATIVE MEASURES

Levels of Meaning	Greek and Japanese myths about the origins and causes of earthquakes; causes and effects; problems and solutions
Structure	two short narratives with illustrations; dialogue; sequence; cause and effect
Language Conventionality and Clarity	descriptive phrases
Knowledge Demands	Greek and Japanese mythology; earthquakes; anthropomorphism

Prepare to Read

LEVELS OF MEANING

In this lesson, students will examine two myths, one Greek and one Japanese, about the origin of earthquakes. In "Earthshaker's Bad Day," Poseidon, god of the seas, is responsible for making earthquakes. In "The Monster Beneath the Sea," a giant catfish named Namazu flips his tail against the ocean floor and makes earthquakes.

STRUCTURE

PREVIEW Have students preview the texts. Students should focus on how the structures compare in the two stories. Ask: How are the structures of "Earthshaker's Bad Day" and "The Monster Beneath the Sea" similar? (There are no chapters. Each story has narrative, dialogue,

ENGLISH LANGUAGE LEARNERS

Use sentence frames to guide student responses in comparing the structures of the two stories. For example, In both texts, I see ___. I see ___ only in the first text. I see ___ only in the second text.

STRUGGLING READERS

Help students better comprehend the stories by learning where the stories take place. Display maps with the locations mentioned in the text. Also display visuals of Greece and Japan.

and illustrations.) Look at the illustrations in the two stories. What do they have in common? (They both have an ocean setting.) How are the illustrations for the stories different? (Illustrations for "Earthshaker's Bad Day" show mostly gods and goddesses. Illustrations for "The Monster Beneath the Sea" show mostly a big fish. There is also a photo of a modern-day earthquake-warning system with Japanese symbols on it.)

LANGUAGE CONVENTIONALITY AND CLARITY

PREVIEW VOCABULARY Use the Preview and Review Vocabulary Routine in Part 3 to assess and build on what students know about the following vocabulary terms: *lair, martial arts, samurai, woodcut, wood block, pagoda, trident, chariot, thunderbolt,* and *tidal wave.*

COGNATES Use the list of Spanish cognates at the beginning of this module to guide your Spanish-speaking students as they read the selections.

KNOWLEDGE DEMANDS

ACTIVATE BACKGROUND KNOWLEDGE Explain to students that they will be reading two myths. A myth is a story that describes the adventures of people, gods, goddesses, or animals and attempts to describe or explain a specific culture's customs or beliefs or something that occurs in nature. Point out that most myths have existed for many years. As a whole group, have students share what they know about myths. Use the Quick Write and Share Routine in Part 3 and ask: Why do you think people make up stories to explain beliefs or things that occur in nature? (Possible response: There may not be technology to research and analyze certain events in nature.) How do you think myths are different from true stories or informational texts? (Possible response: Myths include events or characters that cannot exist in real life.) Have you ever read or heard a myth? If so, what did it explain? (Responses will vary.)

Interact with Text

LEVELS OF MEANING

Ask students to tell the cause of earthquakes in each myth.

> **If . . .** students have difficulty identifying causes,
>
> **then . . .** point out sentences from the myths that show who is present when the earthquakes occur.

For example, display and read aloud the following passages to illustrate the causes of earthquakes.

"Earthshaker's Bad Day," p. 30: [Poseidon] lifted his trident, gave it a mighty whirl, and brought it down with all his power onto the bottom of the ocean floor. When it struck, a giant crack appeared. The ocean floor trembled.

"The Monster Beneath the Sea," p. 31: Namazu was so large that even the smallest flick of his tail caused giant waves to crash on the shore above and stirred earthquakes throughout the island nation of Japan.

Have students find other examples in the myths that point to the cause of earthquakes. Finally, have students find illustrations in the texts that show how the earthquakes happen.

STRUCTURE

Have students tell what impact, or effect, the earthquakes have in each myth.

> **If . . .** students have trouble recognizing impacts or distinguishing causes from effects,
>
> **then . . .** use the Cause and Effect Routine and Graphic Organizer in Part 3 to provide additional guidance.

For example, read the following sentence aloud from p. 31 of "The Monster Beneath the Sea," and explain it in terms of cause and effect: "When Namazu wiggled, even just a tiny bit, the buildings in Japan rattled." Explain that an author can give the cause before the effect or the effect before the cause, but the effect is always the thing that happens second in the order of events. Have students determine the cause and effect in this sentence from p. 30 of "Earthshaker's Bad Day:" "When [the trident] struck, a giant crack appeared."

ENGLISH LANGUAGE LEARNERS

To give students additional support with cause and effect, provide sentence frames, such as: If ___ happens, then ___ happens. When ___ takes place, it makes ___ take place.

STRUGGLING READERS

To help students understand descriptive phrases from "Earthshaker's Bad Day," such as *choppy waters, winged shoes,* or *gleaming helmet,* point to specific illustrations in the selection that help illustrate the description.

LANGUAGE CONVENTIONALITY AND CLARITY

Both authors make frequent use of descriptive phrases. To clarify meaning, help students analyze the descriptive phrases.

For example, display and read aloud the first sentence in "Earthshaker's Bad Day" and underline the descriptive phrases: "Long ago, the great god Poseidon, ruler of the seas, horses, and earthquakes, sat on his golden throne in his glorious and sparkling palace at the bottom of the deep Aegean Sea." Ask: Who was Poseidon? (ruler of the seas, horses, and earthquakes) Where did he live? (in his glorious and sparkling palace at the bottom of the deep Aegean Sea) When did he live? (long ago)

Display and read aloud the first sentence in "The Monster Beneath the Sea" and underline the prepositional phrase: "Deep in the ocean, off the coast of Japan, lived a catfish named Namazu." Ask: What does the underlined phrase modify? (ocean) Where did the catfish live? (deep in the ocean, off the coast of Japan) Have students point out other descriptive phrases in the selections.

KNOWLEDGE DEMANDS

Students may not understand that the gods and animals in myths can have human qualities. Guide students to focus on aspects of each myth that personify the god or animal. For example, have students reread the first page of "Earthshaker's Bad Day." Ask: What is Poseidon's problem? (He is unhappy and lonely because he is all alone at the bottom of the sea and isn't near humans.)

In "The Monster Beneath the Sea," Kashima asks Namazu to stop making earthquakes, and Namazu replies, "No, I won't. I like to smack my tail on the bottom of the sea. I like it when the earth shakes." Ask: What attitude does Namazu show? (He is self-centered and likes to have fun no matter how much trouble it causes others.)

Use the Opinion Writing Routine and Graphic Organizer in Part 3, and have students write about which main character they think has a better personality. Tell them to include details from both texts comparing the characters to support their opinion. After writing, have students share their opinions with a partner.

Express and Extend

EXPRESS Ask pairs of students to list evidence from the text that shows how and why the young man in "The Monster Beneath the Sea" decides to stop being an artist and instead plans to create an earthquake-warning system with his woodcuts.

> **If . . .** students have difficulty finding evidence,
>
> **then . . .** display a list of problems the artist faces during the earthquakes and how he gets help.

EXTEND Have students write a paragraph explaining a situation when they took steps to overcome a setback and accomplish something positive. Model by sharing a personal example: When I was in college learning how to be a teacher, I had one very tough class. I tried my hardest but still did poorly on one of my tests. Instead of giving up, I studied harder for the next test and took better notes in class. When the next test came around, I did very well!

STRUCTURE

EXPRESS Have pairs write short summaries of the two myths. Remind students to include the most important information from the selections and to summarize using their own words. Use the Retell or Summarize Routine in Part 3 to provide additional support.

EXTEND Have student groups use one of their summaries to act out one of the scenes from the myths. They can use props and costumes.

MORE SUPPORT

ENGLISH LANGUAGE LEARNERS

Use sentence frames to help students summarize. For example, Namazu was ___ who lived in the ___. His giant tail caused ___. The result of this was ___.

STRUGGLING READERS

If students have difficulty making predictions, ask guiding questions to provide support. For example, ask: Do you think Poseidon would have created more damaging earthquakes? How would that have affected the people of Athens?

LANGUAGE CONVENTIONALITY AND CLARITY

EXPRESS Talk about Sentences and Words

Display and read aloud the following passage from "Earthshaker's Bad Day."

> Later on, Poseidon returned to visit Athens. He discovered that everyone still worshipped him. They built a temple on the Acropolis called the Parthenon. On the temple were scenes of him and Athena creating their gifts. The spring he created was still there as a deep well. Poseidon felt terrible about having lost his temper, but he also learned he could still be important to the people without being their patron god.

Ask: What evidence does the author give to show that the people still worship Poseidon? (Scenes of his activities were on the temple. The spring he created was now a well.) What does the author imply about Poseidon's change in attitude? (He could accept not having been chosen patron god of Attica because he found that he was still important to the people.)

TEAM TALK Have students work with a partner and explain in their own words what the author is saying about Poseidon's new positive attitude. Then have them tell about a time when they or someone they know changed their attitude.

If . . . students need more support to understand evidence in the passage,

then . . . have them review the personal problems Poseidon experienced earlier in the story.

EXTEND Have students write a short prediction about what might have happened if Poseidon had stayed mad and had not changed his attitude about the town of Attica. Remind students to use text evidence to support their predictions.

KNOWLEDGE DEMANDS

EXPRESS Have pairs or small groups present a brief critique of the two myths, stating their opinions about which one they prefer and why. Use the Express Opinions Routine in Part 3. Have students fill out a T-chart to help them organize information about each myth.

EXTEND Tell students to choose one of the stories. Have them write a fictional extension of that story. Tell them to imagine what happened to Poseidon or Namazu after the story ended. After they have finished writing, allow students time to share in small groups.

ACCELERATED LEARNERS

Have students research another myth that explains a real event. Have them present their research to the class as a short oral presentation. Have students who are not presenting tell which elements of the myth could actually happen and which elements could not really happen.

Cognates

Cognates are words that have similar spellings and meanings in two or more languages. Many words in English and Spanish share Greek or Latin roots, and many words in English came from French, which is closely connected to Spanish (and to Portuguese, Italian, and Romanian). Because of this, many literary, content, and academic process words in English (e.g., *gracious/gracioso; volcano/volcán; compare/comparar*) have recognizable Spanish cognates.

Making the connection to cognates permits students who are native Spanish speakers to understand the strong foundation they have in academic and literary English. These links between English and Spanish are also useful for native speakers of English and other languages because they help uncover basic underlying features of our language.

ANCHOR TEXT Anatomy of a Volcanic Eruption

ENGLISH	SPANISH	ENGLISH	SPANISH
atmosphere	atmósfera	inhabitants	habitantes
atoms	átomos	instruments	instrumentos
avalanches	avalanchas	intervals	intervalos
characteristics	características	island	isla
classification	clasificación	laboratories	laboratorios
collapse	colapsar	lava	lava
column	columna	liquid	líquido
connect	conectar	magma	magma
crater	cráter	planet	planeta
destruction	destrucción	region	región
divergent	divergentes	residents	residentes
eruption	erupción	satellites	satélites
explosive	explosivo	seismograph	sismógrafo
fertile	fértil	separate	separar
float	flotar	structures	estructuras
fragments	fragmentos	vehicles	vehículos
hemisphere	hemisferio		

SUPPORTING TEXT Escape from Pompeii

ENGLISH	SPANISH	ENGLISH	SPANISH
acrobats	acróbatas	mountain	montaña
actor	actor	plants	plantas
air	aire	poets	poetas
archeologist	arqueólogo	politicians	políticos
captain	capitán	protector	protector
destroy	destruir	Roman	romano
eruption	erupción	temples	templos
flowers	flores	theaters	teatros
liquid	líquido	volcanic	volcánico

SUPPORTING TEXT A Tsunami Unfolds

ENGLISH	SPANISH	ENGLISH	SPANISH
alert	alerta	intensity	intensidad
automatically	automáticamente	magnitude	magnitud
contamination	contaminación	messenger	mensajero
destruction	destrucción	nuclear reactor	reactor nuclear
emergency	emergencia	radiation	radiación
epicenter	epicentro	rotation	rotación
eruptions	erupciones	scale	escala
evacuation	evacuación	seismographs	sismógrafos
experience	experiencia	seismologist	sismólogo
generators	generadores	sensors	sensores
government	gobierno	tectonic	tectónica
hydrogen	hidrógeno	vibrations	vibraciones
hypothermia	hipotermia	volcanoes	volcanes

These lists contain many, but not all, Spanish cognates from these selections.

Unlock the Text

QUALITATIVE MEASURES

Levels of Meaning	implicit overall main idea; multiple explicit main ideas in sections; broad range of information about volcanic eruptions in informational text style
Structure	main topic divided into an introduction and five chapters; photographs, drawings, and diagrams with informative captions
Language Conventionality and Clarity	mostly simple and compound sentences; some complex sentences; some domain-specific and academic vocabulary defined within the text
Knowledge Demands	broad scientific knowledge; information about volcanoes; some geography

Prepare to Read

LEVELS OF MEANING

One purpose of *Anatomy of a Volcanic Eruption* is to give information about how and why volcanic eruptions occur. The text also details how scientists try to predict when and where a volcanic eruption will occur.

STRUCTURE

PREVIEW Form small groups and have students read the title of the text and chapter headings, look at the graphic features, and try to predict what each section is about. Ask: How is the text divided? (into chapters) What information do the maps give you? (locations where there are volcanoes) How are the diagrams different from the photographs? (The diagrams show parts of the inside of the earth.) What other text features do you

MORE SUPPORT

ENGLISH LANGUAGE LEARNERS

This selection has many compound words, such as *earthquake, underwater, offshore,* and *landform.* Help students identify the two words in each compound word and explain how the definitions of the two smaller words help them understand the meaning of the compound word.

STRUGGLING READERS

Students may need support with scientific vocabulary. Help students identify trouble words and decide on replacement words that mean the same thing. Use glossary definitions to help students find replacement words for certain scientific terms.

notice? (Responses will vary. The book includes maps, a table of contents, a glossary, and an index.)

LANGUAGE CONVENTIONALITY AND CLARITY

PREVIEW VOCABULARY Use the Preview and Review Vocabulary Routine in Part 3 to assess and build on what students know about the following vocabulary words: *lava, magma, crater, eruption, ash cloud, mantle, crust,* and *summit.*

Throughout this selection, students will encounter compound words that they may not be familiar with, such as *airspace, coastline, mudflow, snowcapped, countryside,* and *landslide.* Use the Compound Words Activity in Part 3 to help students understand the meanings of the compound words.

COGNATES Use the list of Spanish cognates at the beginning of this module to guide your Spanish-speaking students as they read the selection.

KNOWLEDGE DEMANDS

ACTIVATE BACKGROUND KNOWLEDGE Ask students to share what they know about volcanoes. Use the Quick Write and Share Routine in Part 3. Ask students to look at the images throughout the book to help them remember information they might have learned in the past. Have students tell what they know about what volcanoes look like, where volcanoes can be found, and what happens when volcanoes erupt. Model an exemplar response: I have seen volcanoes in many movies and television shows. I remember seeing one on a television show about nature. It looked like a mountain whose top had been broken off. There was a ton of red lava gushing out of the top. It looked very dangerous and frightening. I would like to know more about how and why volcanoes form.

Interact with Text

As you read *Anatomy of a Volcanic Eruption,* periodically stop to assess students' level of understanding of geographic locations. Have students make a list of all of the place names they come across in the text.

If . . . students have difficulty identifying the geographic locations mentioned in the book,

then . . . have them use a globe or map to locate the cities, countries, and continents mentioned. Ask them to describe what happened in each region.

Point out that countries are divided into states. For example, Texas is a state in the United States, which is a country. Then point out that continents are divided into countries. For example, the country of Italy is located in Europe, which is a continent.

STRUCTURE

As students read, periodically stop to assess their understanding of the text's structure. Have students examine one of the illustrations and analyze how it ties into the text to further their understanding.

If . . . students need additional support to understand the relationship between pictures, captions, and the main text,

then . . . model an example of how these elements tie together.

Use a think aloud. Say: When I look at the caption on page 13, it states, "The Hawaiian Islands are volcanic islands that formed over a hot spot." Now I look at the image. It shows an overhead image of the Hawaiian Islands. The text provides information on volcanoes located on the Hawaiian Islands. The caption supports both the image and the text.

Have students independently find another example from the text. Have students give examples of how to use information found in text features, such as diagrams, labeled illustrations, text boxes, and tables, in order to understand words and key concepts in the main text. Remind students to pay attention to how the author uses these types of features as they read this selection.

ENGLISH LANGUAGE LEARNERS

Visuals can be used to help students interpret the meaning of challenging words. Help students understand the meaning of *convergent, divergent, conduit,* and *lahar* by pointing to specific images in the book that help convey the meaning.

STRUGGLING READERS

Using context clues to determine the meaning of new words is one strategy that can be helpful, particularly with informational text. Have students make a list of unknown words from the text. Then guide them in identifying the context clue that helps them determine the definition of an unknown word. Have them use this strategy throughout the selection.

LANGUAGE CONVENTIONALITY AND CLARITY

The language of the selection contains simple, compound, and complex sentences. Many of these sentences are used together to explain scientific information. Use the Simple and Compound Sentences and Combining Sentences Activities in Part 3 to help students access the language.

KNOWLEDGE DEMANDS

To aid students in understanding the specialized words used to describe the anatomy of a volcanic eruption, have students review the text by using the Monitor Understanding: Listening Skills Log in Part 3 to identify details about the text.

For example, display and read aloud the following passage on p. 10: "Some adjacent plates do not move toward each other. Instead, they pull away from each other. These are called divergent plates." Explain to students that the author defines the term *divergent plates* within the text and also includes an illustration to help readers visualize the information.

Circle the term *divergent plates* in the third sentence and underline the second sentence. Point out that the text in the second sentence is a definition/ explanation clue.

Provide more practice. Have pairs of students find the definition/explanation clues for the meaning of *hot spot* in the following example: "Volcanoes occur where two plates meet. Sometimes they also form in the middle of plates in areas called hot spots. A hot spot is a place where magma rises up through the crust and forms a volcano." Have pairs write the sentences, circle *hot spot,* and underline the definition in the text.

Express and Extend

EXPRESS Have pairs of students choose one of the chapters in *Anatomy of a Volcanic Eruption* to show their understanding of implicit and explicit main ideas. Have them identify the main idea of and key details in the section.

> **If . . .** students have difficulty distinguishing between main ideas and details,
>
> **then . . .** use the Main Ideas and Details Routine and Graphic Organizer in Part 3 to help them organize the information.

EXTEND Have pairs write a review of their chosen chapter. Then have each pair share their review with the class. While listening, students should complete the Monitor Understanding: Listening Skills Log in Part 3 to show respect and their comprehension of the other presentations.

EXPRESS Have pairs write one-sentence captions for three of the pictures or illustrations included in the text. In small groups, students can read their captions aloud and have others guess which picture or illustration their captions describe.

> **If . . .** students are struggling to write their own captions,
>
> **then . . .** review captions from the text. Remind students to use their own words in their captions.

EXTEND Have students draw a picture to show their understanding of volcanic eruptions. The drawing must include a caption and labels. Have students share their drawing with a partner.

ENGLISH LANGUAGE LEARNERS

To help students write captions, show them an image from the text and have them use their words to tell about the image in one sentence. Tell them that their sentence can be written as a caption that relates to the image.

STRUGGLING READERS

To help students find supporting details for the main ideas, provide these sentence frames: One main idea in this chapter is ___. One detail that relates to this main idea is ___. Have students look at chapter and heading titles for additional guidance.

LANGUAGE CONVENTIONALITY AND CLARITY

EXPRESS Talk about Sentences and Words

Display the following sentence from *Anatomy of a Volcanic Eruption* and read it aloud:

The richest soil is often found in places with volcanic activity.

Ask: What word does the author use to describe the soil? (*richest*) What does *richest* mean? ("the most rich") Why do you think the author chose to use this word instead of just saying "great soil"? (The word *richest* is more specific and helps the reader better visualize the soil.)

TEAM TALK Have partners use the following sentence frame to rewrite the sentence, using different words with the same meaning as *richest*: The ___ soil is often found in places with volcanic activity.

EXTEND Have students choose other sentences in the text to practice rewriting with words that have the same meaning. Have them record both the original and the edited sentence, and then have them compare the sentences in pairs. Ask: After you read both sentences, did you get a different mental image using the new word? Which word do you think works better in the text? Why?

KNOWLEDGE DEMANDS

EXPRESS Have small groups use details from the text to explain *meteorology* or *geology.* Have them identify paragraphs and captions that deal with these topics. Help students identify the main idea of each paragraph or caption and find details that help them explain the topic.

EXTEND Have students write a short persuasive essay about which career they would prefer: meteorologist or geologist. Tell them to include text evidence to help justify their choice.

ACCELERATED LEARNERS

The text mentions that volcanoes can cause earthquakes and that some people build their homes on post-and-pier foundations as a precaution. Have students research other ways people can take precautions in the event of earthquakes caused by volcanoes. Instruct them to create a public service announcement for the affected area and include tips on how to stay safe and protect belongings.

Unlock the Text

ReadyGEN
Text Collection 4

Escape from Pompeii,
pp. 37–54

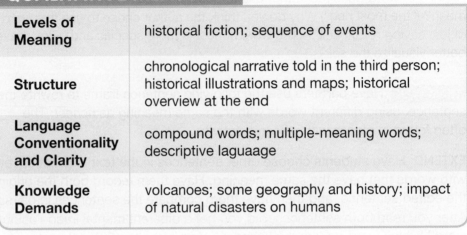

QUALITATIVE MEASURES

Levels of Meaning	historical fiction; sequence of events
Structure	chronological narrative told in the third person; historical illustrations and maps; historical overview at the end
Language Conventionality and Clarity	compound words; multiple-meaning words; descriptive laguaage
Knowledge Demands	volcanoes; some geography and history; impact of natural disasters on humans

Prepare to Read

LEVELS OF MEANING

Escape from Pompeii tells the story of two young children who lived in Pompeii before Mount Vesuvius destroyed the city. It explains how the natural disaster began and what impact it had on the city and its citizens.

STRUCTURE

PREVIEW Form small groups and have students read the title and look at the illustrations and map at the end of the text. Ask students to try to predict what the story is about. Ask: Who do you think is the main character? (a young boy) How do you know? (He appears in most of the illustrations.) When does the story take place? (a long time ago) How do you know? (The clothing and architecture do not look modern.)

ENGLISH LANGUAGE LEARNERS

Have students create a running list of multiple-meaning words from the text. For each word, have students write the definitions and draw illustrations. Tell them they can use this while reading to help decide which definition fits best with the text.

STRUGGLING READERS

To help students correctly pronounce difficult words, such as *politicians, rehearsal,* and *pumice,* say the word aloud. Then have students repeat the word two or three times.

What information does the map at the end of the story give you? (It shows where Pompeii is located.) What do you think the story will be about, based on the title and illustrations? (how the boy had to escape his home because of a volcano)

LANGUAGE CONVENTIONALITY AND CLARITY

PREVIEW VOCABULARY Use the Preview and Review Vocabulary Routine in Part 3 to assess what students know about the following words: *sparkling, glimmered, nervously, frantically, anxious, uncomfortably, grumbling,* and *trembling.* These adjectives and adverbs are used to create a vivid picture in the reader's mind as the story develops, so make sure that students have a strong understanding of them. Miming or acting out each word will help students who are having trouble.

MULTIPLE-MEANING WORDS Work with students to define these multiple-meaning words and determine how they are used in the story: *bars, jack, step, rattle, prop, spot, market, lines, pile,* and *back.*

COGNATES Use the list of Spanish cognates at the beginning of this module to guide your Spanish-speaking students as they read the selection.

KNOWLEDGE DEMANDS

ACTIVATE BACKGROUND KNOWLEDGE Ask students to share what they know about volcanoes or about ancient Rome and Pompeii. Tell students that while reading this story, they will learn about what happened to the city of Pompeii.

Use the Quick Write and Share Routine in Part 3 to assess background knowledge. Have students look at the illustrations throughout the selection to help them remember information they might have learned in the past. Ask: Where is Rome? (in Italy) What might happen to a city when a volcano erupts? (Possible response: There could be a lot of damage or destruction.) What might you see when a volcano erupts? (Possible responses: fire, smoke, ashes, landslides)

Interact with Text

LEVELS OF MEANING

As students read, stop to assess their understanding of the frenzy and devastation the eruption of the volcano brought to the people of Pompeii.

If . . . students have difficulty identifying the effects the volcano had on the people,

then . . . model finding an example of a descriptive phrase in the text.

Use a think aloud. Say: On page 48, I read, "The children could hear dogs barking and people's muffled screams as they ran gasping for air with rags covering their mouths or pillows over their heads." The author uses vivid descriptions, such as *muffled screams* and *gasping for air,* to describe the physical effects the volcano had on people. **Have students find other descriptive phrases that indicate the immediate and lasting impacts the volcano had.**

STRUCTURE

As students read, periodically stop to assess their understanding of the chronology of events in the text. Have students identify sequence words to demonstrate understanding of the progression of events in the text.

If . . . students have trouble following the chronology of events,

then . . . use the Sequence of Events Routine and Graphic Organizer in Part 3 to help students identify the sequence. Guide students in choosing only the most important events to include in their graphic organizers.

For additional support, provide an example. Have students read the following sentences and guide them in identifying the sequence words: "A few years before Tranio was born, there had been a big earthquake in Pompeii, and parts of the town had still not been fully repaired." Point out to students that the phrase *A few years before* indicates a sequence.

MORE SUPPORT

ENGLISH LANGUAGE LEARNERS

Explain to students that sequence is the order in which events happen. Provide a copy of the story and have students highlight sequence words as they see them. Then, have them go back over the story and write whether each word indicates the past, present, or future in a three-column chart.

STRUGGLING READERS

Some students may experience difficulty grasping the vivid, descriptive language used to tell about the frenzy and devastation. Have pairs of students act out parts of the text with these descriptions. Seeing themselves and classmates act out the powerful words will help students create mental images for future texts.

LANGUAGE CONVENTIONALITY AND CLARITY

Use the Compound Words Activity in Part 3 to help students identify and understand the meaning of compound words. Explain to students that the meaning of a word changes when it is combined with another word to form a compound word. Examples of compound words found in the text are *sunlight, fishermen, earthquake, hillside, shopkeeper,* and *overhead.*

Have students work in pairs to separate the two parts of each compound word they find in the text. Then have students define the compound word in their own terms. Remind students that they can determine the meaning of a compound word by defining the two words that make it up. Encourage students to illustrate their definitions. Use a think aloud to model an example. Say: On page 39, I see the compound word *sunlight.* I know that the *sun* is the bright ball in the sky that appears during the daytime, and *light* is how bright something is. So, if I combine these words, I get *sunlight*, which I conclude means "the brightness coming from the sun in the sky during the day."

KNOWLEDGE DEMANDS

One of the major themes in *Escape from Pompeii* is the devastation and loss the volcano creates. Have students identify evidence from the text that helps convey this theme.

> **If . . .** students have trouble finding text evidence that helps convey the theme,
> **then . . .** use the Web Routine and Graphic Organizer in Part 3.

Have students write *Devastation and Loss Caused by Volcano* in the center oval. Then, direct them to the parts of the story that cover events during and after the eruption. Have students write in the outer ovals text evidence and details related to the theme of devastation and loss caused by a volcano. Guide students in understanding how the evidence and details relate to the theme.

If students need additional support, have them tell how the main characters, Tranio and Livia, are different at the end of the story than they are at the beginning of the story. Students can use a web graphic organizer or a Venn diagram to record character traits for Tranio and Livia at the beginning of the story and again at the end of the story.

Express and Extend

EXPRESS Have students summarize sections of the story in their own words. Students will form pairs, and one partner will reread a section from the story aloud. The partner will then summarize the meaning of that section in his or her own words.

EXTEND Have students show their understanding of the main events of *Escape from Pompeii* by writing a two-paragraph summary of the story, including the overall theme and details that support the theme.

EXPRESS Have pairs of students demonstrate their understanding of the relationship between the text and the illustrations. One student should point to an illustration, and the partner should name the event in the story that the illustration depicts. Have students switch roles.

> **If . . .** students have difficulty understanding the connections between the events of the story and illustrations,
>
> **then . . .** help students identify the specific descriptions in the text that are depicted in illustrations.

Encourage students to use illustrations as clues to events in the text. To provide support, use a think aloud. Say: On page 39, I read these sentences: "Beyond the massive city walls he could see Pompeii's greatest protector looming in the distance. They called it Vesuvius, the Gentle Mountain." When I look at the illustration on page 38, I see the city walls with a mountain on the other side. This must be Vesuvius. The picture matches what is stated in the text. Ask students if they can match sentences on p. 44 to the corresponding illustration on pp. 44–45.

EXTEND Have pairs write a one-sentence caption for two of the illustrations in the selection. Partners can read their captions aloud and have the other pairs of students guess which picture each caption describes.

MORE SUPPORT

ENGLISH LANGUAGE LEARNERS

Some students may struggle to summarize sections of the story. Remind these students that when they summarize, they tell the most important parts. Provide students with these sentence frames to use as they summarize: First ___. Next ___. Finally ___.

STRUGGLING READERS

Help students understand the relevance of the illustrations using examples from pp. 40–41. Read p. 40 out loud. As you read a word that is shown in the illustration, such as *river, pots,* or *fishermen,* point to the part of the illustration that depicts the word.

EXPRESS TALK ABOUT SENTENCES AND WORDS

Display this passage from *Escape from Pompeii*. Read it aloud with students and discuss the passage. Clarify any misunderstandings.

> Lightning flashed and thunder roared. Streams of molten liquid flowed in fast rivers down the mountain sloped and covered a nearby town. The walls, streets, and gardens of their beloved Pompeii disappeared beneath a blanket of ash and stones.

Ask: What is the author describing? What vivid or descriptive words did you hear? What mood does the author convey with her use of descriptive words?

TEAM TALK Have students turn to a partner and describe the eruption scene in their own words, using descriptive language.

EXTEND Have small groups produce a skit depicting how the author described people's reactions to Vesuvius erupting. Using the text and illustrations, have them create their own fictional characters that lived in Pompeii to include in their skit. Allow them to use props as appropriate.

KNOWLEDGE DEMANDS

EXPRESS Have students express what they learned about Pompeii from reading *Escape from Pompeii* by creating a short graphic book depicting key scenes in the text with captions that include facts about Pompeii.

EXTEND Have small groups create a poster advertising a new movie called *Escape from Pompeii*. Allow students to use actual photographs taken in Pompeii and their own illustrations. Students should include quotes and reviews as part of their poster presentations, which should outline the most important and exciting parts of the story.

ACCELERATED LEARNERS

Have students research another famous volcanic eruption, such as the eruption of Mount St. Helens in 1980. Have students write a historical fiction story about a person who witnessed it. Tell them to research the event and include real details in their fictional accounts.

MORE SUPPORT

Unlock the Text

QUALITATIVE MEASURES

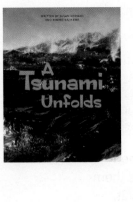

Levels of Meaning	accessible information about the tsunami that devastated Japan in March 2011, including personal anecdotes, maps, photographs, charts, and other text features
Structure	narrative organized in fourteen 2-page chronological parts, each with its own title, purpose, and focus; a list of the parts introduces the contents of the text, and a glossary at the end defines terms
Language Conventionality and Clarity	some high level vocabulary, including Japanese names and words related to the disaster may require direct instruction
Knowledge Demands	understanding about ocean waves, earthquakes, nuclear power, and Japan

Prepare to Read

LEVELS OF MEANING

A Tsunami Unfolds is an informative text about the tsunami that hit Japan in March 2011. It unfolds in fourteen chapters beginning before the devastation occurred, through the earthquake and its aftershocks, the ensuing warnings about the wave, the dangers at the nuclear plant, the search and rescue efforts, and the state of the region one month later. The highly visual text combines objective facts, actual photographs, text box features, and running "Real Life" accounts by a female airport security officer and one account by a cook at a nursery school.

MORE SUPPORT

ENGLISH LANGUAGE LEARNERS

Have students look at the two Japanese characters (called *kanji*) on page 14. Explain that most languages use the Japanese word *tsunami*, which literally means "harbor wave." This means that the word does not translate into a different word in most languages.

STRUGGLING READERS

Pronounce the Japanese nouns that will appear in the text. Ask students to repeat them: Fukushima (foo-koo-SHEE-ma), Honshu (HON-shoo), Sendai (SEN-die), Yumi (YOO-mee), Daiichi (DIE-ee-shee), Setsuko (set-SOO-koh).

STRUCTURE

PREVIEW Remind students that they may have been asked to unfold a piece of paper at some point. Explain that the word *unfold* has another meaning: "to reveal a story one event at a time." The writers unfold their story about the tsunami in fourteen parts. The parts are listed on the Contents page. There is also a Glossary at the end of the story.

LANGUAGE CONVENTIONALITY AND CLARITY

PREVIEW VOCABULARY Use the Preview and Review Vocabulary Routine in Part 3 to assess what students know about the following words: *collapsed, evacuate, scrambling, broadcasted, crisis, stranded, rescue, grim, structures, interior, collide, survive, contamination, radiation.*

COGNATES Use the list of Spanish cognates at the beginning of this module to guide your Spanish-speaking students as they read the selection.

DOMAIN-SPECIFIC VOCABULARY Use the Vocabulary Activities in Part 3 to pre-teach the following domain-specific vocabulary: *epicenter, aftershock, sea wall, tidal wave, seismic wave, nuclear, hydrogen, hypothermia, dormant.* Explain that these words are all associated with ocean geography and earthquakes and their results.

KNOWLEDGE DEMANDS

ACTIVATE BACKGROUND KNOWLEDGE Ask: What do you think of when you hear the word *earthquake*? (Possible responses: land shaking, buildings falling, people in danger.) Say: One of the biggest earthquakes in history happened in Japan at 2:46 pm on March 11, 2011. The earthquake caused an enormous amount of water to move in one big wave. That wave is called a tsunami. This text describes the tsunami and its impact and effect over time. Explain that the events in the text happen during one month, beginning just before the earthquake and ending one month later. Finally, have students ask questions about earthquakes that they'd like to have answered.

If . . . students have difficulty organizing what they know about earthquakes and questions they might have about them,

then . . . use the KWLH Chart with Graphic Organizer in Part 3 to support their understanding.

STRUGGLING READERS

Remind students that *earthquake* is a compound word. Knowing the meaning of the two parts (*earth* and *quake*) will help them understand the meaning of the word. Remind them that compound words can be one word, two words, or hyphenated. Ask them to locate and list other compound words in the text as they read (i.e. *afternoon, fishermen, high-speed, bookshelves, skyscrapers,* and *Ring of Fire,* all on pages 4 and 5).

A Tsunami Unfolds **125**

Interact with Text

LEVELS OF MEANING

As you read *A Tsunami Unfolds*, assess not only the students' understanding of the facts and details, but also their personal reactions to the "Real Life" features on pages 7, 11, 15, 18, 23, 25, and 31. As students read each 2-page spread, ask: What facts do you learn on these pages? Remind them that facts answer questions that begin with *who, what, when, where, why,* and *how*. If the pages include a "Real Life" feature, ask: What feelings or emotions does this personal account express and/or make you feel? Remind them that personal accounts such as these combine facts (such as dates and locations) with words that express emotions and opinions, such as *confused, frightened, stunned,* and *powerful* on page 7. Suggest that news reports might combine both perspectives: the objective and factual with the subjective and emotional.

STRUCTURE

This text has a unique structure that weaves together many different verbal and visual elements to create many layers of meaning. Say: A collage is an assembly of many different elements. These writers create a collage of words and images to tell the story. How many different elements can you name? (Possible responses: narrative, description, photographs, illustrations, a chart, headings, icons, maps, backgrounds, graphic designs, date-and-time blocks, headlines, definitions, colors). Ask: What is the effect of combining so many different elements?

> **If . . .** students have difficulty noting the wide variety of element types in the text,
>
> **then . . .** provide students with the Web Graphic Organizer in Part 3 to organize their notes.

ENGLISH LANGUAGE LEARNERS

Ask each student to choose two illustrations that they think are especially important or powerful. For each one, have them write short answers to these two questions: What does this picture show? Why did the writers decide to include it?

STRUGGLING READERS

Direct students' attention to the headings on each spread of the text. Ask: Which headings are verb phrases that express actions? (*Scrambling* for Safety, *Dealing* with Destruction) Which two ask questions? *A Nuclear Disaster?, Fight or Flight?*)

LANGUAGE CONVENTIONALITY AND CLARITY

Focus students' attention on the warning *Save yourselves!* on page 12. Ask: What does the word *emergency* mean in this text? What are the various factors that made this historical event an emergency? (A tidal wave separated people from their families; it destroyed buildings; it destroyed boats; it swept away boats, cars, trucks, and planes; it left people without clean water and food; it trapped and wounded victims.) Do the words *emergency* and *disaster* mean the same thing? If not, how are they different? (Disasters result in emergencies.)

If . . . students have difficulty organizing details and examples of emergency situations,

then . . . have them use the Web Graphic Organizer or the Main Idea and Details Graphic Organizer in Part 3 to support their analysis.

Finally, ask students to find examples in the text of what Japan and other countries can do to help minimize the impact of another tsunami if one were to happen again. (rebuild stronger buildings; build better warning systems; rethinking nuclear power as an energy source)

KNOWLEDGE DEMANDS

Some students may not be familiar with nuclear generators as a source of power. It is a complex process that may be difficult for most students to imagine. For a simplistic explanation, say: Nuclear power is the use of nuclear reactors to make electricity. Nuclear power plants use a chemical element called uranium. Uranium is found in many rocks and some soils. When the nuclei of uranium atoms are split, a very large amount of energy is released. This process is called nuclear fission. The energy that is released turns water into steam that drives turbines to produce electricity. Make sure students are familiar with related terms such as *reactor, generator, cooling system*, and *radiation* (note that fully understanding these terms and processes will likely be impossible for most students). Also, explain the terms from the text that name what can happen when a nuclear reactor fails: *meltdown* and *evacuation*.

ENGLISH LANGUAGE LEARNERS

Show students the international symbol warning of radioactive hazard. This yellow and black design suggests activity radiating from a central atom. Have them find, reproduce, and discuss other warning or safety signs and symbols such as electricity, biohazards, slippery surfaces, emergency exits, or flammable.

Express and Extend

LEVELS OF MEANING

EXPRESS Remind students that the disaster that unfolds in this text is one of the largest in modern human history. Say: Some disasters are natural, such as earthquakes, landslides, floods, hurricanes, tornadoes, blizzards, and volcanic eruptions. These natural disasters result in destruction around the world every year. Other disasters are caused by humans. These include fires, oil spills, wars, industrial accidents, or even traffic accidents. Explain that preventing disasters is most important.

> **If . . .** students have difficulty brainstorming ways to prevent various kinds of disasters,
>
> **then . . .** use the Three-Column Chart Routine and Graphic Organizer in Part 3 to guide students in listing ways to prevent various kinds of disasters. Have students label the columns *Disaster, Cause,* and *Prevention.*

EXTEND Ask students to choose one of the other four earthquakes listed on page 9 as the basis for a news article written on the date after it happened. Have them do some online research about the earthquake to discover the most important details. Encourage them to use questions that begin with *who, what, when, where, why* and *how* as their starting points.

STRUCTURE

EXPRESS Point out that the six features called "Yumi's Experience" are an internal narrative if they are read together in sequence. Yumi is a heroine who helps other people stay calm and cares for them inside the airport. Have a volunteer read aloud the last part of Yumi's story on p. 31. Ask: What feelings or emotions do the writers express in the conclusion of Yumi's story? Why is this choice of conclusions important to the larger story of the tsunami?

EXTEND Invite pairs of students to create an additional 2-page spread for this text that represents "Several Years Later." Encourage them to find and use photos and facts about Fukushima today. Ask them to make sure the content reflects the optimism and strength that are the main ideas in "A Will to Survive." Give students the opportunity to share and display their pages in your classroom.

MORE SUPPORT

ENGLISH LANGUAGE LEARNERS

Have students write short descriptions of Yumi based on the text. Invite them to combine details from the text with details from their own imaginations. Ask them to write about what they think Yumi might be doing today.

STRUGGLING READERS

Help students explore the word *damage.* Explain that damage is physical harm done to something or someone. Have them scan the text for examples of damage or for words related to *damage.* Have them identify some words that have meanings similar to *damage.* (*harm, injury, destroy, wreck, demolish, mangle, trash, loss, hurt*)

LANGUAGE CONVENTIONALITY AND CLARITY

EXPRESS Talk about Sentences and Words

Display and read aloud the following sentences from *A Tsunami Unfolds.*

Earthquakes are common in Japan. However, the people here instantly knew that something was different about this quake. (p. 6)

Explain that this sentence introduces one of the main ideas of the text that is supported with many details that follow. Say: The writers use descriptive words such as *biggest, strongest, incredible* and *monster*. They use the Richter scale to show the earthquake's magnitude. They show how far it could be felt on the map on page 8. They compare it to other earthquakes in the chart on page 9. Then, ask students to look for ways the authors describe the tsunami that followed. Ask: How do the authors make you understand the tsunami was one of a kind, too?

TEAM TALK Encourage pairs of students to discuss what would happen if an earthquake occurred in your local area during a school day. Where would students go? Who would be in charge? How would teachers and administrators keep you safe?

EXTEND Ask students to use their imaginations to write fictional news stories that happen in your community that begin this way: _____ are common in _____. However, the people here instantly knew that something was different about this _____. Encourage them to describe a humorous and fun event rather than a disaster story.

KNOWLEDGE DEMANDS

EXPRESS Challenge students to use the details of this text to write short journal entries by either Yumi or Setsuko using the first-person pronoun "I." Remind them to use as many of the five senses as possible in their journal entries, as well as details that answer *who, what, when, where, why,* and *how.*

EXTEND Challenge students to find out more about normal ocean waves. Ask: What causes ocean waves? How large are normal waves? What do the words *trough* and *crest* mean as they apply to ocean waves? Have them use what they learn to write short reports about waves. Ask them to include photographs, illustrations, or their own drawings in their reports.

If . . . students have little or no experience with ocean waves,
then . . . have them locate and play videos or audio of actual ocean waves online.

ACCELERATED LEARNERS

Some people think nuclear power is a safe, reliable, and sustainable energy source that reduces carbon emissions. Others think that nuclear energy is dangerous to the health of humans, other creatures, and the planet itself. This debate has intensified since the Fukushima disaster of 2011. Encourage students to choose one side of this debate, research facts, and give an oral argument either for or against nuclear power as a source of the world's electricity.

MORE SUPPORT

Creating Innovative Solutions

MODULE A **Cognate Chart** 132

Anchor Text Lunch Money 134

Supporting Text Max Malone Makes a Million 140

Supporting Text Coyote School News 146

TEXT SET

ANCHOR TEXT
Lunch Money

SUPPORTING TEXT
Max Malone Makes
a Million

SUPPORTING TEXT
Coyote School News

MODULE B **Cognate Chart** 152

Anchor Text Using Money 154

Supporting Text A Tale of Two Poggles 160

Supporting Text The Boy Who Invented TV 166

TEXT SET

ANCHOR TEXT
Using Money

SUPPORTING TEXT
A Tale of Two Poggles

SUPPORTING TEXT
The Boy Who
Invented TV

Cognates

Cognates are words that have similar spellings and meanings in two or more languages. Many words in English and Spanish share Greek or Latin roots, and many words in English came from French, which is closely connected to Spanish (and to Portuguese, Italian, and Romanian). Because of this, many literary, content, and academic process words in English (e.g., *gracious/gracioso; volcano/volcán; compare/comparar*) have recognizable Spanish cognates.

Making the connection to cognates permits students who are native Spanish speakers to understand the strong foundation they have in academic and literary English. These links between English and Spanish are also useful for native speakers of English and other languages because they help uncover basic underlying features of our language.

ANCHOR TEXT Lunch Money

ENGLISH	SPANISH	ENGLISH	SPANISH
accept	aceptar	interrupt	interrumpir
audience	audiencia	lesson	lección
author	autor	license	licencia
bank	banco	logic	lógica
cancel	cancelar	necessary	necesario
celebrate	celebrar	obvious	obvio
committee	comité	opportunity	oportunidad
compare	comparar	pause	pausa
competitor	competidor	permission	permiso
convince	convencer	plastic	plástico
curiosity	curiosidad	politics	política
decide	decidir	probably	probablemente
details	detalles	process	proceso
disputes	disputas	public	pública
dozens	docenas	repeat	repetir
economics	economía	section	sección
energy	energía	social studies	estudios sociales
experience	experiencia	special	especial
fortune	fortuna	spectacular	espectacular
generous	generoso	student	estudiante
incident	incidente	talent	talento
initiative	iniciativa	titles	títulos
insist	insistir	university	universidad
intelligence	inteligencia	volunteers	voluntarios
interesting	interesante		

SUPPORTING TEXT **Max Malone Makes a Million**

ENGLISH	SPANISH	ENGLISH	SPANISH
part	parte	ingredients	ingredientes
affect	afectar	interest	interés
appreciate	apreciar	interrupt	interrumpir
athlete	atleta	line	línea
cement	cemento	million	millón
combine	combinar	moment	momento
definitely	definitivamente	park	parque
difference	diferencia	practice	práctica
especially	especialmente	product	producto
finally	finalmente	supermarket	supermercado
fortune	fortuna	vacation	vacaciones
human	humano	victory	victoria
imagine	imaginar		

SUPPORTING TEXT **Coyote School News**

ENGLISH	SPANISH	ENGLISH	SPANISH
contributed	contribuir	perfect	perfecto
electricity	electricidad	ranch	rancho
graduate	graduar	sardines	sardinas
guitars	guitarras	secret	secreto

These lists contain many, but not all, Spanish cognates from these selections.

Unlock the Text

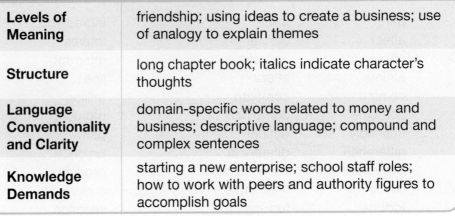

QUALITATIVE MEASURES

Levels of Meaning	friendship; using ideas to create a business; use of analogy to explain themes
Structure	long chapter book; italics indicate character's thoughts
Language Conventionality and Clarity	domain-specific words related to money and business; descriptive language; compound and complex sentences
Knowledge Demands	starting a new enterprise; school staff roles; how to work with peers and authority figures to accomplish goals

Prepare to Read

LEVELS OF MEANING

Lunch Money tells the story of a money-loving boy who wants to create a comic book business in his school in order to make money. He must learn to work with peers and adults to accomplish his goals. The story also addresses the importance of money, working with peers and school administrations, and learning to be a good friend.

STRUCTURE

PREVIEW Have students preview the text, focusing on the title of the book, the chapter titles, and the illustrations. Ask: Look at the cover. What do you think the book will be about? (Possible response: money and homemade comic books) Why do you think the writer chose to break the book into twenty-four chapters? (Using chapters helps break a long

---

MORE SUPPORT

ENGLISH LANGUAGE LEARNERS

To give students practice using the vocabulary words, have them work in groups to act out scenes using the vocabulary words. For example, a student could act out asking a bank teller, "What are your lending fees?"

STRUGGLING READERS

Students may not have much background with business or banking. Explain that stores are businesses where people go to buy things with money. Give students sentence frames to help them discuss money: One store I go to is ___. I go there with my family to buy ___.

story into smaller, more manageable parts.) Why do you think the author included illustrations? (to show what is being described in the text) Why do you think most of the drawings are small? (Possible response: The text gives more details than the drawings, so the author wants the reader to focus on the text.)

LANGUAGE CONVENTIONALITY AND CLARITY

PREVIEW VOCABULARY Use the Preview and Review Vocabulary Routine in Part 3 to assess what students know about the following words: *consumer, competitor, investment, profit, marketing, publishing, editor, designer,* and *print.*

DOMAIN-SPECIFIC VOCABULARY Use the Vocabulary Activities in Part 3 to teach critical, domain-specific vocabulary words, such as *accounting, deposit, lending fee, sales force, bind,* and *mass produce.*

COGNATES Use the list of Spanish cognates at the beginning of this module to guide your Spanish-speaking students as they read the text.

KNOWLEDGE DEMANDS

ACTIVATE BACKGROUND KNOWLEDGE Ask students to share what they know about starting a club or business at school. Use the Quick Write and Share Routine in Part 3 and ask: What are some things that require special permission to do at school during the school day or after school? How would you start a school club? Who do you think you would need to ask? How many people would be needed to run the club? What responsibilities would these people have?

Interact with Text

At the end of each chapter, have students summarize what has happened so far and identify emerging themes. Have students refer back to the text and cite text evidence in their summaries. Help students identify themes by asking them guided questions.

For example, after reading Chapter 9, ask: Why is Greg surprised that Mr. Z's brother lives in Idaho? (He could make more money if he lived somewhere else.) What is the Zentopoulous Toilet Theory? (People can only use one bathroom at a time.) Why does Mr. Z tell it to Greg? (Greg said he wanted a house with fifteen bathrooms.) What themes are developing here? (money, the importance of wealth, the issue of whether money can buy happiness)

STRUCTURE

As students read, periodically stop to assess their understanding of the story's use of italicized words. Ask: How does the writer show what a character is thinking? (by setting the thoughts in italics) Why doesn't the writer use quotation marks for this? (The story is told from the narrator's point of view. Quotation marks show what characters say out loud, and italics show what characters think. This separates the characters' words and thoughts from the narrator's words.)

> If . . . students have difficulty understanding the purpose of the italics,
>
> then . . . provide specific examples that include quotation marks and italics to model how the two are used.

Model analyzing the use of italics to show what Greg is thinking. Use a think aloud. Say: On page 74, I read this dialogue: "'But what?' Greg called after her. 'Later,' she called back." This text is in quotes to show that Greg and Maura are talking to each other. The word *called* gives me a clue that they are saying these words out loud. The next paragraph reads, "And Greg thought, *Later? Oh yeah. 'Cause we have to go to see Mr. Z.*" This text is in italics to show that Greg is thinking to himself. The word *thought* gives me a clue that he is not speaking out loud. Repeat with other examples as needed.

MORE SUPPORT

ENGLISH LANGUAGE LEARNERS

If students are confused by certain uses of italics in the text, explain that italics are also used to indicate when words are being emphasized. On p. 114, italics are used for words spoken by characters. These words are meant to be stressed.

STRUGGLING READERS

As the class or students finish reading chapters, have them write or draw a sketch in a journal about what they just read. Tell them to include main events, how characters have changed, and any predictions they have. This will help students summarize the text.

LANGUAGE CONVENTIONALITY AND CLARITY

The story includes detailed descriptions of the characters, the different things the characters see, and the things the characters do. Have students practice reading segments of text that have a lot of details and deciding what the author is trying to show. Have students draw a sketch of the scene or take notes on what the author is describing with the details that are present.

For example, have students read the description on p. 6 of the way that Greg worked to make money when he was very young. Ask: What do you learn from this description? (Greg was obsessed with making money. He was willing to work all the time.)

KNOWLEDGE DEMANDS

Explain that the role of a teacher is different from the role of a school administrator, like a principal. Have students compare Mr. Z as a teacher and Mrs. Davenport as a school administrator. Have students use text evidence to cite differences.

If . . . students have difficulty identifying differences,

then . . . have them complete a T-chart graphic organizer.

Tell students they can organize their information in a T-chart, using *Mr. Z* and *Mrs. Davenport* as the column headings. As students record the differences they find, ask them if they find any similarities.

Express and Extend

EXPRESS In the story, Mr. Z tries to show Greg that he cannot own an idea and expect nobody else to use it. He uses an analogy about ancient Sumerians to help illustrate his point. Reread the analogy on p. 82 with students and ask students to explain what would have happened if the Sumerians did not allow other people to use their idea.

EXTEND Have students write a letter to Mr. Z telling him whether they agree with what he said about people owning ideas. Have them include specific reasons as well as evidence from the text to support their opinions.

STRUCTURE

EXPRESS Assign two or three chapters to pairs of students. Using the book for text evidence, have partners come up with their own chapter titles that summarize the chapters. Write all of the suggested titles on the board and have the class vote on the best title for each chapter.

EXTEND Ask students to think about which chapter they enjoyed reading the most. Have students write two paragraphs that summarize the chapter and explain why this is their favorite part of the book.

MORE SUPPORT

ENGLISH LANGUAGE LEARNERS

Provide students with sentence frames they can use to tell which chapter they liked the most: I liked chapter ___ the most because ___. I liked when ___. The best part of the story is ___. My favorite character is ___ because ___.

STRUGGLING READERS

To help determine whether students agree or disagree with Mr. Z, use the Express Opinions Routine in Part 3. When students communicate their opinions, ask whether they are the same as or different from Mr. Z's opinion.

LANGUAGE CONVENTIONALITY AND CLARITY

EXPRESS Talk about Sentences and Words

Display the following sentences from p. 196 of *Lunch Money*. Read them aloud with students, and point out the use of rich, detailed language used to create a detailed image of Maura in words.

> From a file folder cradled in one arm, she took a slim stack of stapled pages and handed one packet to each committee member. She walked to the table, sat lightly on the front edge of the chair, spread some papers out in front of her, and said, "Good evening" into the microphone.

Ask: How did Maura hold the pages before she handed them out? (She held them in one arm.) What words give you more details about the way Maura conducts herself at the meeting? *(cradled, slim stack, walked, lightly on the front edge, spread)* How does the writer use commas in the second sentence? (to separate each of the actions that Maura takes) Why do you think the author wrote in this style, rather than using simple sentences? (to show a process that includes many actions)

TEAM TALK Have partners restate the ideas in these sentences using simple sentences. Ask students to discuss how simple sentences affect the impact of the text.

EXTEND Have pairs choose a paragraph from the story and rewrite it using only simple sentences. Then have them discuss which paragraph is more interesting to read and why.

KNOWLEDGE DEMANDS

EXPRESS Review the different steps that Greg and Maura take in order to get permission to sell comic books at school. Have small groups discuss what they learned about the process of getting something changed in a school or another organization.

EXTEND Have students write an essay explaining the importance of showing respect for authority, even when trying to get changes implemented. Tell students to cite examples from the story in their essays.

ACCELERATED LEARNERS

Have students write interview questions for a principal or school board member to find out the process your district has for starting a school club. If possible, have students conduct the interview and create a diagram that explains the different steps in the process and why each step exists.

MORE SUPPORT

Unlock the Text

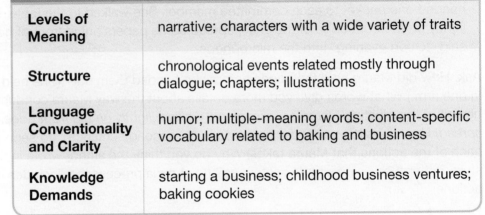

QUALITATIVE MEASURES

Levels of Meaning	narrative; characters with a wide variety of traits
Structure	chronological events related mostly through dialogue; chapters; illustrations
Language Conventionality and Clarity	humor; multiple-meaning words; content-specific vocabulary related to baking and business
Knowledge Demands	starting a business; childhood business ventures; baking cookies

Max Malone Makes a Million, pp. 74–93

Prepare to Read

LEVELS OF MEANING

This narrative text is about a boy who decides to get rich quickly by starting a business with his friend. The boy learns that there is no easy way to make a million dollars.

STRUCTURE

PREVIEW Have students preview the text, focusing on the title, the chapter titles, and the illustrations. Ask: Based on the title, what do you think the story will be about? (Possible response: a boy who earns a lot of money) Look at the small picture on page 76 of the text next to the chapter title. What do you think this chapter will be about? (The picture shows cookies with dollar signs over them. Maybe Max is going to make a lot of money baking cookies.)

ENGLISH LANGUAGE LEARNERS

Provide students with sentence frames they can use when discussing businesses that are run by young people: Many young people try to sell ___. Young people can also ___. I can make money by ___. To start this business, I need ___.

STRUGGLING READERS

Have students create index cards for the vocabulary words and then categorize and sort the words. Then have students create new, more specific categories and re-sort the words. For example, students might sort some words into the category "things," and then re-sort them into "things related to money" and "things related to people."

LANGUAGE CONVENTIONALITY AND CLARITY

PREVIEW VOCABULARY Use the Preview and Review Vocabulary Routine in Part 3 to assess what students know about the following words: *interrupted*, *millionaire*, *personalized*, *ingredients*, *appreciate*, *businesslike*, *customer*, *hesitated*, *insulted*, and *construction*. Have partners use the words in sentences as they talk about everyday life.

COGNATES Use the list of Spanish cognates at the beginning of this module to guide your Spanish-speaking students as they read the text.

MULTIPLE-MEANING WORDS The following words in the story each have more than one meaning: *chip*, *jar*, *counter*, *check*, *bowl*, *switch*, *batter*, *sheet*, *pad*, *park*, *stand*, *handle*, and *beat*. Use the Analyze Multiple-Meaning Words Routine in Part 3. Have students work with partners to list some of the multiple meanings for each word. For example, *batter* can mean "dough for baking" or "the person who hits a ball in baseball."

KNOWLEDGE DEMANDS

ACTIVATE BACKGROUND KNOWLEDGE Ask students to discuss what they know about businesses started by children. Use the Quick Write and Share Routine in Part 3 and ask: What are some businesses that many children have been involved in? (Possible responses: mowing lawns, shoveling snow, selling lemonade, walking dogs) Why do you think children often open the same types of businesses? (Possible responses: Certain businesses don't require much money to start. Children have the skills required for certain kinds of businesses.) What type of business would you choose to create? (Responses will vary.)

Before students get started, model describing a childhood experience related to running a business: Many young people want to earn money so they can buy something they want. When I was young, I really wanted a new bike. I decided to mow lawns for people in my neighborhood. I made money, and I was proud of how it felt to have a job and to be responsible.

Interact with Text

As you read *Max Malone Makes a Million*, periodically assess students' understanding of the plot and the characters. Ask students to describe what has happened so far in the story, as well as how the characters relate to one another.

> **If . . .** students have difficulty describing plot events,
>
> **then . . .** use the Story Map Routine and Graphic Organizer in Part 3 to help students record the main events in a chapter.

Instruct students to not only use their own words when recording main events, but also to include vocabulary words whenever possible.

STRUCTURE

Some students may find it difficult to follow the events of the story, since the events are mostly described through dialogue. Assess students' comprehension of story events by having them describe events in chronological order.

> **If . . .** students have difficulty putting events in order,
>
> **then . . .** use the Sequence of Events Routine and Graphic Organizer in Part 3.

As students read, have them record information about the steps Max takes to try to become a millionaire. Instruct students to record the events in their own words, without using dialogue from the selection.

MORE SUPPORT

ENGLISH LANGUAGE LEARNERS

To help students with the concept of sequence, name three events from the story in random order. Provide students with these sentence frames: The first thing that happened was ___. The next thing that happened was ___. The last thing that happened was ___.

STRUGGLING READERS

Show students a recipe. Start a dialogue about the importance of following a recipe. Allow students to share the experiences they have following a recipe or another set of step-by-step instructions. Discuss what might happen if students skip a step in the recipe or instructions.

LANGUAGE CONVENTIONALITY AND CLARITY

The story uses humor to show what happens to Max and his friend. Have students give examples of humor in the story.

Read aloud the cookie-baking scene, pointing out humorous dialogue exchanges:

"Oops," said Gordy. "I think there is something seriously wrong with these chocolate-chip cookies."

"What?" asked Max.

"We forgot the chocolate chips."

Point out that the writer does not provide any type of reaction to what happened. Instead, the writer presents the situation and allows the reader to figure out that it is humorous.

KNOWLEDGE DEMANDS

Students may not have experience baking cookies or other baked goods. Thus, they may not know the importance of each specific ingredient in the recipe. However, students should be able to find clues in the text to support the idea that the cookies will not turn out right. Ask: What are some clues that the writer uses to help the reader predict that the cookies will not turn out right? (Max tells his mom that following a recipe will take too much time. As this section of the story continues, the writer gives several specific examples of ways the boys do not follow the recipe.)

If . . . students have trouble identifying text clues,

then . . . use the Story Prediction Chart Routine and Graphic Organizer in Part 3 to help students record predictions, text clues, and eventual outcomes.

Express and Extend

EXPRESS Have students compare and contrast the characters of Max and Austin Healy. Brainstorm the personality traits that Austin exhibits and that enable him to succeed. Have students look at the characteristics one by one and decide whether Max displays a similar or opposite trait. For example, Austin chooses his sales location carefully, while Max carelessly adds ingredients when he bakes his cookies.

> If . . . students have trouble comparing and contrasting,
>
> then . . . use the Venn Diagram Routine and Graphic Organizer in Part 3 to help students record similarities and differences.

EXTEND Have students describe the character traits they think are important for someone who wants to become a successful business owner. Tell students to use vocabulary words and give examples from the story to show how those character traits can help a person succeed.

EXPRESS Have students analyze the ways in which dialogue relates story events and develops the plot and the characters. Ask: How does the writer use dialogue to develop the story's plot and the characters?

Have students focus on specific examples of dialogue for the same character in order to analyze what they learn about the plot and the character from dialogue. Model an example by saying: Rosalie tells Max that he cannot use the recipe from the package of chocolate chips. Her dialogue with Max tells the reader that she is not afraid to say what she thinks, even if her brother does not want her advice.

EXTEND Have students choose one event from the story about which to create a comic book. Have them include in their comics dialogue from the text, using speech bubbles.

ENGLISH LANGUAGE LEARNERS

Students may need additional help describing the character traits needed for a successful business. Provide them with the following sentence frames: It is important for a businessperson to ___. A businessperson should not be ___. Very successful people are usually ___.

STRUGGLING READERS

To help students follow who is speaking in a dialogue, remind them that the author begins a new paragraph each time the speaker changes. Have students look for other clues, such as a character's name that follows the word *said*.

EXPRESS Talk about Sentences and Words

Display the following sentences from *Max Malone Makes a Million*. Read them aloud with students.

> "You picked a pretty good spot to set up your stand," said Max. He hated to admit it, but it was true.
>
> "Yeah," said Austin. "I knew these men would be here today. I knew they'd be thirsty. <u>You just have to be in the right place at the right time. You've got to know your market. Know your customers.</u> Too bad they won't be here tomorrow. I'll have to figure out something else to do."

Discuss the meaning of the underlined sentences, explaining that these are common business expressions. Ask: How does Austin show that he knows his market and knows his customers? (He sets up his lemonade stand in a place where he knows he will find thirsty people who will buy his lemonade.)

TEAM TALK Have students work with a partner to discuss why they think the author wrote such complicated phrases for the dialogue of a six-year-old boy. Ask: Why does the author have Austin say these phrases even though he is only six years old? What does this tell the reader about the character? (Austin is very smart and knows more about business than Max.)

EXTEND Have partners discuss what tone they think Austin may have used when he made the statement quoted above. Allow students to share their ideas with the class, using evidence from the story to support their viewpoints.

EXPRESS Have students write their own ending to the story showing how Max succeeds or fails. Tell students that their story conclusion should develop the characters based on what has already happened in the story. Students should include dialogue and narrative text. To help students get started, ask: From what you have gathered reading the text, do you think that Max is going to become a successful businessperson? Why or why not?

EXTEND Have students create a tip list for Max for becoming a successful businessperson. Tell them to include the top five things a person should do in order to be successful. Have students share their lists with the class and underline any tip on their list that also appears on another student's list.

ACCELERATED LEARNERS

Have students create a business plan for a new business selling cookies or some other product. Tell them to include how and where they will market the product, how their product will be unique, and what supplies they will need to create the business.

Unlock the Text

QUALITATIVE MEASURES

Levels of Meaning	multiple points of view; importance of family
Structure	first-person narrative; newspaper issues are interspersed within the narration
Language Conventionality and Clarity	mixed verb tenses; Spanish words; content-specific vocabulary related to ranching
Knowledge Demands	Mexican American culture; cowboy culture; rural community life in pre–World War II Arizona; one-room schoolhouses

Coyote School News,
pp. 58–73

Prepare to Read

LEVELS OF MEANING

Coyote School News is different from many of the stories that students read because it presents the story in an unusual way. Narrated sections give first-person accounts of what happens to the main character. Issues of a school newspaper present information from the points of view of other characters.

STRUCTURE

PREVIEW Have students preview the text, focusing on the section titles, illustrations, and pages from the *Coyote News.* Say: Look at pages labeled *Coyote News.* How might these sections of the story be different from the rest of the story? (These look like pages from a homemade newspaper. These pages might be written more like news stories than fictional stories.) What do the map and the illustration on pages 60 and 61 tell you about the story? (The story takes place in the southwestern United States.

MORE SUPPORT

ENGLISH LANGUAGE LEARNERS

To give students additional background knowledge about cowboys and ranchers, display photographs of real cowboys from books and the Internet. Include pictures of items, such as cowboy hats, lassoes, and spurs, and explain how these items are useful.

STRUGGLING READERS

Have students use a T-chart or Venn diagram to compare and contrast their school with a one-room schoolhouse. Have them consider aspects of school, such as who teaches various subjects, nonacademic activities they enjoy, and modern conveniences of their school.

The story will probably be about ranchers or cowboys.) What do you notice about the definitions that appear at the bottom of many of the pages? (The definitions are for Spanish words, and there are pronunciations given for the words.) Why do you think the author included these definitions? (The story must contain a lot of Spanish words, and the author wants the reader to know what these words mean and how to say them.)

LANGUAGE CONVENTIONALITY AND CLARITY

PREVIEW VOCABULARY Use the Preview and Review Vocabulary Routine in Part 3 to assess what students know about the following words: *coyote*, *roundup*, *spurs*, *bawling*, *mimeograph*, *mesquite*, *buckle*, *lassoes*, *steer*, and *chuck wagon*. Use the words to discuss life on a ranch or things related to cowboys. Provide pictures for the words when possible.

COGNATES Use the list of Spanish cognates at the beginning of this module to guide your Spanish-speaking students as they read the text.

KNOWLEDGE DEMANDS

ACTIVATE BACKGROUND KNOWLEDGE This story is about a boy who attends a one-room school in the late 1930s. Prompt students to think about sharing a classroom with students in kindergarten, first grade, and sixth grade. Use the Quick Write and Share Routine in Part 3 and ask: What do you think it is like to learn in a one-room schoolhouse? (Possible responses: It might be nice because you could get to know your teacher and the other students very well. But it might be challenging because the teacher has to give attention to students of many different grade levels.) How is a one-room school different from your school? (Possible responses: Students of different ages and grade levels are in one room. The teacher has to teach different subjects and different information for the various grade levels.) How is it similar to your school? (Possible responses: There would be a teacher giving lessons. Students would be learning information. Different subjects would be taught.)

Before students begin writing, model describing a one-room schoolhouse by comparing and contrasting it with a specific aspect of a modern school. Say: When I think about what it would be like to teach in a one-room schoolhouse, I start by thinking about how it is similar to our school. I come to school each day to teach you all. I have a desk and books. Then I think about how the one-room school would be different from our school. I would have students of all ages. The school would not have a music teacher or an art room.

Interact with Text

LEVELS OF MEANING

As students read *Coyote School News,* periodically stop to assess their level of understanding of the multiple points of view in the story.

> **If . . .** students struggle to identify the various points of view,
>
> **then . . .** provide support by asking guiding questions.

Ask: How can you tell when the story is told from Monchi's point of view? How can you tell when the point of view changes? How can you tell whose point of view is expressed in the newspaper?

STRUCTURE

As students read, periodically stop to assess their understanding of the story's structure. **Say:** Issues of the *Coyote News* are mixed in with Monchi's first-person narration. **Ask:** How do these two different ways of telling the story work together?

Have small groups discuss why the author chose to write the story in this style. Distribue the Venn Diagram Graphic Organizer from Part 3. Have students label one circle *Monchi's Narration* and the other *Coyote School News*. Have groups look through the text and record information they learned from Monchi in the appropriate circle and record points they learned from the newspaper in the other. Have them add information they learned from both sources in the center of the diagram. Lastly, have students discuss what information they would have missed if the author had written the story from only one point of view.

MORE SUPPORT

ENGLISH LANGUAGE LEARNERS

Review present- and past-tense verbs with students. To help them distinguish between past and present, provide sentence frames, such as: Yesterday, one thing I ate was ___. Right now, I am thinking about eating ___.

STRUGGLING READERS

Changes in point of view might confuse some students. Explain that point of view only changes on the pages that show the newspaper. Students can point to the names at the end of each article to identify which character's point of view is given.

LANGUAGE CONVENTIONALITY AND CLARITY

The writer uses both the present and past tenses in a deliberate way that helps to create meaning. The writer uses the past tense to describe a specific event that happened. The writer uses the present tense to describe things that happen often or to create an overall context.

Review the section "Chiles," and say: The first two paragraphs are in the present tense because the narrator is describing what happens every day during the harvesting season. The third paragraph is in the past tense because it tells about a specific event that happened—how Monchi broke his hand. Ask: Why does the writer switch between the present tense and the past tense?

KNOWLEDGE DEMANDS

The story includes many aspects of rural Mexican American culture in the late 1930s. Have students describe various aspects of the culture that are shown through the actions of the characters in the story.

For example, Monchi's family expects him to stay home from school during roundup. Even though Monchi wants to get the Perfect Attendance Award, he does not complain about missing school. He knows that going to roundup is more important to his family than him winning the Perfect Attendance Award.

If . . . students have difficulty understanding the role of culture and setting in this story,

then . . . have them look at the illustrations to get additional information about the culture and the setting.

Explain that illustrations can also provide information about things that were important in the culture, such as growing crops, participating in the roundup, and taking part in family celebrations.

MORE SUPPORT

Express and Extend

EXPRESS The story develops the theme of family. Ask: What does the story show about the importance of family in this culture? Use examples from the story to support your answer.

> **If . . .** students have difficulty identifying examples of this theme,
>
> **then . . .** have them reread the section titled "Roundup." Have students look for the text that tells why Monchi missed school and what his brother told him about what was most important.

EXTEND Have students debate whether Miss Byers should have students work for a Perfect Attendance Award, given the culture and the importance of ranching. Tell students to write a letter to Miss Byers in which they state their opinion about having students work for the Perfect Attendance Award. Students should use vocabulary words in their letters. They should provide reasons and cite examples from the story to support their opinions.

EXPRESS Have small groups choose one character besides Monchi and use information in the text to create a poster about this character. They should include how Monchi describes this character, as well as how the character is portrayed in the rest of the text. Have students present their poster to the class.

EXTEND Have students write a review of the story for someone who is deciding whether to read the book. Students should tell whether they would recommend the story to other readers and give reasons for their recommendation. Tell students to include information about their favorite character or event, but to not reveal too much of the plot in their review.

ENGLISH LANGUAGE LEARNERS

If students are confused by some of Monchi's English, explain that this structure helps show that Monchi lives in a Spanish-speaking household. Help students reword sentences. For example, "In my family we are six kids" can be reworded as "There are six kids in my family."

STRUGGLING READERS

Before students begin to write their letters to Miss Byers, review opinion writing with them. Use the Express Opinions Routine in Part 3. Once students have written their letters, have partners exchange papers and check for the various opinion elements.

LANGUAGE CONVENTIONALITY AND CLARITY

EXPRESS Talk about Sentences and Words

Display the following sentences from p. 70 of *Coyote School News*. Read them aloud with students.

> The vaqueros were hollering, "¡Ándale!" ¡Ándale!" They were cutting through the cattle on their horses, swinging their lassoes in the air to rope out the steers. My tío Chaco threw his saddle up on his horse, Canelo, and joined them.

The author uses Spanish words throughout the story. Ask: What words and proper names in this passage are in Spanish? (*vaqueros, ándale, tío, Chaco, Canelo*) Why do you think the author uses Spanish words? (The Spanish words help to show that the characters are Mexican American. They would have used the Spanish words in their speech, and they would have used Spanish words to describe themselves.)

TEAM TALK Have students work with a partner to replace the Spanish words with English words and rewrite the sentences. Instruct students to use the definitions at the bottom of the page to find possible replacement text. Have students explain how the use of Spanish is important to the text.

EXTEND Ask: Suppose the writer could use Spanish for only one of the events in the story. Which event should he have chosen and why? Have partners discuss their response to this question. Provide time for partners to share their answers with the class.

KNOWLEDGE DEMANDS

EXPRESS Have students cite evidence from the text and use it to discuss what they learned about life in this part of Arizona in the 1930s.

If . . . students have difficulty discussing what they learned,

then . . . provide sentence frames, such as the following, for them to complete: In the 1930s, life was different from today because ___. One thing I learned about school at that time is ___.

EXTEND Have students write interview questions for the students in the text. Tell them to ask about things they still want to know about learning in a one-room schoolhouse, how they created the newspaper, or any other lingering questions.

ACCELERATED LEARNERS

Have students create a classroom newspaper detailing the events of the past week. Tell them to choose one student to name the paper, one student to design the paper, one student to draw illustrations for the paper, three or four students to write stories, and at least one editor-in-chief to make sure everyone is working together. The remaining students can read the finished newspaper and compare it to *Coyote News*.

MORE SUPPORT

Cognates

Cognates are words that have similar spellings and meanings in two or more languages. Many words in English and Spanish share Greek or Latin roots, and many words in English came from French, which is closely connected to Spanish (and to Portuguese, Italian, and Romanian). Because of this, many literary, content, and academic process words in English (e.g., *gracious/gracioso; volcano/volcán; compare/comparar*) have recognizable Spanish cognates.

Making the connection to cognates permits students who are native Spanish speakers to understand the strong foundation they have in academic and literary English. These links between English and Spanish are also useful for native speakers of English and other languages because they help uncover basic underlying features of our language.

ANCHOR TEXT Using Money

ENGLISH	SPANISH	ENGLISH	SPANISH
bank	banco	limit	límite
benefits	beneficios	magnetic	magnético
check	cheque	minimum	mínimo
convenient	convenientes	opportunities	oportunidades
cost	costo	organizations	organizaciones
decide	decidir	philanthropist	filántropo
denominations	denominación	plan	planear
deposit	depositar	problem	problema
donate	donar	pronounce	pronunciar
electricity	electricidad	require	requerir
emergencies	emergencias	reserve	reservar
European	europeo	restaurants	restaurantes
frugal	frugal	services	servicios
identity	identidad	strict	estricto
important	importante	using	usar
information	información	values	valores
interest	interés		

SUPPORTING TEXT A Tale of Two Poggles

ENGLISH	SPANISH	ENGLISH	SPANISH
announcement	anuncio	importance	importancia
batteries	baterías	inventor	inventor
cafeteria	cafetería	machine	máquina
carnival	carnaval	messages	mensajes
carousel	carrusel	park	parque
compartments	compartimientos	pilot	piloto
connection	conexión	reappeared	reapareció
designer	diseñador	rumor	rumor
election	elección	satisfied	satisfecha
engineer	ingeniero	sections	secciones
enormous	enorme	station	estación
explained	explicó	text	texto
furious	furiosa	train	tren
immediately	inmediatamente	tunnels	túneles

SUPPORTING TEXT The Boy Who Invented TV

ENGLISH	SPANISH	ENGLISH	SPANISH
announce	anunciar	inventors	inventores
bicycle	bicicleta	lines	líneas
catalog	catálogo	magnetism	magnetismo
credit	crédito	mechanical	mecánico
convert	convertir	model	modelo
diagram	diagrama	obsession	obsesión
electrons	electrones	particle	partícula
elements	elementos	phonograph	fonógrafo
experiment	experimento	possession	posesión
explanation	explicación	reporter	reportero
generator	generador	scientist	científico
hero	héroe	stimulate	estimular
include	incluir	theory	teoría

These lists contain many, but not all, Spanish cognates from these selections.

Unlock the Text

QUALITATIVE MEASURES

Understanding Money
Using Money

Levels of Meaning	informational text about money, banking, and the use of credit cards and debit cards
Structure	chapters; text features, including boxed text, graphs, and charts
Language Conventionality and Clarity	dense and detailed information; domain-specific vocabulary
Knowledge Demands	basic understanding of buying and selling goods; math skills and concepts; concepts of money

Prepare to Read

LEVELS OF MEANING

Using Money is an informational text that tells the history and purpose of money. The text explains issues related to money and banking, including earning, spending, borrowing, and investing.

STRUCTURE

PREVIEW Have students preview the text, looking at the cover, chapter titles, photos, and graphic elements. Ask: Why does the author put some of the words in boldface, or dark, type? (to let the reader know that these words are defined in the glossary) What do you notice about the chapter titles? (They are all questions.) Why do you think the author divided the book into chapters? (Each chapter is about a different topic related to money.) Why do you think the author included text boxes and captions on almost every page of this book? (to give the reader additional information about the text, photos, or graphics on the page)

ENGLISH LANGUAGE LEARNERS

Remind students to use the glossary for help with difficult words. Say: When you encounter a difficult word, look it up in the glossary. Be sure you understand the word as it is used on the page. Rewrite the sentence on a sticky note, using your own words. Model this strategy for students.

STRUGGLING READERS

For unfamiliar words that are not in the glossary, have students create their own book of banking words that they can add to as they read the text. For each word, students should define the word, give examples, and use it in a sentence.

PREVIEW VOCABULARY Use the Preview and Review Vocabulary Routine in Part 3 to assess what students know about the following words: *check*, *credit cards*, *expenses*, *relatives*, *business*, *income*, *purchase*, *fee*, *percentage*, *provide*, *insures*, *unexpectedly*, *appointed*, *philanthropist*, and *chairman*.

COGNATES Use the list of Spanish cognates at the beginning of this module as a reference to guide your Spanish-speaking students as they read the text.

DOMAIN-SPECIFIC VOCABULARY Use the Vocabulary Activities in Part 3 to preteach domain-specific vocabulary words, such as *deposit*, *loans*, *interest*, *debt*, *savings account*, *checking account*, *balance*, *debit card*, *ATM*, *personal identification number*, and *budget*.

ACTIVATE BACKGROUND KNOWLEDGE Ask students to share what they know about how money is used. Use the Quick Write and Share Routine in Part 3. Ask: How do you or your parents buy something you want or need? What kinds of things do you or your parents always pay for with cash? What about with checks or credit cards?

If students need more support, model with an example such as the following: There are many different ways to buy something I want or need. Sometimes I buy things on the Internet. When I do that, I pay with a credit card. I don't hand anyone my card. I just enter the card information into a form on the Web site and pay electronically.

Interact with Text

As students read *Using Money,* periodically stop to assess their level of understanding of the main idea of each chapter.

If . . . students have difficulty identifying main ideas,

then . . . use the Main Idea and Details Routine and Graphic Organizer in Part 3.

Remind students that the chapter titles tell readers what each chapter will be about. Explain that each section heading within a chapter gives details about the main idea of the chapter. Remind students to look at chapter titles and section titles to get information about the topics being covered. Students can write chapter titles in the top box of the graphic organizer and write section titles in the Details boxes. Then, as they read, students can take notes in each of the boxes.

Review some graphic organizers that students can use to take notes as they read.

STRUCTURE

As students read, periodically assess their understanding of the purpose of the text features within the text. Ask: What types of information does the author present in boxed text, graphs, and charts?

If . . . students have difficulty describing how the author presents information using text features,

then . . . choose one type of text feature to focus on, go through the text looking for specific examples of that text feature, and explain what kind of information is provided.

For example, have students look at the text in the yellow boxes on pp. 15, 18, 27, and 28. Ask: What type of information do you learn from these boxes? (Each box gives a specific example or useful tip about how the reader can use, save, or protect his or her own money.) Have students find other examples of boxed text and explain how those are related to the text and how they are helpful.

MORE SUPPORT

ENGLISH LANGUAGE LEARNERS

To put information into their own words when summarizing, provide sentence frames: The main idea of this chapter is ___. One important detail is ___. The text features are helpful because ___.

STRUGGLING READERS

Some students may have difficulty with the Solve It! problems, not because they have difficulty with math, but because they have difficulty reading. Distribute a photocopy of the problem and have students highlight what they need to find out or solve, underline important details, and cross out nonessential information.

LANGUAGE CONVENTIONALITY AND CLARITY

Using Money contains a fair amount of dense and detailed information within the text. Have students choose a chapter from the book and write a two-paragraph summary of that chapter, using information from the main body of text, as well as information from the text features.

> **If . . .** students have difficulty summarizing information,
>
> **then . . .** use the Retell or Summarize Routine and Graphic Organizer in Part 3 to help students organize information. Remind students that summaries should include the most important details from the text, stated in their own words.

KNOWLEDGE DEMANDS

Students need to use their math skills and math knowledge to fully understand the charts and to work through the Solve It! problems. Go back to the text and have students explain the math that is used in the various charts and the math skills they used for each Solve It! box.

> **If . . .** students have difficulty explaining the math,
>
> **then . . .** break the problem into more manageable parts.

For example, direct students to the Solve It! box on p. 32. Reread the problem aloud with students. Then say: The text says that the game costs $25, and Reggie has $13. How do you know that Reggie needs to save $12? ($25 – $13 = $12) To find out how many weeks it will take Reggie to save $12 for the game, will you add, subtract, multiply, or divide? (divide; 12 ÷ 2 = 6. So it will take Reggie 6 weeks to save $12.) What math skill do you need to use to find out how many weeks it will take Reggie to save $12 for the game if he saves $3 a week? (division; 12 ÷ 3 = 4. So it will take Reggie 4 weeks to save $12.) Remind students that they can check their answers to the Solve It! boxes by looking on p. 45.

Express and Extend

LEVELS OF MEANING

EXPRESS The text explains concepts related to banking and money. The information about credit cards may be particularly challenging for students. Ask: How is a credit card different from a debit card? Why isn't a credit card a form of money?

Have students use the Venn Diagram Graphic Organizer in Part 3 to compare debit cards and credit cards. Have them reference the text for specific examples.

EXTEND Have students reread p. 25 and write a letter to Seth with advice about how to pay off his credit card balance more quickly. Students should explain why it is important to pay more than the minimum payment each month.

STRUCTURE

EXPRESS Assign small groups of students a chapter of the text. Have groups discuss how the concepts in the chapter are related to the book's overall topic—using money.

> **If . . .** students have difficulty explaining how the various concepts relate to the bigger topic,
>
> **then . . .** use the Web Routine and Graphic Organizer in Part 3.

Instruct students to write Using Money in the center circle of the web, then write concepts from their assigned chapter in the outer circles. This will give them a better visual guide to how their assigned chapter is connected to the bigger topic of using money.

EXTEND Have students write an introductory paragraph for their chapter. Paragraphs should clearly identify the main idea of the chapter and explain how the chapter is related to using money. Tell students to use vocabulary words in their paragraphs.

ENGLISH LANGUAGE LEARNERS

Provide sentence frames to help students discuss the differences between debit cards and credit cards: People use ___ to ___. Debit cards are not ___. Debit cards are ___. Credit cards are not ___. Credit cards are ___.

STRUGGLING READERS

If students struggle to write an introductory paragraph for a chapter, remind them to break the task into manageable chunks. Students should write a sentence that explains how the chapter relates to using money as a whole. Then have students write two or three sentences to show the connection.

LANGUAGE CONVENTIONALITY AND CLARITY

EXPRESS Talk about Sentences and Words

Display and read aloud the following sentence from p. 35 of *Using Money*.

> The group that oversees the banking system (including interest rates on loans) and makes sure that it works well is the Federal Reserve System, also known as the Fed.

Ask: What does the word *Federal* in the name of this organization tell you about the organization? (It is part of the federal or national government.) What does it mean to oversee something? (to watch what happens and make sure that things are done the right way) What are some things the Fed is watching over? (the banking system overall and interest rates on loans)

TEAM TALK Have students work with a partner to discuss why it is important to have an individual or group, such as the Fed, watch over the banking system. Students should cite examples from the text during their discussion.

EXTEND Have students discuss what might happen if no one oversaw the banking system. Students can look through the book to identify problems that can arise in banking, and they can predict additional problems that might develop over time.

KNOWLEDGE DEMANDS

EXPRESS Using the text for support, have students write a paragraph about the most important thing they learned about money from *Using Money*.

EXTEND Have students think of something that requires saving money in order to purchase. Students should research the cost of the item and then create a budget and a savings plan. Tell students to explain how they will earn the money they will save, and how long it will take to save enough money.

ACCELERATED LEARNERS

Have students synthesize what they learned from this text by creating a pamphlet outlining important information for people who want a credit card. Have them include how credit cards work, how to pay off debt, and the pros and cons of taking on debt.

MORE SUPPORT

Unlock the Text

A Tale of
Two Poggles

WRITTEN BY MARGI MCALLISTER
ILLUSTRATED BY MARK BEECH

QUALITATIVE MEASURES

Levels of Meaning	accessible and fun narrative in which two clever children convince the greedy owner of an envelope factory to let the workers purchase the factory and transform it into an amusement park; includes table of contents, lively illustrations, and lots of dialogue
Structure	narrative organized in six straight chronological chapters; first-person narrator quickly transforms to a third-person omniscient voice
Language Conventionality and Clarity	mostly grade-level vocabulary, including some domain-specific words about factories and amusement parks
Knowledge Demands	understanding about envelopes, factories, and amusement parks

Prepare to Read

LEVELS OF MEANING

A Tale of Two Poggles is a humorous tale about a town's transformation of a factory to a creative place owned by its citizens. It unfolds in six chapters beginning with descriptions of the factory and its owner, Gloria Grabber, and a contest in which the school children are asked to write about their ambitions. Two children, Nina and Alejandro, write essays about wanting to be an inventor and an astronaut which kicks off a series of comical yet transformative events, told with an abundance of descriptive details, rich dialogue, and lively illustrations.

STRUCTURE

PREVIEW Direct students' attention to the talk bubbles and illustrations on page 7. Say: These three back-and-forth conversations illustrate the

ENGLISH LANGUAGE LEARNERS

Point out that *Poggle* is a made-up name of a town – it is not a real place. Say the word *Poggle* aloud and ask children to repeat it. Explain that there are two towns in the story that use this name, *Nether Poggle* and *Upper Poggle*.

STRUGGLING READERS

Ask students to predict what the story will be about. Have them write their predictions on pieces of paper, fold them, and tuck them into an envelope addressed to themselves. Collect them. After reading, return their envelopes so they can see if their predictions were accurate.

conflict in this story. They are between Gloria Grabber and people who work in the factory that she owns. Ask four students to read the conversations on this page aloud, with three students reading the voices of the townspeople on the left and one student reading the voice of Gloria Grabber on the right. Then ask: What kind of person is Gloria Grabber? Does she remind you of anyone else that you have read stories about? (Students may recall other female antagonists, such as the Queen of Hearts in *Alice in Wonderland* or the Stepmother in *Cinderella*.)

LANGUAGE CONVENTIONALITY AND CLARITY

PREVIEW VOCABULARY Use the Preview and Review Vocabulary Routine in Part 3 to assess what students know about the following words: *sternly, scornful, rotten, grimmer, miserable, cautious, local,* and *clever*. Explain that these words are all adjectives that describe people, places, and things in this story.

COGNATES Use the list of Spanish cognates at the beginning of this module to guide your Spanish-speaking students as they read the selection.

DOMAIN-SPECIFIC VOCABULARY Use the Vocabulary Activities in Part 3 to pre-teach the following domain-specific vocabulary: *operate, chute, compartment, revolve, automatic,* and *enormous*. Explain that these words are all related to the factory that is at the center of this story.

KNOWLEDGE DEMANDS

ACTIVATE BACKGROUND KNOWLEDGE Ask: What do you already know about factories? Make a list of students' responses. Say: Factories are places that include large buildings with machinery inside. Factories employ many workers who manufacture products that are sold to the general public. Point students to the illustrations on pages 4–5, 17, 18–19, 22, 23, and 24–25 that show the inside of the factory. If there are factories in your town or city, make a list of them. Ask if any students have relatives or know people who work in these factories. Ask: What do you think it is like to work in a factory? What might be good about it? (steady paychecks, steady work, good benefits) What might be bad about it? (indoors all day, repetitive work)

If . . . students have difficulty organizing what they know about factories and questions they might have about them,

then . . . use the KWLH Chart with Graphic Organizer in Part 3 to support their understanding.

STRUGGLING READERS

Focus students' attention on two key words in the story: *Poggle* and *Grabber*. Explain that *Poggle* is the name of a town that has two parts: Upper and Lower (Nether). Ask students to name words that rhyme with *poggle* (toggle, goggle). Then, focus students' attention on the mayor's last name. Ask: What does grabber mean? (a person who grabs) What does *grab* mean? (to physically take something from someone else)

Interact with Text

LEVELS OF MEANING

As you read *A Tale of Two Poggles,* assess not only students' understanding of the events but also their understanding of the characters: Grabber, Nina, Alejandro, and Nina's father. Encourage students to complete a web using the Web Graphic Organizer in Part 3 for each character with their names in the center of the webs. Ask: What words describe each of the main characters? Remind them that sometimes, descriptive words will be explicit in the text (e.g. Grabber is *greedy, sharp, sneaky,* and *scornful,* and performs actions such as *grumbled* and *glared*). They can also make inferences based on details in the text (e.g. Grabber is *unfair, mean, evil,* or *tricky*). Remind them that if they make inferences, they must be able to cite specific textual evidence as support.

STRUCTURE

This story happens in strict chronological order; one event leads to the next which leads to the next in an uninterrupted sequence. However, help students recognize that pages 4–8 contain exposition. That is, they contain background information about the town, the factory, and the mayor that readers need to understand the events. Say: The action of the story, the plot, begins on page 9 with the words "One wet morning." Can you find other words and phrases in the story that show that time has passed and show when events take place? ("That evening," on page 12; "The next week" on page 13; "The next Monday morning" on page 16) Ask: What does page 15 contain? (This page, like pages 4–8, contains exposition or background information about Upper Poggle. Nothing actually happens on this page; it contains no plot events.)

If . . . students have difficulty keeping track of the chronological events in the text,

then . . . use the Sequence of Events Routine with Graphic Organizer in Part 3 to take notes. Help them understand how one event leads to the next.

ENGLISH LANGUAGE LEARNERS

Ask each student to choose two illustrations that they think are especially important or funny. For each one, have them explain what the picture shows and why the illustrator included it.

STRUGGLING READERS

Ask students to read the last sentence on p. 12. Have them tell you which of the five senses the words *whirled, rolled, whizzed,* and *shone* connect to. (sound and sight) Have them look for other places in the story that use words that connect to the senses. Have them explain how words like these help the reader relate to the story.

LANGUAGE CONVENTIONALITY AND CLARITY

Focus students' attention on the word *transform* on page 41. Ask: How do the two word parts in *transform* help you understand its meaning? (The prefix *trans-* means "across." The base word *form* refers to something's shape or appearance. The word means "to change across one shape to another.") Then, challenge students to list as many ways as possible, based on details in the story, that Nether Poggle transforms (brightly colored paint, store becomes bowling alley, mezzanine and carts become roller coasters, chute and disks become slide and carousel, skate park and skating rink outside, new chairs and tables in cafeteria, office becomes gift shop). Finally, ask: In general, how is the envelope factory transformed? What does this transformation mean? (It becomes fun. It becomes lively. It serves the people instead of the people serving it.) Explain that their answer to this question is a conclusion based on evidence from the text.

> **If . . .** students have difficulty seeing the connection between specific details and a conclusion,
>
> **then . . .** encourage them to use the Draw Conclusions Graphic Organizer in Part 3 to support their analysis.

KNOWLEDGE DEMANDS

Some students may not be familiar with amusement parks. Help them locate and observe photographs from online sources that show the various components mentioned in the story, such as roller coasters, carousels, bouncy castles, and ball pits. Challenge them to locate an amusement park near you using an online search engine. Let students who have visited this amusement park or another park share their experiences aloud. Encourage them to share details that appeal to all five senses: sight, sound, taste, smell, and touch. Students can also use the illustrations on pages 42–45 as support. They also might be interested in the history of amusement parks and be interested to know that the earliest one opened in 1583 in Denmark.

ENGLISH LANGUAGE LEARNERS

Make sure students understand the word *mayor* and its importance in this story. Explain that *Mayoress* is a feminized version of the word. A mayor or mayoress is the elected leader of a town or city government. Invite them to share words from their native languages that name similar offices.

MORE SUPPORT

A Tale of
Two Poggles

WRITTEN BY MARGI MCALLISTER
ILLUSTRATED BY MARK BEECH

Express and Extend

EXPRESS Focus students' attention on the sequence of the lunchroom (pages 28-29), Nina and Alejandro's playtime (page 30-32), and their "bright ideas" (pages 33-36). Say: The lunchroom represents the past; the children play in the present; and their dreams and plans represent the future. This is how innovative solutions happen. Characters and real people describe their past, dream in the present, and make plans for the future. Then, have them apply these three concepts (past, present, and future) to the rest of the story. How many ways can they apply them? (For example, how do they apply to Gloria Grabber?)

> **If . . .** students have difficulty organizing their ideas and supporting details,
>
> **then . . .** use the Three-Column Chart Routine and Graphic Organizer in Part 3. Have students label the columns *Past (How It Used to Be), Present (How the Children Used It)* and *Future (What It Became).*

EXTEND Ask students to choose one specific thing or person that is important in the story (i.e. the mezzanine, Upper Poggle, or the cafeteria) and write a three-part description of it in the story's past, present, and future, showing how it changed.

EXPRESS Ask a volunteer to read the first paragraph of the story aloud to remind students of the "I" voice that the writer uses and then abandons. Model by saying: The story's first sentence introduces a first-person narrator, but we never "hear" this voice again. The narrator appears to be someone who lived in Nether Poggle before it changed and describes it as it used to be. **Ask:** Why do you think the writer used this first-person point of view in the first sentence? Why do you think she never uses it again in the story?

EXTEND Invite pairs of students to write and illustrate the news story as it might have appeared in the *Post of the Poggles*, referred to on page 44. Have them begin with the sentence quoted on page 25. Have them include interviews with Nina, Alejandro, Nina's father, and other factory workers. Have them write interesting headlines. Invite them to include illustrations. Remind them to include linking words to connect their ideas.

MORE SUPPORT

ENGLISH LANGUAGE LEARNERS

Have students imagine that they are Gloria Grabber. Have them answer the following questions using the first-person pronoun "I." Where did you go when you left Nether Poggle? What did you do there? Why did you return? What kind of job do you have now? Do you like it? Why do you always wear the same red dress?

STRUGGLING READERS

Remind students to pause after reading a page to summarize what happened in their own words in one or two sentences. Display sentence frames, such as: On this page, _____. Gloria Grabber _____. Alejandro and Nina _____.

LANGUAGE CONVENTIONALITY AND CLARITY

EXPRESS Talk about Sentences and Words

Display and read aloud the following sentences from *A Tale of Two Poggles*.

> Gloria Grabber had just stood up to open the door, but at the word *money*, she immediately sat down again. Nina gave a small, satisfied smile.

Explain that this sentence represents the turning point of the story, the point at which the children begin to succeed with their plan. Say: This is the moment in which Gloria Grabber begins to change her mind. It's the word *money* that does it. Nina has tricked Gloria into thinking that she could make money from an amusement park. On the next page, Nina even tricks her into thinking that she might get credit for the idea. Nina is a very clever girl. Then, invite three students to read the dialogue on pages 38–40 between the three characters. Encourage them to pay close attention to how Nina and Alejandro trick the mayoress into agreeing to their plan.

TEAM TALK Encourage pairs of students to discuss how and why the prospect of *money* can change people's minds. Ask them to think of another example, either from a story, a film, or real life, where this is true. Let them share their examples with the whole group and compare them with what happens in this story.

EXTEND Challenge students to write rhyming poems that tell the story of Gloria Grabber. Encourage them to use some of the more colorful words and images from the story in their poems, such as her red dress, her gold jewelry, her funny hairstyle, or the way her high heels *click-clack* on the floor to signal her coming.

KNOWLEDGE DEMANDS

EXPRESS Ask students whether they agree or disagree with Gloria Grabber's idea that people should write letters by hand and mail them instead of relying on emails and text messages. Have them create charts that show the advantages and disadvantages of both kinds of communication.

EXTEND Challenge students to combine some research with their imaginations to write one of the essays, either by Nina or Alejandro, about what they want to be when they grow up (an astronaut or an engineer). Have them use details from the story as a jumping off point, but encourage them to make their essays entertaining, informative, and fun.

ACCELERATED LEARNERS

Challenge students to find out about a real city or town that has gone or is going through a transformation. Have them enter the words *town* and *transform* into an online search engine. They may discover, for example, the Texas town that transformed wastewater into drinking water, the Ohio town transformed by a wind farm, or the small New Mexico town that is being transformed by space tourism. Give them the opportunity to share what they learn in short oral reports and to share photographs of the projects they discover.

Unlock the Text

QUALITATIVE MEASURES

Levels of Meaning	narrative biographical account of a real person; theme of dedication and believing in oneself; theme of overcoming obstacles
Structure	sequence of events; illustrations that convey meaning
Language Conventionality and Clarity	quotation marks used to show Philo's words and thoughts; difficult sentence structures; domain-specific vocabulary and multiple-meaning words
Knowledge Demands	early inventions; how the first televisions worked

The Boy Who Invented
TV, pp. 94–120

Prepare to Read

LEVELS OF MEANING

The Boy Who Invented TV is the biography of Philo Farnsworth, the inventor of the first television. One purpose of this text is to inform readers about Farnsworth's quest to create new inventions. The other is to show how his passion changed life as we know it today.

STRUCTURE

PREVIEW In pairs, have students read the title and look at the illustrations. Afterward, say: Look at the cover page. Who might this person be, and how do you know? (It is probably Philo Farnsworth. His name is on the cover page.) When do you think the story takes place? How can you tell? (a long time ago; The people in the illustrations are all wearing old-fashioned clothes.) What do you think the story will be about? (the man who first invented television) Do you think this is a true story? Why or

ENGLISH LANGUAGE LEARNERS

Students can help each other learn, use, and remember key vocabulary words by playing a vocabulary guessing game. Students choose a vocabulary word and make up a clue. The rest of the class guesses the word from the context of the clues.

STRUGGLING READERS

Remind students to use the strategies they've learned for dealing with difficult vocabulary. Have them create a glossary by first recording the vocabulary words from the lesson. They can add unfamiliar words they encounter while reading. Have them include the word, a definition, and a sentence or an illustration.

Why not? (I think it is a true story because the illustrations look like things that could really happen, and TV is a real invention.)

LANGUAGE CONVENTIONALITY AND CLARITY

PREVIEW VOCABULARY Use the Preview and Review Vocabulary Routine in Part 3 to assess what students know about the following words: *phonograph, electricity, magnetism, engineer, generator, electrons,* and *relativity.*

COGNATES Use the list of Spanish cognates at the beginning of this module as a reference to guide your Spanish-speaking students as they read the text.

MULTIPLE-MEANING WORDS Use the Analyze Multiple-Meaning Words Routine in Part 3 with these multiple-meaning words from the text: *harness, switch, spare, plain, beam, fetching,* and *credit.* Have students work with partners to list some of the multiple meanings for each word. Have one student say a sentence using one meaning. Then, have the partner say a sentence using a different meaning. For example, one student could say: "Let's switch places so I can be closer to the window." Then, the partner could say: "Flip the switch to turn the light on."

KNOWLEDGE DEMANDS

ACTIVATE BACKGROUND KNOWLEDGE Use the Quick Write and Share Routine in Part 3 and ask students what they know about early inventions, such as the telephone and radio. Ask: What do you think early televisions and radios were like? Why do you think that? Have you heard your parents or grandparents describe older technology? What do you think has been improved since then?

Interact with Text

LEVELS OF MEANING

As students read *The Boy Who Invented TV*, periodically stop to assess their level of understanding of the characteristics that Philo Farnsworth had that led to his success. Ask: What words would you use to describe Philo Farnsworth? What personality traits did Philo have that helped him make his dreams a reality?

> **If . . .** students have trouble understanding how Philo's personality helped lead to his success,
>
> **then . . .** have students use the Draw Conclusions Graphic Organizer in Part 3.

Have students focus on Philo's early childhood and young adult life and look for text evidence that exemplifies characteristics and personality traits that helped lead Philo to success. For example, students might note in the Supporting Details boxes text evidence of Philo's determination, persistence, and curiosity. Help students use details from the text to draw conclusions about how Philo became successful and famous.

STRUCTURE

As students read, periodically stop to assess their understanding of the sequence of events in Philo Farnsworth's life.

> **If . . .** students have difficulty identifying the sequence of events in Philo's life,
>
> **then . . .** use the Sequence of Events Routine and Graphic Organizer in Part 3.

Once students have completed the sequence of events graphic organizer, write four or five events from Philo's life in random order on the board or chart paper. Then draw a horizontal time line, and have volunteers write the events on the time line in the correct order, from first to last. Remind students that they can refer to their graphic organizers for help.

MORE SUPPORT

ENGLISH LANGUAGE LEARNERS

Have students find the prepositions in compound sentences and cross out the prepositional phrases. This will help them simplify the ideas and break the compound sentences into two distinct simple sentences.

STRUGGLING READERS

Explain to students that sequence is the order in which events happen. Have them look for clue words and phrases, such as *at first*, *then*, *next*, and *last* or *first*, *second*, and *third*. Also have them look for days, months, and years to help them follow the order of events for the time line activity.

LANGUAGE CONVENTIONALITY AND CLARITY

Some of the sentences in the text are compound, containing two or more ideas. Have students identify compound sentences in the text and rewrite them as simple sentences. Model how to identify and simplify a compound sentence. For example, display the following sentence from the text and read it aloud to students:

> By then the family had moved back to Utah, to the town of Provo, and Philo supported them by working at all sorts of jobs in nearby Salt Lake City.

Explain that there are two separate events taking place in the sentence: the family moving back to Utah and Philo working to support the family. Rewrite the sentence as *The family moved back to Provo, Utah. Philo worked many jobs to support them.* Use the Simple and Compound Sentences Activity in Part 3 for more support.

KNOWLEDGE DEMANDS

Most students will not know how the first televisions worked. Have them work in groups to make a diagram based on Philo's description of an early TV. Emphasize that it is more important to record the details from the text than to make a completely accurate diagram. Afterward, show students a photo or illustration of an early TV.

Express and Extend

LEVELS OF MEANING

EXPRESS Have pairs of students work together to show their understanding of the theme by writing, in their own words, what obstacles Philo faced and how he overcame these obstacles. Have students use evidence from the text for support.

> **If . . .** students have difficulty identifying Philo's obstacles,
>
> **then . . .** use the Problem and Solution Routine and Graphic Organizer in Part 3.

Students can start by focusing on just one obstacle. Instruct students to write one of Philo's obstacles in the Problem box, then write the outcome in the Solution box. The outcome should include information about how Philo overcame the obstacle.

EXTEND Have students write their opinion about what was the most important step in Philo's problem-solving process and why. Remind them to use text evidence to support their opinion.

STRUCTURE

EXPRESS Explain to students that illustrations are often key to conveying the meaning of a text. Have partners choose two illustrations from the text that they feel add meaning to the text. Have them explain why they chose the illustrations and what information the illustrations contribute to the text.

EXTEND Have students create an alternative illustration for one part of the story, using the text for support. Tell them to pay special attention to how the author describes the event or scene and to include these details in their illustrations.

MORE SUPPORT

ENGLISH LANGUAGE LEARNERS

Provide students with the following sentence frames for writing their opinions: It was important when Philo ___. If Philo had not ___, ___ would not have happened. The TV was invented because Philo ___.

STRUGGLING READERS

Help students illustrate an event from the text. Have students choose one event from the text and describe what makes this event different from the other events. Encourage students to include these unique elements in their drawings.

LANGUAGE CONVENTIONALITY AND CLARITY

EXPRESS Talk about Sentences and Words

Display the following sentence from *The Boy Who Invented TV.* Read it aloud with students.

> On weekends he organized "radio parties" so his friends could gather around one of the bulky wooden cabinets and listen to the new stations.

Ask: What words does the author use in this sentence to describe radios? (*bulky wooden cabinets*) Why do you think the author chose these words? (to let the reader know that old radios were large enough for groups of people to gather around) Why are the words *radio parties* set in quotation marks? (to show that these are words that Philo used to describe something)

TEAM TALK Have students turn to a partner to discuss how the use of quotation marks is important to the text.

EXTEND Have students search the text for other places where quotation marks are used. Have them record these examples and discuss what purpose they serve.

KNOWLEDGE DEMANDS

EXPRESS Have small groups discuss what they learned about how people get ideas for inventions. Have them review how Philo came up with the idea for breaking down images into lines of light. Ask them if the inspiration for his idea had anything to do with television or with using electricity. Instruct students to write a conclusion statement about how inventors get ideas for new inventions. For example, "Ideas can come from anywhere" or "Ideas can come from observing everyday surroundings."

EXTEND Have small groups brainstorm a new invention that will help students and teachers complete classroom tasks. Have them create a proposal for their new invention, as well as how they will sell it to the rest of the class. Explain that the invention does not need to be something that can actually be built, just something that will help around the classroom and has not been invented before.

ACCELERATED LEARNERS

Have students research the history of another everyday object, such as a computer. Give them the time and resources to create a skit or presentation about the history of the object, how it has changed, and how it is used now.

MORE SUPPORT

Unlock the Writing

Part 2 Unlock the Writing

Scaffolded Lessons for the Performance-Based Assessments
Unit 1, Module A: Informative/Explanatory 175
Unit 1, Module B: Informative/Explanatory 181
Unit 2, Module A: Narrative 187
Unit 2, Module B: Opinion 193
Unit 3, Module A: Opinion 199
Unit 3, Module B: Informative/Explanatory 205
Unit 4, Module A: Narrative 211
Unit 4, Module B: Opinion 217

Scaffolded Lessons for the Writing Types
Unlock Opinion Writing 224
Unlock Informative/Explanatory Writing 234
Unlock Narrative Writing 244

Scaffolded Lessons for the Performance-Based Assessments

Unit 1
Module A: Write a Biographical Spotlight 175
Module B: Create an Infographic 181

Unit 2
Module A: Write a Tall Tale 187
Module B: Write About Native American Cultures 193

Unit 3
Module A: Identify Effective Writing 199
Module B: Write a News Report 205

Unit 4
Module A: Write a Short Story 211
Module B: Write About Innovations 217

Unlock the Task: Write a Biographical Spotlight

BREAK APART THE TASK

Distribute copies of the writing task found on page 196 of the Teacher's Guide. Read the task together. Have students name and discuss important key words or phrases to highlight within the task.

Complete a short investigative project about a scientist or researcher who has made a difference. Conduct research and use that information to write a biographical spotlight about your subject.

After conducting your research, introduce the subject of your biography and come up with a main idea about your subject. Then, create a biography that uses facts and details that explain your subject's life and work. Organize your information logically, clearly link ideas using transitional words and phrases, and provide an effective concluding statement.

ANSWER QUESTIONS ABOUT THE TASK

Display the questions below. Have students look at the words and phrases they highlighted to help them answer the questions.

- **What type of writing is this?** (informative/explanatory)
- **What will the text of my writing look like?** (a biographical spotlight)
- **What texts should I reference?** (*Mary Anning: The Girl Who Cracked Open the World,* library, Internet)
- **What information should I give?** (information about the person being researched and how that person made a difference in the world)
- **What do I need to include?** (main idea about my subject, facts that support my main idea, organized ideas, precise language, links between ideas, a concluding statement)

RESTATE THE TASK

Have students restate the task in their own words. Check for misunderstandings or missing elements.

ENGLISH LANGUAGE LEARNERS

If . . . students have difficulty understanding what a biographical spotlight is,

then . . . explain that a biography is the story of someone's life. Tell students to imagine pointing a flashlight at someone. Explain that the purpose of a biographical spotlight is to show important facts about a person's life. Point out that the two words used together mean to provide a clear view, or spotlight, on certain aspects of a person's life story. It might help to use a flashlight to illustrate. Explain that a biographical spotlight provides mainly important details about the person.

STRUGGLING WRITERS

If . . . students have difficulty identifying a scientist or researcher to investigate,

then . . . provide library resources, such as books and articles about scientists and inventors. Have students read the title of each resource and guess who the article or book is about and what contribution that person made. Keep a list of students' responses for reference. Have students use names and contributions from the list to identify someone or something they are interested in finding out more about.

Prepare to Write

Once students understand the writing task, have them review the selection *Mary Anning: The Girl Who Cracked Open the World,* as well as any topic-related texts you may have gathered about scientists or researchers. Have students look through the materials to identify which scientist or researcher they want to write a biographical spotlight about.

Have students gather facts and details about their scientist or researcher from texts and the Internet. Urge students to use a graphic organizer to better organize the facts and details they find. Tell students who are using multiple sources to list facts and details under the associated title of each text or Internet article. Remind students that organizing their information by source will make it easier to remember where each detail or fact is from.

GATHER IDEAS

Have students organize the facts and details for their biographical spotlights. Tell students to arrange their facts and details to tell a story about their scientist or researcher. Remind students that they can use sticky notes or colored ink to write linking words before facts and details to show how the ideas are connected. Remind students that it might be helpful to move facts, details, and linking words around to improve the flow of the thoughts represented.

Remind students that a biographical spotlight highlights the main idea about their subject's life and then provides facts and details that support that main idea. Explain that the main idea will center on their subject's contribution to the world. Students will explain in their biographical spotlight why this person is important and what helped this person accomplish what he or she did. It is important for students to realize that their biographical spotlight cannot include all the facts and details about their subject. Students should select only the most important facts and details that will help the reader understand the main idea of their biographical spotlight.

ACCELERATED WRITERS

If . . . students use language that is not precise or domain specific,

then . . . have students reread their notes and think specifically about their word choice. Remind students that precise language helps convey ideas in a way that readers can clearly understand. Point out that domain-specific language relates to the topic, such as scientific words used by a scientist. Have students circle words that are too vague or generic and substitute more precise or domain-specific word choices for them. Students should look in their sources for words specific to their subject.

Have students talk through their biographical spotlight with a partner to help them refine their ideas. Students may benefit from modeling these prewriting conversations or reviewing some questions the writer might ask a listener.

Questions a Writer Might Ask

- Who am I researching?
- What contribution did this person make to the world?
- What sources am I using?
- What is my main idea about this person?
- What facts and details am I providing to support my main idea?
- What precise or domain-specific vocabulary can I use to make my ideas clearer?
- Is there anything that I should leave out?
- How can I use linking words to connect my ideas more smoothly?
- What sort of concluding sentence would support or extend my main idea?

Have students also formulate questions of their own.

GET ORGANIZED

Have students think about the feedback they received after talking through the topic with a partner. Remind them that using that feedback to organize their biographical spotlight will save them time and effort when writing.

Remind students that a biographical spotlight does not provide every fact or detail about a person. Instead it provides highlights about the person that help the reader understand why he or she is important. Have students group similar facts and details together. Tell students to use linking words and phrases to connect ideas. Once they have gathered their information, have them revisit their main idea about the subject, and rework their main idea if their facts and details do not support it.

ENGLISH LANGUAGE LEARNERS

If . . . students have difficulty understanding domain-specific vocabulary in the books and articles they are using,

then . . . have them write words they do not understand on note cards. Have students draw pictures or write clue words on each note card that help explain the meaning of each word. Students should use the cards to practice pronouncing each word and using it in a sentence.

STRUGGLING WRITERS

If . . . students are not able to form a main idea about the person they are researching,

then . . . have them look at the text *Mary Anning: The Girl Who Cracked Open the World* and answer these questions: Why is this person famous? What contribution did this person make to the world? Explain that the answers to these questions can be used to form the main idea about *Mary Anning: The Girl Who Cracked Open the World*. Have students then answer the same questions about the person they are researching and use their answers to write a main idea.

Write

BREAK IT DOWN

Work with students to create a chart that describes the elements of a biographical spotlight. Tell them that informational/explanatory writing should always be supported by facts and details, and that there should be a clear link between these facts and details. Remind students that a biographical spotlight has a concluding statement that summarizes the main idea.

Element	Definition	Example
Title	• Catches the attention of a reader • Gives a quick idea of the topic	Tim Berners Lee Creates the Web Who Invented the Internet?
Introduction	• States the main idea, includes the name of the scientist/researcher and his or her main contribution	Tim Berners Lee is a computer scientist who created the idea for the World Wide Web, also called WWW.
Body	• Provides facts and concrete details to support the main idea • Includes precise and domain-specific language to document the subject's experiences • Includes quotations from source material • Includes linking words and phrases to connect the ideas and present information logically	As a child, Tim Berners Lee learned about electronics by playing with model railroad trains. He used his passion for electronics to study engineering in college. Originally, the Internet was used mainly by scientists, but as Tim Berners Lee said, "The situation was very difficult." Tim Berners Lee wanted to communicate more easily with other scientists on the web. He had an idea he called hypertext, which let articles be interconnected.
Conclusion	• Summarizes the main idea, leaves the reader with something to think about	Tim Berners Lee's idea of using hypertext grew into the hyperlinks we use on the Web today. Where would we be without this invention?

MONITOR AND SUPPORT

ENGLISH LANGUAGE LEARNERS

If . . . students have difficulty punctuating quotations,

then . . . remind them that a quotation is the exact words that a person said. Tell students that they should set off quotations with a quotation mark at the beginning and end of spoken text. Review the placement of commas and speaker tags with these sentences: *Amy said, "Let's go home." "Let's go home," said Amy.* Have students find examples of quotations in their sources, and use those examples to continue the discussion.

STRUGGLING WRITERS

If . . . students have difficulty coming up with a title for their biographical spotlight,

then . . . have students look for key words or phrases that are similar across their source titles, and also in their main idea statement. Remind students that their title should catch the reader's attention. Have students create word associations between their subject and their subject's contribution, such as Edison and the light bulb. Show how these words can help students think of a title. For example, *Edison Lights Up the World.*

Look Closely

LOOK AT CONVENTIONS

SENTENCES Remind students that they have worked recently on writing complete sentences. Point out that a complete sentence has a subject and a verb and expresses a complete thought. Explain that a fragment is not a complete sentence and that a run-on is a sentence that has too much information in it. Have students review their writing to revise any sentence fragments or run-on sentences.

MODAL AUXILIARY VERBS Focus attention on the use of modal auxiliary verbs, which always come before a main verb. Remind students that *can* is used to tell ability, possibility, probability, and permission; *may* is used to tell permission and prediction; and *must* is used for a strong obligation, a strong recommendation, and to show certainty. Have students find examples of modal auxiliary verbs in their writing.

ADJECTIVES Remind students that adjectives are used to tell more about a noun. Tell students that using specific adjectives can help make their writing more precise. Explain that using precise language helps the reader know exactly what the author is saying. Point out examples of precise adjectives in *Mary Anning: The Girl Who Cracked Open the World.* Have students determine if a more precise word could be used. Have students evaluate their use of adjectives.

LOOK AT CRAFT

SENTENCES Have students look closely to see that their sentences work together within each paragraph to support the main idea. Remind them that, in a biographical spotlight, the facts and details must support the main idea. Tell students to review their work for facts and details that clearly support their main idea regarding their subject and his or her contribution to the world.

DEMONSTRATE SEQUENCE Remind students that sequence is how the author establishes time order. Explain that it is important for the reader to understand the sequence of events that led up to the contribution made by the person they are researching. Point out good examples of sequence from the texts as models.

ENGLISH LANGUAGE LEARNERS

If . . . students have difficulty using the correct modal verb form,

then . . . write *can*, *may*, and *must* and these sample sentences: *I can go to the store. I may go to the store. I must go to the store.* Read each sentence and discuss its meaning. Remind students that *can* means "has the ability," *may* means "has permission," and *must* means "obligated to." Then write: *I ___ go to the library.* Have students use *can, may,* or *must* to complete the sentence and tell the meaning of the sentence. Repeat with other examples.

STRUGGLING WRITERS

If . . . students have difficulty with sequencing,

then . . . write simple actions on note cards, such as *take two slices of bread, spread peanut butter, spread jelly,* and *put sandwich together.* Also write sequence words, such as *first, next, then,* and *finally.* Have students draw on their own knowledge and experience to put the action cards in order. Then help them place the sequence cards between the action cards. Discuss how the sequence words help students know in what order to perform the actions.

Name _____

Title _____

Write a Biographical Spotlight
Writing Checklist

☐ Did I introduce the main idea clearly?

☐ Did my biographical spotlight help the reader understand my subject and why he or she is important?

☐ Did I support my main idea using facts and details?

☐ Did I use precise and domain-specific vocabulary?

☐ Did I use linking words and phrases to connect my facts and details? Example:

_____

☐ Did I organize my facts and details in a logical order?

☐ Did I use modal auxiliary verbs correctly? Example: _____

_____

☐ Did I use specific, precise adjectives correctly? Example: _____

_____

☐ Did I include a strong conclusion?

☐ Did I review my work for correct capitalization, punctuation, and spelling?

☐ (Optional) Did I correctly cite the texts I found on the Internet and in the library?

Unlock the Task: Create an Infographic

Distribute copies of the task found on page 396 of the Teacher's Guide. Read the task together. Have students look for important words or phrases to highlight within the task. Discuss why these words or phrases are important.

Conduct a short investigative project on an animal of your choice, researching the key features of the animal.

Write a brief introduction that clearly introduces your topic. Then create an infographic about the animal, developing your topic with facts, concrete details, and domain-specific vocabulary. Provide a brief conclusion to sum up the information.

Remind students of the questions they must answer to show they understand the task. Tell students to look at the words and phrases they highlighted to help them answer the questions below.

- **What type of writing is this?** (informative/explanatory)
- **Who is my audience?** (people who want to learn more about animals)
- **What will the text of my writing look like?** (an infographic)
- **What texts should I reference?** (*Skeletons Inside and Out, Movers and Shapers,* library resources, and the Internet)
- **What information should I give?** (key features about the animal)
- **What do I need to include?** (a clear introduction, an infographic, facts, concrete details, domain-specific vocabulary, and a conclusion)

Have students restate the task in their own words. Check for misunderstandings or missing elements.

ENGLISH LANGUAGE LEARNERS

If . . . students are intimidated by the task,

then . . . review with them what an infographic is. Ask: Who can remind us what an infographic is? How can we define it using the words *info* and *graphic*? Who can give us examples of an infographic that we have studied in this unit? As students answer the questions, assess their understanding of an infographic. Clear up any misconceptions.

STRUGGLING WRITERS

If . . . students have difficulty identifying the information they want to include in their infographic,

then . . . provide library resources, such as books or articles about animals. Have students skim the books and articles, looking specifically for pictures of animals. Have them keep a list of information they learn from looking at the pictures. Remind students that important information, such as skeletal structure, habitat, and animal tracks, should be added to their lists. Tell students to keep in mind what information could best be presented in picture form while they research their animal.

Prepare to Write

Once students clearly understand the writing task, have them review the selections *Skeletons Inside and Out, Movers and Shapers,* and any topic-related texts you may have gathered about animals. Have students look through the materials to identify which pictures provide the most information in infographic format.

Remind students that they will write a short introductory paragraph about their selected animal, create an infographic that provides key features, and then write a brief conclusion. Point out that an infographic groups information clearly and provides concrete details that help readers understand and visualize textual information. Explain that infographics include diagrams, pie charts, and maps.

GATHER IDEAS

Have students write each fact and detail they have gathered from their research on a separate note card. Tell students to group cards with related facts and details about their animal and then use those groupings to decide which facts and details could best be presented in an infographic. Remind students that the captions and labels in their infographic must also provide information. Point out specific examples of captions in the texts students have read. Help them understand how the captions provide additional information about the picture or drawing. Make sure students understand how the caption relates to main text. Point out to students that their introductory paragraph will provide the main idea and supporting details about their animal, and the infographic will help readers visualize that information.

Remind students that an infographic provides facts, details, and domain-specific vocabulary that support the main idea. Students will explain the main purpose of their writing in their introductory paragraph. Their infographic will support that main idea. It is important for students to realize that their infographic cannot include all the facts and details about their animal. Students must select only the facts and details that help the reader understand the main idea about their animal.

ACCELERATED WRITERS

If . . . students are finding conflicting information about their animal,

then . . . remind students to use multiple sources and to check the authority of any sources they are using. Point out that students might find the same part of an animal with two different labels, such as the top of a bird's head labeled as *crown* or *crest.* Remind students that if they find conflicting facts, they need to do additional research to find out which fact is correct. In the bird example, the crown is the top or peak of a bird's head, and the crest is a tuft of feathers on the crown. Have students review their domain-specific vocabulary against several sources in order to create the best definition and drawing for the term.

MONITOR AND SUPPORT

Have students talk through their main idea and infographic with a partner to help them refine their ideas. Students may benefit from modeling these prewriting conversations or reviewing some questions the writer might ask a listener.

Questions a Writer Might Ask

- What animal am I researching?
- What main idea do I want the reader to understand?
- What resources am I using?
- What facts and details should I include with my infographic?
- How well does my infographic support my main idea?
- Does my concluding sentence summarize or extend both my main idea and my infographic?
- What might be missing?
- Is there anything I should leave out?

Have students also formulate questions of their own.

Have students think about the feedback they received when talking about their topic with a partner. Remind them that using that feedback to organize their infographic will save them time and effort when writing and rewriting.

Remind students that an infographic does not provide every fact or detail about a topic or subject. Instead it provides facts and details about one focused idea. Have students group similar facts and details together. Tell students to review groups of their facts and details to see which group they can most easily visualize in a drawing. Once they have gathered information for their infographic, have them revisit their main idea about the animal, and rework their main idea if the infographic they intend to draw does not support their main idea.

ENGLISH LANGUAGE LEARNERS

If . . . students have difficulty understanding how to include domain-specific vocabulary in their infographic,

then . . . have them look at the infographics in *Skeletons Inside and Out* and *Movers and Shapers.* Point out domain-specific vocabulary associated with some of the infographics, such as *skull, rib cage,* and *spine* on page 6 of *Skeletons Inside and Out.* Discuss how the drawing helps the reader understand the vocabulary. Have students select domain-specific vocabulary about their animal and talk about how to include those words in a drawing.

STRUGGLING WRITERS

If . . . students are focused on creating a perfect drawing,

then . . . remind students that readers will use their drawing to gain information. The drawing should be as precise as possible but does not need to be perfect. A successful infographic is one that provides helpful information to readers. Have students discuss the techniques used in sample infographics, such as line or pen-and-ink drawings. Point out that the details are often found in the captions and the callouts and not the drawing itself.

Write

Work with students to create a chart that describes the elements of an infographic. Remind them that their infographic should support the main idea expressed in their introductory paragraph and that it should contain facts, details, and domain-specific vocabulary in the captions and callouts. Also remind students that their infographic must be followed by a concluding statement that summarizes their main idea.

Element	Definition	Example
Title	• Catches the attention of a reader • Gives a quick idea of the topic	Birding: On the Fly How to Identify Birds in the Field
Introduction	• Includes the main idea, the name of the animal, and the main point you want to make with the infographic	Do all birds look the same to you? If you are a birder, someone who likes to identify birds in the wild, then you know all birds are not alike. You know how to spot differences to help you identify each bird type.
Infographic	• Provides facts and concrete details to support the main idea • Includes precise, domain-specific language associated with the animal • Provides drawings, diagrams, or photos with labels or captions containing information about specific parts of the animal	All birds have similar features or parts. This infographic identifies common parts of a bird, such as the crown, the eye ring, and the tarsus. This line drawing of a bird with its body parts labeled will help you identify the body parts of a bird. You can use the names of these body parts to write lots of details about the birds you see. After you learn the parts of a bird, then you can identify these parts on birds you see in the wild.
Conclusion	• Summarizes the main idea and leaves the reader with something to think about	Knowing the parts of a bird will help you make accurate notes about birds you see. You can use these notes to help you identify birds.

ENGLISH LANGUAGE LEARNERS

If . . . students have difficulty summarizing their main idea in their conclusion,

then . . . have them review their introduction and infographic and take notes about the most important information presented in these sections of their writing. Remind students that when they summarize, they retell only the most important information. Review the notes with students to determine what information they want their reader to remember most. Explain that this should go in the summary.

STRUGGLING WRITERS

If . . . students have difficulty labeling their infographic,

then . . . have them make several copies of their drawing and then use the drawings to practice fitting the labels to the drawing space. Remind students that readers will use their drawings to gather information, so the drawings and labels must be clear. Suggest that students use a ruler to help draw straight lines from the image to the callout. Remind students that, like their written work, an infographic must present information logically.

Look Closely

SENTENCES Remind students that they have worked recently on writing simple and compound sentences. Point out that a simple sentence has a subject and a verb and expresses an idea. Remind students that a compound sentence is two simple sentences joined together using a coordinating conjunction. Have students review their writing to locate examples of simple sentences that can be combined into a compound sentence.

PREPOSITIONAL PHRASES Focus attention on the use of prepositional phrases in the texts. Read this sentence from p. 7 of *Skeletons Inside and Out*: Without protection, even a small bump on the head might affect your thinking, senses, and movement. Have students identify the prepositional phrases. Then read the sentence again, but omit *on the head*. Discuss how the meaning of the sentence changes. Encourage students to use prepositional phrases to add details to their writing.

FREQUENTLY CONFUSED WORDS Remind students that some words sound the same but are spelled differently, such as *there* and *their* or *its* and *it's*. Tell students it is important to use the correct form and spelling of these words because these words have different meanings. If they use the wrong word, their readers might be confused. Have students review their writing for words that sound the same and confirm they have used the correct spelling of the word.

SENTENCES Have students look closely to see that their sentences work together within the introductory paragraph and the concluding paragraph to support the main idea. Remind them that sentence structure is key to a well-written selection.

ESTABLISH A PURPOSE Remind students their infographic must support the main idea of their introductory paragraph. Explain that, after reading the introductory paragraph, it should be clear to the reader why the infographic was included. Have students review their introductory paragraph to be sure they have established the purpose for their infographic.

ENGLISH LANGUAGE LEARNERS

If . . . students have difficulty using the correct form of words that sound the same but have different meanings,

then . . . write these types of words on note cards, such as *there* and *their*, *write* and *right*, *for* and *four*. Pick a pair, read the words, and use them in sentences, such as, "I write on the paper. My answer was right." Have students say the words that sound the same in each sentence and then use each word in a sentence. Repeat with other examples.

STRUGGLING WRITERS

If . . . students have difficulty establishing a purpose,

then . . . have them talk about the animal they selected to research. Discuss with each student what he or she wants the reader to know about that animal. Take notes during this discussion and give the notes to the student so that he or she can use them to write an introduction that establishes his or her purpose.

Name _____

Title _____

Create an Infographic
Writing Checklist

☐ Did I establish the purpose for my infographic clearly?

☐ Did my infographic help my reader know more about the animal I researched?

☐ Did I support my purpose using concrete facts and details in my infographic?

☐ Did I use precise and domain-specific vocabulary in my infographic?
Example:

_____

☐ Did I use linking words and phrases to connect my facts and details?

☐ Did I organize my facts and details in a logical order?

☐ Did I use prepositional phrases to add details? Example: _____

_____

☐ Did I use correct sentence structure? Example: _____

_____

☐ Did I include a strong conclusion?

☐ Did I review my work for correct capitalization, punctuation, and spelling?

☐ (Optional) Did I correctly cite the texts I found on the Internet and in the library?

Unlock the Task: Write a Tall Tale

Distribute copies of the task found on page 196 of the Teacher's Guide. Read the task together. Have students look for important key words or phrases to highlight within the task. Discuss why these words or phrases might be important.

> Write a tall tale that includes an element of nature and includes larger-than-life characters, a problem that is solved in a humorous way, and exaggeration of characters and events. Establish a situation that introduces the narrator and/or characters, and organize a clear sequence of events using transitional words and phrases. Use dialogue, description, and sensory details. Provide a conclusion that makes sense based on the events of the tall tale.

ANSWER QUESTIONS ABOUT THE TASK

Remind students of the questions they must be able to answer to show they understand the task. Tell students to look at the words and phrases they highlighted to help them answer the questions below. You may wish to provide this as a handout for students to complete individually.

- **What type of writing is this?** (narrative)
- **What will the text of my writing look like?** (a tall tale)
- **What texts should I reference?** (*Why the Sea Is Salty*, "Pecos Bill," "John Henry," and *How the Stars Fell into the Sky*)
- **What do I need to include?** (an element of nature, larger-than-life characters, a problem that is solved in a humorous way, exaggeration of characters and events, descriptive details, clear event sequences, a conclusion that makes sense)

RESTATE THE TASK

Have students restate the task in their own words. Check for misunderstandings or missing elements.

ENGLISH LANGUAGE LEARNERS

If . . . students are unfamiliar with the concept of a tall tale,

then . . . explain that tall tales can be a fictional, exaggerated telling of an event that may be true. The story often involves larger than life characters such as giants, and talking animals or trees. The story *Why the Sea Is Salty* is a tall tale that tells why seas and oceans contain only salt water.

STRUGGLING WRITERS

If . . . students feel overwhelmed by the number of things they need to include in their tall tale,

then . . . identify the following features of a tall tale from one of the unit texts: the use of larger-than-life characters, solving a problem in a humorous way, and the exaggeration of characters and events. Record the information in a three-column chart. Tell students that the tall tale they write will be a story that contains these features. Help them understand how these elements work together in a tall tale.

Prepare to Write

Once students understand the writing task, have them look through the following materials: *Why the Sea is Salty,* "Pecos Bill," "John Henry," and *How the Stars Fell into the Sky*. Tell students to identify in each selection the parts of a tall tale, such as an element of nature, larger-than-life characters, a problem that is solved in a humorous way, and an exaggeration of characters and events.

Have students use this information to help them determine the focus of their own tall tale. Students will answer questions such as the following: Who will be the main characters in my tall tale? What characteristics will make them seem larger than life? Where will my tall tale take place? What problem will my characters resolve? What element of nature will be included in my tall tale? Tell students that the answers to these questions will help them narrow the focus of their tall tale.

GATHER IDEAS

Remind students that, like each of the unit selections, their tall tales should explain a naturally occurring process or event, as well as the resolution to a problem. Students should consider starting their tall tale by establishing the situation that needs to be explained or resolved. Then have students put together the details for their tall tale. Urge students to organize their details into the following areas: a situation to be explained or resolved, the setting for their tall tale, their larger-than-life characters, and the exaggeration of characters and events. Students can record details about each area using a word web or other graphic organizer.

Remind students that when writing a tall tale, they should create characters that are believable but that also have larger-than-life skills or attributes. This can include a power or resource that allows them to do things that others can't. Explain to students that an example of a larger-than-life attribute is the ability of Pecos Bill's lasso to reach the moon. Students should use dialogue and descriptive details to develop their characters and the setting. Suggest that students go online to find appropriate sound effects or background music to enhance the setting of their tall tale.

ACCELERATED WRITERS

If . . . students' details suggest that the situation they have identified will be explained or resolved in a common or expected way,

then . . . tell students that readers like a twist or an unexpected turn of events, because they make the story memorable. Have students make their situation more robust by answering questions similar to the following: How can I make the situation more unique? What twist or element of surprise can I add to my situation to make it more interesting for the reader? How can my characters make the situation different from what the reader is expecting? Tell students that their answers can help them create a more interesting tall tale.

TALK IT THROUGH

Have students talk about the characters and events for their tall tale with a partner to help them refine their ideas. Students may benefit from modeling these prewriting conversations or reviewing questions the writer might ask a listener.

Questions a Writer Might Ask

- What element of nature will I try to explain?
- Who will my characters be?
- What situation will my characters resolve?
- What will be the setting for my tall tale?
- What larger-than-life traits will my characters have, and how will those traits help the characters resolve a situation?
- What is the time line for my events, and how does the time line help the events to unfold naturally?
- Is there anything missing or anything that I should leave out?

Have students also formulate questions of their own.

GET ORGANIZED

Have students think about the feedback they received when talking about their tall tale with a partner. Remind them that using their partner's feedback to organize their tall tale will save them time and effort when writing and rewriting.

Tell students they will use transitional words and phrases to connect the sequence of events. Once they have gathered their information, have them revisit the situation that will be explained or resolved in their tall tale to be sure that their characters and setting fit with their conclusion. Tell students to rework the elements that do not support their situation or to add more details as needed.

ENGLISH LANGUAGE LEARNERS

If . . . students have difficulty identifying a topic for their tall tale,

then . . . have them ask questions about naturally occurring processes or events, such as the following: Where do rainbows come from? Why does the moon change shape? Why do oceans have waves? Tell students their tall tale does not provide a scientific explanation to the question. Model how to make up a story to answer one question. Have students follow your model to write their tall tale.

STRUGGLING WRITERS

If . . . students are having difficulty creating their sequence of events,

then . . . have students write on note cards key words and details regarding each event they plan on including in their tall tale. Next, have them arrange the note cards from left to right in the order in which they think the events should occur. Review the events with students to determine if they occur in a logical order. Have students rearrange the note cards as needed.

Write

Work with students to create a chart that describes the elements of a tall tale. Remind them that a tall tale includes an element of nature, larger-than-life characters, a problem that is solved in a humorous way, and exaggerated characters and events. Also remind students that a tall tale has a conclusion that makes sense based on the events of the tall tale.

Element	Definition	Example
Title	• Catches the attention of a reader • Gives a quick idea of the topic	The Squirrel's Tail Why do squirrels curl their tail?
Introduction or Lead	• Establishes a situation to be resolved • Introduces a narrator and characters	A long time ago, in a forest far away, lived an old gray squirrel. The other forest animals thought he was foolish, but he was really wise.
Body	• Uses natural dialogue to develop larger-than-life characters • Uses concrete words and phrases as well as sensory details to provide elements of truth to convey experiences and events precisely • Uses descriptive language to establish setting • Uses transitional words and phrases to manage a sequence of events	"What if the food runs out?" asked the old gray squirrel. "I don't care about tomorrow!" exclaimed the deer. "I want to eat this now, not save it for later." So, while the other forest animals ate their fill, the old gray squirrel went about his business, gathering nuts. Soon, every tree in the forest bulged with the squirrel's supply of food. Each year, the weather got worse, and the dry ground cracked from lack of rain. Then, the forest animals noticed there was no more food to eat. And, the old squirrel with his hidden supply of nuts did not look so foolish now.
Conclusion	• Provides a logical conclusion that follows the narrated events	To this very day, the squirrel's tail forms a question mark to remind all who see it to ask "What if?"

ENGLISH LANGUAGE LEARNERS

If . . . students have difficulty using descriptive language or precise wording,

then . . . remind them that adjectives are used to describe nouns. Tell them that the more precise the adjective, the easier it is for the reader to understand the description. For example, have students name other words for *red*, such as *rosy*, *apple-red*, or *crimson*. Repeat with other examples. Tell students to use words that create clear pictures in their minds when they write their tall tale.

STRUGGLING WRITERS

If . . . students are having difficulty creating natural dialogue between characters,

then . . . have students work with a partner to carry on a short conversation similar to one their characters might have. After having the conversation, tell students to write as much of the conversation as they can remember. Have partners read the written dialogue, and make adjustments as needed. Remind students to use opening and closing quotation marks and proper punctuation in their written dialogue.

Look Closely

LOOK AT CONVENTIONS

SENTENCES Remind students that they have worked recently on writing complete sentences. Point out that a complete sentence has a subject and a verb and expresses a complete idea. Explain that a fragment is not a complete sentence and that a run-on is a sentence that has too much information in it. Have students review their writing to locate and revise sentence fragments and run-on sentences.

ADJECTIVES Remind students that adjectives are used to tell more about nouns. Tell students that using the adjectives can help make their writing more precise. Point out that adjectives should be used in proper order, such as size, age, shape, and then color. Have students evaluate their use of adjectives in their writing, revising to make sure they use the most precise adjectives in the proper order.

USING A DICTIONARY Remind students that a dictionary provides the pronunciation of a word, the meaning or meanings of a word, and often synonyms, or words that mean the same or almost the same as the key word. Have students review their tall tale for word choice and then use a dictionary to help them identify more precise words as needed.

LOOK AT CRAFT

SENTENCES Have students look closely to see that their sentences work together within each paragraph to support the organization of that paragraph. Remind them that their sentences need to flow in a natural order and that they can use transitional words and phrases to help establish the order. Point out that sentences used in dialogue will be punctuated differently from other sentences. Have students review their tall tales to be sure all sentences are complete, are punctuated properly, and are in a logical order.

ESTABLISH TONE Remind students that tone is the writer's attitude toward the subject of the narrative and that tone can be developed through careful word choice. For example, the tone of a story can be serious, playful, optimistic, or pessimistic. Point out good models of word choice used to establish tone from the students' texts whenever possible.

ENGLISH LANGUAGE LEARNERS

If . . . students have difficulty using adjectives in the proper order,

then . . . write adjectives, such as *large, small, tiny, old, young, new, oval, circular, teal, crimson,* and *green,* on note cards. Have students sort the adjectives into the following groups: size, age, color, and shape. Tell students to select one adjective from each group and use them in a sentence, such as The tiny, green leaves floated to the floor. Discuss the order of the adjectives used before repeating the exercise. Provide examples of sentences with adjectives in an incorrect order, and discuss with students how the incorrect order makes the description hard to follow.

STRUGGLING WRITERS

If . . . students have difficulty using precise words,

then . . . have students circle two or more words in their tall tales that they would like to make more precise. For example, if they use the word *run*, students might like to find a more precise word, such as *flee* or *scamper*, to help convey tone. Model how to use a dictionary or thesaurus to find another more precise word for *run*. Then have students use the dictionary to find more precise synonyms for the words they circled in their tall tales.

Name _____

Title _____

Write a Tall Tale
Writing Checklist

☐ Did I introduce my tall tale clearly?

☐ Did my tall tale include:

　☐ an element of nature

　☐ a setting that fits the tall tale

　☐ larger-than-life characters

　☐ a problem that is solved in a humorous way

　☐ exaggeration of characters and events

☐ Did I introduce a narrator or characters to help move the story forward?

☐ Did I use dialogue to help develop my characters?

☐ Did I organize my events in a logical order so that the sequence unfolds naturally?

☐ Did I use adjectives correctly and in the proper order? Example: _____

_____

☐ Did I use a dictionary to find better word choices? Example: _____

_____

☐ Did I include a strong conclusion?

☐ Did I review my work for correct capitalization, punctuation, and spelling?

☐ (Optional) Did I include sound effects to set the mood of my tall tale?

Unlock the Task: Write About Native American Cultures

Distribute copies of the task found on page 396 of the Teacher's Guide. Read the task together. Have students look for and discuss important key words or phrases to highlight within the task.

> Write to state an opinion, providing reasons for your opinion and using text evidence to support it. You will write an opinion essay examining the various Native American cultures you read about in *Three Native Nations: Of the Woodlands, Plains, and Desert* and *Northwest Coast Peoples*. In your essay, explain which of the groups you read about you would have liked to grow up in. Provide a conclusion that restates your opinion.

ANSWER QUESTIONS ABOUT THE TASK

Remind students of the questions they must be able to answer to show they understand the task. Tell students to look at the words and phrases they highlighted to help them answer the questions below.

- **What type of writing is this?** (opinion)
- **What will the text of my writing look like?** (an opinion essay)
- **What texts should I reference?** (*Three Native Nations* and *Northwest Coast Peoples*)
- **What information should I give?** (how the two books give similar, yet different, information about Native American life in order to support my opinion about which culture would have been more interesting to have grown up in)
- **What do I need to include?** (a clearly stated opinion, text details and evidence supporting my opinion, a conclusion that summarizes my opinion)

RESTATE THE TASK

Have students restate the task in their own words. Check for misunderstandings or missing elements.

ENGLISH LANGUAGE LEARNERS

If . . . students have difficulty choosing the words to express their opinion,

then . . . provide them with sentence frames they can complete. For example: I think Haudenosaunee life was interesting because ___. The Native American culture I wish I had grown up in is ___.

STRUGGLING WRITERS

If . . . students have difficulty understanding the writing task,

then . . . help clarify for them that they need to form an opinion about which Native American culture would have been more interesting to grow up in. Provide them with the following questions: Which selection helps me better understand what Native American life was like? If I had to explain to someone what Native American life was like, which selection would I refer to? Students can refer back to the questions as they determine their focus and gather information.

Prepare to Write

Once students understand the writing task, have them review *Three Native Nations* and *Northwest Coast Peoples*. Have students look through each text to locate facts about the Native American way of life. Tell students to place sticky notes next to each fact they find.

Remind students that they will write an opinion piece that explains in which Native American culture they would like to have grown up in and why. Tell students to state their opinion clearly at the beginning to ensure that readers understand the purpose of their essay. Students must support their opinion with facts and evidence from each selection before restating their opinion in the conclusion.

GATHER IDEAS

Have students put together the facts for their opinion essay. Tell students to group the facts by book. Remind them that, while both selections present information on life in a particular Native American culture, the way the information is presented differs. If possible, have students research Native American culture on the Internet.

Once students have identified facts about the Native American way of life from both selections, have them highlight facts from both selections that are similar. Tell students they can use these facts to help them form their opinion about which selection does a better job presenting a clear picture of Native American life. Point out that the selection with the most facts doesn't necessarily present a clearer picture about Native American life. Discuss other factors as well, including author's point of view, tone, transitions, and precise word choice, all of which might affect their opinion. Also remind them that there is no right or wrong answer. They just need to support their opinion with facts and evidence from the books.

ACCELERATED WRITERS

If . . . students are basing their opinion solely on the number of facts presented in each book,

then . . . have students dig deeper into why they think one selection more clearly presents information about the Native American way of life than the other. Have students answer the following questions: Which book provides pictures to help the reader understand the facts? Which book uses domain-specific vocabulary to present the facts? Which book uses precise word choice and detailed descriptions to help the reader better understand the topic? After answering these questions, have students revisit their opinion statement and make changes to it and to the evidence from the text as needed to support their opinion.

Have students talk about their plans for their opinion essay with a partner to help them refine their ideas. Students may benefit from modeling these prewriting conversations or reviewing some questions the writer might ask a listener.

Questions a Writer Might Ask

- What is my opinion about which selection presented the most interesting information about Native American culture?
- What reasons should I give to support my opinion?
- What facts should I include to convince the reader of my opinion?
- What evidence from the text should I provide to support my opinion?
- How will my evidence show that I compared the cultures in each book to form my opinion?
- How can I effectively organize my information?
- How will my conclusion help convince the reader of my opinion?
- Is there anything missing or anything that I should leave out?

Have students also formulate questions of their own.

GET ORGANIZED

Have students think about the feedback they received when talking about their topic with a partner. Remind them that using their partner's feedback to organize their opinion essay will save them time and effort when writing and rewriting.

Remind students that an opinion essay is based on facts and supported by evidence. Tell students that one reason for writing their opinion essay is to convince the reader to agree with their opinion. Point out that their essay should include not only details about the ways in which the cultures described in each selection are alike, but also how they are different. Have students review their facts and evidence from the text to be sure they support their opinion.

ENGLISH LANGUAGE LEARNERS

If . . . students have difficulty understanding how to convince a reader of their opinion,

then . . . remind students that reasons supported by facts are most convincing. For example, show two balls. Point to one and give an opinion with reasons, such as the following: I like this ball more because it is smaller, it will fit in my pocket, and it bounces higher. Have students say whether these reasons convinced them that the smaller ball is better and why. Repeat with other examples.

STRUGGLING WRITERS

If . . . students have difficulty expressing an opinion for their essay,

then . . . point out that they are not only examining the facts but also the ways in which those facts are presented. Have students use a Venn diagram to record similarities and differences between the cultures described in each selection. After students have completed their Venn diagrams, they can review the information they recorded to help form their opinion about which Native American culture they would have liked to grow up in.

Write

Work with students to create a chart that describes the elements of an opinion essay. Remind them that their essay should clearly state their opinion, provide reasons and facts to support that opinion, organize the information in a logical manner, and link ideas smoothly. Also remind students that their essay will have a conclusion that summarizes their opinion and tries to convince the reader to agree with their opinion.

Element	Definition	Example
Title	• Catches the attention of a reader • Gives a quick idea of the topic	*Northwest Coast Peoples* Wins *Growing Up in a Northwest Coast Village*
Introduction or Lead	• Clearly states an opinion so the reader knows the author's point of view	In my opinion, *Northwest Coast Peoples* does the better job of telling about Native American life.
Body	• Includes information from both texts • Provides reasons supported by facts that support the main opinion • Includes precise and domain-specific language associated with the topic • Groups related ideas to support the author's purpose	While *Three Native Nations explains life in three different cultures, Northwest Coast Peoples* provides lots of facts about each area of Native American life along the Pacific coast. I learned new terms, such as *moieties, clans,* and *phraties,* specific to the Northwest Native Americans.
Conclusion	• Summarizes the main idea and encourages the reader to agree with the stated opinion	Through its use of colorful maps and pictures, domain-specific vocabulary, and lots of interesting facts, I think the text *Northwest Coast Peoples* does the better job of writing about Native American life. Don't you agree?

ENGLISH LANGUAGE LEARNERS

If . . . students have difficulty finding the words to support their opinion about which culture they prefer,

then . . . have them draw pictures about what they find most interesting about their preferred culture. Then have them talk about their pictures while you record any words or phrases they use that could be used to write about them.

STRUGGLING WRITERS

If . . . students have difficulty supporting their opinion,

then . . . remind them to draw evidence directly from the selection. For example, students might write that a selection mentions that Native Americans used cedar, "which the people used to make shelter, clothing, and transportation." Point out how this evidence from the selection adds more detail, which helps the selection do a better job presenting a clear picture of Native American life. Have students find other evidence from the text to support their opinion.

Look Closely

SENTENCES Remind students that they have worked recently on writing complete sentences. Point out that a simple sentence has a subject and a verb and expresses an idea. Remind students that a compound sentence is two simple sentences joined together with a coordinating conjunction. Have students review their writing to locate examples of simple sentences. Tell students to combine two simple sentences into a compound sentence, if using a compound sentence makes the meaning more clear.

NOUNS Remind students that a common noun names a person, place, thing, or idea. Point out that a proper noun names a specific person, place, thing, or idea. Tell students that a proper noun begins with a capital letter. Provide examples of common and proper nouns, such as *school* and *Emerson School.* Have students review their use of common and proper nouns.

UNDERSTAND PRONOUNS Remind students that a pronoun takes the place of a noun. Point out that the pronoun must be the same number (singular or plural) and the same gender (female, male, or neutral) as the noun it replaces. Provide examples of matching nouns and pronouns. Then have students find examples of pronouns in their essay and be sure they can name the noun it replaces and that the correct pronoun is used.

SENTENCES Have students look closely to see that their sentences work together within the introductory paragraph and the concluding paragraph to support the stated opinion. Remind them that sentence structure is the key to a well-written selection.

DRAW EVIDENCE FROM TEXT Remind students that they should draw evidence from the text to support their opinion. Tell students that when they quote a passage directly from the text, they must be sure to set the words in quotation marks. Have students review their essay for examples of evidence from the text and to be sure the evidence is punctuated properly.

ENGLISH LANGUAGE LEARNERS

If . . . students have difficulty using the correct pronoun form,

then . . . write these nouns and pronouns on note cards: *Ed*, *Kim*, *bus*, *classmates*, *he*, *she*, *it*, and *they*. Have students match each noun with its pronoun, and then use both in a sentence. For example: Ed is reading the book he got from the library. Repeat with other nouns and pronouns. Then have students skim the text *Northwest Coast Peoples* for pronouns and identify the noun each pronoun replaces.

STRUGGLING WRITERS

If . . . students have difficulty remembering when to capitalize a noun,

then . . . point out that proper nouns begin with a capital letter. Remind students that a proper noun names a specific person, place, thing, or idea. Have students skim the text *Northwest Coast Peoples* for words that begin with a capital letter and make a list of the words they find. Tell students not to include words that are capitalized because they are the first word in the sentence. Review the list and point out that the words on the list name proper nouns.

Name _____

Title _____

Write About Native American Cultures Writing Checklist

☐ Did I clearly state which culture I would like to have grown up in?

☐ Did I support my opinion with reasons and facts?

☐ Did I include facts and information from the two texts?

☐ Did I organize my reasons and facts in a logical order?

☐ Did I use linking words and phrases to connect my reasons and facts?

☐ Did I use common and proper nouns correctly? Example: _____

_____

☐ Did I use pronouns correctly? Example: _____

_____

☐ Did I draw evidence from the text to support my opinion? Example: _____

_____

☐ Did I include a strong conclusion that helps readers understand why they should agree with my opinion?

☐ Did I review my work for correct capitalization, punctuation, and spelling?

☐ (Optional) Did I support my opinion with research I found on the Internet?

Unlock the Task: Identify Effective Writing

Distribute copies of the task found on page 196 of the Teacher's Guide. Read the task together. Have students identify key words or phrases to highlight within the task. Discuss why each word or phrase might be important. When students agree that the word or phrase is important, have them highlight it.

> Think about two of the texts you have read in this module—*Earthquakes* and *Quake!* Write an opinion that states which text you think more effectively shows the impact of earthquakes on human beings.

ANSWER QUESTIONS ABOUT THE TASK

Remind students of the questions they should be able to answer to show they understand a task. Have students look at the words and phrases they highlighted to help them answer the questions below. You may wish to provide this as a handout for students to complete individually. Scan the group to determine who needs more support and who is ready to work independently.

- **What type of writing is this?** (opinion)
- **What will the text of my writing look like?** (an opinion piece)
- **Which texts should I reference?** (*Earthquakes* and *Quake!*)
- **What information should I give?** (my opinion regarding which text more effectively shows the impact of earthquakes on human beings)
- **What do I need to include?** (a clearly stated opinion, reasons based on evidence from the texts, a conclusion that summarizes my opinion)

RESTATE THE TASK

Ask students to restate the task in their own words. Check for possible misunderstandings or missing elements.

ENGLISH LANGUAGE LEARNERS

If . . . students confuse the task with a book review,

then . . . explain that instead of telling which text they like best, they should compare and contrast *Earthquakes* and *Quake!* Point out that both texts teach about the impact of earthquakes on human beings. Their job is to write an opinion about which one does a better job of teaching about the impacts and why.

STRUGGLING WRITERS

If . . . students are confused about how facts are connected to opinions and reasons,

then . . . explain that for this task, they need to provide reasons that support their opinion. Point out that reasons that are supported by facts and details from the text are stronger than reasons that are not. Provide examples of both and help students understand why one is stronger than the other.

Prepare to Write

Once students clearly understand the task, have them review the selections *Earthquakes* and *Quake!* Ask students to write their opinion regarding which text they think more effectively shows the impact of earthquakes on human beings. Have students label this statement My Opinion.

Ask students to gather facts and details from the texts that support their opinion. Suggest they use a graphic organizer to organize the evidence they find. Some students might like to list facts and details under the associated title of the text. Once they have listed this information, ask students if their opinion is the same or if the evidence they collected has changed their mind. Allow students time to change their My Opinion statement, if needed.

GATHER IDEAS

Have students put together the information for their opinion piece. If they made lists of the facts and details for each text, they might like to cut apart the list that supports their My Opinion statement. Have students arrange the facts and details in an order that supports their opinion. Suggest students use sticky notes or colored ink to write linking words before each item to help show how the ideas are connected. Encourage students to keep moving facts, details, and linking words around to improve the flow of the thoughts represented.

Remind students that in an opinion piece, the facts and details must support the opinion. If students become stalled, ask them to think about how a specific example helps explain the impact of earthquakes on human beings. If they cannot explain the relationship, ask them to decide whether this fact or detail belongs in the opinion piece. It is important for students to realize that not all of the information in a selection will support the writer's opinion. Students need to know that they do not need to use all of the facts and details in their opinions.

ACCELERATED WRITERS

If . . . students have many more facts than needed to support their opinion,

then . . . ask them to prioritize the facts and details by deciding which ones best support their opinion statement. Remind students that they do not need to include every supporting fact and detail but only those that will help readers understand their point of view. Encourage students to consider whether any of their examples could be used to support an opposing opinion. If so, suggest they eliminate them and use only the ones that support their opinion.

Encourage students to talk through their opinion and supporting facts and details with a partner to help them clarify their ideas. Students may benefit from modeling these prewriting conversations or reviewing some questions the writer might ask his or her partner.

Questions a Writer Might Ask

- What is my opinion regarding which text better shows the impact of earthquakes on human beings?
- What is one thing the texts have in common?
- How do the texts differ?
- Which facts and details should I use to support my opinion?
- Is there anything I should add or leave out?
- How can I connect my ideas?
- How will my conclusion support and summarize my opinion?

Encourage students to formulate questions of their own as well.

GET ORGANIZED

Ask students to think about the feedback they received when talking through the task with a partner. Remind them that using that feedback to organize their opinion piece will save them time and effort when writing and editing.

Remind students that an opinion is not simply something the writer likes or dislikes. Instead, an opinion is formed after examining facts and details related to the topic. Tell students to group similar facts and details together, using linking words and phrases to connect the ideas. Once they have gathered their information, have them revisit their opinion statement and rework it if their facts and details do not support it.

ENGLISH LANGUAGE LEARNERS

If . . . students have difficulty using appropriate linking words and phrases to connect ideas,

then . . . have them brainstorm possible linking words and phrases, such as *first, next, then, in addition to, therefore, for example, for instance, in order to, because,* and *since.* Then use the linking words and phrases in sample sentences. Have students identify the linking word or phrase and explain how it helps connect the ideas. Repeat the activity with other linking words and phrases.

STRUGGLING WRITERS

If . . . students are not able to form an opinion about the topic,

then . . . help students use the texts to identify facts and details about the impact of earthquakes on human beings. To help students see the relationship among the facts and details, ask questions, such as *What does this fact tell you about earthquakes?* Then discuss how students can use their answers to form an opinion about which text is more effective.

Write

Work with students to create a chart that describes the elements of an opinion piece. Remind them that opinion writing must be supported by facts and details and that there should be a clear link between these facts and details. Also remind students that an opinion piece has a concluding statement that summarizes the writer's opinion. Work with students to provide examples for the chart.

Element	Definition	Example
Title	• Catches the reader's attention • Gives a quick idea of the topic	Earthquakes – My Opinion All Shook Up by Earthquakes
Introduction	• Includes the opinion the writer plans to support	In my opinion, the book *Quake!* more effectively shows the impact of earthquakes on human beings.
Body	• Provides details to help the reader understand the reasons behind the opinion • Includes adjectives to help the reader understand the setting • May include visuals to help explain the facts • May include quotations from people involved or source material	The dog was jittery. The dog pushed Jacob out of the way of the horses. Buildings began weaving in and out. Bricks were raining all over the street. Jacob tried to make sense of what was happening. Jacob was tense. The picture shows the destruction caused by the earthquake.
Conclusion	• Summarizes the writer's opinion	The story does more than state facts. It helps the reader grasp the emotional and physical impacts of an earthquake.

ENGLISH LANGUAGE LEARNERS

If . . . students have difficulty phrasing comparisons,

then . . . review forming comparative and superlative adjectives and adverbs. Explain that adjectives and adverbs of one or two syllables often end in -er and -est to make the comparative and superlative forms, but that adjectives and adverbs of three or more syllables use *more* and *most* to make the comparative and superlative forms of the words. Provide examples as needed.

STRUGGLING WRITERS

If . . . students are intimidated by the task,

then . . . encourage students to work on one section at a time. Breaking the task into smaller, more manageable pieces can remove some of the anxiety and make the task seem more achievable.

Look Closely

SENTENCES Remind students that they have recently worked on writing sentences that use prepositional phrases and relative adverbs. Using examples from the texts, show students both prepositional phrases and relative adverbs that can be used to answer when, where, and why questions. Encourage students to add variety to their writing by using prepositional phrases and relative adverbs in their sentences.

MODAL AUXILIARY VERBS Focus attention on the use of modal auxiliary verbs, which always come before another verb. Remind students that *can* is used to tell ability, possibility, probability, and permission; *may* is used to tell permission and prediction; and *must* is used for strong obligations, strong recommendations, and to show certainty. Ask students to find modal auxiliary verbs in their writing.

COORDINATING CONJUNCTIONS Review with students that a coordinating conjunction is a connecting word placed between words, phrases, or clauses. Discuss how coordinating conjunctions are similar to linking words and how they are different. Encourage students to check for coordinating conjunctions in their writing and use them to join two simple, related sentences.

SENTENCES Ask students to look closely to see that their sentences work together within each paragraph to support the main idea. Remind them that in an opinion piece, the facts and details must support the opinion. Tell students to review their work to make sure the information they included clearly supports their opinion regarding which text more effectively shows the impact of earthquakes on human beings.

LINKING WORDS Remind students that writers use linking words in an opinion piece to connect the reasons with the opinion. Encourage students to look for linking words and phrases in their writing and to check for opportunities to add more. Also ask students to look for variety in the linking words they have used. Point out good examples from the texts as models whenever possible.

ENGLISH LANGUAGE LEARNERS

If . . . students have difficulty using coordinating conjunctions,

then . . . write coordinating conjunctions on notecards and give one to each student. Have students skim one of the texts to find their word. After students find their word, read the sentence aloud. Have the other students name the conjunction they heard. Then read the two ideas aloud without the conjunction. Discuss how the conjunction helps join the two ideas into one sentence.

STRUGGLING WRITERS

If . . . students have difficulty with prepositional phrases,

then . . . have students follow simple directions that include prepositional phrases, such as "Set the pencil on the table." After they complete the action, have students identify the prepositional phrase and the preposition. Then have students use that same prepositional phrase in a different sentence. Repeat this activity with other prepositional phrases.

Name _____

Title _____

Identify Effective Writing
Writing Checklist

☐ Did I clearly state my opinion regarding which text more effectively shows the impact of earthquakes on human beings?

☐ Did I support my opinion using facts and details from the texts?

☐ Did all of my facts relate to the topic?

☐ Did I organize my facts and details in a logical order?

☐ Did I use modal auxiliary verbs correctly? Example: _____

_____

☐ Did I use coordinating conjunctions correctly? Example: _____

_____

☐ Did I use linking words and phrases when needed? Example: _____

_____

☐ Did I include a strong conclusion?

☐ Did I review my work for correct capitalization, punctuation, and spelling?

☐ (Optional) Did I include images or videos from the Internet to support my opinion?

Unlock the Task: Write a News Report

BREAK APART THE TASK

Distribute copies of the task found on page 396 of the Teacher's Guide. Read the task together. Have students identify and discuss important key words or phrases to highlight in the task.

> During this unit you read *Anatomy of a Volcanic Eruption* and *A Tsunami Unfolds*. Choose a natural event to research. Write a news report that explains the effects of the natural event on both living things and Earth.

ANSWER QUESTIONS ABOUT THE TASK

Remind students of the questions they should be able to answer to show they understand the task. Tell students to look at the words and phrases they highlighted to help them answer the questions below. You may wish to provide this as a handout for students to complete individually.

- **What type of writing is this?** (informational)
- **What will the text of my writing look like?** (a news report)
- **What texts should I reference?** (*Anatomy of a Volcanic Eruption* and *A Tsunami Unfolds*)
- **What information should I give?** (an explanation of the effects of change to Earth's surface)
- **What do I need to include?** (a clear topic, paragraphs with headings, facts, pictures, details, linking words that connect ideas, precise and domain-specific vocabulary, a concluding statement)

RESTATE THE TASK

Ask students to restate the prompt or task in their own words. Check for possible misunderstandings or missing elements.

ENGLISH LANGUAGE LEARNERS

If . . . students are intimidated by the task,

then . . . show students examples of informational news reports from magazines, newspapers, or the Internet. Work with them to identify the different features of the news reports. Have them identify features they think are helpful to readers. Exposing students to additional examples will help eliminate anxiety surrounding the task and product.

STRUGGLING WRITERS

If . . . students have difficulty rewording the task,

then . . . ask students to go back to the key words they highlighted and say one sentence using each highlighted phrase. Example: I need to write a news report. It needs to explain how changes to Earth's surface can be caused by natural events.

Prepare to Write

DETERMINE FOCUS

Once students clearly understand the task, have them review the selections *Anatomy of a Volcanic Eruption* and *A Tsunami Unfolds,* and any other topic-related texts you have gathered. Ask students to quickly record ideas of what they might want to include in their news report. Some students may benefit from putting sticky notes on pictures and features that spark ideas for them.

Ask students to prioritize their list to one or two big ideas that will be the focus of their news report. If students have difficulty choosing between two topics, ask them to make a quick list of the information they might include in the news report, including words specific to the topic and pictures that illustrate the topic. One topic may have much more information than the other. If both seem rather equal, ask students which topic they find more interesting.

GATHER IDEAS

Have students put together ideas for their news reports. They might use note cards or sticky notes to gather ideas without putting them in any particular order yet. Encourage students to gather facts, definitions, concrete details, quotations, or other information and examples related to the topic. Tell students to be sure they understand and can use domain-specific vocabulary.

Ask students to review the information they have gathered and to include only information that conveys the topic clearly. Suggest they chunk similar details together and think of a main idea that unifies that information. Be sure students understand that their news report should have multiple paragraphs with headings.

If a writer becomes stalled, ask him or her to pretend to be the person reading the news report that explains the effects of the natural event on both living things and Earth. What information does the reader need to know to understand the topic? What information will help the reader remember the topic? Are there charts or images that will help the reader understand the topic better?

ACCELERATED WRITERS

If . . . students have many more facts than needed for their news report,

then . . . ask them if they can narrow the focus of their topic. Perhaps the topic they have chosen is too broad or perhaps they are trying to share too much information about each main idea. Remind students that a news report must be tightly focused to keep the readers' interest. Have students organize their main ideas and then provide three or four of the most interesting and informative details for each main idea.

Encourage students to talk through their news report with a partner to help them get their ideas together. Students may benefit from modeling these prewriting conversations or reviewing some questions the writer might ask a listener.

Questions a Writer Might Ask

- What will I include in my introduction?
- How will I group my information in a meaningful way?
- How do the illustrations or other forms of multimedia I plan on including support my topic?
- How can I develop the topic with appropriate facts and details?
- What pictures would be good to include?
- What information might be missing from my report?
- Is there anything I should leave out?
- How will my conclusion summarize the topic?

Encourage students to also formulate questions of their own.

GET ORGANIZED

Ask students to think about the feedback they received when talking through the topic with a partner. Remind them that using that feedback to organize their news report will save them time and effort when writing and rewriting.

Have students group similar information together and determine what is the strongest and most important information they need to share. Explain that a news report begins with attention-grabbing information. Suggest students start their report by asking a question about the topic, such as "Have you ever wondered how mountains were made?" Explain that a well-formulated question will grab the readers' attention and help them focus on the information that follows.

ENGLISH LANGUAGE LEARNERS

If . . . students have difficulty using domain-specific vocabulary related to their news reports,

then . . . have them write domain-specific words on note cards. Help students find pictures in magazines, newspapers, or clip art software that illustrate each word. Have students describe the pictures in their home language and then use that information to help them describe the pictures in English.

STRUGGLING WRITERS

If . . . students have difficulty finding pictures or other forms of multimedia to include in their reports,

then . . . work with them to identify the main ideas they plan to write about. Then help them brainstorm a list of pictures or other multimedia they think would be helpful to readers. Provide suggestions as needed. Then direct students to print or online resources where they might find these items.

MONITOR AND SUPPORT

Write

Work with students to create a chart that describes the elements of a news report. Remind them that, like any good reporter, they should include the information that answers the questions who, what, where, when, why, and how. Creating a chart such as the one below can be especially helpful for struggling writers. Invite students to give examples for each row in the chart. This chart may also be used to assess student understanding.

Element	Definition	Example
Headline	• Catches readers' attention • Gives a quick idea of the topic	The Day the Ground Moved! Our Shifting Landscape
Introduction	• Includes most important information • Answers many of the who, what, when, where, and how questions	Earthquakes help shape the surface of the Earth. They can cause land to rise and fall, change how rivers flow, and create tsunamis.
Body	• Provides details • Includes facts, beginning with the most important • Includes details to help readers understand the topic • Includes precise, domain-specific language • May include visuals to help explain the facts • May include quotations from people involved or source material	The Earth's crust is made of plates. When these plates vibrate, they cause an earthquake. An earthquake can produce a seiche. The picture of the fence shows how the Earth moved about six feet. Dr. Wills, a scientist with the USGS explained, "Slow earthquakes build mountains."
Conclusion	• Gives readers a short summary • Gives suggestions for next steps	Earthquakes will continue to shape the surface of the Earth. If you live in an earthquake area, have an emergency kit ready.

ENGLISH LANGUAGE LEARNERS

If . . . students are intimidated by answering the who, what, when, where, and how questions in their writing,

then . . . provide examples of each type of question. For example, ask: What is an earthquake? Who do earthquakes affect? When do earthquakes occur? Where do earthquakes occur? How can people prepare for earthquakes? Help students formulate similar questions about their topic and identify facts that answer the quesitons.

STRUGGLING WRITERS

If . . . students have difficulty organizing their news report,

then . . . have them begin by putting the visuals they would like to use in order. Encourage them to write about each image. Then ask them what additional information is needed to make their news report more complete.

Look Closely

LOOK AT CONVENTIONS

SENTENCES Remind students that they have worked recently on writing sentences that use relative adverbs and relative pronouns. Using examples from the texts, show students how relative adverbs and relative pronouns can help answer the questions who, which one, where, when, and why—important elements of a news story. Encourage students to add variety to their sentences by using relative adverbs and relative pronouns.

RELATIVE ADVERBS Focus attention on the use of relative adverbs to answer the questions where, when, and why. Point out that these questions are part of the 5Ws used in news reports. Encourage students to review their writing to find places where inserting or revising a relative adverb would make the action clearer or more interesting. For example, the phrase *plates when they bump vibrate* provides more detail than *vibrating plates*.

QUOTATIONS Remind students that they have worked recently on including quotations in their writing. Point out that they should include a comma before and quotation marks around a direct quotation. Ask students to explain why it is important to include quotations in a news report. Encourage students to review their news report and add at least one direct quotation to support their topic.

LOOK AT CRAFT

SENTENCES Ask students to look closely to see that their sentences work together within each paragraph to support the main ideas. Remind them that, in a news report, the most interesting information should be presented first. Tell students to review their work for facts and details that clearly show how natural events affect the Earth's surface.

MAKING EFFECTIVE WORD CHOICES Remind students that a news report needs to be clear. Point out that using precise language, especially words related to the topic, help make the message clear. Encourage students to look for domain-specific words in their reports and to add additional ones if they make the topic more clear. Point out examples from the texts of topic-related and precise word choice.

ENGLISH LANGUAGE LEARNERS

If . . . students have difficulty with run-on sentences,

then . . . help students break a run-on sentence into two or more manageable sentences. Ask which is easier to understand, the run-on sentence or the rewritten sentences. Discuss why. Provide as many models and opportunities to practice as possible.

STRUGGLING WRITERS

If . . . students only use simple sentences,

then . . . remind students that when sentences are different lengths, the news report will be more interesting for the reader. Model how to use relative adverbs or relative pronouns to add details to a sentence. Encourage students to review their work and find at least one sentence they can enhance by adding a relative adverb or relative pronoun.

MONITOR AND SUPPORT

209

Name _____

Title _____

Write a News Report
Writing Checklist

☐ Did I include an attention-grabbing introduction?

☐ Did I make it clear how a natural event can affect the Earth's surface?

☐ Did I use information from *Anatomy of a Volcanic Eruption, A Tsunami Unfolds,* or other appropriate sources to support my topic?

☐ Did I use paragraph headings effectively?

☐ Did my illustrations or other visuals help make the report more interesting or easier to understand?

☐ Did I use concrete details and examples?

☐ Did I use relative adverbs and relative pronouns correctly?

Example: _____

_____

☐ Did I use quotations effectively? Did I format them correctly?

Example: _____

_____

☐ Did I use topic-specific words correctly?

Example: _____

_____

☐ Did I include a strong conclusion?

☐ Did I review my work for correct capitalization, punctuation, and spelling?

Unlock the Task: Write a Short Story

Distribute copies of the task found on page 196 of the Teacher's Guide. Read the task together. Have students name and discuss important words or phrases to highlight within the task.

In both *Lunch Money and Coyote School News,* the characters have to work together to come up with creative solutions. Write a short story about a character who solves a problem or overcomes a challenge with an innovative solution. You will establish a situation, introduce the narrator and/or characters, and organize logical event sequences. Use dialogue and a variety of transitional words and phrases. Use specific words, phrases, and sensory details to describe experiences and events. Provide an effective conclusion that follows from the narrated events.

ANSWER QUESTIONS ABOUT THE TASK

Remind students of the questions they must be able to answer to show they understand the task. Tell students to look at the words and phrases they highlighted to help them answer the questions below. You may wish to provide this as a handout for students to complete individually.

- **What type of writing is this?** (narrative)
- **What will the text of my writing look like?** (a short story)
- **What texts should I reference?** (*Lunch Money* and *Coyote School News*)
- **What do I need to include?** (a character who solves a problem in an innovative way, descriptive details, dialogue, clear event sequences, sensory details, a conclusion)

RESTATE THE TASK

Ask students to restate the task in their own words. Check for misunderstandings or missing elements.

ENGLISH LANGUAGE LEARNERS

If . . . students are not sure what *innovative* means,

then . . . explain that *innovative* is an adjective that means "introducing or using new ideas, methods, or ways of doing something." Brainstorm with students synonyms for *innovative,* such as *clever, imaginative, creative,* and *inventive.*

STRUGGLING WRITERS

If . . . students have difficulty understanding the task,

then . . . discuss a story students are familiar with, such as *Lunch Money,* and have them identify the characters, problem, and solution in the story. Discuss why the solution in the story was innovative, or creative, and what it means to be innovative. Then have students name the steps in the story the character followed to solve the problem.

Other students might move on to gathering ideas with independence.

Prepare to Write

DETERMINE FOCUS

Once students understand the writing task, have them review the selections *Lunch Money, Coyote School News,* and any other short stories you have gathered. Tell students to record ideas for their short story. Have students identify a character, problem, and at least one creative or innovative solution to that problem. Encourage students to think of more than one solution and then focus on the most innovative or unusual solution. Remind students that readers like stories that end with a creative twist.

Have students think about the steps their character must follow to solve the problem. Remind students that these steps will provide a sequence of events that will improve the flow of their story. If students have difficulty thinking of a problem, brainstorm a list of problems and allow students to choose a problem from the list for their short story.

GATHER IDEAS

Have students put together ideas for their short story. They might use different colored note cards or sticky notes to organize their ideas. They can use one color for ideas about their character, one color for ideas about the problem the character faces, and another color for possible solutions to the problem. Ask the following questions to help students add details to their three big ideas: Who is the main character? What do you want the reader to know about this character? What problem does this character face? Is there more than one solution to the problem? Which is the most creative solution? Does the solution fit with the character? Is it believable that the character would think of this solution?

Remind students that the sequence of events in their story must unfold naturally. They should use dialogue and descriptive words to create their character, and transitional words and phrases to create the sequence of events leading from the problem to the solution. Point out that including sensory details that tell more about how things look, sound, smell, taste, and feel will help readers understand the story better.

ACCELERATED WRITERS

If . . . students have solved the character's problem using an expected or common solution,

then . . . ask students to think of a different, surprising, creative, or humorous solution to the problem. Remind students that their solution can be real or imaginary. Suggest that students give their main character an unusual skill that can help solve the problem. Also remind students that even though the solution can be imaginary, it still needs to be believable to the reader.

Encourage students to talk about their short story with a partner to help them refine their ideas together. Students may benefit from modeling these prewriting conversations or reviewing the questions below.

Questions a Writer Might Ask

- Who is my main character?
- How can I provide enough detail for my reader to know my character?
- What problem will my character face?
- What events will lead to the solution of the problem?
- How well does one event lead to another event?
- Does my solution fit my character?
- How surprising is my solution?
- How can I use dialogue successfully?

Encourage students to formulate questions of their own.

Ask students to think about the feedback they received when talking about their short story with a partner. Remind them that using that feedback to organize their short story will save them time and effort when writing and rewriting.

Have students write descriptive words to describe how their character reacts to his or her problem. For example, is the character angry about the problem, overwhelmed by the problem, determined to solve it, or afraid of it? Then ask questions to help students think about creative or innovative solutions to their character's problem. Remind them that the solutions should flow from the character's reaction to the problem. For example, ask: Is there another way to solve the problem? Is this problem unique to this character, or is it a problem that others might have as well? Would the creation of a new product help to solve the problem?

ENGLISH LANGUAGE LEARNERS

If . . . students have difficulty punctuating dialogue in English,

then . . . review speaker tags, commas, and quotation marks and how they are used to show who is speaking and the exact words each characters says. Also explain that they should start a new paragraph each time a different character speaks. Provide an example such as:

Greg said, "Mrs. McCormick, I left my lunch at home. May I borrow fifty cents?"

"I'm sorry, but no, I will not lend you the money," replied Mrs. McCormick.

STRUGGLING WRITERS

If . . . students are having trouble thinking of a problem their character might have,

then . . . talk about popular television or book characters and the problems those characters have encountered. Then talk about the solutions those characters found to their problems. Help students understand how these characters' problems are often similar to everyday problems others might encounter. Suggest students adapt one of these problems to write about.

Write

Work with students to create a chart that describes the elements of a short story. Remind them that their short story must include a believable main character, a problem their character faces, a sequence of events leading to the solution of the problem, and a conclusion that ties the story together. Creating a chart, such as the one below, can be especially helpful for struggling writers. Invite students to give examples for each row in the chart. This chart may also be used to assess student understanding.

Element	Definition	Example
Headline	• Catches the attention of a reader • Gives an idea of the problem	Smears No More! Write Without Worry!
Introduction or Lead	• Introduces the main character and sets the scene for the story • Includes the problem the main character faces	Meet Will, a fourth grader who is excited about getting to write with a pen instead of a pencil. But Will is frustrated because as he moves his hand across the paper, his words smear, creating a mess.
Body	• Includes details about the characters, setting, and plot • Uses concrete words and phrases as well as sensory details to convey experiences and events precisely • Includes dialogue and descriptions to move the plot along and to provide insight into characters' thoughts and actions • Uses transitional words and phrases to manage a sequence of events	Will is left-handed. Will is a perfectionist. He likes things just right. Will is frustrated because as he writes, he drags his left hand through the ink creating a mess. Will told a classmate, "I've tried lots of solutions, but none work." Then, Will has an idea. He draws a sketch of his solution.
Conclusion	• Provides a conclusion that follows the narrated events	Will creates a mini-wagon. He rests his left arm on the wagon, and it rolls freely over his words as he writes. Will knows he has a million-dollar idea!

ENGLISH LANGUAGE LEARNERS

If . . . students have difficulty using sequence words and putting events in sequence,

then . . . have students begin by listing each event on a separate note card. Then have students move the note cards around to show the order of the events. Have students read the note cards aloud. Ask if the order makes sense. If not, have students move the ideas that seem out of order. Finally, provide a list of transitional words and phrases, and review with students how to use those to connect their ideas.

STRUGGLING WRITERS

If . . . students are having difficulty writing a conclusion,

then . . . remind students that the conclusion is based on the events in the story. Explain that the conclusion tells how the story ends, and it may get the reader thinking about the story's main character, problem, and solution in a new way. Tell students to name the main idea of their story, describe the events that support the main idea, and then use that information to write their conclusion.

Look Closely

SENTENCES Remind students that they have worked recently on writing dialogue. Have students review their writing to locate examples of dialogue. Using examples from the texts, show students how dialogue can be used to develop character. Encourage students to add variety to their writing by using dialogue to let the reader get to know their character. Be sure students understand the conventions of using quotation marks and commas when writing dialogue.

USE RELATIVE ADVERBS Focus attention on the use of relative adverbs, such as *before, first, second, next, then,* and *eventually*, to sequence events in a story. Encourage students to underline relative adverbs in their writing. Suggest students read their stories aloud to a partner, first leaving out the words they underlined, then including the words they underlined. Have partners discuss how the use of relative adverbs adds meaning to the story.

FORM AND USE PREPOSITIONAL PHRASES Remind students that prepositional phrases can be used to provide vivid details about when, where, how, and which. Tell students to find prepositional phrases in their writing. Have students identify the question the prepositional phrase answers, name the preposition in the phrase, and tell what word the prepositional phrase describes.

SENTENCES Have students look closely to see that their sentences work together within each paragraph to support the main ideas. Remind them that character development is often a main element of a short story. Tell students to review their work for facts and details that help the reader understand more about the main character of the story.

USE TRANSITIONAL WORDS AND PHRASES Remind students how writers use transitional words and phrases to help establish a sequence of events. Encourage students to look for transitional words and phrases in their short stories and to check for additional opportunities to use transitional words and phrases. Have them make sure they have used a variety of transitional words and phrases. Point out good examples from the texts as models whenever possible.

ENGLISH LANGUAGE LEARNERS

If . . . students have difficulty using prepositional phrases,

then . . . help students create prepositional phrases to answer the questions when, where, how, and which. For example, place a book on a table and ask: Where is the book? Write *on the table*. Have students repeat the response. Underline the preposition *on* and have students use that preposition in another sentence. Repeat with other examples.

STRUGGLING WRITERS

If . . . students use only simple sentences,

then . . . remind students that when sentences are different lengths, the text will be more interesting for the reader. Model how to put two related sentences together using coordinating conjunctions, such as *and, but, or,* and *so,* and a comma. Encourage students to review their writing and combine two simple sentences using a coordinating conjunction and a comma.

Name _____

Title _____

Write a Short Story
Writing Checklist

☐ Did I include an attention-grabbing introduction?

☐ Did I make clear who the main character is?

☐ Did I make clear what problem the main character faces?

☐ Did my main character solve the problem creatively?

☐ Did I provide details to clearly show the main character and the problem?

☐ Did I create a clear sequence of events?

☐ Did my main character's actions match the details provided about the character in the story?

☐ Did I use dialogue correctly? Did I punctuate the dialogue correctly?

Example: _____

_____

☐ Did I use relative adverbs correctly? Example: _____

_____

☐ Did I use transitional words and phrases to help my sequence of events flow

naturally? Example: _____

_____

☐ Did I include a strong conclusion?

☐ Did I review my work for correct capitalization, punctuation, and spelling?

☐ (Optional) Did I type my story, draw illustrations, scan and upload them to the word processing document, and put them in appropriate places?

Unlock the Task: Write About Innovations

Distribute copies of the task found on page 396 of the Teacher's Guide. Read the task together. Have students identify and discuss important key words and phrases to highlight within the task.

> You will create an opinion statement about the technology-based innovation that you feel has had the greatest impact on people's daily lives. With the text *Using Money* as a reference, you will choose one innovation and tell why you think that innovation is important and write about the impact that innovation has had on people's daily lives.

ANSWER QUESTIONS ABOUT THE TASK

Remind students of the questions they must be able to answer to show they understand the task. Tell students to look at the words and phrases they highlighted to help them determine the answers to the questions below. You may wish to provide this as a handout for students to complete individually. Scan the group to determine who needs more support and who is ready to work independently.

- **What type of writing is this?** (opinion)
- **What texts should I reference?** (*Using Money*)
- **What information should I give?** (an innovation and my opinion on why this innovation is important)
- **What do I need to include?** (facts, details, and an organizational structure to support my opinion; linking words and phrases to connect the reasons to the opinion; a conclusion that summarizes my opinion)

RESTATE THE TASK

Ask students to restate the task in their own words. Check for misunderstandings or missing elements.

ENGLISH LANGUAGE LEARNERS

If . . . students have difficulty identifying a technology-based innovation,

then . . . display everyday objects, such as a pencil, a book, or a ruler. Provide the English word or words for each item and have students talk about the purpose of each object and why the invention was successful. Have students think about their day-to-day routines and name objects that could make those routines easier. Explain that one of these ideas could become the innovation that they write about. Provide English words if needed.

STRUGGLING WRITERS

If . . . students have difficulty stating an opinion about their chosen innovation,

then . . . explain that their reasons for their opinion should be supported by facts. Then, have students talk about why they think their chosen innovation is important. Help students separate their statements into those that are their opinion and those that are facts.

Prepare to Write

DETERMINE FOCUS

Once students understand the task, have them review the selection *Using Money* and any other topic-related texts you may have gathered. Have students record ideas for their chosen invention/innovation. Some students may benefit from making a list of everyday tasks and then explaining how technology has helped to make those tasks easier to complete.

Tell students to prioritize their list to one or two innovations that they think should be the focus of their opinion statement. Remind them that they should choose the idea about which they have the strongest opinion and the most supporting facts to share. If students have difficulty choosing between two innovations, have them make a quick list of the information they might include and then select the innovation that has the most information to support it.

GATHER IDEAS

Tell students to gather ideas for their opinion statement. Remind students that their statement will include their opinion about why this innovation has become important and must include facts that support their opinion. As students gather their facts, tell them to decide whether the fact is one that will be cited with a source, in which case it should be copied carefully word for word, or whether the fact is information that should be summarized and not copied exactly. For example, information regarding specific names, dates, times, etc. should be cited. Information that is more general, such as a well-established fact that is common knowledge, should be summarized.

Remind students that when they write about their chosen innovation, they should state their opinions clearly so that readers can understand what they are trying to achieve. Then they must include facts, details, and quotations that will convince their reader that their innovation has changed the way people do things. They should organize the text so that their facts and details make sense. Have them make sure they provide enough information to convince their readers that the innovation has changed everyday life.

ACCELERATED WRITERS

If . . . students are concerned about convincing readers how their chosen innovation has changed everyday life,

then . . . have students think of how everyday life would be different if their chosen innovation did not exist. What would be harder or take more time to do? Then help students arrange their facts in such a way as to make a convincing argument for why they feel their innovation is the most important.

Encourage students to talk about their innovation with a partner to help them refine their ideas. Students may benefit from modeling these prewriting conversations or reviewing some questions the writer might ask a listener.

Questions a Writer Might Ask

- What technology-based innovation am I focusing on?
- What is my opinion about the impact of this innovation?
- What facts should I provide to support my opinion?
- Should I provide any quotations from experts to support my opinion?
- Will my presentation convince the reader of the importance of my opinion?
- What connecting words should I use to transition smoothly from one fact to another?
- How will my conclusion support my opinion?

Encourage students to also formulate questions of their own.

GET ORGANIZED

Ask students to think about the feedback they received when talking about their chosen innovation with a partner. Remind them that using that feedback to organize their opinion statement will save them time and effort when writing and rewriting.

Tell students that when they write an opinion, they must state their opinion clearly to make sure their readers understand it. Remind students that an opinion is more than just a feeling. Explain that opinions are supported by facts and details. Suggest students use a graphic organizer to help visualize their opinion and its supporting facts and details.

ENGLISH LANGUAGE LEARNERS

If . . . students come from a culture in which it is considered impolite or argumentative to strongly state an opinion,

then . . . help them practice stating opinions about everyday objects. Ask students a series of questions to elicit opinions, such as: Do you like peanut butter? Do you like the color red? Do you like science or social studies better? Using their answers, ask students to give facts or reasons for their opinions and explain that it is okay to voice their opinion when they support it with facts and reasons.

STRUGGLING WRITERS

If . . . students are unable to identify an innovation of their own to write about,

then . . . suggest they take a common household item, such as an energy efficient light bulb, and form an opinion about it. Then have students find facts about the item and use those facts to support their opinion. Remind students that their facts should not only support their opinion but also try to persuade others to agree with their opinion. Students can use these skills to think of an innovation of their own.

Write

Work with students to create a chart that describes the elements of an opinion paper. Remind them that they should state their opinion clearly and then provide facts and details that support that opinion. Creating a chart such as the one below can be especially helpful for struggling writers. Invite students to give examples for each row in the chart. This chart may also be used to assess student understanding.

Element	Definition	Example
Headline	• Catches the attention of a reader • Gives a quick idea of the topic	Smartphones: The Smartest Innovation
Introduction	• Includes a strong, clear statement of the opinion	Smartphones have made a big difference in the way people live every day. We can make or receive calls anywhere we are. We can send emails and text messages and look things up on the Internet.
Body	• Provides details • Includes facts beginning with the most important • Includes details to help others understand the topic • May include visuals to help explain the facts • Uses linking words and phrases to connect ideas	Smartphones combine the best features of a cell phone with the best features of a computer. The first version of a "smartphone" was introuced in 1992. Steven Jobs introduced the first iPhone in 2007.
Conclusion	• Gives readers a short summary • Provides suggestions for next steps	Almost everyone uses a smartphone every day. It has made communication with family and friends easier than ever before.

ENGLISH LANGUAGE LEARNERS

If . . . students have difficulty using appropriate linking words,

then . . . help them create a list of linking words, such as *for instance, in order to,* and *in addition.* Have students talk about when to use each phrase, such as using *for instance* when providing an example or *in addition* when adding more information or another fact. Have students revisit their opinion paper and use the linking words to connect ideas.

STRUGGLING WRITERS

If . . . students have provided lots of facts but the facts don't seem to fit together or support the opinion,

then . . . remind students that the facts must support the stated opinion and flow together so that their opinion paper is easy to read and understand. Have students read each fact they have gathered, and then ask: Does this fact support your opinion? Does it help the reader understand your point of view? If students answer *no,* have them remove that fact from their paper.

Look Closely

SENTENCES Remind students that they have worked recently on using a comma before a coordinating conjunction in a compound sentence. Use examples from the texts to show students how a coordinating conjunction can help connect two simple sentences. Have students review their writing to locate examples of compound sentences connected with a coordinating conjunction. Be sure they included the comma before the conjunction.

USE RELATIVE PRONOUNS Focus attention on the use of relative pronouns. Remind students that a relative pronoun introduces an adjective clause that relates to the noun or pronoun it describes. Encourage students to review their writing to find places where using a relative clause would provide more details about a noun or pronoun. Use the following example of a relative pronoun and adjective clause from *Using Money*: "WaMu offered special loans, called adjustable-rate mortgages, which had low interest rates and low monthly payments."

ORDER ADJECTIVES Help students recall the order in which to use adjectives when using two or more to describe the same noun: number, opinion or judgment, size, weight, age, shape, color, and material. Encourage students to review their writing and check that multiple adjectives for the same noun are used in the correct order.

SENTENCES Have students check that their sentences work together within each paragraph to support the main ideas. Remind them that they need to state their opinion and then support that opinion with facts. Tell students to review their work for facts and details that clearly support their opinion.

ESTABLISH A PURPOSE Remind students that as writers, they must establish a purpose, or reason, for their writing. When they write an opinion piece, their opinion at the beginning of the text helps establish the purpose. Therefore, they must state their opinion clearly. Their opinion must be more than just a feeling, and it must be supported through clear facts and details. Have students review their opinion to be sure it clearly states their purpose for writing their paper.

ENGLISH LANGUAGE LEARNERS

If . . . students have difficulty deciding when to use *who* and when to use *that*,

then . . . remind students that *who* is used to describe a person and *that* is used to describe an idea or a thing. Provide a sentence frame, such as: Mary, ___ is wearing a red coat, raised her hand. Ask students which word, *who* or *that*, is needed to complete the sentence. Have them explain their answer. Repeat with other sentence frames.

STRUGGLING WRITERS

If . . . students have difficulty placing adjectives in the correct order,

then . . . write a variety of adjectives on note cards. Have students read each adjective and tell what type of adjective it is: a number, an opinion or a judgment, a size, a weight, an age, a shape, a color, or a material. Tell students to use two adjectives before a noun, such as *large, red ball*, and explain the order. Once they can order two adjectives consistently, have them use three adjectives, such as *three small, yellow balls*, and explain the order.

Name _____

Title _____

Write About Innovations
Writing Checklist

☐ Did I clearly state my opinion?

☐ Did I support my opinion with facts and details?

☐ Did I present the information using a structure that supports my opinion?

☐ Did all of my facts relate to my opinion?

☐ Did I use linking words to help establish the sequence?

☐ Did I use relative pronouns correctly? Example: _____

_____

☐ Did I use the correct order for adjectives when I used two or more adjectives to describe the same noun? Example: _____

_____

☐ Did I use a comma before a coordinating conjunction in a compound sentence? Example: _____

_____

☐ Did I include a strong conclusion?

☐ Did I review my work for correct capitalization, punctuation, and spelling?

☐ (Optional) Did I research my chosen innovation online and type my opinion paper?

Scaffolded Lessons for the Writing Types

Unlock Opinion Writing 224
Introduce an Opinion 225
Organize Writing.. 226
Support an Opinion 227
Link Opinions and Reasons 228
Write a Conclusion... 229
Support for Extended Writing 230
Checklists 232

Unlock Informative/Explanatory Writing.......234
Plan and Introduce a Topic.. 235
Use Illustrations and Multimedia 236
Develop a Topic.. 237
Use Linking Words 238
Write a Conclusion.. 239
Support for Extended Writing 240
Checklists 242

Unlock Narrative Writing 244
Establish a Situation and Introduce Characters 245
Organize an Event Sequence.. 246
Use Transitional Words and Phrases 247
Use Dialogue, Descriptions, and Sensory Details ... 248
Write a Conclusion.. 249
Support for Extended Writing 250
Checklists 252

Unlock Opinion Writing

INTRODUCE

Display an opinion text that students have read during the school year. Point out that the writer is explaining something he or she believes to be true. Allow students to look through the text and summarize the text as they remember it. Have them tell what the topic of the writing is and what the author's opinion is.

Explain to students that when they read opinion writing, they may or may not agree with the writer's position. The ideas may be based on the writer's feelings, or what the writer has learned about the topic. Some opinion writing may be supported with facts and evidence to explain the author's opinion. Other opinion writing may simply include reasons to support the opinion. Ask questions to get students to express opinions: "Should teachers be required to wear school uniforms?" or "Which character was most admirable?" Explain that when they write an opinion piece, they must give reasons to support their opinion. Provide some opinion articles from newspapers or magazines, and have students tell each writer's opinion.

UNDERSTAND TASK AND TONE

Explain that opinion writing often takes on an emotional or spirited tone because the writer may feel strongly about the topic. Explain that expressive words can help a writer get his or her opinion across to the reader. Show students examples of assignments that require them to write opinion texts. Tell students that they are often provided with a topic to write about, but that they are usually responsible for deciding what their opinion about the topic is. Remind them that before they begin writing, they should carefully read the assignment and understand all of its parts. Explain that most school assignments should use a formal tone because they will be read by you, their teacher. Explain that as they write, they should pay attention to making their topic seem important to the reader and worth getting excited about.

REFOCUS ON THE WRITING TYPE

Throughout the year as students read or are asked to write opinion texts, remind them of the key features of this text type. Opinion writing

- introduces a topic and states an opinion about the topic.
- makes a claim about the topic.
- gives reasons for the writer's opinion.
- may include facts and details about the topic.
- may offer a possible solution to a problem.

Introduce an Opinion

What Students Should KNOW	What Students Will DO
• Identify how topics are introduced in texts students have read. • Recognize elements of a clear introduction.	• Introduce a topic or text clearly.
• Identify opinions.	• State an opinion.

MODEL AND PRACTICE

Help students focus on how to introduce an opinion topic and state an opinion in a clear and concise way for the reader. Choose a topic that most students show an obvious interest in, such as games, movies, sports, or personal friendships. Explain that the first step in good opinion writing is stating the topic and opinion clearly.

MODEL We read a nonfiction book about the history of baseball. Then I was asked to write about my favorite sport. Instead of jumping right in and saying that I love swimming best, because it popped into my mind first, I thought about all of the possible choices. I do like baseball a lot, and I've played soccer every year since I was six, but swimming really is my all-time favorite sport. If I think about introducing the topic and opinion, I might begin by saying, "There are so many great sports, but swimming is my favorite by far."

PRACTICE Have students work in small groups. Provide each group with a different topic and ask them to work together to come up with a collective opinion about the topic. Invite each group to present their topic and opinion to the class.

DEEPER PRACTICE Using the information from the group practice, have students work independently to write an introductory sentence or two to introduce their topic and opinion. Then have students regroup to compare their introductions.

ENGLISH LANGUAGE LEARNERS

If . . . students have trouble expressing their opinion,

then . . . help them practice by asking questions about the topic: Do you like ___? What do you like about it? Then have them complete a sentence frame to express their idea: My favorite part of ___ is ___.

STRUGGLING WRITERS

If . . . students have trouble summarizing an opinion they read in an existing work,

then . . . ask partners to work together to summarize the opinion together. Provide them with a copy of the written work, and ask them to underline key words that indicate opinions, such as *think, feel, good, best, favorite,* or *bad.* Once students have identified the opinion, help them summarize the opinion in their own words.

Organize Writing

What Students Should KNOW	What Students Will DO
• Know and apply the organizational steps for an opinion essay. • Develop a paragraph that introduces a topic and states an opinion related to the topic.	• Create an organizational structure in which related ideas are grouped to support the writer's purpose.

MODEL AND PRACTICE

Explain to students that once they understand their assignment and topic and decide on their opinion, it's time to organize what they will write. Explain that their introduction should be more than just a sentence. They should develop a paragraph that introduces and starts to organize what they will be discussing.

MODEL Now that I know I'll be writing about swimming, I should organize and develop an introductory paragraph. One sentence will introduce the topic, and the next will state my opinion about the topic. I can revise and expand my first idea and write, "There are many sports that people can do for fun and exercise. The sport that I enjoy most is swimming." Then I can complete the paragraph with something like, "I swim every week in swimming class, and I swim all summer long." This helps me to introduce my topic more fully before I discuss it.

PRACTICE Provide students with two samples of opinion writing. Ask groups of students to analyze the introductions to both samples. Have them discuss each, tell which one they think is better, and explain their choice.

DEEPER PRACTICE Ask students to write an introductory paragraph to describe their favorite sport. When they are done, have students read their paragraphs to a partner.

ENGLISH LANGUAGE LEARNERS

If . . . students have trouble comparing introductions,

then . . . have them hold the two samples side by side. Model how to summarize the main points of each introduction. Say: This introduction states the topic ___. Then it gives the writer's opinion. The writer thinks ___. Encourage students' attempts to summarize the second sample.

STRUGGLING WRITERS

If . . . students have trouble expressing which introduction they like best and why,

then . . . break students into small groups or pairs based on the introduction they like best. Have students brainstorm a list of things they like about the introduction. Then invite them to combine their ideas into a summarizing sentence to defend their choice.

Support an Opinion

What Students Should KNOW	What Students Will DO
• Understand the value of supporting an opinion. • Distinguish between facts and details that do and do not support an opinion.	• Provide reasons that are supported by facts and details.

MODEL AND PRACTICE

Explain that good opinion writing must provide reasons to support the writer's opinion. Reasons need to relate to the topic and help explain the opinion. Opinion writing often uses facts and details to support an opinion. Give students an example of a book or movie review. Show how the writer uses facts from the book or details from the movie as reasons to support his or her opinion.

MODEL When I write about how much I love swimming, I'll let the reader know my reasons. I can think of these reasons from my personal experience. I can write, "I like swimming because it makes my body strong, and it's a lot of fun to be in the water." I can also research facts about the health benefits of swimming. But suppose I was asked to write my opinion of a book that I just read about dogs. I would state my opinion and then use details from the book as my reasons. I might say, "I didn't like the book about dogs, because there were not enough pictures to show me the kinds of dogs that were being described." I couldn't support my opinion about the book without using the book to give reasons.

PRACTICE Make a list of the following facts and details about swimming on the board: It can be done with friends; Many pools are 25 meters long; Swimming builds muscle and strength; Many pools are over 3-feet deep; Swimming makes people healthy; Lifeguards watch swimmers. Then have students work in pairs to identify the reasons that support the opinion, "Swimming is my favorite sport."

DEEPER PRACTICE Have students work with a partner to brainstorm a list of facts and details that support their opinion about a favorite sport. Ask them to review the list when they are done to weed out any reasons that do not support their opinion.

ENGLISH LANGUAGE LEARNERS

If . . . students have trouble with vocabulary to describe reasons,

then . . . work together to discuss the favorite sport. Ask questions about the sport such as these: How does the sport make people feel? What makes the game fun to play? Help turn each question into a statement. For example: People feel strong when they swim. Baseball is fun because you are part of a team.

STRUGGLING WRITERS

If . . . students have trouble understanding which facts and details support an opinion,

then . . . provide students with practice by writing the words *supports* and *does not support* on index cards. Then give students an example of an opinion. As you give examples of facts and details that support and do not support that opinion, ask students to hold up the card that correctly identifies the fact or detail. Have students explain why the example did or did not support the opinion. Correct any misunderstandings.

Link Opinions and Reasons

What Students Should KNOW	What Students Will DO
• Identify linking words and phrases. • Determine how to use linking words and phrases in opinion writing.	• Link opinion and reasons using words and phrases (*for instance, in order to, in addition*).

MODEL AND PRACTICE

Explain to students that they can make their writing more clear and understandable to the reader by using linking words and phrases. List linking phrases for students, such as *for instance, in order to,* and *in addition*. Explain the meaning of each phrase and use each in a sample sentence. Describe the importance of using linking words to help clarify opinions. Ask students to identify linking words in opinion texts you have in the classroom. Add any additional linking words to the list.

MODEL Linking words help me express my opinion. I rely on them to help me say things clearly. I can write, "In addition to loving what swimming does for my muscles, I think swimming is a lot of fun. For instance, I can race my friends or play Marco Polo in the pool." Without these linking words, my writing would not be as interesting, and it might not make as much sense. Model reading the sentences without the linking words, and note how choppy it sounds.

PRACTICE Have students use linking phrases to complete these sentences:

- ___ to swimming, I also love warm, summer weather. (*in addition*)
- Readers may need a dictionary ___ understand everything in the book. (*in order to*)
- The book told about many dogs. ___, it told about the eating habits of Dalmatians. (*For instance*)

DEEPER PRACTICE Have students write a short paragraph about their favorite sport, using one or all of the linking phrases mentioned. Have them give the paragraph to a partner and ask the partner to underline all of the linking words and phrases in the paragraph.

ENGLISH LANGUAGE LEARNERS

If . . . students have trouble choosing the correct linking words or phrases,

then . . . show students examples of the words or phrases used in real sample opinion pieces. Invite students to find and underline the words or phrases. Then rephrase the sentences for students so that they can clearly understand the idea in more than one way.

STRUGGLING WRITERS

If . . . students use linking words or phrases incorrectly,

then . . . have them work in pairs to write a sentence that uses one of the words or phrases. Invite students to verbally explain how the linking word or phrase connects the two parts of the sentence. Ask: Does the word/phrase help add examples? Does it describe something in more detail? Encourage students to repeat the activity until they have used all of the phrases.

Write a Conclusion

What Students Should KNOW	What Students Will DO
• Identify the components of a strong concluding sentence or paragraph. • Write a strong concluding sentence or paragraph that relates to the presented opinion.	• Provide a concluding statement or section related to the opinion presented.

MODEL AND PRACTICE

Explain to students that opinion writing should have a strong concluding statement or section. The conclusion should relate to the opinion presented, preferably by summarizing or restating the opinion. Explain that the conclusion should give a definite ending point to the writing without introducing new ideas or concepts. Explain that some writers include a clincher in their conclusion, which is a strong statement that creates an impression on the reader. Have students look for examples in texts they have read.

MODEL Now that I've written the reasons to explain why swimming is my favorite sport, I can wrap up my opinion by writing a strong concluding section. I can write something like this: "I can stay in shape *and* have fun with my favorite sport—swimming. What's your favorite sport?" When I ask the reader a question, I'm getting the reader involved and making an impression. That will leave the reader with something to think about.

PRACTICE Provide several small, student groups with a copy of the same opinion text. Ask students to analyze the conclusion and discuss it in their group. Then ask each group to explain to the class one thing that they like about the conclusion, and one thing that they think needs improvement.

DEEPER PRACTICE Ask each student to write a sample conclusion about their favorite sport that they have been writing about. Invite volunteers to share their conclusions with the class. Have listeners identify the restatement and the clincher in each conclusion.

ENGLISH LANGUAGE LEARNERS

If . . . students have trouble coming up with a clincher for their conclusion,

then . . . help them to first focus on what it is they want the reader to think or feel when he or she finishes reading. Encourage students to express their thought in a complete sentence. Then guide students to use that idea to write a clincher ending for their opinion.

STRUGGLING WRITERS

If . . . students write conclusions that are too abrupt or do not summarize their opinion,

then . . . give students copies of additional samples to analyze for their conclusions. Invite them to circle the entire concluding section and then underline the summary or restatement of the writer's opinion. Then ask students to discuss what is left off of their conclusion and how they can make their conclusion similar to the sample conclusion.

Support for Extended Writing

Refer to this process when students are writing a longer passage that requires development and organization to produce an opinion text. Remind students of the importance of the revising and editing stages of the writing process. Explain that these steps are necessary to make their work as strong as possible.

UNDERSTAND THE TASK Tell students to review their writing prompt or writing assignment carefully to be sure they understand what is being asked. Have them answer these questions: What is the writing task? How can I restate the task in my own words? What topic will I be writing about? Do I already know my opinion about this topic? Should I cite information from another text to provide support for my opinion? How many parts are there to this writing assignment? Do I understand what I am being asked to do?

BRAINSTORM Provide students with guidance and support to brainstorm ideas that will help form their opinion writing. Explain that they may need to list possible opinions about the topic so that they can choose the best one. They need to also identify possible ways to organize their writing so that it is presented clearly.

PROVIDE REASONS Have students focus on the part of their writing in which they give reasons to support their opinion. Guide students to decide if their assignment requires that they find evidence to support their opinions. If so, encourage them to find facts or details from outside sources, such as books or online material. Remind students that they should be able to tell from their assignment whether they should be providing facts and details. Assignments about books or nonfiction topics will require text evidence, while assignments about personal experiences may not. If students do not need to provide evidence, ask them to list several reasons, even if they may not end up using them all in their writing.

ORGANIZE INFORMATION Have students focus on the way they will organize their writing into distinct paragraphs. Have them list the reasons and evidence that will support their opinion. Have them decide whether they will list reasons from least important to most important, or from most important to least important. Have students plan their concluding statement or section before they begin to write.

WRITE

Provide students with encouraging tips to guide them through their writing process. Some tips might include:

- Remind students that their draft should focus on clearly organizing their opinion and reasons, and they should feel free to explore making their writing as strong as possible.

- Explain to students that they can organize their writing in lists, notes, or graphic organizers, and refer to them repeatedly as they write.

- Tell students to give their honest opinion about the topic and not to worry about what other people think of their opinion.

- Encourage students to use descriptive words, emotional language, and logical reasoning to express their opinions and reasons.

- When students are finished, have them double check that they have answered all parts of the writing prompt or assignment and cited or referenced any related texts included in the prompt.

REVISE AND EDIT

Guide students through the revising and editing process. Work with students to develop writing and reviewing checklists to help them look for details that they might address in their revision. You may choose to reproduce the checklists on the following pages and work with students to add task-specific items to the lists. After revising their work, have students review each other's work to further strengthen their writing.

PUBLISH

Provide students with support in presenting their final version. If students are writing book reviews, you may wish to have students presenting the same book read their final drafts one after the next. Then pause to have a class discussion about the reviews and the ways in which they were alike and different. You might provide students with time to enter their final drafts into a computer software program and add images that support their opinion pieces. Allow students to print their final drafts, if possible, and bind them into a classroom book.

ACCELERATED WRITERS

If . . . students are using library or online resources for their project,

then . . . guide them to keep track of the appropriate information so they can cite it correctly in a bibliography. Have them fill out an index card for each source with the name of the source, author, publication date, and any other information they should track to create a bibliography for their work.

Writer's Checklist

Name _____

Title _____

❏ Did I include a clear introduction that stated the topic
   and my opinion?

❏ Did I give an important reason early on to support my opinion?

❏ Are my paragraphs organized clearly and in a logical order?

❏ Did I use facts and details to support my reasons if necessary?

❏ Did I cite evidence from text if required?

❏ Did I explain my opinion clearly so that the reader understands it?

❏ Did I use linking words and phrases to make ideas clear?

❏ Did I summarize my opinion and reasons in the concluding statement
   or section?

❏ Did I include a clincher in the conclusion to make an impression
   on the reader?

❏ Did I answer all parts of the prompt or address all parts of the writing
   assignment?

❏ Did I review my work for correct capitalization, punctuation,
   and spelling?

❏ _____

❏ _____

Peer Review Checklist

Name _____

Writer's Name_____

Title _____

❏ Does the introduction describe the topic and the writer's opinion about it?

❏ Is the writing clearly organized into paragraphs?

❏ Does the writer give reasons to support his or her opinion?

❏ Does the writer cite evidence if required in the task?

❏ Does the writer use facts or details from different sources when necessary?

❏ Is the writing organized in a logical way that gives reasons?

❏ Does the writing have linking words or phrases to connect or clarify ideas?

❏ Does the writing have a strong concluding statement or section?

❏ Does the writing clearly address all parts of the prompt or assignment?

❏ _____

❏ _____

❏ _____

Unlock Informative/ Explanatory Writing

Hold up an example of an informative/explanatory text from your classroom library that students are familiar with. Explain to students that the text is an example of informative/explanatory writing. Tell them that the writer researched facts and details to give the reader information about a specific topic, and the writer refrained from giving opinions about the topic. Allow students to look through the text and decide what the topic is.

Explain to students that the purpose of informative/explanatory writing is to teach or explain a topic and to convey ideas and information clearly without opinions. Informative/explanatory writing also helps the reader gain content knowledge about the topic. Explain that the writer's job is to examine the topic and research it thoroughly enough to be able to write about it. Give students a few examples of this type of writing, and work with students to brainstorm a more comprehensive list. You may add to the list throughout the year.

UNDERSTAND TASK AND TONE

Have volunteers talk about informative/explanatory writing they have come across in their own experiences. Discuss how this type of writing is different from opinion or narrative writing, including in the tone or voice. Point out that this type of writing generally has a more serious and formal tone. Show students examples of informative/explanatory writing prompts. Tell them that they will usually be provided with the topic they should write about. Explain that before they begin writing, students must carefully read the assignment and understand all of its parts. They should also make sure they understand the purpose of their writing and who their audience is.

REFOCUS ON THE WRITING TYPE

Throughout the year as students read or are asked to write informative/explanatory texts, remind them of the key features of this text type. Informative/explanatory writing

- gives information accurately.
- explains a topic by describing the "how" or "why" behind a topic.
- includes facts and definitions.
- may include visuals to make information as clear as possible.
- may explain a process or the relationship between events or ideas.

Plan and Introduce a Topic

What Students Should KNOW	What Students Will DO
• Identify clear introductions in texts that students read. • Identify and use introductory words and phrases to write strong introductory sentences.	• Introduce a topic clearly.
• Identify how information is grouped in texts students read. • Gather and categorize information and organize information into paragraphs or sections.	• Group related information in paragraphs and sections.

MODEL AND PRACTICE

Display examples of introductions to familiar informative/explanatory texts. Explain that an introduction should let the reader know the topic and describe what the reader might learn. An introduction should be clear and use introductory words, phrases, and sentences. Discuss where writers get the information they research. Mention both print and online sources as ways that students can research topics.

MODEL I'm going to write a short piece to teach about the American Revolution. In order to start with a clear introduction, I need to do some research and organize my facts. I'll use a graphic organizer to keep track of the information I find on dates, people, and events. I'll organize the information to show what I want to cover in each paragraph. If I research and organize beforehand, I can write a clearer introduction.

PRACTICE Ask students to work in small groups to choose a topic they already know about, such as places to visit near where they live. Have them list facts they know about the topic. Have them research at least four new facts. Then ask them to make a graphic organizer to show what might be covered in each paragraph of an informative/explanatory text about the topic.

DEEPER PRACTICE Have students work individually and use their group's graphic organizer to write a clear introduction to the topic that includes introductory words and phrases. Have them share their introductions, discuss what parts are clear, and explain why.

ENGLISH LANGUAGE LEARNERS

If . . . students have trouble naming places people can visit near where they live,

then . . . display a book or travel guide about the area. Ask pairs of students to name places they see in the pictures. Guide them to list their ideas on a sheet of paper and talk about them in complete sentences.

STRUGGLING WRITERS

If . . . students have trouble writing an introduction,

then . . . ask them to refer to the graphic organizer their group put together. Have them place a star next to three of the places in the organizer that they would like to mention in the introduction. Then guide students by providing the following sentence frame: There are many places to visit here, such as ___.

Use Illustrations and Multimedia

What Students Should KNOW	What Students Will DO
• Identify how illustrations, headings, and multimedia are used in texts students read. • Determine what to include in an illustration and how information is best illustrated. • Determine how to use multimedia in a useful manner.	• Include formatting (e.g., headings), illustrations, and multimedia when useful to aid comprehension.

MODEL AND PRACTICE

Review an example of a textbook with students. Point out examples of graphics, such as photos, artwork, diagrams, and charts. Then point out any captions or labels that go with these graphics. Point out references to multimedia, and show students how to access the videos or Web sites to gain additional information about a topic. Explain that headings also help direct readers to understand the topic more clearly and narrow down a topic to aid the reader's comprehension.

MODEL Informative/explanatory texts are not just straightforward writing about a topic. I need to add some headings to help break up the topic, and I'll use graphics to clarify details that may be hard for the reader to grasp. Charts, graphs, and maps help me to explain information in a visual way, and a diagram of a battle can call out important parts. I think I'll include references to Web sites that I found interesting.

PRACTICE Provide students with examples of various graphics and multimedia in informative/explanatory texts. Invite groups of students to make their own chart to list each graphic, header, table, or multimedia. Then have them write how each formatting element helps the reader comprehend different aspects about the topic.

DEEPER PRACTICE Have students write down and describe three different examples they could use for graphics that would make their writing about places to visit near where they live clearer to the reader.

ENGLISH LANGUAGE LEARNERS

If . . . students have trouble explaining how graphics aid the reader's comprehension,

then . . . show students an example of an illustration or other graphic. Ask: What does the picture show? What is the topic about? What does the picture tell about the topic? Ask students to write their own sample caption for the graphic.

STRUGGLING WRITERS

If . . . students have difficulty describing three ways to use graphics to describe places to visit,

then . . . provide them with three sample graphic types and ask: How could this kind of graphic describe where we live? What would you write as a caption? Ask them to make a sample drawing of one of the graphics they describe.

Develop a Topic

What Students Should KNOW	What Students Will DO
• Identify facts, definitions, concrete details, and quotations in familiar texts and how the facts help develop the topic. • Know how to state facts clearly to help develop a topic. • Identify important words to define. • Use proper conventions for including quotations when writing.	• Develop a topic with facts, definitions, concrete details, quotations, and other information and examples.

MODEL AND PRACTICE

Explain to students the importance of developing a topic. Point out that facts, definitions, and details help to make a topic clear and give a topic depth. Quotations and examples are also ways to help develop a topic.

MODEL When I write about the American Revolution, I will need to use facts that help explain my topic. Terms such as *colonists, patriots, loyalists,* and *taxes* are important for my reader to understand, and I will need to define them. I must make them clear as I write. I will also include events that were important, such as the Boston Tea Party and the writing of the Declaration of Independence. I think a quotation from a soldier could also be useful to make the event real to readers.

PRACTICE Gather examples of informative/explanatory texts that students can mark up. Have them highlight definitions and underline facts that clarify the topic. Ask them to circle any quotes from experts or historical figures that further explain the topic.

DEEPER PRACTICE Ask students to choose one of the sites they listed on their graphic organizer, and have them write a paragraph about that place. Ask them to focus on including facts and details about the location. Guide them to use the library or the Internet to locate facts. Challenge them to find a quotation to include in their paragraph. Then ask students to exchange paragraphs with a partner and identify the definitions, facts, and details in the text.

ENGLISH LANGUAGE LEARNERS
If . . . students have trouble identifying which words should be defined in a text,

then . . . help students make a visual dictionary for the topic. Based on research they have done, have partners list topic words they think readers should know. Students can draw a picture for each word. Then have them look up each word in the dictionary and include its definition in their visual dictionary. As they write, students can refer to their visual dictionary. Explain that they should define words from the dictionary that they use often in their writing or that may be unfamiliar to those without the dictionary.

STRUGGLING WRITERS
If . . . students cannot express facts and details clearly,

then . . . ask them to find facts in a resource and read them aloud. Then have them try to restate the same fact in their own words. They may wish to make a two-column chart, with the exact text from the research source on one side and their restated, summarized text on the other side.

Use Linking Words

What Students Should KNOW	What Students Will DO
• Identify linking words and phrases in texts students have read. • Determine the appropriate linking words and phrases to use.	• Use linking words and phrases (e.g., *another, for example, also, because*) to connect related ideas.
• Identify precise language and domain-specific vocabulary in texts students read. • Determine which precise language and domain-specific vocabulary should be used to examine a topic.	• Use precise language and domain-specific vocabulary.

MODEL AND PRACTICE

Discuss with students the importance of good word choices. Give examples of informative/explanatory texts that use words specific to that topic. Tell students that linking words, such as *another, for example, also,* and *because,* can help writers connect ideas clearly and easily.

MODEL When I write facts and details about a topic, I try to use specific words and precise language to express ideas. I also use linking words or phrases to connect the ideas. For example, "The British Parliament placed many taxes on the colonists. For example, taxes were placed on paper, tea, sugar, and stamps." The phrase *for example* connects the idea of taxes to the specific things that were taxed.

PRACTICE Model how to use each linking word and phrase (*another, for example, also, because*), and have students say a sample sentence that uses the linking word or phrase correctly.

DEEPER PRACTICE Invite students to find examples in familiar texts that include the linking words or phrases *another, for example, also,* and *because.* Have students write each sentence with a blank space for the linking word or phrase. Have partners trade papers and try to fill in the missing word or words.

ENGLISH LANGUAGE LEARNERS

If . . . students have trouble understanding linking words or phrases or using them in their writing,

then . . . ask them to look for additional examples of the linking words and phrases *another, for example, also,* and *because* in sample texts. Have them underline each linking word and phrase. Then ask them to highlight which words have a meaning similar to the word *more* (*another* and *also*).

STRUGGLING WRITERS

If . . . students do not use the correct linking words or phrases to combine ideas,

then . . . provide students with practice by giving them a sample paragraph that has the four linking words and phrases mixed up. Ask students to first highlight each of the four linking words or phrases in the paragraph—*another, for example, also,* and *because.* Then have them rearrange the words and phrases so that they appear in the correct places in the paragraph.

Write a Conclusion

What Students Should KNOW	What Students Will DO
• Understand the goal of a concluding statement or section. • Identify the components of a strong conclusion.	• Provide a concluding statement or section related to the information or explanation.

MODEL AND PRACTICE

Begin a discussion with students with students about the importance of having a good concluding statement or section in their writing. Tell students that the conclusion summarizes, or restates, the topic and the most important ideas about the topic. It does not include any new information, and it sometimes provides the reader with a clincher, which is a statement that gives the reader something to think about.

MODEL When it's time to conclude, or end, my text, I think about what I want the reader to remember. I can mention the main ideas that I wrote about the American Revolution. For example, I can write, "There were many problems between the colonists and the British. Yet after years of fighting, the colonies became a free and independent nation. We can be thankful for the hard work and difficult times that the colonists experienced during the war. The colonists helped us to gain our freedom." These last lines are not new information, but they do help to make the reader think.

PRACTICE Provide students with several examples of informative/explanatory texts. Ask students to read each conclusion and analyze them in small groups. Ask students to vote on which conclusion is the strongest, and invite volunteers to give reasons for their vote.

DEEPER PRACTICE Ask each student to write a sample conclusion to the text they are writing about places to visit. Have students trade papers with a partner, and ask the pairs to provide each other with feedback about their conclusions.

ENGLISH LANGUAGE LEARNERS

If . . . students have trouble summarizing the events of their text into a conclusion,

then . . . ask students to name the three main points they would like to mention in their conclusion. Provide sentence frames for students to complete, such as the following: When visiting here, a person might ___.

STRUGGLING WRITERS

If . . . students cannot express a clincher that relates to the topic,

then . . . ask them to consider what they want the reader to ponder when they think of visiting. Have them create a bulleted list of ideas. Guide them to circle their favorite idea and use it to form a clincher sentence for their concluding section.

Support for Extended Writing

Refer to this process when students are writing longer passages that require development, organization, revising, and editing to produce informative/ explanatory texts.

UNDERSTAND THE TASK Tell students to review their writing prompt or writing assignment carefully to be sure they understand what is being asked. Have them answer these questions: What am I asked to write about? What do I already know about my topic? What must I find out about my topic? Where can I find good research information about my topic? Should I cite evidence from texts in my writing? In what order should I organize my ideas and paragraphs? How can I restate the task in my own words? How many parts are there to this writing assignment?

RESEARCH Provide students with guidance and support to research the details of their writing topic. You might wish to have students visit the school library or computer lab in small groups. Make sure they are prepared with the topics they wish to research and questions they hope to answer. Ask students to preview the books they find about their topic before they check them out of the library so that they are sure the books will help them write their response to the prompt. Demonstrate ways they can indicate which pages they want to return to later without damaging the books. Suggest sticky notes instead of folding down pages, and remind them not to write in library books.

TAKE NOTES Model for students how to use their research to take notes about their topic. Introduce various graphic organizers that might help their organization, such as a concept web or a cause-and-effect chart. Remind them to research and take notes about all parts of their writing prompt. You may also help students develop a bank of related words by working with a partner who is writing on a similar topic. Encourage the pairs to group the words into logical categories. Explain how these words may be helpful in searching for information as well as in their writing.

ORGANIZE INFORMATION Ask students to choose the best organization form for their writing topic. Suggest that they choose from compare-and-contrast, cause-and-effect, sequence, description, or problem-and-solution formats. Provide an example of each, and show students graphic organizers that can help them to visually understand how their content would be organized and discussed.

WRITE

Provide students with encouraging tips to guide them through their writing process. Some tips might include:

- Remind students that they are writing a draft, and that their drafts should concentrate on the facts and details of the topic. They should not worry about making everything perfect at this point.

- Explain to students that they must use their own words when they summarize their research notes.

- If students have difficulty beginning to write their first draft, encourage them to look at their notes and write one sentence. Then ask them where that sentence would best fit into the whole text. Encourage them to take it one sentence at a time.

- Remind students to concentrate on an effective introduction and conclusion.

- When students are finished, have them double check that they have answered all parts of the writing prompt or assignment and cited or referenced any related texts included in the prompt.

REVISE AND EDIT

Guide students through the revising and editing process. Work with students to develop writing checklists for details they might wish to address in their revision. Then work with students to develop a peer review checklist to help them review one another's work and further strengthen their writing. You may use the checklists on the following pages and add details specific to the assignment.

PUBLISH

Provide students with support in presenting their final version. You may wish to set up a news reporter's desk and record students as they sit behind the desk and read their final drafts aloud. Provide students with enough time to enter their work into a computer and include illustrations or photos to go with their work.

ACCELERATED WRITERS

If . . . students have difficulty finding research about their topic,

then . . . ask them to divide their topic into several smaller keywords that they might use to look up the topic in a library's card catalog or database. Encourage them to also use these keywords to research the topic online. Help students learn how to narrow or broaden their topic as needed, based partly on information that is available. Model for students how to record the necessary information to include in a bibliography.

Writer's Checklist

Name _____

Title _____

❏ Did I include an effective introduction that presents the topic?

❏ Are my paragraphs organized clearly and correctly?

❏ Did I cite or reference other texts as needed?

❏ Did I group related information?

❏ Did I use illustrations to help make the topic clearer?

❏ Did I include definitions when necessary?

❏ Did I develop the topic with facts and details?

❏ Did I use quotations effectively?

❏ Did I use linking words and phrases to connect related ideas?

❏ Is my concluding section clear and engaging?

❏ Did I address all parts of the prompt or writing assignment?

❏ Did I review my work for correct capitalization, punctuation, and spelling?

❏ _____

❏ _____

Peer Review Checklist

Name _____

Writer's Name _____

Title _____

❏ Does the introduction describe what the text will be about?

❏ Is the writing clearly organized into paragraphs?

❏ Did the writer cite or reference other texts as needed?

❏ Do illustrations or graphics help make the topic easier to understand?

❏ Are there helpful quotations included?

❏ Does the writing include definitions, facts, and details?

❏ Does the writing have linking words that correctly connect ideas?

❏ Does the writing have a strong conclusion?

❏ Are all parts of the prompt or assignment addressed clearly in the writing?

❏ _____

❏ _____

❏ _____

❏ _____

❏ _____

Unlock Narrative Writing

Hold up an example of a narrative text that students have read as part of one of their reading assignments. Explain that it is an example of narrative writing because the writer is telling about a real or imagined experience or event. Allow students to look through the text and recall what the story is about, and then identify whether the event being described is real or imaginary.

Explain to students that the word *narrative* comes from the word *narrator*. Be sure that students understand that the narrator of a story is the person telling the story. Remind students that the narrator may be a character in the story, or it may be an unseen voice or character who is describing the events. Ask students to work in small groups to brainstorm a list of additional examples of narrative stories they have read. Remind them that narratives can be set in the past, present, or future. As students list examples of narratives, ask them to tell whether the narrator is someone in the story or an unseen voice and when the story is set. After students have successfully listed their own examples of narratives, present students with a mix of different book genres and ask them to identify the narratives.

UNDERSTAND TASK AND TONE

Have volunteers talk about times they have written a story or described their own experiences. Show students examples of narrative writing prompts. Tell students that they will usually be provided with the narrative topic they will be writing about. Remind them that before they begin writing, they must carefully read the assignment and understand all of its parts. They should also make sure they understand the purpose of their writing and who their audience is. Explain that most school assignments will be read by you, their teacher, and students should use a formal but natural tone when writing their story.

REFOCUS ON THE WRITING TYPE

Throughout the year as students read or are asked to write narrative texts, remind them of the key features of this text type. Narrative writing

- tells about a real or imagined experience or event.
- gives descriptive details about events or characters.
- includes a logical sequence of events.
- describes characters and events that the narrator may or may not be part of.
- may include dialogue to help tell a story or to make it more interesting.

Establish a Situation and Introduce Characters

What Students Should KNOW	What Students Will DO
• Identify how a situation is established in narrative texts students have read.	• Orient the reader by establishing a situation.
• Identify what a narrator is and the part it plays in a narrative. • Identify ways that narrators and characters are introduced.	• Orient the reader by introducing a narrator and/or characters.

MODEL AND PRACTICE

Explain that the first part of a narrative situates the reader into the story by establishing the general situation and introducing the narrator and characters. Point out that sometimes the narrator is one of the characters, and sometimes the narrator is only the storyteller. Show examples of situations, narrators, and characters in familiar texts.

MODEL When I write a narrative, I must spend some time at the beginning to orient the reader to the story. My story will be about what I did during my favorite summer as a child. I am the narrator and the main character, so I will use the words *I* or *me* to talk about myself. My story will be set at my grandmother's beach house when I was eight, and it will tell what I did week by week through the whole summer. Other characters will be my parents, my little sister, and my grandmother. I'll make a web to help me think about ways I can describe each person.

PRACTICE Provide students with a short narrative text they have read before. Ask pairs of students to identify the situation, the narrator, and the characters in the text.

DEEPER PRACTICE Have students work individually to make a list of things they would write about if they had to write about their own summer break. Ask them to include the situation and characters and identify the narrator.

ENGLISH LANGUAGE LEARNERS

If . . . students have trouble identifying the narrator of a story,

then . . . display a picture book that is narrated by the main character and one that is not. Point to the narrator character and say: This character is the narrator. He/She is telling the story. Then point to the main character in the other story. Say: This character is not the narrator. We cannot see who is telling this story.

STRUGGLING WRITERS

If . . . students have trouble expressing what they will be writing about,

then . . . ask them to use the notes they wrote about the situation in their story. Ask: What was the most interesting thing that happened? Provide students with a sentence frame, if necessary: My narrative will be about ___.

Organize an Event Sequence

What Students Should KNOW	What Students Will DO
• Retell events in the correct sequence from familiar texts. • Determine how to organize a sequence of events in a logical, natural way.	• Organize an event sequence that unfolds naturally.

MODEL AND PRACTICE

Begin a discussion about the sequence of events in a story. Explain that stories make the most sense when they are told in a logical order, from beginning to end. Create a non-example by asking what would happen if one of the stories they are familiar with had been told in a different, illogical order.

MODEL If I wrote my family story out of order, it wouldn't make much sense. The reader would be confused, and the story would not be as enjoyable. So I will organize my writing and think about using a paragraph for each week of my vacation. This is how the vacation happened, so I'm going to tell the story that way, too.

PRACTICE Ask students to think about a narrative that they have read as a class together. Invite students to recall the events of the story and write them down. Remind students to arrange the events in the order they were told in the story. Start a class discussion about why it makes sense to tell the events in this order.

DEEPER PRACTICE Have students write a sentence about each event for their narrative in a list. Tell them to leave a few inches between each item on the list. Have students cut out each item on their list, shuffle them, and give them to a partner to put in the correct order.

ENGLISH LANGUAGE LEARNERS

If . . . students have trouble describing events in the correct order,

then . . . read them a short story from the classroom library. Have them draw each scene on a separate piece of paper. Then shuffle the drawings and ask students to put them in the correct order, using sequence words, such as *first, second, next, then,* and *finally,* to describe each picture.

STRUGGLING WRITERS

If . . . students have difficulty retelling events in a logical order,

then . . . encourage them to draw a comic strip with four panels to help them think about a logical progression from left to right as it relates to the events from beginning to end. Have them explain each event on the comic strip in the correct order.

Use Transitional Words and Phrases

What Students Should KNOW	What Students Will DO
• Identify transitional words and phrases in texts students read. • Identify how transitional words and phrases help readers understand the sequence of events.	• Use a variety of transitional words and phrases to manage the sequence of events.

MODEL AND PRACTICE

Explain to students the importance of using transitional words and phrases to help show the sequence of events and to tell the story in a way that makes sense.

MODEL Now that I know the order in which I will tell my story about my summer vacation as a child, I will use transitional words and phrases to help make my story clear and flow well for the reader. I'll use transitional words to help the reader understand the sequence. I can write, "First, Grandma bought us new beach toys, and then we dug in the sand for hours. After dinner, we walked along the beach to see the sunset."

PRACTICE Gather examples of narratives from the class library or from the reading program. Have small groups of students look through the books and write down transitional words that signal the sequence of events. Invite students to compare their lists when they are finished.

DEEPER PRACTICE Ask students to write a paragraph about their own summer vacation, using at least three different transitional words to signal the sequence of events. Have them underline each transitional word or phrase.

ENGLISH LANGUAGE LEARNERS

If . . . students have trouble using the correct transitions between events,

then . . . show students the comic section of a newspaper, and focus on one comic to read together. Point to each panel, saying *first, next, then,* and *finally* before you read the panel to students. Then invite students to retell the events of the comic in order, using the correct transition words.

STRUGGLING WRITERS

If . . . students have trouble indicating when transition words are needed,

then . . . ask them to place a star on their writing page to show where one event ends and the other begins. When they are done placing all of the stars, explain that these are the places where sequence words belong. Challenge them to place the correct words themselves, and then guide them to find the best word for the situation.

Use Dialogue, Descriptions, and Sensory Details

What Students Should KNOW	What Students Will DO
• Identify dialogue and descriptions in texts students read. • Know how to write dialogue correctly.	• Use dialogue and description to develop experiences and events or show the responses of characters to situations.
• Identify concrete words and phrases and sensory details in texts students read. • Improve sentences by adding concrete details and phrases and sensory details.	• Use concrete words and phrases and sensory details to convey experiences and events precisely.

MODEL AND PRACTICE

Discuss with students the importance of dialogue, descriptions, and sensory details in narrative writing. Review what the senses are and how they relate to details. Tell students that these are ways to develop experiences and events, or to show the responses of characters to situations. They keep the reader's interest.

MODEL I like to include dialogue in my narratives so that the reader can get a sense of what the characters are like and how they respond to different events and situations. Descriptive and sensory details also help me tell my story. I can write, "My first sandcastle of the summer glistened in the hot sun and caught the eye of every beachgoer. 'Wonderful work, kids,' said Grandma, showing her pride in us." I need to be careful about how I punctuate dialogues.

PRACTICE Have small groups work together, and assign each group an object in the classroom or on the playground. Have students brainstorm a list of descriptive words and sensory details about the object. Then have them write a short dialogue that two students might say to each other about the object.

DEEPER PRACTICE Invite the groups to break further into pairs. Each pair will use the notes their group took about the object to write a descriptive paragraph that includes dialogue and sensory details.

ENGLISH LANGUAGE LEARNERS

If . . . students have trouble using sensory words or details,

then . . . show them a photo and have them choose one part of the photo to describe. Ask them to describe color, shape, size, and any other details about the photo. List the words, and work together to incorporate those words into a complete sentence.

STRUGGLING WRITERS

If . . . students have trouble thinking of dialogue that characters might say,

then . . . invite pairs of students to act out an event in a narrative. Remind students to talk naturally about what is happening as part of the story's event. When they finish, ask writers what of the spoken dialogue they might include in their writing. Review how to punctuate dialogues using models from familiar texts.

Write a Conclusion

What Students Should KNOW	What Students Will DO
• Identify examples of closure in narrative texts students read. • Explain how the conclusion follows from the narrated experiences or events in texts students read. • Identify the components of a strong conclusion.	• Provide a conclusion that follows from the narrated experiences or events.

MODEL AND PRACTICE

Explain to students that narrative writing should have a sense of closure, or a clear conclusion. Tell students that a conclusion should be straightforward and to the point and that it should summarize the moral, lesson, or theme of the story if one exists. Explain that a conclusion to a narrative should signal a definite end to the story, solve any story conflicts, and be memorable for the reader.

MODEL When I get to the end of my narrative, I'll include a paragraph that sums up my feelings about the summer I spent as a child and lets the reader know why it was special. For example, I could write, "After weeks at the sunny beach, taking care of my dad's vegetable garden at home and reading some great books, I was sad to see the relaxing summer end. I wished it could go on forever. But I was also happy to return to school to see my friends."

PRACTICE Provide students with several examples of narrative texts. Ask students to read each conclusion and analyze them in small groups. Have them identify whether the conclusion summarizes a moral, lesson, or theme. Ask students to vote on which conclusion is the strongest, and invite volunteers to give reasons for their vote.

DEEPER PRACTICE Ask students to write a conclusion for their own narrative about their summer vacation. Have students trade papers with a partner, and then have the pairs provide each other with feedback.

ENGLISH LANGUAGE LEARNERS

If . . . students have trouble summarizing the events of their narrative into a conclusion,

then . . . ask students to underline the three main points of their narrative. Provide sentence frames for students to complete: During the summer, I ___, ___, and ___. I felt ___ when summer was over.

STRUGGLING WRITERS

If . . . students write a conclusion that does not relate well enough to the narrative topic,

then . . . ask them to fold a sheet of paper into three parts and write three ideas from their writing that they think should be included in their conclusion. Have them use the notes to guide them in writing the concluding section.

Support for Extended Writing

Refer to this process when students are writing a longer passage that requires development, organization, revising, and editing to produce a narrative text.

UNDERSTAND THE TASK Tell students to review their writing prompt or writing assignment carefully to be sure they understand what is being asked. Have them answer these questions: What am I asked to write about? How can I restate the task in my own words? What should I include in my narrative? In what order should I write about the events or experiences? Am I the narrator or one of the characters in this narrative? Have I referenced any texts that are part of the assignment? How many parts are there to this writing assignment? Is there a lesson or moral I want the reader to learn?

BRAINSTORM Provide students with guidance and support to brainstorm the details of their narrative. Explain that just because they think of an idea first does not mean that the idea is the best one to use. Encourage them to continue brainstorming additional ideas, even after they think they have found the idea they want to write about. Then have students review their lists carefully and choose the strongest idea that could be used to answer the prompt fully.

TAKE NOTES Model for students how to take notes about the narrator, characters, and sequence of events in their story. Have them write down details about the story, including the story's setting and characters. Encourage them to refer back to the notes regularly as they write. They should use it as a checklist to see that they have covered everything they wanted to and have written the story the way they intended to during their planning stage.

ORGANIZE INFORMATION Use a story map graphic organizer. Explain that the organizer has a box for each of the parts of their story: the beginning, the middle, and the end. Show them how to use the boxes to record the major events of the plot. Explain that each box on the organizer can represent a paragraph or group of paragraphs in the story.

WRITE

Provide students with encouraging tips to guide them through their writing process. Some tips might include:

- Remind students that they are writing a draft, which should concentrate on the major events of their story, not the small details of making everything perfect.
- Explain to students that the more planning they do ahead of time, the easier their narrative will be to follow.
- If students have difficulty beginning to write their first draft, encourage them to look at their notes and write one sentence. Then ask them where that sentence would best fit into the whole text. Encourage them to take it one sentence at a time.
- Encourage students to think of details that can be added to help the reader imagine how things in the story looked, smelled, sounded, tasted, or felt.
- Remind students to concentrate on an effective introduction and conclusion.
- When students are finished, have them double check that they have answered all parts of the writing prompt or assignment and cited or referenced any related texts included in the prompt.

REVISE AND EDIT

Guide students through the revising and editing process. Work with students to develop writing checklists for details they might wish to address in their revision. Then work with students to develop a peer review checklist to help them review one another's work and further strengthen their writing. Use the checklists on the following pages and add details specific to the assignment.

PUBLISH

Provide students with support in presenting their final version. You may want to set up a time for students to illustrate their final work and read it aloud to classmates. You may wish to record their presentations and help students load the presentations to a class or school Web site or blog.

ACCELERATED WRITERS

If . . . students have difficulty deciding when their final drafts are ready to be reviewed,

then . . . suggest that students focus on the writer's checklist and point to a specific place in their narrative where they feel the item was met. When they have gone through the whole list and found that they met all of the criteria, ask them to hand in their paper. Explain that they will always be free to go back later, after the paper has been reviewed or graded, to make additional changes if they wish.

Writer's Checklist

Name _____

Title _____

❑ Did I include an effective introduction that presented the topic?

❑ Are my paragraphs organized clearly and correctly?

❑ Did I choose a real or imagined experience to write about?

❑ Did I establish the setting and situation of the narrative?

❑ Did I establish and introduce the narrator and/or characters?

❑ Did I organize the events in a sequence that unfolds naturally?

❑ Did I develop the story with dialogue?

❑ Did I develop the story with descriptions and sensory details?

❑ Did I use linking words and phrases?

❑ Did I provide a strong conclusion?

❑ Did I address all parts of the prompt or writing assignment?

❑ Did I reference or cite any texts called for in the assignment?

❑ Did I review my work for correct capitalization, punctuation, and spelling?

❑ _____

❑ _____

Peer Review Checklist

Name _____

Writer's Name _____

Title _____

❏ Does the introduction describe what the narrative will be about?

❏ Is the writing clearly organized into paragraphs?

❏ Are the narrator and characters clearly identified?

❏ Does the writing organize events in a sequence that unfolds naturally?

❏ Does the writing include dialogue, descriptions, and sensory details?

❏ Does the writing have linking words that show a sequence of events?

❏ Does the writing have a strong conclusion that summarizes and ends the story?

❏ Are all parts of the prompt or assignment addressed clearly in the writing?

❏ _____

❏ _____

❏ _____

❏ _____

❏ _____

PART 3

Routines and Activities

Part 3 Routines and Activities

Reading Routines

Quick Write and Share. 258
Ask and Answer Questions 259
Three-Column Chart with Graphic Organizer 261
Venn Diagram with Graphic Organizer. 263
Web with Graphic Organizer. 265
Story Map with Graphic Organizer. 267
Story Prediction Chart with Graphic Organizer 269
Story Comparison with Graphic Organizer 271
KWLH Chart with Graphic Organizer. 273
Main Idea and Details with Graphic Organizer 275
Problem and Solution with Graphic Organizer 277
Cause and Effect with Graphic Organizer 279
Steps in a Process with Graphic Organizer. 281
Sequence of Events with Graphic Organizer. 283
Time Line with Graphic Organizer 285
Draw Conclusions with Graphic Organizer 287

Writing Routines

Narrative Paragraph Writing with Graphic Organizer. 289
Narrative Essay Writing with Graphic Organizer. 291
Informative/Explanatory Writing with Graphic Organizer 293
Opinion Writing with Graphic Organizer 295
Description: Sensory Details with Graphic Organizer 297

Listening and Speaking Routines

Retell or Summarize with Graphic Organizer 299
Monitor Understanding: Listening Skills Log 301
Express Opinions 303
Prepare for Discussions 304
Understanding Media 306

Language Routines and Activities:
Vocabulary and Conventions

Preview and Review Vocabulary. 307
Act Out or Draw Meaning with Graphic Organizer 308
Analyze Cognates 310
Word Knowledge Strategy 313
Multisyllabic Word Strategy 314
Analyze Idioms and Expressions 315
Analyze Multiple-Meaning Words. 316

Noun Activities

Common Nouns 317
Proper Nouns 317
Titles and Abbreviations 318
Days, Months, and Holidays 318
Singular and Plural Nouns. 319
Irregular Plural Nouns 319
Singular Possessive Nouns. 320
Plural Possessive Nouns. 320

Pronoun Activities

Possessive Pronouns. 321
Subject Pronouns. 321
Object Pronouns 322
Indefinite Pronouns 322
Reflexive Pronouns 323
Pronouns and Antecedents. 323

Verb Activities

Verbs in Present Tense 324
Verbs in Past Tense 324
Irregular Verbs 325
Verbs in Future Tense 325
Principal Parts of Regular Verbs. 326
Principal Parts of Irregular Verbs 326
Helping Verbs 327
Linking Verbs 327
Troublesome Verbs *Lie/Lay, Sit/Set* 328
Troublesome Verbs *Leave/Let, Rise/Raise* 328
Contractions. 329
Negatives 329

Articles and Adjective Activities

Articles 330
Adjectives: Size, What Kind, How Many 330
Adjectives: Comparative and Superlative 331
Adjectives: Demonstrative 331

Adverb Activities

Adverbs for *When, Where,* and *How* 332
Comparative and Superlative Adverbs 332

Preposition and Conjunction Activities

Prepositions and Prepositional Phrases 333
Conjunctions 333

Sentence Activities

Subjects and Predicates 334
Subject-Verb Agreement 334
Word Order 335
Complete Sentences and Sentence Fragments 335
Types of Sentences: Statements 336
Types of Sentences: Questions 336
Types of Sentences: Exclamations and Interjections 337
Types of Sentences: Commands 337
Simple and Compound Sentences 338
Combining Sentences 338
Complex Sentences 339
Independent and Dependent Clauses 339

Punctuation Activities

Commas: In a Series and in Direct Address 340
Commas: With Appositives and Introductory Phrases 340
Quotation Marks 341
Parentheses 341

Word Study Activities

Plurals and Possessives 342
Verb Endings: *-s, -ed, -ing* 343
Compound Words 344
Related Words 345
Homophones 346
Prefixes: *un-, re-* 347
Prefixes: *im-, in-, mis-, over-* 348
Prefixes: *pre-, mid-, over-, out-, bi-* 349
Suffixes: *-ly, -ful, -less, -ness* 350
Suffixes: *-tion, -sion, -able, -ible* 351
Suffixes: *-er, -or, -ess, -ist* 352
Suffixes: *-y, -ish, -hood, -ment* 353
Words with Greek Roots 354
Words with Latin Roots 355
Syllable Patterns: V/CV and VC/V 356
Syllable Patterns: CV/VC 357
Syllable Patterns: VCCCV 358
Syllable Patterns: C + *-le* 359

Vocabulary Activities and Games
. . . . 360

Quick Write and Share

PURPOSE

Use this routine to activate and build on students' prior knowledge before reading a selection.

PROCEDURE

1. Before reading a selection, pose a question to activate students' prior knowledge about a topic they will read about. Give students a few minutes to immediately jot down their ideas. Because this is a quick write, tell students that they do not need to worry about grammar or spelling.

2. Review class rules for discussion. Remind students of the proper methods for sharing ideas, such as who goes first, what to do while someone else is speaking, and when it is okay to take a turn.

3. As a class, or in small groups or pairs, ask students to share their ideas with others in their group. Encourage students to make comments that contribute to the discussion and elaborate on the remarks of others. Again, remind them that each person should speak without interruption so that everyone has a chance to share. Walk around to assess the prior knowledge of each group and to clarify questions.

TEACHING TIPS

- When creating questions for step one, make sure they are text specific and that answering them will help students unlock ideas in the text. For example, before starting a book on jungle frogs and their habitats, it would be appropriate to ask questions such as: *How might a jungle frog look or act differently than a frog in your backyard?* or *Why might a frog live in the jungle?* These questions are appropriate because they are specific to the text and ask students to recall information that will help them when reading. An inappropriate question would be *Do you like frogs?* because it is not text specific, and responding to the question will not help students unlock ideas in the text.

- Additionally, it may benefit students to read a short paragraph or excerpt relating to a key idea or topic in the text. This will help students gain confidence going into the text because it will ensure that everyone will have some foundational understanding of the text.

EXTEND

- Have one student from each group share ideas from their discussion with the class. Use student responses to create a class list or web of prior knowledge, and display the list/web permanently in the classroom. This will act as a continual reminder to students of what they already know. As students acquire new knowledge, the information can be added to the list/web so they can see how their understanding is growing.

- After reading an excerpt relating to a key idea or topic of the text, have pairs discuss and write one or two questions on what they hope to learn as they read the rest of the text. Students may revisit their questions after reading to check whether their initial questions have been answered. Point out that further research may be needed to find the answers to questions that might not have been answered by reading. Guide students to appropriate resources to assist research.

Ask and Answer Questions

PURPOSE

Use this routine to build on students' use of asking and answering questions to better understand a text.

PROCEDURE

1. Use text that the class is currently reading. As a warm-up activity, review *how* and *wh-* questions, such as *Where does the princess live with the frogs? How do tarantulas shed their skin? What is a tall tale? Where are earthquakes most likely to happen? Why do glaciers melt?* Go around the class and have students take turns asking questions orally. (If students want to answer questions, give them the chance to do so.)

2. Choose a short passage, paragraph, or chapter from the text the class is currently reading. If the passage is short, you may want to read the text aloud as students follow along.

3. Model specific examples of questions relating to the selection, such as *Why are roots different shapes? Where do you find long, skinny roots? Which kind of root lives in water?* Invite students to think of their own questions to ask about the text.

4. If the class has completed reading the entire selection, you can have students ask questions based on the text as a whole, including questions about main idea, themes, or character development.

5. Hand out copies of the worksheet on the following page and direct students to the selection or passage. Explain that students should refer directly to the selection to ask and answer questions about it.

TEACHING TIPS

- Encourage students to ask themselves questions as they read on their own. For fiction, students might ask: *What is the problem in the story? What is the main character like? What is happening in the story now?* For informational text, students might ask: *What interesting facts did I learn so far? What else do I want to learn?* Answering these questions will help students understand and remember what they read.

- Students may go beyond the text and ask, *How could he or she have acted differently? How could the conflict have been resolved differently?* In informational texts, help students make connections between the facts. Have them consider the kinds of sources and how they are used to support opinions.

EXTEND

After completing Step B on the worksheet, ask students to share their most challenging questions with the class and have other students try to answer them. This will allow students to understand the text more fully and share what they already know. Encourage students to discuss ideas for further reading or research to find the answers to their questions and build overall knowledge about the topic.

Ask and Answer Questions

A. Read the text. On the first lines below, write three questions you think of as you read the text. The questions may be about details in the text, or they may be about ideas the text brings up.

1. Question: _____

_____

_____

2. Question: _____

_____

_____

3. Question: _____

_____

_____

B. Exchange papers with a classmate. Read your classmate's questions in Step A. Write your responses to the questions below.

1. Response: _____

_____

_____

2. Response: _____

_____

_____

3. Response: _____

_____

_____

Three-Column Chart

PURPOSE

Use this routine with the Three-Column Chart Graphic Organizer. This is a multipurpose organizer that works well for exploring and organizing ideas for three concepts, words, or ideas. It works well with many selections and can aid students in exploring or classifying ideas, story elements, genres, or vocabulary features. It can also help students recognize comparisons and contrasts or chart ideas within and across texts.

PROCEDURE

1. Display the organizer. Choose three headings and write them on the chart, such as three different concepts.
2. Ask students for details or examples for each heading and record them on the chart. Details or examples should directly reference the text.
3. Point out that this chart helps students organize information and explore new ideas.
4. Ask students for any comparisons, contrasts, or patterns they notice in the chart.

TEACHING TIPS

- Once you have modeled how to use the organizer, students can complete the organizer independently, in pairs, or in small groups.
- Students can include quoted text in the charts, as well as list ideas.
- Students can use the three-column chart to explore story characteristics or characteristics of a genre.
- Students can use the chart to organize ideas they generate during brainstorming.
- Students can use the chart to organize synonyms, antonyms, and multiple-meaning words. Create a class chart to model using the chart for vocabulary study.

EXTEND

- Students can use the organizer to record events or happenings that follow the *before*, *during*, and *after* format in a selection. For example, ask students to record key points of character development in one selection. *How do the characters resolve the main conflict? As you read about them from the beginning to the end of the story, how does their way of thinking or behavior change?* Remind them to include examples from the text to support their responses.
- Students can use the organizer to compare a variety of selection elements, such as characters within or across selections, structures across selections, or themes across selections.
- After completing the class activity, have students use the chart in pairs or individually with another selection. Then have them share their charts in small groups.

Three-Column Chart

Venn Diagram

PURPOSE

Use this routine with the Venn Diagram Graphic Organizer. This graphic organizer works well in any situation that lends itself to comparing and contrasting. Students can use this organizer to record similarities and differences between places, ideas, characters, or other elements of fiction or nonfiction.

PROCEDURE

1. Start by comparing and contrasting something simple, such as plants and animals. Write the names of the subjects you are comparing at the top of the circles of the Venn diagram.

2. Point to where the circles overlap. Let students know that in this section you'll write similarities, or how the two things are alike. Ask how the two subjects are alike. Record students' responses. (Both plants and animals need water to survive.)

3. Point to an individual circle and let students know that in this section they will write details that describe only what is labeled at the top of the circle. Then ask how the two subjects are different and record students' responses. (Animals need shelter. Plants need soil.)

TEACHING TIPS

- Ask questions that lead students to share details for the diagram, such as: *Where is the village located? Describe the weather.*

- Display sentence frames to guide students. Examples: These two characters are alike because ___. These two settings are different because ___.

- List words that signal comparing and contrasting, such as *alike*, *different*, and *but*. Students can point out those words and supporting examples in the text.

EXTEND

- Have students create Venn diagrams to compare characters in two fictional texts. Ask them to draw details from the texts to fill out the Venn diagram. Ask volunteers to present their ideas to the class.

- Have students use Venn diagrams to compare topics in informational texts, such as two different accounts of a historical event, two locations, or two time periods.

- Have students use Venn diagrams to compare structural elements of literary and informational texts. Point out that informational texts contain facts and visuals, such as photographs that may have labels, graphs, charts, and diagrams. Literary texts contain a made-up story with illustrations or photographs. Both texts may be organized by chapter and include a table of contents.

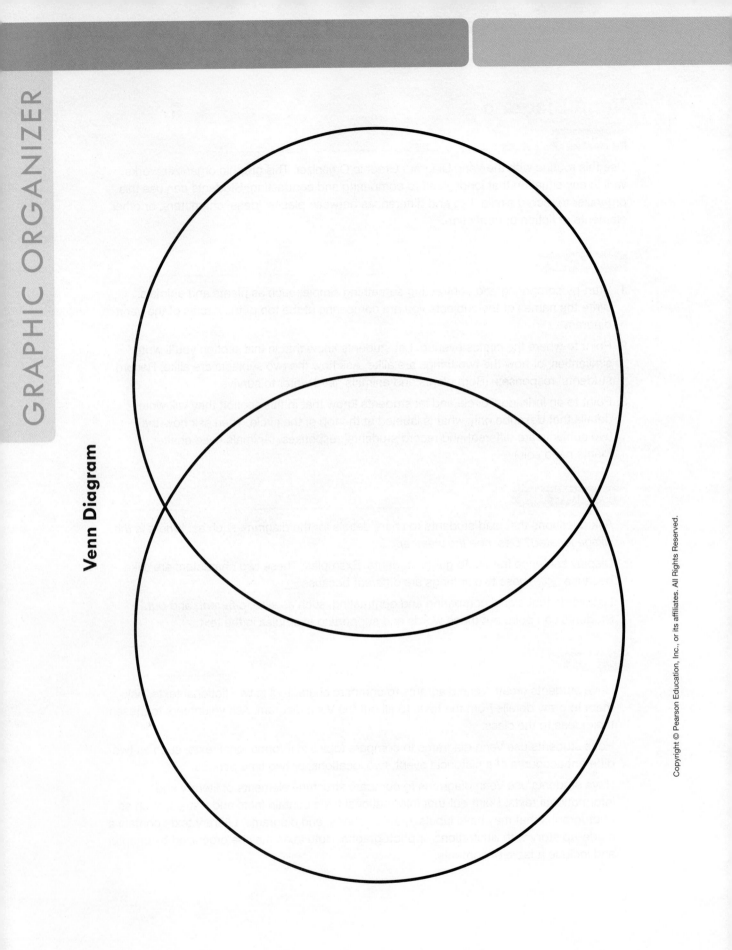

Venn Diagram

Web

PURPOSE

Use this routine along with the Web Graphic Organizer to help students activate their background knowledge as they brainstorm related ideas, recognize concept relationships, or organize information. This organizer can also be used to highlight a central concept and connect it to related words, ideas, or details.

PROCEDURE

1. Display the organizer. Write a central idea or topic in the middle of the web.
2. Ask students for ideas that are related to the central idea. Record those ideas in the circles attached to the middle circle.
3. You can add ideas related to the "subideas" in additional ovals.

TEACHING TIPS

- Once you have modeled how to use the organizer, have students complete the organizer independently, in pairs, or in small groups.
- Ask students to explain how the ideas on the web are related to the central idea. Display sentence frames to help students talk about the web: The main idea is ___. One related idea is ___.
- Use this web to help students to record and organize information, such as main ideas and details, theme or topic, characters and their traits, and vocabulary words with their synonyms.
- As an aid to understanding what they've read, students may use this graphic organizer to record ideas and concepts across texts. For example, they may take notes about one topic from two separate texts. Recording main points and related details will help students classify ideas and examine the relationships between texts.

EXTEND

- Have students use the web to record background knowledge about a topic. Use the webs to assess gaps in understanding as you plan instruction.
- After students create a web, have them write a paragraph telling how the concepts are connected.

Web

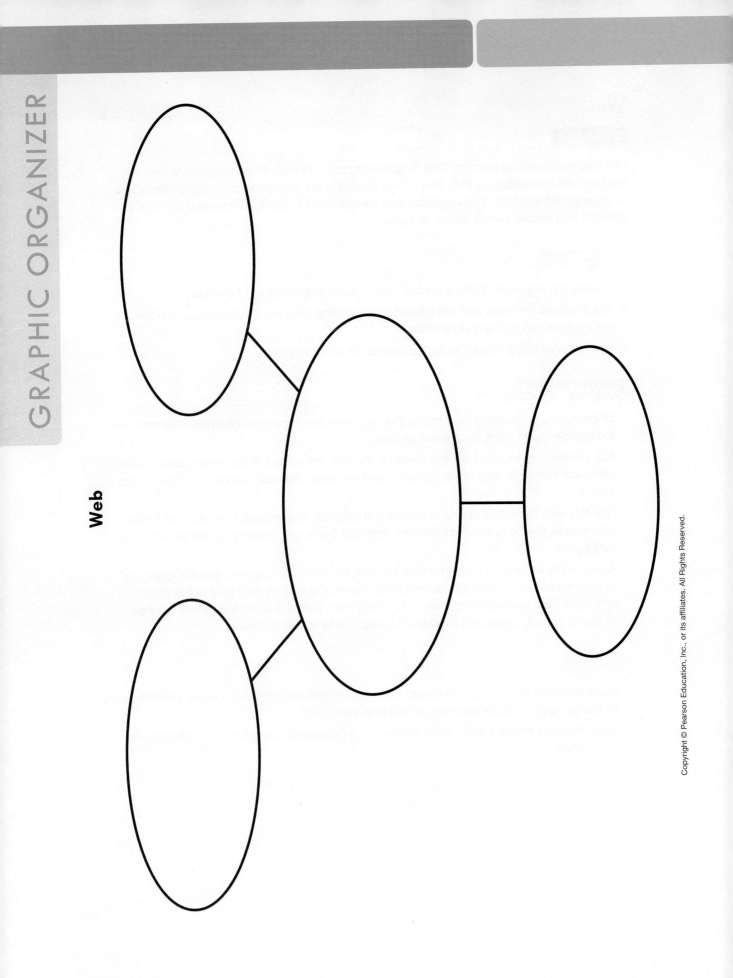

Story Map

PURPOSE

Use this routine with the Story Map Graphic Organizer. This organizer works well with any text that has a clear sequence of events. This graphic organizer can aid students in recording the sequence of events in a text.

PROCEDURE

1. Display the organizer. Write the title of the text on the graphic organizer.
2. As you read, record information about characters on the graphic organizer.
3. Read the text. Ask students where and when the story takes place. Record those details in the Setting section.
4. As you read, pause to record information about the sequence of events.

TEACHING TIPS

- Model talking about characters and setting: ___ *is a person/an animal in this story. This story takes place (in the future, in the past, today).*
- Help students look for clue words for sequence. Make a list of clue words to display for students' reference.
- Students may not need all the lines, or they may need more. Help them modify the organizer depending on the story.
- Help students look for details that tell more about a character's thoughts, words, and actions.

EXTEND

- After completing this activity as a class exercise, have students use the graphic organizer in pairs, small groups, or independently.
- Students can draw events in the organizer and label those events.
- Help students think of words to describe characters or events. Make a list and have students add to it. As they list the descriptive words and phrases, help them identify any antonyms in the text. For example, a character may be introduced as competitive and unwilling to share and then later be described as friendly, helpful, and collaborative.

Story Map

Title

_____

Characters

Who is in the story?

_____

Setting

Where does the story happen?

_____

When does the story happen?

_____

Events

What happens in the story?

_____

_____

_____

_____

_____

_____

_____

Story Prediction Chart

PURPOSE

Use this routine with the Story Prediction Chart Graphic Organizer. Students preview the text's title and illustrations and then predict what might happen in the text. This graphic organizer works well with any text in which the title and/or pictures suggest predictions about the events in a story. Consider using it for content-area texts as well.

PROCEDURE

1. Display the graphic organizer.

2. Preview the text with students. Read the title and lead a picture walk. Tell students: You make predictions when you use clues from the story, such as these pictures and what you know from your own experiences, to figure out what will happen next. Record their predictions in the graphic organizer in the first column.

3. Ask students how they figured out what would happen. Ask: Have you read a story like this before? What evidence from the pictures helped you figure out what would happen next? Record the clues they used in the graphic organizer in the second column.

4. After reading, look back at the predictions. Write what actually happened in the third column. Ask students if their predictions were different from what happened. Ask: Why do you think the story turned out differently than you predicted? Why might making predictions be a useful skill?

TEACHING TIPS

- Focus on clues in illustrations. What details in the illustrations help students make predictions?

- Provide sentence frames for predicting, such as: I think ___ will happen. I think this will happen because ___.

- Remind students that good readers need to think ahead to get a better understanding of the story. As they read, have them pay attention to characters, setting, and events so far. For example, they may wonder why a character is behaving a certain way. Have students make continual adjustments to their predictions as they read.

EXTEND

- After completing this activity as a class exercise, have students use the graphic organizer in pairs, small groups, or independently.

- Use the graphic organizer with content-area texts. Focus on the content, giving students a sentence frame to use: I think I will learn about ___ because ___.

Story Prediction Chart

Title _____

What might happen?	What clues do I have?	What did happen?

Story Comparison

PURPOSE

Use this routine with the Story Comparison Graphic Organizer. Students can use this graphic organizer to record how two texts are similar and different. This organizer works well with texts that have something in common. It is a great tool for comparing texts by the same author, about the same topic, or in the same genre.

PROCEDURE

1. Display the graphic organizer for students.
2. Choose two stories to compare. Write their titles on the graphic organizer.
3. Ask questions to elicit characters, setting, and plot events. Guide students to think about the comparisons they will make. For example, ask: How are these accounts of legends similar? What qualities do the characters share or not share?
4. Record details on the graphic organizer.

TEACHING TIPS

- After you model how to use the graphic organizer, students can work on their graphic organizer with partners or in small groups.
- Provide sentence frames for comparison and model how to use them, such as The characters in this story are ___, but the characters in that story are ___.
- Invite students to use the graphic organizer to retell stories.

EXTEND

- Students can use this graphic organizer to compare a fictional story and a nonfiction text about the same topic.
- Have students use one half of the graphic organizer to plan the writing of their own stories. Ask volunteers to share their original stories with the rest of the class. You may wish to display the graphic organizer and lead a discussion in filling it out after two stories have been shared.

Story Comparison

Title A _____

_____

Title B _____

_____

Characters

Who is in the story?

Characters

Who is in the story?

Setting

Where and **when** does it happen?

Setting

Where and **when** does it happen?

Events

What happens in the story?

Events

What happens in the story?

KWLH Chart

PURPOSE

Use this routine with the KWLH Chart Graphic Organizer. Students can use what they know to explore prior knowledge about a text, set purposes for reading, and record what they learn and how they learned it as they read. This graphic organizer works well with expository texts.

PROCEDURE

1. Display the graphic organizer for students. Have volunteers read aloud the question at the top of each column.

2. Before students begin reading, ask them for ideas to answer the first two questions of the KWLH chart: What Do I **K**now? What Do I **W**ant to Learn? Model recording responses on the graphic organizer. Explain that answering these questions sets objectives for reading and helps students focus on what they read.

3. Read the text together or have students read on their own.

4. After reading the text, model recording students' responses to the questions in the *L* and *H* columns: What Did I **L**earn? **H**ow Did I Learn It?

TEACHING TIPS

- After your modeling, students can complete the graphic organizer in pairs or small groups. Have students take turns reading parts of the chart aloud with their partner or within the group. Have volunteers share their work with the class.

- Modify the graphic organizer, if necessary, by changing the headings into sentence frames: I know ___. I want to learn ___. I learned ___. I learned it by ___.

EXTEND

- Use the graphic organizer as you read in various content areas, such as social studies and science. Post the organizers around the room. Students can add to them as they learn more about a topic over time.

- After reading, challenge students to identify information they wanted to learn that was not provided in the text. Have them do research online or at the library to find that information. For any questions that will require further research, ask what kind of resources they will use to find answers.

KWLH Chart

Topic ———

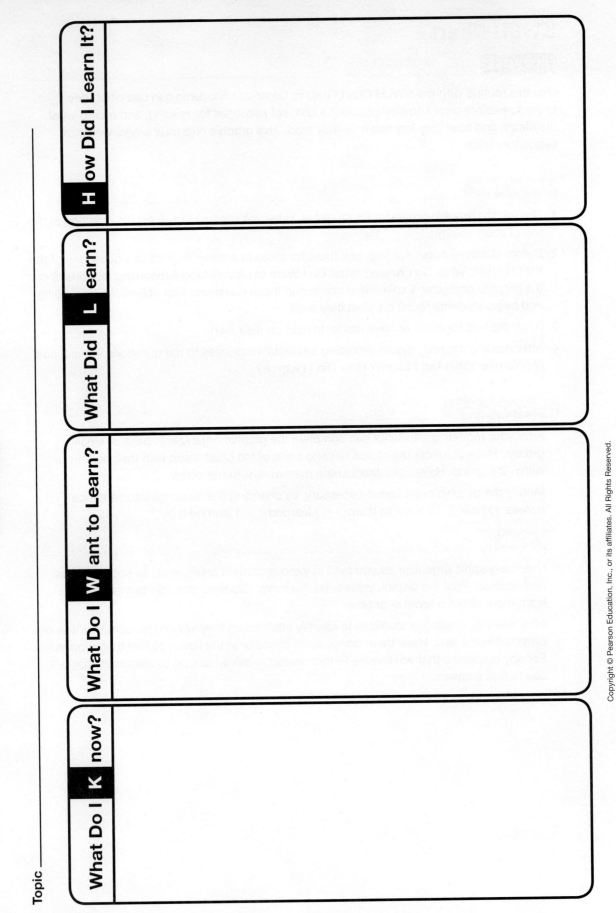

What Do I **K** now?	What Do I **W** ant to Learn?	What Did I **L** earn?	**H** ow Did I Learn It?

Main Idea and Details

Use this routine with the Main Idea and Details Graphic Organizer. This graphic organizer works especially well with nonfiction selections that are organized around main ideas and details. Students recognize a main idea and distinguish between the main idea and the details. Use it with an entire selection, individual chapters, a section, or a paragraph in a selection.

PROCEDURE

1. Read the selection. Record the main idea in the top box. Define *main idea* as the most important idea.

2. Use a think aloud to model how to find a detail in the selection that supports, or tells more about, the main idea. For example, say We found that the main idea of this paragraph is to tell why roots have different shapes. As I read, I will look for information that tells about different-shaped roots.

3. Have students supply additional details as you record them. Details should directly refer back to the text.

TEACHING TIPS

- Supply a sentence frame about main ideas, such as: The most important idea is ___. Supply a sentence frame about details, such as: One detail about this idea is ___.

- Model how to tell a supporting detail from a detail that is not a supporting detail. Let students know that some ideas are important to know and other ideas are interesting to know. Display part of a selection and model highlighting important ideas.

- Sometimes the main idea isn't included, as in fiction. Teach students that when reading stories, they will need to come up with their own main idea based on details they read. They may ask: *What is this text about? What details best support this idea? Which are unimportant ideas?*

- Extend or add boxes if necessary to add more details.

EXTEND

- Have students use the organizer to record ideas for writing pieces of their own. Have students write a paragraph using the information they record in the graphic organizer.

- As students become more independent, use the organizer in pairs or small groups to record important ideas and details from selections.

Main Idea and Details

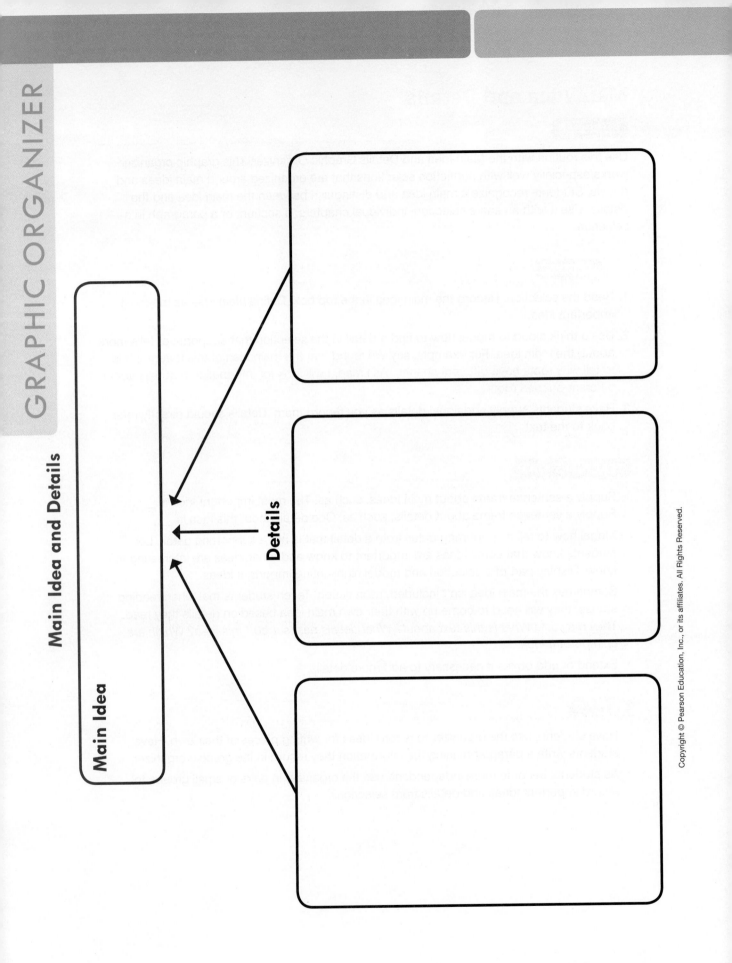

Main Idea

Details

Problem and Solution

PURPOSE

Use this routine with the Problem and Solution Graphic Organizer. This graphic organizer works well with any selection with clear problems and solutions. The organizer can aid students in identifying problems and solutions presented in fiction or nonfiction texts.

PROCEDURE

1. Ask students what they think a problem is, and record answers. Tell students that a problem is something that needs to be solved. Explain: Good readers need to pay attention to the problems and solutions in the text so that they can understand what the important message is, or what the author is telling them. Give an example of a problem from a selection.

2. Record it in the organizer in the Problem section.

3. Ask students what happens in the selection to fix the problem. Tell students that fixing a problem is the same as solving a problem.

4. Record their responses in the Solution section. Student responses should reference the text directly.

TEACHING TIPS

- Point out that not all solutions are "good." Sometimes the way a character solves a problem might result in an unhappy ending for the story. Lead a discussion that prompts students to think about how they might solve a problem better, and have them explain why their solution is better.

- Provide the following sentence frames to help students discuss problems and solutions: One problem in the text is ____. One way to solve it is ____.

- Explain that a text might have one main problem and also many smaller problems that get solved throughout the story. Point out examples of each of these types and have students record them on the organizer.

EXTEND

- Have students work individually or in pairs to brainstorm a problem in the school, classroom, or community. Tell them to write this problem in the first box and brainstorm solutions in the bottom section.

- After reading and identifying a selection's problems and solutions, have pairs review their graphic organizers and discuss alternative solutions to the problems in the text. How would they solve one of the problems differently? They may work together or independently to write a brief paragraph describing a different solution. In their paragraphs, they should explain why this choice is better than the one in the selection. Have volunteers share their ideas with the rest of the class.

Problem and Solution

Problem

Solution

Cause and Effect

PURPOSE

Use this routine with the Cause and Effect Graphic Organizer. This graphic organizer works well with any fiction or nonfiction selection that has clear cause-and-effect relationships.

PROCEDURE

1. Discuss the meaning of the word *effect* with students. Explain that something that happens is an effect. Record or draw an effect on the graphic organizer.

2. Then ask students: Why did it happen? Explain that the reason something happens is a cause. Record or draw the cause on the graphic organizer.

3. Summarize: To find cause-and-effect relationships, let's look at one event that caused another event. For example, *I was late for school because I slept late.* Ask students to identify the cause and the effect in this situation. Prompt students to come up with more examples from the reading selection.

TEACHING TIPS

- It is usually easier to identify effects first, before the causes. Remind students to ask themselves *What happened?* and *Why did it happen?* to identify causes and effects.

- List clue words that signal causes and effects, such as *because* and *so.* Remind students that not all causes and effects in selections have clue words. Guide them in examining the text to find effects and then to determine what caused them.

EXTEND

- Students can write causes and effects from reading selections from science, math, or social studies classes. They could record, for example, causes of thunderstorms or events in history. Ask volunteers to share their work with the class.

- Once students are able to use this organizer, point out that in some cases there are many causes for one effect or many effects for one cause. Alter the organizer with students so they can use it with multiple causes and effects.

- If students need extra assistance, fill in either causes or effects before distributing the organizer.

ROUTINE

Cause and Effect

Causes   **Effects**

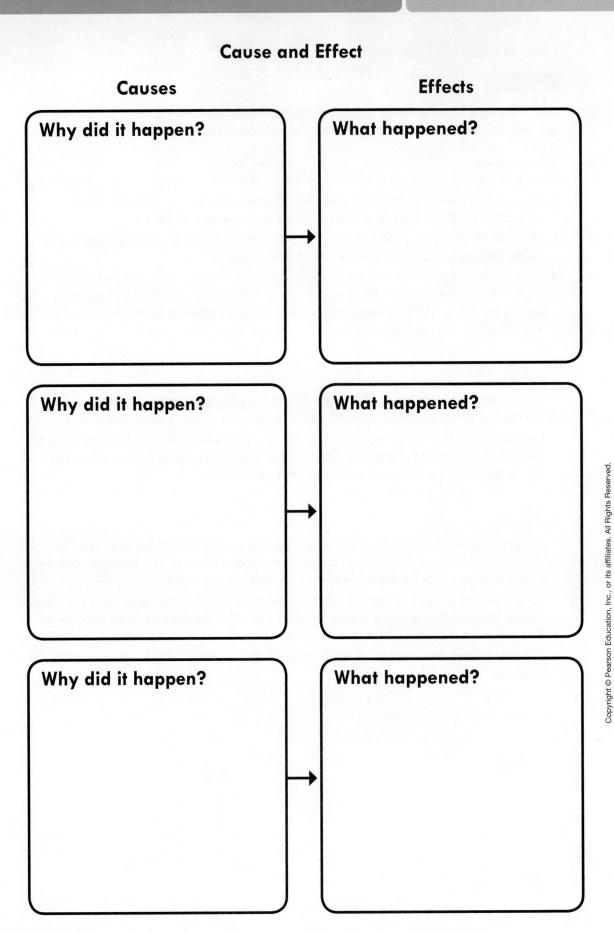

Why did it happen?

What happened?

Why did it happen?

What happened?

Why did it happen?

What happened?

Steps in a Process

PURPOSE

Use this routine with the Steps in a Process Graphic Organizer. This organizer aids students in breaking down a process into simple steps or directions. This graphic organizer works well with any procedure that has relatively few steps. If students need more or fewer steps, help students redesign the organizer.

PROCEDURE

1. Read the text. It may be the whole selection or an individual chapter. Identify a process or procedure that takes place.
2. Display the graphic organizer. Write the process on the organizer, such as Solving the Case.
3. Ask students what the first step is. Record the first step in the organizer.
4. As a group, write the remaining steps in the organizer in order as students supply them.

TEACHING TIPS

- Once students can contribute to a group Steps in a Process Graphic Organizer, have them work in pairs or small groups to write the steps of a simple process, such as how to make a salad.

- Tell students to look for clue words such as *first*, *next*, and *later* to help them sequence the steps. Ask students to review their processes and check that each step is clear. They may ask themselves, *Is this process easy to follow? Which step might be broken down into two or three additional steps?*

EXTEND

- Students may illustrate the steps in the organizer and label them with words or phrases.

- Have students use the organizer to show steps in a recipe, a science project, or in another content area. Have volunteers share their work with the class and allow classmates to offer feedback on the procedures.

Steps in a Process

Process _____

Step 1

Step 2

Step 3

Sequence of Events

PURPOSE

Use this routine with the Sequence of Events Graphic Organizer. This graphic organizer works well with any fictional selection that has a clear series of events. It can help students understand the connection between the characters, setting, and events in the story. Use it with a selection or with individual chapters in a selection.

PROCEDURE

1. Display the organizer. Write the title of the selection or chapter on the organizer.

2. Read the text. Ask students where and when the story takes place. Record those details in the Setting section.

3. As you read, use a think aloud to model how to record information about the characters. I noticed Drake talks about Nell. I wonder who Nell is and how Drake knows her. I will write her name in the left column under Characters. As I read, I will look for information about Nell and other characters I read about.

4. Pause to record information about the sequence of events in the boxes under Character and Setting.

TEACHING TIPS

- Provide sentence frames for talking about characters and setting. Examples: ___ is a person/an animal in this story. This story takes place in ___.

- Help students look for clue words for sequence. Make a list of clue words to display for students' reference, such as *first, next, then, finally*.

- Modify the organizer as needed to include more or fewer boxes or, for example, to focus on a single character and how each event affected that character.

EXTEND

- After completing this activity as a class exercise, have students use the chart in pairs, small groups, or independently with other selections.

- Help students think of words that describe the characters. Make a list and have students add to it as they read.

- After completing the chart, have students summarize, orally or in writing, information about the story from the graphic organizer.

- After reading a fictional selection, provide a list of its major events to small groups, leaving one event out. Have each group identify which event is missing. Ask students: How does the story change if one event is missing?

Sequence of Events

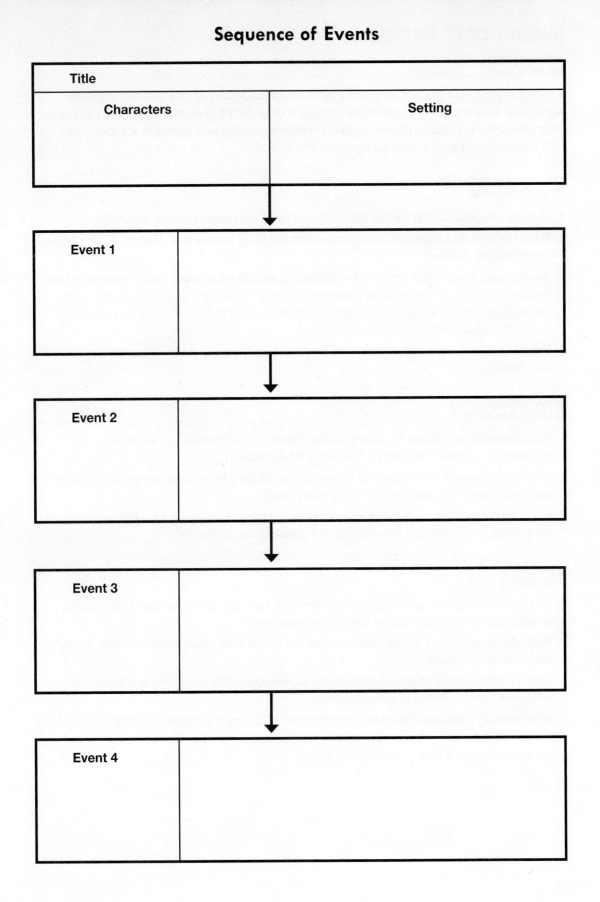

Title	
Characters	**Setting**

Event 1

Event 2

Event 3

Event 4

Time Line

PURPOSE

Use this routine with the Time Line Graphic Organizer to organize events from fiction or nonfiction texts in sequential order. This organizer works well with any selection that presents events in sequential order. It can also help students organize events in order. It can be used with a selection, individual chapters, or a small section of a selection, depending on the complexity.

PROCEDURE

1. After reading a selection, ask students what happened first. Record the first event on the chart.
2. Continue asking students to name events in order, placing them on the continuum.
3. It may be helpful to list all of the events first and then place them in order on the time line to ensure that all of the important events are included.
4. If there are specific dates or references to a specific time (for example, *summer* or *January*), record those under the event.

TEACHING TIPS

- Remind students to look for clues in the text to the order in which things happen. They might find dates or clue words such as *first*, *next*, *then*, and *last*.
- If students need extra support, write events from the text on sentence strips. Have students work in pairs or small groups to place the strips in order and then write the events on the time line.
- Some texts are not written in chronological order. For example, some fiction texts include flashbacks in the narrative that interrupt the sequential flow of events. Students can use the Time Line Graphic Organizer as they read to understand a complex text structure. Help them identify these occurrences and record them in the proper place on the continuum.

EXTEND

- After students have created their time lines for a selection, point out how events are sometimes related, occurring because of something that happened previously. Show students how events are connected by cause and effect.
- Share time lines from social studies texts with students. Have them discuss what the time lines have in common. Identify those features.

Time Line

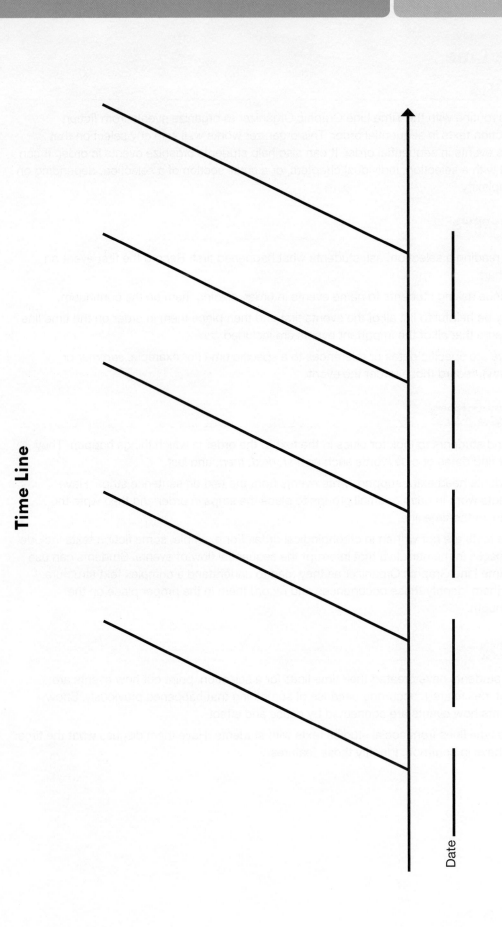

Date

Draw Conclusions

PURPOSE

Use this routine with the Draw Conclusions Graphic Organizer. Students preview the text and learn to draw conclusions from it. This graphic organizer works well with fiction and nonfiction texts.

PROCEDURE

1. Display the graphic organizer. Say: When you draw conclusions, you are getting at the meaning of a text. You are referring to information that is not clearly stated and forming a conclusion based on what you know and what you have read.

2. Preview the text with students. Read the title and ask students what they think will happen in the text. Remind them to use what they know about the topic to make educated guesses.

3. Present a section of the text to students. Ask them to analyze it and draw conclusions from it. Write their conclusions in the appropriate section of the graphic organizer.

4. Ask students to look for evidence to support their conclusions. Add their evidence to the appropriate section of the graphic organizer.

TEACHING TIPS

- Demonstrate how to use this graphic organizer to help students draw conclusions about fiction.

- Guide students to analyze informational texts and draw conclusions based on facts.

- Help students walk through the thought process of how to draw conclusions. Provide sentence frames, such as the following: I conclude that ___ because the text says ___ and I know that ___.

EXTEND

- Encourage students to think critically and compare and contrast their conclusions.

- Have volunteers debate their conclusions and support their positions with evidence from the text.

Draw Conclusions

Conclusions:

Supporting Evidence:

Supporting Evidence:

Narrative Paragraph Writing

PURPOSE

Use this routine with the Narrative Paragraph Writing Graphic Organizer to help students plan and write a narrative paragraph or story or to add details to a description of a place or an event. (See also the Unlock Narrative Writing lesson in Part 2 of this handbook.)

PROCEDURE

1. Ask students: What is narrative writing? Say: It is a story told by a narrator.

2. Show examples of narrative writing that students have read recently. Say: Narrative writing may be fiction, such as a short story or folk tale, or nonfiction, such as a news article or magazine article. Ask students for other examples of narrative writing.

3. Explain that a narrative paragraph usually describes one meaningful event or happening.

4. Distribute the graphic organizer. Review the parts of a paragraph with students: topic sentence, body, and closing sentence.

5. To demonstrate how to begin writing a narrative paragraph, provide story-starter sentence frames, such as the following: It was a dark and stormy night ___. We walked to the end of a long, crooked hall and pushed open the heavy door ___. When the phone rang in the middle of the night, ___.

6. Brainstorm ideas with the class about how the narrative might develop. Explain to students that they may include sensory details, or words and phrases that help a reader visualize what something may look, sound, smell, taste, or feel like, in their narrative paragraphs. Refer to the sentence frames and point out examples of sensory details. Write these ideas on the board. Work with students to choose the best ideas. Display the graphic organizer and model how to fill it in.

7. Repeat the process with the body and closing sentence.

8. Now ask students to write their own narrative paragraph using the graphic organizer. Provide them with several sentence frames to start.

9. Invite students to read aloud their paragraphs to a partner or small group. Have the class identify examples of sensory details in volunteers' paragraphs.

TEACHING TIPS

- Make sure students understand the story starters. Supply an alternative sentence frame if needed.

- Remind students to pay attention to the self-monitoring questions in Step C on the graphic organizer.

EXTEND

Have students publish their paragraphs in a class booklet or on a class or school Web site. Check for proper grammar, capitalization, and spelling prior to publishing.

Narrative Paragraph Writing

A. Read the story starters. Choose one and brainstorm ideas for your paragraph. Write down these ideas on a separate sheet of paper.

B. Use your ideas to write sentences in the graphic organizer. Read the information in the left column, and write your ideas in the right column.

A **topic sentence** tells what the paragraph is about.	
The **body** of a paragraph gives information to help readers understand the narrative. Write three to five sentences here.	
In a narrative paragraph, the **closing sentence** tells the end of the narrative.	

C. Read your narrative paragraph. Ask yourself:

- Does the paragraph have a topic sentence that sets up the narrative?
- Do the sentences in the body of the paragraph tell the story?
- Does the closing sentence tell the end of the narrative?

D. Read aloud your narrative paragraph to a partner, a small group, or the class.

Narrative Essay Writing

PURPOSE

Use this routine along with the Narrative Essay Writing Graphic Organizer to help students plan and write a narrative essay. (See also the Unlock Narrative Writing lesson in Part 2 of this handbook.)

PROCEDURE

1. Remind students that narrative writing tells a story. Say: Narrative writing may be fiction, such as a short story or folk tale, or nonfiction, such as a news story or a biography. Explain that a narrative essay tells a story that has a point. The reader should gain insight or learn a lesson. The final paragraph should come to an important conclusion.

2. Distribute the graphic organizer. Go over the parts of an essay with students: beginning (introduction), middle (details), and end (conclusion).

3. Brainstorm ideas with the class about how the narrative might develop. Write these ideas on the board.

4. Model filling out the graphic organizer:

   - In the Subject box, fill in the name and a brief description of the situation or experience you are writing about.
   - In the Setting box, write when and where the experience takes place.
   - In the Beginning, Middle, and End boxes, describe the events of the experience in the order they occurred.

5. Now ask students to write their own narrative essays using the graphic organizer.

6. Invite student volunteers to read aloud their narrative paragraphs to a partner, small group, or the class. Ask listeners to identify the subject, setting, and where the narratives begin, are at midpoint, and end. Ask them to also identify the lesson or moral of the story.

TEACHING TIPS

- Use sentence frames to help students get started. For example, It was a dark and stormy night ___. We walked to the end of a long, crooked hall and pushed open the heavy door ___. The phone rang in the middle of the night ___.

- Remind students that the order of events must flow logically and end in a manner that makes sense. Look for transitional words and phrases that will signal to readers where they are in the story and show the flow of the story from one part to the next. Students should also use a variety of descriptive details to highlight characters, places, or events. Finally, narratives may incorporate dialogue; check for the proper use of punctuation for what characters say. Remind students that their essays should teach readers something.

EXTEND

- Have students publish their narratives in a blog or on a class or school Web site.
- Have them create illustrations and post their work in the classroom.

Narrative Essay Writing

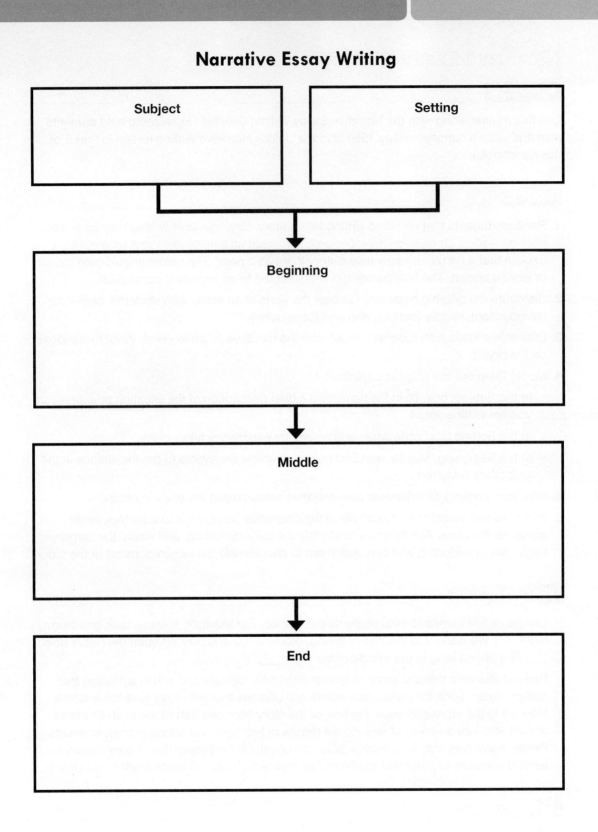

Subject

Setting

Beginning

Middle

End

Informative/Explanatory Writing

ROUTINE

PURPOSE

Use this routine along with the Informative/Explanatory Writing Graphic Organizer to help students plan and write an informative/explanatory piece of writing. (See also the Unlock Informative/Explanatory Writing lesson in Part 2 of this handbook.)

PROCEDURE

1. Ask students: What is informative/explanatory writing? Say: It explains a topic and clearly conveys ideas and information about the topic.

2. Show examples of informative/explanatory writing that students have read recently. Say: Informative/explanatory writing is factual, or nonfiction. Newspaper articles, magazine articles, and textbooks are examples of informative/explanatory writing. What other examples of explanatory/informative writing can you think of?

3. Display the graphic organizer. Explain that the first step in creating an informative/explanatory piece of writing is to choose a topic. For example, if students choose to write about natural disasters, they may ask questions such as: *Why do they occur? Where do they happen the most? How can people best prepare or protect themselves from disasters?* The next step is to do some research and gather facts and information about the topic.

4. Then tell students that they will develop their topic and organize the information they have gathered. The topic is developed with facts, definitions, and details in the middle. They will write a draft and make sure they have a strong conclusion for their piece of writing.

5. Model how to complete the graphic organizer.

6. Now ask students to write their own informative/explanatory piece, using their graphic organizer.

TEACHING TIPS

- Have students use linking words and phrases *(because, therefore, since, for example)* to connect ideas within categories of information. Look for the use of precise language in students' writing.

- Have students refer to the checklist on the graphic organizer as they write.

EXTEND

- Have students publish their informative/explanatory writing with illustrations, photographs, and/or diagrams that support their writing.

- Invite volunteers to share their work with the rest of the class. Have students review the graphic organizer as they listen to check whether the essays meet the checklist criteria.

Informative/Explanatory Writing

Topic: _____

Facts About Topic

Conclusion

Use this checklist to remind yourself to

☐ introduce the topic.

☐ develop the topic with facts, definitions, and details.

☐ provide a concluding section.

Opinion Writing

PURPOSE

Use this routine with the Opinion Writing Graphic Organizer to help students plan and write an opinion piece, including formulating an opinion and identifying reasons that support the opinion. (See also the Unlock Opinion Writing lesson in Part 2 of this handbook.)

PROCEDURE

1. Explain that an opinion is how a person feels or what a person believes about something. Say: *An opinion cannot be proven true or false because it is not a fact. A fact can be proven to be true.* Select two topics about which students can formulate an opinion. For example, *Should all elementary students learn a foreign language?* or *Should television be turned off for one night every week?* Use one topic to model instruction and the other for independent writing.

2. Explain that opinion writing involves the following steps:

    a. Students will first introduce the topic that they are writing about. This includes stating their opinion about the topic.

    b. Next, students will provide reasons that support their opinion.

    c. Finally, students will provide a concluding statement that revisits the topic and restates the opinion.

3. Display the graphic organizer and model filling it in. Begin by brainstorming some topic choices and making a decision about the best idea. Model writing a statement of opinion.

4. Next, fill in the reasons for the opinion. Remind students to provide strong reasons that support their point of view about the topic. The reasons should be based on fact. Remind students to keep in mind the reasons for their opinion as they write.

5. Finally, model writing an opinion piece using the information in the graphic organizer. Students should have several good supporting reasons for their opinion and a strong conclusion.

TEACHING TIP

Have students use linking words and phrases *(for instance, in order to, in addition)* to connect their reasons to their opinions.

EXTEND

- Have students publish their writing in a classroom book, or have them create cartoon illustrations and display them for the school to enjoy.

- Invite volunteers to share their work with the class. Have classmates review their graphic organizer's checklist as they listen to check whether the opinion pieces meet the checklist criteria.

- Encourage class discussion by allowing classmates to ask additional questions or offer opposing opinions and reasons.

Opinion Writing

Topic: _____

Information About Topic

Opinion Statement: _____

Reasons for Opinion

Use this checklist to remind yourself to

☐ introduce the topic and your opinion.

☐ give reasons to support your opinion.

☐ provide a concluding statement that revisits the topic and restates the opinion.

Description: Sensory Details

PURPOSE

Use this routine along with the Description: Sensory Details Graphic Organizer to help students break down and understand descriptive-rich passages. The organizer can also aid students in using sensory details to write their own description of a place or an event.

PROCEDURE

1. Because teaching sensory details has both a reading and writing component, find a paragraph that is rich in sensory details. Remove them one by one so that students can see what is lost in the description without them. Then put them back in so students can evaluate the role that sensory details play in making meaning.

2. Explain that writers use sensory details (sight, sound, smell, taste, and touch) when sharing important experiences. These sensory details also make the text more interesting to read because they create vivid images for the reader.

3. Display the graphic organizer. Choose a piece of text that contains examples of sensory details and read it aloud. Model how to fill in the chart with details from each sense that the author uses. Discuss how this makes writing more interesting for readers.

4. Use and display a new Sensory Details Graphic Organizer when assisting students in writing their own descriptive passages. As a class, choose a classroom object or an area of the classroom to describe. Ask questions, such as *What does it feel like? How does it smell? What colors and shapes do you see? What are the sounds that it makes?*

5. Next, divide the class into five groups and give each group a sense. Students can work with their group or on their own to brainstorm words for their sense. For example, if your object is a bell and your sense is "hear," you would write down words like *loud, pealing,* or *clanging.*

6. Fill out the displayed organizer as a class. Go in order and have each group share their sensory words.

7. Use a think aloud to demonstrate how students can use the sensory words from the organizer to describe the object or place.

TEACHING TIPS

- The above activity works well as a guided collaborative writing activity.
- Use *I see, I hear, I feel, I smell,* and *I taste* as sentence starters.
- Display lists of vivid sensory words in the classroom for students to reference.

EXTEND

Have students work alone or in pairs and use the graphic organizer to write a description of an object or place. When they finish their descriptions, they can read them aloud and have others guess what is being described.

Description: Sensory Details

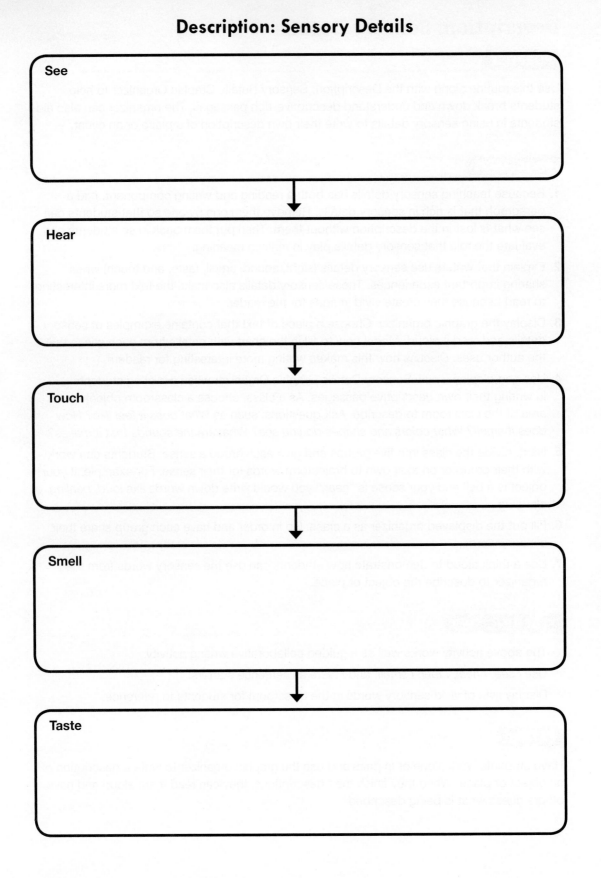

See

Hear

Touch

Smell

Taste

Retell or Summarize

PURPOSE

Use this routine with the Retell or Summarize Graphic Organizer.

PROCEDURE

1. Model thinking aloud an example of summarizing: I saw a movie yesterday. When my friends asked me about it, I didn't tell every detail from the beginning to the end. Instead, I told the most important ideas and events. This is called summarizing. I summarize things I see, things I read, and things I hear. When I summarize, I know that I must sort out the most important details. A summary includes important ideas and events, not everything. Retelling is a little different. When you retell something, you listen to or read the message and then say it in your own words to show you understand it.

2. Ask students to listen carefully as you read a short passage aloud. After you read, ask students to contribute to a summary of the passage. Say: A summary should answer the question What was it about?

3. Help frame their thinking as you list their ideas to create a summary. Tell them they are only noting main ideas. Have pairs of students read the complete summary together.

4. Then reread the passage. Have pairs decide if the summary lists the most important details. Ask: What should be added or changed? What can be left out? Discuss and clarify answers. Repeat this process with another story to focus on retelling. Remind students that for both summarizing and retelling, they must use their own words.

TEACHING TIP

Students can use the sentence starters at the bottom of the graphic organizer to guide their writing.

EXTEND

Have students use the graphic organizer to list details from a written or spoken passage. In the box at the bottom, students can write their summaries. Encourage them to keep their summaries short and to the point. Ask them to read their summaries aloud to a partner.

Retell or Summarize

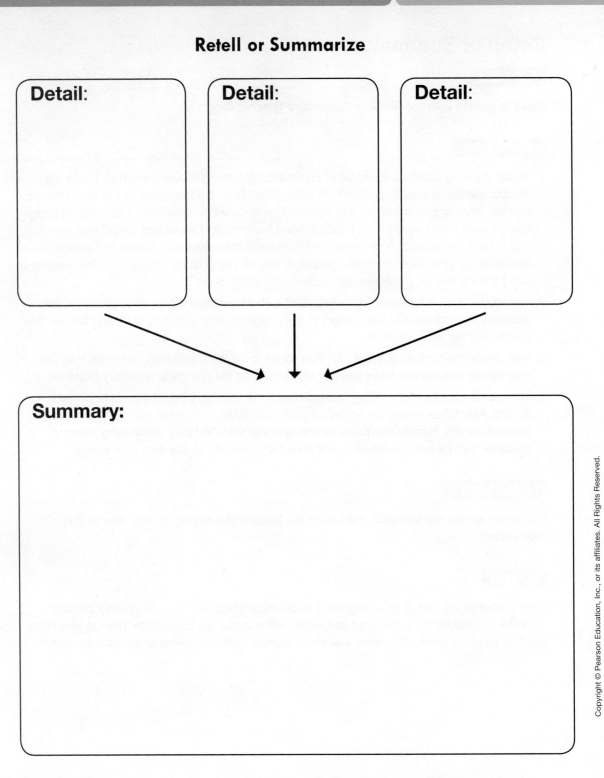

Use the summary starters below if you need to.

In summary, . . .

The most important ideas are . . .

What we need to remember is . . .

Monitor Understanding: Listening Skills Log

PURPOSE

Use this routine with the Listening Skills Log Graphic Organizer to help students monitor their understanding and learn how to take helpful class notes.

PROCEDURE

1. Explain the purpose of the Listening Skills Log to students. Begin with questions, such as *Why is it important to listen?* or *Why is it important to take notes?*

2. Distribute the Listening Skills Log and model filling it out. Explain to students that good note takers do not write down every word a speaker says. Instead, they listen for main ideas. Review the difference between a key idea and a detail.

3. Display the log you created in Step 2 as a model. Have students view the log while listening to the same media or audio selection. Afterward, discuss why you chose to write down what you did, and allow students to ask questions.

4. Read a text aloud, or present information using a form of media. When using media, preview the selection so you can pause after main ideas. This will allow students to practice listening for and writing down main ideas.

5. Have students compare their log entries in small groups prior to discussing them with the class. Encourage students to ask about any words they did not understand.

TEACHING TIPS

- Speak at a normal rate and enunciate clearly. Pause at appropriate places to allow students to process the information and ask clarifying questions or seek further explanation. Prompt students to think critically about the text by giving example opinions or making connections to their own life experiences.

- If students have difficulty with a passage, pause to explain new words and concepts. As students become more proficient listeners, gradually increase the length and difficulty of the passages.

- Reread or replay the same text or media so students have multiple chances to catch main ideas. During each reread or replay, students should work on a different portion of the Listening Skills Log to hone their focus.

- Allow students to reread the selection to compare their Listening Skills Log with what was in the text. As they reread a selection, students can code parts of the text with sticky notes to indicate *I understand. I need further explanation. I figured it out.*

- If appropriate, post an essential question that students can refer to as they listen.

EXTEND

- Students can write a paragraph from their notes.

- After students listen to a selection or read aloud and fill out the log, have them get in pairs and use classroom resources to find answers to their own questions, define unknown words, and clarify any misunderstandings. Pairs can present their findings to the class and explain how they came to their answers.

Listening Skills Log

Topic	
Main Idea	
What did I learn?	
What was hard to understand?	
Questions I Have	
New Words	

Express Opinions

INTRODUCE

Use this routine to guide students in expressing opinions.

PROCEDURE

1. Explain to students that we express opinions to show what we think or believe about something. We cannot prove if an opinion is true or false. Say: If someone says, "It is raining outside," that's a fact. I can look outside and see rain falling. If someone says, "Rainy weather is the best weather," that's an opinion. That person may like rainy weather because it helps flowers grow. But others may not like rain. They have a different opinion.

2. Display the following opinion words and phrases:

I think	I disagree	best
I believe	I like	worst
my opinion is	I do not like	good
I agree	better	bad

   Say: We use these words to give our opinions. These words tell what we think or believe. Model creating an opinion using one of the words or phrases.

3. Have students work with partners to state opinions about the text they are currently reading. Remind them that they need to refer directly to the text to show evidence that supports their opinion. Have them use the displayed opinion words and phrases. Provide sentence frames as needed, such as: I like ___. I think ___. I believe ___. I do not like ___. My opinion is ___.

TEACHING TIPS

- Students may think of facts as true and opinions as false. Locate statements of opinions in the text that are supported by facts and discuss them with students. Point out that people trust opinions when they are supported with facts.

- If students have trouble distinguishing fact from opinion because the opinion words/ phrases are not used in the text, help them by providing some hints. Facts may include dates and numbers and can be proven. Opinions tell an attitude or belief and cannot be proven.

EXTEND

For additional practice, have students elaborate by giving reasons for their opinions, referring directly to the text. Students can use the following sentence frames as needed: I like ___ because ___. Her opinion is ___ because ___. Have volunteers share their opinions and reasons with the class. Remind students to be respectful of others' opinions.

Prepare for Discussions

Use this routine to help students prepare for and engage in collaborative one-on-one, group, and teacher-led discussions.

PROCEDURE

1. **Ask:** What does it mean to engage effectively in a range of collaborative discussions? (It means you can have a conversation with a partner, in a small group, or with the whole class. It also means that you communicate your ideas in a way that other people can understand.)

2. **Ask:** How can you communicate your ideas in a way that other people can understand? (by preparing for the discussion, including reading and understanding the text ahead of time; by asking questions before, during, and after the discussion to make sure you understand; by staying on topic; by building on others' ideas; by expressing your own ideas clearly; by linking comments made by different people in the discussion)

3. Review the rules of discussions from the worksheet on the following page.

4. Model a discussion with several student volunteers. Tell them that you are planning a party for a relative; list which of your family members you intend to invite to the party and what you will have to do to prepare for it. Ask students questions about how you should decorate for the party and what foods you should prepare for it. Reiterate what they say, and expand upon it.

5. Have students use the worksheet to rate themselves when they have a discussion with classmates.

TEACHING TIP

Set roles for class discussions, such as timekeeper, leader, note taker, and summarizer.

EXTEND

- Peruse a local newspaper for an article presenting a local controversy (a large department store opening next to a series of small businesses or a new traffic light proposal). Present this article to your students for discussion.

- Ask students to suggest topics for discussion. Have a few volunteers participate in the discussion while the rest of the class listens. Have the listeners rate the discussion using the worksheet. Ask students to point out things that the volunteers did well or could improve upon.

Prepare for Discussions

Rate what you do during discussions with your classmates.

1 I need to practice this skill.

2 I do this sometimes.

3 I almost always do this.

I listen carefully to others when they speak.	1 2 3
I speak one at a time.	1 2 3
I talk about the topic when it is my turn.	1 2 3
I ask questions when I don't understand.	1 2 3
I come prepared.	1 2 3
I gain the floor respectfully.	1 2 3
I stay on topic.	1 2 3
I explain my own ideas.	1 2 3

What topics would you like to discuss with classmates?
List them here. Then **discuss!**

_____

_____

_____

Understanding Media

PURPOSE

Use this routine when watching a video or listening to an audio recording to help students understand the main idea.

PROCEDURE

1. Introduce a guiding question to help students focus while watching a video or listening to a recording.

2. Play the media once from beginning to end. Then replay the media, pausing at critical points, such as when new information is taught. Ask questions to monitor students' comprehension.

3. Confirm that students understand what they have seen or heard by asking them to summarize each section.

4. Once students have watched or listened twice, have them answer the guiding question.

5. Replay the media a third time so that students can confirm their answers.

TEACHING TIPS

- Ask students to discuss any background knowledge they have about the guiding question.

- Have struggling speakers draw a picture that illustrates their background knowledge.

- If students are unable to summarize sections, watch or listen to each section again. Ask questions that will guide them to understand the main idea of the section.

EXTEND

Use the Three-Column Chart Graphic Organizer. Title one column What I Knew, the second What I Learned, and the last What I Want to Know. Have students fill in the columns using information that they already knew about the guiding question and information they learned while watching or listening. For any questions they still have under What I Want to Know, lead a class discussion to arrive at answers or guide students in conducting further research.

Preview and Review Vocabulary

PURPOSE

Use this routine to assess what students know about words they will encounter in a reading selection. This activity also is a way to review the vocabulary from previous selections so that students internalize the words.

PROCEDURE

1. Select 12–14 words for vocabulary study. Use words from the vocabulary list in the Teacher's Guide and select the remaining words based on the needs of your students. Include three or four words from a previous selection in the list.

2. Display the words and read each one aloud to students. Have students write each word in a vocabulary notebook for later reference. Then have students read each word with you.

3. Ask students first to decide which words they think will be in the selection before joining a partner for the following step.

4. Have students explain to a partner why they chose each word and why they didn't choose others. Afterward, pairs can explain their choices to the class. Explaining why is a very important step because students will use their understanding of the words to predict the content of the selection. These explanations also demonstrate what students know about a word. Sharing the explanations helps to provide more background to students who may not be familiar with the words.

OPTIONS FOR VARYING THIS ROUTINE Replace Steps 3–4 with one of the following:

- Select words they want to know more about.
- Select words they don't know or understand.

EXTEND

- Have students create word webs relating the vocabulary terms to other words they know. These can be words with similar affixes, suffixes, sounds, or meanings.

- Before students read a fiction selection, choose 10 words from the text that exemplify the story's characters, setting, and problem. Have students sort the words into three categories: characters, setting, and problem. Then, work together as a class to create a one- to three-sentence prediction about the story. Make sure the prediction includes all of the words. The purpose is to have students use new words to practice making predictions, so it is okay if the predictions are "wrong."

- In small groups, have students discuss the words they are unfamiliar with. Guide them in making educated guesses about the words' meanings, referring to the selection for context. Once they have defined the words, have them work together to write new sentences using the words.

Act Out or Draw Meaning

Use this routine with the Act Out or Draw Meaning Graphic Organizer to help students learn and remember new vocabulary.

PROCEDURE

1. Explain that one way to learn and remember new words is to draw or act out the meaning. For example, I just read the word *fault* in a science text. A *fault* is a place in the earth where an earthquake happens. To remember the word, I can draw a picture of a circle to show the earth and draw a line on it. I put arrows to show how the earth shifts at the fault line. (Display a picture.) I can also act out the meaning by rubbing my hands together to show what happens at a fault to make an earthquake.

2. Divide the class into small groups. Introduce words from the selection. Choose "picturable" words and give each group a word.

3. Have students work together to create a picture and/or demonstrate the meaning of the word. Say: Talk about what this word means. Then explain by drawing a picture of it or showing us what it means.

4. Have volunteers explain their drawings to the class. Clear up any misconceptions.

5. Ask: How did drawing the word or acting it out help you remember what it means?

TEACHING TIPS

- Drawing a word aids understanding because it requires students to express ideas in a different format. If students doubt their artistic ability, reassure them that they will not be evaluated based on the way their drawings look, but rather on their ability to explain how their drawings help them understand new words.

- Note that while almost all words can be made into drawings and can serve as pictorial reminders as students read, not all words transfer well into actions. It is also important to consider whether or not acting out a word will be more helpful or distracting to classroom learning.

- Consider modifying the graphic organizer to include synonyms and antonyms as well as dictionary definitions.

EXTEND

- Play a guessing game with students. Distribute index cards with words that students have learned in class. Students can take turns drawing pictures or acting out word meanings for the class to guess.

- Use the graphic organizer on the next page for students to create their own dictionary of pictures. Distribute copies of the drawing frames when students learn new words. Have students keep and add to their own personal dictionaries.

- Challenge students to distinguish shades of meaning with words that describe the same general action, such as: *walk, stroll, prowl, march.* Provide a list of words for students in small groups to expand by adding synonyms. Then have each group act out the words on their expanded list.

Act Out or Draw Meaning

Word: _____

Drawing

This word means _____
_____.

Word: _____

Drawing

This word means _____
_____.

Analyze Cognates

Identifying cognates in texts is a useful strategy for expanding vocabulary, helping students understand more words in English, validating the home language, and making clear connections between the home language and the target language, English. Use this routine with the Personal Cognate Chart to help students who are literate in languages that have many English cognates, such as Spanish, Portuguese, French, and Italian.

PROCEDURE

1. Present a chart like the one below. Read the words with students, and note the similarities across various languages. Explain: When words look and mean the same in different languages, they are called cognates. Let's look at the word *demand* and its cognates. What other words can we add to this chart? Tell students that cognates can help them understand more words in English.

English	Spanish	French	Italian
demand	demanda	demande	domanda

2. Explain to students that cognates in different languages usually have the same origins. For example, the different words for *demand* are all based on the Greek word part *-mand,* which means "order." Explain that because many scientific words have Greek or Latin origins, they are often cognates.

3. Point out that sometimes words in different languages are "false friends," which means they look almost the same, but they don't mean the same thing. For example, the Spanish word *sopa* looks and sounds similar to the English word *soap*, but it means "soup." Ask students to give other examples of these or false cognates, which are words that are not true cognates. Together, find an example of a word from a text that students think is a cognate and discuss their rationale.

4. Copy and distribute the Personal Cognate Chart. Have students look for English cognates of home-language words in an English text they are reading. Help them decide whether or not the words really are cognates.

5. Ask students to say or write five examples of cognate pairs in English and their home language and one example of a "false friend." Ask: How does knowing cognates help you to understand the meaning of words?

TEACHING TIPS

- Suggest that students consult resources such as bilingual dictionaries, other students, or the Internet (with your guidance) to find translations and word meanings.
- Students might make a class chart showing words such as *computer* in various languages.
- Ask students to pay attention to the context. If they believe they have identified a cognate, have them think of the meaning and check if it makes sense in context.

EXTEND

Assist students in labeling and defining Latin and Greek roots of new words they encounter in classroom texts. Identifying and understanding the meaning of these roots will be a useful tool in helping students decode new words in the future, and it also allows them to make connections between words. Use the Personal Cognate Chart for this activity by relabeling the headings of each column. In column one, write New Word, and have students write the word in English with its definition in the space provided. In column two, write Latin and Greek Roots, and have students write the various Greek and Latin roots of the new word. In column three, write Definition of Latin and Greek Roots, and have students define each of the Greek or Latin roots.

ENGLISH LANGUAGE LEARNERS

Cognates are words that share origins and appear in similar forms in different languages. For example, the English word *school* is of Greek origin, and it is similar to the Spanish *escuela*, the French *école*, the Polish *szkoła*, and the German *schule*. For speakers of languages that share word origins with English, the study of cognates can be a powerful vocabulary-building tool.

* Have students work together in pairs or small groups to write sentences in English using the English words they have listed in their Personal Cognate Charts. Ask volunteers to share their sentences with the class.

Personal Cognate Chart

English Cognate	Cognate in Other Language	Meaning

Word Knowledge Strategy

PURPOSE

Model these strategies to show students what to do when they come across a word they do not know. These strategies can be modeled through a think aloud or demonstrated explicitly through a mini lesson. The goal is that over the course of several units, students will become independent users of these strategies.

PROCEDURE

Begin with a question: *What do I do when I come to a word I don't know?*

- **Decode/Pronounce** Have students read the word aloud. Sometimes just hearing it will show them that they know it. Say it again and tap out the parts of the word as you say it. Check: *Does the word sound right?* If the answer is "no," go to the next step.

- **Word Structure** Look at the word parts, affixes, and roots. If students see a word part they know, have them underline it and define it. For example, *unknown*: *un-* means "not," so *unknown* means "not known or understood." This can also be done with compound words or word parts. For example, *know* means "to understand," so *knowledge* has to do with the ability to understand something. Check: *Does the word sound right?* If the answer is "no," go to the next step.

- **Related Words and Cognates** Is there another word that is similar in spelling and/or sound that can help? For example, if the unknown word is *medicate*, can knowing the meaning of the word *medicine* help students determine its meaning? If the answer is "no," go to the next step.

- **Context Clues** Read what comes before and after the word to find clues that will help students understand the meaning of the word. For fiction, think about the setting, characters, events, and actions taking place. For nonfiction, look for examples, explanations, and definitions within the text. Model a think aloud considering these elements. Check: *Does the word make sense?* If the answer is "no," go to the next step.

- **References** The final step is looking in a reference source such as a dictionary, glossary, or thesaurus. Remind students that words are listed in reference books in alphabetical order. Also discuss what to do if two words start with the same letter (*simulate* and *synthesize*).

TEACHING TIPS

- Remind students that there are times when they might know what a word means but that the meaning can change based on how it is used in a sentence. ("I am simply stumped" versus "The directions are written simply.")

- After students understand the word, have them use the new word in a sentence and record the new vocabulary word in a notebook. Have students exchange sentences with a partner to identify those that are correctly constructed and those that are not. Guide students to correct any mistakes in one another's sentences.

Multisyllabic Word Strategy

Use this routine to help students understand and decode multisyllabic words that do not have prefixes, suffixes, or roots.

PROCEDURE

1. **Introduce the Strategy** Explain that word parts, or chunks, help us to read larger words. They also help students learn to spell correctly.

   Display the word *rabbit* as an example.

2. **Connect to Sound-Spellings** Explain that the parts of a word are called syllables. Break the word into syllables.

   Say: *Rabbit* has two syllables: *rab* and *bit*.

3. **Model** Explain that syllables help us say and read words. Say each syllable as you run your hand from one syllable to the next. Then read the syllables together as you say the word. Then show students how they can use clapping to help identify syllables. Demonstrate by clapping once after saying each syllable.

4. **Read the Word** Read the syllables as you run your hand beneath them, and then read the syllables together as you say the word.

   Say: This is how I read this word. First I read each syllable, and then I read the syllables together: *rab/bit, rabbit.*

5. **Practice** Display more examples. Have students read the syllables, and then read the word as you run your hand beneath the parts.

TEACHING TIP

If students have difficulty using sound-spellings and syllabication to read word parts, then read one part at a time as you cover the remaining parts.

EXTEND

Choose an excerpt from a selection that contains several multisyllabic words. Have volunteers read aloud to practice decoding and pronunciations.

Analyze Idioms and Expressions

Idioms are phrases that have a figurative meaning, such as *hit the road*. An expression is a group of words used as a unit, such as *wise guy*.

Because the meanings of idioms and expressions are not literal, students may need extra support to understand them. Students who speak other languages at home might have added difficulty, since there may not be similar idioms in their own language. The best approach to teaching idioms and expressions is to discuss them in the context of a classroom text or in conversation. By being exposed to idioms and expressions, students will be better able to recognize and understand them when reading or listening to conversations and media.

1. Explain that idioms are phrases that communicate an idea or feeling that cannot be understood based on what they say. When I use an idiom, I don't mean exactly what the words say. For example, what do I mean when I say that Carl talked too much and he spilled the beans about the surprise party? Did he literally spill some beans? No, I mean to say that he told the secret about the surprise party.

2. Ask students for other examples of idioms and expressions, or supply examples, such as *jumping down my throat, feeling under the weather, bite the dust.*

3. Write the examples on the board and discuss what they might mean based on the context in which they were heard or read. Talk about why someone might be confused by a particular idiom. For example, *to sleep on it* can be confusing because students might visualize someone sleeping on top of something.

4. Point out idioms and expressions in selections that students are reading or that you read aloud to them. Ask them to figure out the meanings. Clarify any misunderstandings and provide corrective feedback.

- Have volunteers practice using idioms and expressions in everyday conversation. Provide a prompt. For example: Convince your friend to try something new. Use the phrase "give it a shot" in conversation. Or have students suggest examples of idioms and use them in conversation.

- Have pairs work together to write sentences using idioms and then explanations of what they mean. Ask volunteers to read their sentences to the class.

Analyze Multiple-Meaning Words

PURPOSE

Use the Analyze Multiple-Meaning Words Routine to help students determine or clarify the meaning of words and phrases that have more than one meaning.

PROCEDURE

1. Explain that some words have more than one meaning. Say: Words like *leaves* have multiple meanings. *Leaves* can mean "the thin, flat, green parts of plants that grow from stems," but *leaves* can also mean "departs." When you come across a word in a text that has more than one meaning, how can you figure out which meaning is being used?

2. Present different strategies that students can use to determine or clarify the meaning of a word that has more than one meaning:

    a. Tell students that they can often use the context of the sentence to figure out what a word or phrase means. Using the context means looking at the other words in the sentence for clues. Say: If I told you that I jumped in a pile of leaves, you would know that I am talking about the thin, green parts of plants.

    b. If the text does not provide enough context to help students figure out the meaning of a word, tell them they can also use prefixes and suffixes that they do know to figure out the meaning of a word. For example, the prefix *un-* means "not" and the suffix *-able* means "can" or "able to."

    c. Another strategy is to use root words with which they are familiar. For example, *bio-* means "life."

    d. Finally, remind students that they can always use a dictionary or other reference tool if they need help finding the meaning of a word.

TEACHING TIPS

- To avoid too many interruptions while reading, have students use self-stick notes to flag unknown words, especially those with multiple meanings, while they read.

- Point out that words may be used as different parts of speech. For example, *work* may be used as a noun (We like doing our *work*) or as a verb (Our teachers *work* hard).

EXTEND

- Draw a two-column chart. Title one column Word and the other Meanings. Have students brainstorm additional multiple-meaning words and fill in the columns accordingly.

- Provide pairs with multiple-meaning words and have them write sentences using the words in two different contexts (for example, *button* as a noun and as a verb). Have volunteers share their work with the class.

Common Nouns

INTRODUCE Remind students that we have names for the things around us. A noun is a word that names something or somebody.

TEACH/MODEL Present the concept and provide examples of common nouns such as:

Person	Place	Animal	Thing
girl	country	dog	statue

PRACTICE Have pairs find more examples of common nouns to add to the chart. Fill out the chart with the class. Clarify questions students might have.

ASSESS Have students find other examples of nouns from new selections they are reading. Have them share their examples and explain why their choices are common nouns.

ENGLISH LANGUAGE LEARNERS

In languages such as Spanish and French, nouns have gender (masculine or feminine). You can point out that while some nouns in English refer to males or females (*boy, girl, uncle, aunt*), English nouns are not grouped by gender.

Proper Nouns

INTRODUCE Write a student's name on the board. Point out that everyone's name begins with a capital letter and that each of us has our own specific name. Explain that a proper noun is the specific name of a person, place, animal, or thing. Proper nouns all begin with capital letters. The word *city* is not a proper noun because it is not a specific place. *New York City* and *Chicago* are proper nouns because they are specific places. Likewise, the word *girl* is not a proper noun because many people are girls. However, *Sandra* is a proper noun because it is specific to a particular girl.

TEACH/MODEL Present the concept and provide examples:

- A proper noun names a specific person, place, animal, or thing.
- A proper noun begins with a capital letter.

Specific Person	Specific Place	Specific Animal	Specific Thing
Sandra	Africa	Fifi	Statue of Liberty

PRACTICE Model finding a proper noun in a text and recording it. Circle the capital letter. Have pairs work together to provide more examples to add to the chart.

ASSESS When students understand the concept, have them work independently to find examples from texts they read to add to the chart.

ENGLISH LANGUAGE LEARNERS

Students who are literate in nonalphabetic languages such as Chinese, Korean, and Japanese may not be familiar with capitalizing proper nouns and may need more practice.

Titles and Abbreviations

INTRODUCE Write the names of various school staff members on the board, including titles such as *Mr., Mrs.,* and *Dr.* Read the names aloud with students, and underline the titles as you say them. Point out that these titles are abbreviations, or shortened forms of words.

TEACH/MODEL Present the concept and provide examples:

* Proper names may begin with a title such as *Mrs., Mr., Ms.,* or *Dr.*
* A title begins with a capital letter. If a title is an abbreviation, it ends with a period.

Abbreviated Title	Example
Mr. (mister)	Mr. Garza
Ms. (miz)	Ms. Prince
Mrs. (missus)	Mrs. Dexter
Miss (miss)	Miss Wong
Dr. (doctor)	Dr. Marco

PRACTICE Have students expand the chart by adding adults they know. Next, have pairs find examples from a recent selection. Remind students that some titles, such as *Senator, President,* and *Professor,* are not abbreviated. Have them keep a running list of examples of the various titles they find in their reading.

ENGLISH LANGUAGE LEARNERS

* Explain that in English the title *Doctor* is used for both men and women.
* In some countries, the word *teacher* is used as a title. Point out that in the United States, teachers are addressed with a title such as *Mr., Ms., Mrs.,* or *Miss.*

Days, Months, and Holidays

INTRODUCE Ask students to name today's day and date. Write them on the board, and point out that the names of the day and month begin with capital letters.

TEACH/MODEL Present the concept and provide several examples:

* Days of the week, months of the year, and holidays begin with capital letters.

Days of the Week	Months of the Year		Holidays (Examples)
Sunday	January	July	New Year's Day
Monday	February	August	Labor Day
Tuesday	March	September	Thanksgiving
Wednesday	April	October	
Thursday	May	November	
Friday	June	December	
Saturday			

PRACTICE Students can write sentences featuring days of the week, months of the year, and holidays. Provide sentence starters such as: ___ is my favorite day of the week. The weather is often ___ during the month of ___. On ___, I celebrate by ___.

Singular and Plural Nouns

INTRODUCE Point to one book and say: book. Point to two books and say: books. Repeat with *(lunch)box* and *(lunch)boxes.* Have students name other singular and plural nouns as you point to them. Say: Some nouns name one thing. They are called singular nouns. Some nouns name more than one thing. They are called plural nouns. The word *plural* means "more than one."

TEACH/MODEL Present the concept and provide examples:

- Add *-s* to most nouns to form the plural.
- If the noun ends in *-ch, -sh, -s, -ss,* or *-x,* add *-es.*
- If the noun ends in a consonant + *y,* change the *y* to *i* and add *-es.*

Add *-s*	Add *-es*	Change *y* to *i* and Add *-es*
girl/girls	box/boxes	berry/berries

PRACTICE Have students make a three-column chart with the following headings: Add *-s;* Add *-es;* Change *y* to *i* and Add *-es.* Invite students to look through magazines to find nouns that fit each category.

Irregular Plural Nouns

INTRODUCE Write this sentence on the board: *The <u>children</u> brushed their <u>teeth</u>.* Ask a volunteer to name the singular of the underlined nouns *(child, tooth).* Tell students: Most nouns add *-s* or *-es* to form the plural. Some nouns form the plural in a special way. They are called irregular plural nouns.

TEACH/MODEL Present the concept and provide examples:

- Most nouns add *-s* or *-es: books, girls, boxes, brushes.*
- Irregular plural nouns have special forms. Here are some examples:

Irregular Plural Nouns			
child/children	foot/feet	life/lives	man/men
ox/oxen	tooth/teeth	leaf/leaves	woman/women

PRACTICE Have pairs create "singular noun" word cards: *child, tooth, leaf, foot, man.* Then have them create "irregular plural noun" cards, including incorrect forms: *childs, children, teeth, tooths, leafs, leaves, feet, foots, men, mans.* Have students place the "singular" and "plural" cards facedown in two separate groups, then take turns drawing correct pairs.

Singular Possessive Nouns

INTRODUCE Display and read aloud these sentences, gesturing as appropriate: This is Maya. This is Maya's desk. **Explain:** The first sentence is about Maya. The second sentence says that Maya has something. To show that a person, place, or thing has or owns something, add an apostrophe **(point to apostrophe)** and the letter *s*. The word *Maya's* is called a singular possessive noun.

TEACH/MODEL Present the concept and provide examples:

- A singular possessive noun ends in *'s.*

Singular Nouns	Singular Possessive Nouns	Examples
Sam	Sam's	Sam's mom
friend	friend's	friend's house
class	class's	class's pet
child	child's	child's jacket

PRACTICE Have students place school supplies on their desks. Then have students point to and name a classmate's supplies, using a singular possessive noun. For example: *This is Lin's book. This is Lin's calculator.*

Plural Possessive Nouns

INTRODUCE Display and read aloud these sentences: All my friends have desks. These are my friends' desks. Encourage students to discuss the meaning of each sentence. Explain: To show that two or more people, places, or things have or own something, use a plural possessive noun.

TEACH/MODEL Present the concept and provide examples:

- If the plural noun ends in *-s, -es,* or *-ies,* add an apostrophe (') to make it possessive.
- If the plural noun does **not** end in *-s, -es,* or *-ies,* add *'s* to make it possessive.

Plural Nouns	Plural Possessive	Examples
friends	friends'	friends' houses
classes	classes'	classes' teachers
puppies	puppies'	puppies' tails
children	children's	children's jackets

PRACTICE Provide sentences such as the following and ask students to choose the correct plural possessive noun in each sentence: *This is the* (childrens', children's) *cake. These are my* (friends', friend's) *chairs. The* (lady's, ladies') *book club chooses a book.* Have students choose a plural possessive noun from the sentences and use it in their own sentence.

Possessive Pronouns

INTRODUCE Hold a book and say: This is my book. This book is mine. **Explain:** The words *my* and *mine* are possessive pronouns. They show that I have this book. Possessive pronouns show who or what has or owns something.

TEACH/MODEL Present the concept and provide examples from the current reading selection. Use *my, your, her, our,* and *their* before nouns. Use *mine, yours, hers, ours,* and *theirs* alone. *His* and *its* can be used before nouns and alone.

Possessive Pronouns	
Before Nouns	This is <u>your</u> pen. It is <u>her</u> doll.
Alone	The shoes are <u>mine</u>. The doll is <u>hers</u>.
Both	The pen is <u>his</u>. This is <u>his</u> home.

PRACTICE Have students look around the room and identify objects that belong to them or to someone else. Have them use each item in a sentence with a possessive pronoun and underline the possessive pronoun: Here is *my* pencil. This calculator is *yours*.

ENGLISH LANGUAGE LEARNERS

Students who speak Asian languages may try various forms for possessive pronouns (*the hat of her, you hat*) or may not always state the pronoun (*Mo Yun took off hat*). Provide additional practice with possessive pronouns.

Subject Pronouns

INTRODUCE Point to yourself and say, I am a teacher. Point to the students and say, You are students. **Point** to a boy and say, He is a student. **Point** to a girl and say, She is a student. Indicate everyone in the room and say, We are at school. **Explain:** Pronouns such as *I, you, he, she, we,* and *they* are used in place of nouns or noun phrases, such as people's names. These pronouns are used for subjects of sentences. We do not say, "*Me* am a teacher" or "*Him* is a student."

TEACH/MODEL Present the concept and provide examples from the current reading selection. A subject pronoun is used as the subject of a sentence.

	Subject Pronouns
Singular	I, you, he, she, it
Plural	we, you, they

PRACTICE Say the following sentences, or choose examples from the text, and have students rephrase them using the correct subject pronoun: Ana sits in the third row. Max sits here. Ana and Max are cousins. The sandwich is the teacher's lunch.

ENGLISH LANGUAGE LEARNERS

In Spanish, unlike English, speakers may omit subject pronouns because Spanish verbs can indicate the subjects. Korean speakers may add a subject pronoun after the noun, reflecting a pattern in Korean, such as "Nathan, he is my brother."

Object Pronouns

INTRODUCE Display these sentences: *Give the book to me. Mom made us a snack. They talked with Tom and her.* **Explain:** Pronouns such as *me, you, him, her, us,* and *them* are used after verbs or after words such as *for, at, with,* or *to.* We do not say, "Give the book to I" or "Mom made we a snack."

TEACH/MODEL Present the concept and provide examples. An object pronoun is used in the predicate, after an action verb or preposition.

	Object Pronouns
Singular	me, you, him, her, it
Plural	us, you, them

PRACTICE Pose open-ended sentences, cueing object pronoun endings by gesturing to different people in the room: I will help ___ [gesture toward a girl]. Students should finish the sentence with the word *her.*

ENGLISH LANGUAGE LEARNERS

Spanish, Chinese, and Vietnamese speakers and other English learners may use subject pronouns as objects, for example, "Give the book to she." Additional practice in English will help clarify the different pronoun forms.

Indefinite Pronouns

INTRODUCE Display this sentence: *Someone wrote you a note.* **Ask:** Who is this someone? If we don't know, then we can use the indefinite pronoun *someone.* Other singular indefinite pronouns are: *anybody, everyone, everything, either,* and *each.* Some plural indefinite pronouns are: *few, several, both, others, many, all,* and *some.*

TEACH/MODEL Present the concept and provide examples from the current reading selection. Indefinite pronouns may not refer to specific nouns. Use the correct verb forms with singular indefinite pronouns and with plural indefinite pronouns.

	Indefinite Pronouns
Singular	<u>Everyone</u> is clapping. <u>Somebody</u> has sung very well.
Plural	<u>Some</u> are standing. <u>Others</u> are sitting.

PRACTICE Show students a picture of a concert. Have them describe it, using similar sentences: *Everyone is in the concert. Some are singers.* Give other examples using illustrations or pictures from the text or related to the text.

ENGLISH LANGUAGE LEARNERS

In some languages, the words *everyone* and *everybody* take a plural verb. Students may try using verbs such as "Everyone are" or "Everybody say."

Reflexive Pronouns

INTRODUCE Display these sentences: *I will write a note to myself. She will buy herself a snack.* **Explain:** *Myself* and *herself* are reflexive pronouns.

TEACH/MODEL Present the concept and provide examples. Reflexive pronouns reflect the action back on the subject, for example, *They gave themselves a chance to rest.*

	Reflexive Pronouns
Singular	himself, herself, myself, itself, yourself
Plural	ourselves, yourselves, themselves

PRACTICE Write these subject pronouns on index cards: *I, you, he, she, it, we, they.* Make another set with reflexive pronouns. Have students draw a card from the reflexive set and match it to its subject pronoun. Then, have them write a sentence with the words they chose.

ENGLISH LANGUAGE LEARNERS

Chinese speakers learning English may omit a second reference to one person in a sentence. Rather than "I enjoyed myself," a student may feel that "I enjoyed" is complete.

Pronouns and Antecedents

INTRODUCE Display and read aloud this sentence: <u>Sam</u> says <u>he</u> will go. **Explain:** In this sentence, the pronoun *he* replaces the name *Sam.* The sentence does not have to say "Sam says Sam will go." *Sam,* the noun being replaced, is called the antecedent. A pronoun must agree in number and gender with the noun or noun phrase it replaces. Sam is one person, a boy. So we use the pronoun *he,* which is singular and masculine. The pronoun for a girl is feminine: *she.* Lisa says she will go.

TEACH/MODEL Present the concept and provide examples:

• A pronoun and its antecedent must agree in number and gender.

Pronouns and Antecedents
<u>Laura</u> knows what <u>she</u> wants.
<u>Ravi</u> and <u>Ben</u> called me when <u>they</u> got home.
<u>The parrot</u> repeats what <u>it</u> hears.

PRACTICE Display this sentence: <u>*The cat* eats what *it* likes.</u> Write the following on cards and distribute to students: *The girl; My brother; The children; The dog; she; he; they; it.* Invite students to use the cards to substitute antecedents and pronouns in the sentence.

Verbs in Present Tense

INTRODUCE Perform these actions as you narrate: I walk to the front of the room. I point to the board. Explain that the words *walk* and *point* are verbs. The tense of a verb tells when something happens. A verb in present tense, like *walk* or *point*, tells what happens now. To talk about one other person or thing, add *-s*: *He walks. She points.*

TEACH/MODEL Present the concept and provide examples from the text. Verbs in present tense tell what happens now.

	Verb	Example
I, you, we, they	see	I <u>see</u> my sister.
he, she, it	sees	She <u>sees</u> me.

PRACTICE Write these subjects on index cards: *The baby, The girls, Sam, my brother, I.* Write these verbs on another set: *work, sleep, run, jump,* and *play.* Have students draw a card from each set and create a sentence. You can also use characters, information, and verbs from the reading.

ENGLISH LANGUAGE LEARNERS

English verb endings differ from verb endings in languages such as Spanish and Polish, which use different endings for person and number. However, students may need practice adding *-s* or *-es* to present-tense verbs with third-person singular subjects.

Verbs in Past Tense

INTRODUCE Display these sentences: *I <u>walked</u> to the front of the room. I <u>pointed</u> to the board.* Explain: I did these things in the past. Many verbs in past tense end with *-ed.* If a verb ends in *e*, like *move*, drop the *e* and then add *-ed: moved.* If a verb has one syllable and ends with a vowel followed by a consonant, such as *shop,* double the consonant before adding *-ed: shopped.*

TEACH/MODEL Present the concept and provide specific examples from the current reading selection. Verbs in past tense tell what happened in the past.

	Verbs in Past Tense
Add *-ed*	He *jumped* over the chair.
Drop the Final *e* and Add *-ed*	I *moved* the chair.
Double the Consonant and Add *-ed*	He *slipped* on the rug.

PRACTICE Display a list of verbs: *walk, play, jump, call, move, push, listen,* and *watch*. Begin to tell a story: Yesterday, I walked to the park with my friend. Have students add to the story, using the verbs from the list in the past tense. Alternatively, use a list of verbs from the text.

ENGLISH LANGUAGE LEARNERS

In Chinese, Hmong, and Vietnamese, verbs do not change to show the tense. Adverbs or expressions of time indicate when an action has taken place. Explain that regular past-tense verbs in English always have an *-ed* ending.

Irregular Verbs

INTRODUCE Display these sentences: *I think about you. I write a note. I thought about you. I wrote a note.* **Explain:** Usually, you add *-ed* to a verb to form the past tense. But here, I didn't use *thinked* or *writed*. Some verbs are not regular verbs. They are called irregular verbs. An irregular verb has a different spelling in the past tense.

TEACH/MODEL Present the concept and provide specific examples from the current reading selection. Irregular verbs do not add *-ed* to form the past tense. Irregular verbs have different spellings in the past tense.

Irregular Verbs	Past Tense
write	I *wrote* a poem yesterday.
sing	I *sang* a song last night.
eat	I *ate* an apple earlier today.

PRACTICE Prepare index cards with irregular verbs. On one side, write the present tense. On the other side, write the past tense: *write/wrote; sing/sang; make/made; give/gave; eat/ate; have/had*. Have pairs dictate sentences to each other using the words on both sides.

ENGLISH LANGUAGE LEARNERS

Many English learners need extra practice with the variety of irregular verbs that also feature unfamiliar phonics elements, such as *catch/caught, buy/bought,* and *can/could*.

Verbs in Future Tense

INTRODUCE Say: What will I do after school today? I will go home. I will eat a snack. I will read my e-mail. **Explain:** To talk about the future, we use verbs in the future tense. The future may be later today, next week, or even next year. Write one of the statements and point out the word *will*. Say: We use the helping verb *will* to form the future tense.

TEACH/MODEL Present the concept and provide examples from the current reading selection. Verbs in future tense tell what will happen in the future.

Verbs in Future Tense
I *will go* home.
I *will eat* a snack.
I *will do* my homework.

PRACTICE Have pairs tell each other what they will do when they get home from school or at some point in the future. If students can pantomime the action, have them act out the verb. Then, have them write or say the complete sentence.

ENGLISH LANGUAGE LEARNERS

Spanish, Haitian Creole, and Hmong speakers may use present tense in places where English calls for future tense. Help students practice verbs in statements using the word *will*.

Principal Parts of Regular Verbs

INTRODUCE Display these sentences: *I talk to you. I am talking to you. I talked to you. I have talked to you many times.* Explain: A verb's tenses are made from four basic forms: present, present participle, past, and past participle. These are called the verb's principal parts. The present form is used in the first sentence. The second sentence uses the present participle form. The third sentence uses the past form, which is the -ed form of the regular verb. The fourth sentence uses the past participle.

TEACH/MODEL Present the concept and provide examples from the current reading selection. The four basic forms are called the principal parts. The present participle can use *am, is,* or *are* and the -*ing* form. The past participle uses *has, have,* or *had* and the -*ed* form.

	Principal Parts: Regular Verbs
Present	The baby *plays* all day.
Present Participle	The baby *is playing* now.
Past	You *helped* me yesterday.
Past Participle	You *have helped* me before.

PRACTICE Say and display these verbs: *jump, walk, talk, wave, laugh.* Have students give the present participle of each verb with the subjects *I, you, she,* and *they*. Have them pantomime the actions and point to the corresponding subject.

ENGLISH LANGUAGE LEARNERS

Speakers of several languages, including Arabic, may find the English distinction between the past and present perfect tenses unfamiliar. Show contrasting examples, and explain how the sense of time differs.

Principal Parts of Irregular Verbs

INTRODUCE Display these sentences: *You grow every day. You are growing so much! You grew an inch last year. You have grown an inch every year.* Point out the past form and past participle. Irregular verbs change spelling in these forms.

TEACH/MODEL Present the concept and provide examples from the current reading selection. The principal parts of irregular verbs are the same four kinds as the principal parts of regular verbs. The -*ing* form is made the same way, such as *growing* or *going*. But irregular verbs do not use the -*ed* ending for the past and the past participle. For example, we do not say *growed*; we say *grew*. We do not say *have growed*; we say *have grown*.

PRACTICE Write the principal parts of *go, sing, take,* and *write* on index cards. Give each student a card. Students circulate to find others with principal parts of the same verb.

ENGLISH LANGUAGE LEARNERS

Spanish, like English, has irregular verbs (such as *ser*, which means "to be," and *ir*, which means "to go"). Challenge students who are literate in Spanish to identify irregular Spanish verbs, and see whether English verbs with the same meanings are irregular.

Helping Verbs

INTRODUCE Display these sentences: *I <u>am planting</u> seeds. They <u>will grow</u> fast. I <u>have planted</u> seeds before.* Explain: The underlined parts are called verb phrases. The main verbs—*planting, grow,* and *planted*—show action. The helping verbs—*am, will,* and *have*—tell more about the action. The helping verb *am* tells what I am doing now. *Will* tells what the seeds will do in the future. *Have* tells what I have done in the past.

TEACH/MODEL Present the concept and provide examples from the current reading selection. Helping verbs can tell the time of the action.

	Helping Verbs
Present	The dog *is* wagging his tail.
Past	He *was* barking last night.
Future	He *will* stay inside tonight.
Started in the Past	You *have* helped me before.

PRACTICE Have each student create three index cards labeled Present, Past, and Future. Say these sentences and have students hold up the corresponding card: You *were* playing basketball yesterday. You *are* listening to me now. You *will* go to the library later. Encourage students to say other sentences with helping verbs.

ENGLISH LANGUAGE LEARNERS

The uses of *have* and *had* as helping verbs may be familiar to Spanish-speaking students once they learn the English words. The Spanish verb *haber* is used similarly.

Linking Verbs

INTRODUCE Display these sentences: *I <u>am</u> tired. I <u>feel</u> sick. She <u>seems</u> sad. He <u>is</u> the leader. The car <u>was</u> new.* Explain: In these sentences, the underlined words are called linking verbs. They tell what the subject is or what the subject is like.

TEACH/MODEL Present the concept and provide examples. Linking verbs do not show actions. They tell what the subject is or what the subject is like.

Linking Verbs	Examples
is	Summer *is* here.
are	The days *are* longer.
feels	The sun *feels* warmer.

PRACTICE Have pairs tell three nice things they observe about each other: *You seem happy. You are smart. You are funny.* Have them identify the linking verbs. Students can also find three sentences in a text that describe a character using linking verbs.

ENGLISH LANGUAGE LEARNERS

In languages such as Chinese and Korean, linking verbs often are not required: *she tired* or *they sad.* Help students practice English sentences with linking verbs. Vietnamese speakers may use the English verb *have* in place of *there are* or *is,* as in *Inside the box have a gift.* Help students practice with sentences using forms of *be.*

Troublesome Verbs *Lie/Lay, Sit/Set*

INTRODUCE Write and say: The boy lays his book on the table. Then, he lies down on his bed to take a nap. Explain that in the first sentence, the boy puts his book down on a table. In the second sentence, he goes to bed to rest. Write and say: Miguel sets the plates on the table. Then, he sits at the table. Show the difference between *set* and *sit* in these sentences by pantomiming the actions.

TEACH/MODEL Present the concept and provide examples from the text that the students are currently reading. Some verbs look similar or have similar meanings. Think of the meanings and the main parts of verbs. Tell students that the verbs *set* and *lay* usually take a direct object. Display the sentences: *She set her keys on the counter. He lays his wallet on the table.* Use the sentences to show students that a direct object (*keys, wallet*) is a noun or pronoun that receives the action of a verb (*set, lays*) or shows the result of the action.

Troublesome Verb	Past	Past Participle
lie: "rest" or "recline"	lay	(has, have, had) lain
lay: "put" or "place"	laid	(has, have, had) laid
sit: "sit down"	sat	(has, have, had) sat
set: "put something somewhere"	set	(has, have, had) set

PRACTICE In pairs, have students take turns creating sentences that include troublesome words. The partner accepts a correct example and offers a new example.

Troublesome Verbs *Leave/Let, Rise/Raise*

INTRODUCE Write and say: The girl will leave with her friends. Her mother let her go. Explain that first the girl is going away. Her mother allows, or permits, her to go. Write and say: The sun will rise every day. The children raise their hands in class. Use pantomime or pictures to discuss the differences between *rise* and *raise* in these sentences.

TEACH/MODEL Present the concept and provide examples from the students' reading. Some verbs look similar or have similar meanings. Think of the meanings and principal parts of the verbs to use them correctly.

PRACTICE Display several incomplete sentences, asking students to complete each sentence with a troublesome verb. For example: *The teacher _____ (let) the children go home. The children _____ (left) quickly.*

ENGLISH LANGUAGE LEARNERS

Have English learners study the meanings and principal parts of troublesome verbs. Then, provide additional examples of the verbs used correctly.

Contractions

INTRODUCE Display these sentences: <u>*You're*</u> *calling me.* <u>*I'm*</u> *far away. I* <u>*can't*</u> *hear you.* Explain: The underlined words are contractions. A contraction is a shortened form of two words. An apostrophe (point to an apostrophe) takes the place of one or more letters. Look at these contractions: *You* and *are* become *you're. I* and *am* become *I'm. Can* and *not* become *can't.*

TEACH/MODEL Present the concept and provide examples:

- A contraction is a shortened form of two words.

- An apostrophe takes the place of a letter or letters that are removed when you write a contraction.

Two Words	Contractions
<u>I</u> and <u>have</u>	<u>I've</u> eaten breakfast.
<u>should</u> and <u>not</u>	You <u>shouldn't</u> run in the hall.
<u>can</u> and <u>not</u>	She <u>can't</u> come to my party.

PRACTICE Say the following sentences and have students rephrase them using contractions: You are hiding. I do not see you. I am going to find you. I could not stop looking. If necessary, help students learn the contractions for each of the sentences: *you're, don't, I'm,* and *couldn't.*

Negatives

INTRODUCE Display these sentences: *I* <u>*never*</u> *eat fish. I* <u>*don't*</u> *ever eat fish.* Explain: The underlined words are negatives. They mean "no" or "not." Contractions with *n't* are negatives. In English, we use only one negative with one verb. *I* <u>*don't*</u> <u>*never*</u> *eat fish* has a double negative. Take away one negative. (See the first two examples.)

TEACH/MODEL Present the concept and provide examples:

- Use only one negative with one verb.
- Use a positive verb in a sentence with *not.*

Type of Word	Examples
negative word + verb	<u>Nothing</u> is on the table.
positive verb + *not*	I don't see <u>anything</u> there.
verb + negative word	They went <u>nowhere</u>.
positive verb + *not*	We didn't go <u>anywhere</u>.

PRACTICE Write these sentences on the board: *I can't never tell you. I won't say nothing. I don't want nobody to hear.* Invite students to come up and show how they would fix the double negative. Ask them to read the new sentence.

ENGLISH LANGUAGE LEARNERS

In Spanish, Haitian Creole, and some other languages, double negatives (similar to *We did not do nothing*) are correct. Tell students that standard English does not use double negatives.

Articles

INTRODUCE **Say:** I need a pencil. **Hold up a pencil and say:** Here is a pencil with an eraser. The pencil is yellow. **Show some pencils and say:** The pencils are new. **Explain that** *a, an,* **and** *the* **are called articles:** Articles are these words that come before nouns: a pencil, the paper, an ink pen. Use *a* or *an* before a singular noun. You can use *the* before singular nouns or plural nouns.

TEACH/MODEL Present the concept and provide several examples:

* *A, an,* and *the* are articles.

* Use *a* before a singular noun that begins with a consonant sound; use *an* before a singular noun that begins with a vowel sound.

Articles
I want <u>a</u> banana. Sue wants <u>an</u> apple.
<u>The</u> fruit salad was good. <u>The</u> girls ate it all.

PRACTICE Have students identify the articles in the following sentences.

1. Cali, Beth, and Ling found (an, a) rope in their garage.

2. (An, The) rope was six feet long.

3. Beth knew (a, an) song for jumping rope.

4. (The, A) girls jumped rope for (a, an) hour.

Adjectives: Size, What Kind, How Many

INTRODUCE **Say:** You know that nouns are words that name people, places, animals, or things—for example, *girls* and *house.* Adjectives are words that tell more about the nouns: *small house, four girls, blue car, long hair.* Which words are the adjectives? *(small, four, blue, long)*

TEACH/MODEL Present the concept and provide examples:

* An adjective tells more about a noun or pronoun.

	Adjectives
What Kind?	a <u>good</u> friend; The food is <u>spicy</u>.
How Many?	<u>two</u> men; <u>many</u> apples
Size	a <u>big</u> hat; The school was <u>small</u>.

PRACTICE Have students identify the adjectives in the following sentences: *My two brothers and I have a small garden. We have three plants. The plants have many tomatoes that are big and red. They are delicious!*

Adjectives: Comparative and Superlative

INTRODUCE Draw three long lines of different lengths on the board. Point to the different lines and say: This line is long. This line is longer. This line is the longest. **Say:** *Long* is an adjective. *Longer* compares two nouns, such as two lines. To compare two nouns, add *-er* to most adjectives. *Longest* compares three or more nouns. To form a superlative adjective that compares three or more nouns, add *-est* to most adjectives.

TEACH/MODEL Present the concept and provide examples:

- Many comparative adjectives end in *-er: faster, thinner, tinier.* Change the spelling of some adjectives, like *tiny,* when you add *-er.*
- Many longer adjectives use the word *more* instead of *-er: more exciting, more beautiful.*
- Many superlative adjectives end in *-est: brightest, loudest, tallest.* Use *most* with longer adjectives: *most beautiful.*
- Some adjectives have irregular forms, such as *good, better, best.*

Comparative	Superlative
bigger; more important	fastest; most difficult

PRACTICE Have students choose the correct adjective to complete the following sentences: *The squirrel is* (smaller, smallest) *than the dog. Chico is the* (largest, larger) *of the three dogs. My bird is* (more beautiful, most beautiful) *than my friend's bird. The big dog should have a* (gooder, better) *name. My friend Buffy is the* (funniest, funnier) *person I know.*

Adjectives: Demonstrative

INTRODUCE Present three girls and three boys, with the boys farther away. Ask: Which students are girls? These students are girls. Those students are boys. Which girl is Audrey? This girl is Audrey. That boy is Oliver. *These, those, this,* and *that* are called demonstrative adjectives. They help you demonstrate, or show, which one or which ones. Use *this* and *these* when things are close. Use *that* and *those* when things are farther away.

TEACH/MODEL Present the concept and provide examples:

- Demonstrative adjectives: *this, that, these, those*

	Demonstrative Adjectives
Singular	<u>This</u> book is longer than <u>that</u> book.
Plural	<u>These</u> shoes are bigger than <u>those</u> shoes.

PRACTICE Have students choose the correct adjective to complete the following sentences: (These, This) *flowers are called poppies. Each spring,* (this, these) *field is full of poppies.* (That, Those) *tree on the hill looks like a person. People ride their bikes across* (those, this) *hills. Many people take pictures of* (this, these) *place.*

Adverbs for *When, Where,* and *How*

INTRODUCE Say and act out this chant: Slowly I turn. Loudly I clap! I walk here and there. I end with a tap. Say: *Slowly, loudly, here,* and *there* are adverbs. They tell how, when, or where something happens.

TEACH/MODEL Present the concept and provide examples:

* Adverbs tell more about the actions of verbs.
* Adverbs that tell how something happens often end in *-ly.*

	Adverbs
When?	I <u>always</u> walk to school.
Where?	I like to walk <u>outside</u>.
How?	I walk <u>quickly</u>.

PRACTICE Write the following adverbs on slips of paper: *slowly, quickly, loudly, sleepily.* Display them. Have a volunteer choose one. Give a command such as: Walk to the door. The volunteer must walk in the manner of the adverb. The student who guesses the adverb takes the next turn.

ENGLISH LANGUAGE LEARNERS

Point out to Spanish speakers that the adverb suffix *-ly* is like the ending *-mente* in Spanish. Give examples with cognates such as *rapid/rápidamente.*

Comparative and Superlative Adverbs

INTRODUCE Say each sentence: I speak quietly. Katya speaks more quietly. Rob speaks most quietly. *More quietly* is a comparative adverb. It compares two actions: I speak, Katya speaks. *Most quietly* is a superlative adverb. It compares three or more actions. If an adverb does not end in *-ly,* add *-er* or *-est* to compare.

TEACH/MODEL Present the concept and provide examples:

* A comparative adverb compares two actions.
* A superlative adverb compares three or more actions.
* Some adverbs are irregular: *well, better, best.*

Comparative and Superlative Adverbs
Julia runs <u>fast</u>. Anil sings <u>beautifully</u>.
Pat runs <u>faster</u>. Kenji sings <u>more beautifully</u>.
Tere runs the <u>fastest</u>. Ivan sings <u>most beautifully</u>.

PRACTICE Display three pictures of athletes. Have students compare them using *well, better, best* or *fast, faster, fastest* with the verbs *run, play,* or *swim.*

Prepositions and Prepositional Phrases

INTRODUCE Stand behind a chair, and have students do the same. Say: Behind the chair. Have students repeat. Continue moving and speaking, using the words *beside, around,* and *on* (sit). Explain: *Behind, beside, around,* and *on* are prepositions. *Behind the chair* and *on it* are prepositional phrases. *Behind* is a preposition, and *chair* is a noun. *On* is a preposition, and *it* is a pronoun.

TEACH/MODEL Present the concept and provide examples:

- A prepositional phrase can tell where, when, how, or which one.
- A prepositional phrase begins with a preposition (*above, across, at, behind, for, from, in, near, with,* and so on).
- A prepositional phrase ends with a noun or pronoun.

Preposition	around
Prepositional Phrase	around the chair

PRACTICE Model as you give students directions to follow: Walk to this side of the room. Walk across the room. Stand by a desk. Look under the desk. Have volunteers take turns giving directions that include prepositional phrases.

Conjunctions

INTRODUCE Use colored pens or markers to illustrate the following: I have a red pen and a green pen. The word *and* joins two similar things: two colors of pens. Do you like red or green better? The word *or* gives a choice: red or green. You can use the green pen, but don't use the red pen right now. The word *but* joins two different ideas: use and don't use. *And, or,* and *but* are called conjunctions.

TEACH/MODEL Present the concept and provide examples:

- A conjunction joins words, phrases, and sentences.

Related Ideas: Diego <u>and</u> I are friends.
Different Ideas: We live far apart, <u>but</u> we talk often.
Choice: We talk on the phone, <u>or</u> we send e-mail.

PRACTICE Share these common phrases with conjunctions: *salt and pepper; thanks, but no thanks; stop-and-go traffic; left or right; boy or girl.* Invite students to say them while using gestures to help show the meanings.

ENGLISH LANGUAGE LEARNERS

Speakers of Chinese and some other languages may build sentences using two conjunctions where English typically uses one. For example: *Because the sun came up, so I could see the clock.* Help students practice English patterns.

Subjects and Predicates

INTRODUCE Display this sentence: _The girl walks to school._ Explain that _The girl_ is the subject of the sentence, or what the sentence is about. Explain that _walks to school_ is the predicate. A predicate tells something about the subject.

TEACH/MODEL Present the concept and provide examples:

- The subject of a sentence tells whom or what the sentence is about.
- The predicate of a sentence tells what the subject is or what the subject does.

Subject	Predicate
Sam	went to the store.
The students	write a paper.
The vegetables	are fresh.

PRACTICE Write these sentences on strips of paper: _My friend rides a bike. My dog barks at cats. The fish smells good. The clown is funny._ Cut each strip into subject and predicate. Have students use the strips to form new sentences such as: _My friend is funny._

ENGLISH LANGUAGE LEARNERS

The typical English sequence of subject then predicate is not standard in some languages. For example, in Spanish the verb often appears before the subject, while in Korean and Hindi the verb typically appears at the end of a sentence.

Subject-Verb Agreement

INTRODUCE Display these sentences: _The bird sings a song. The birds sing a song._ Discuss the differences between the underlined parts: The first sentence has a singular subject: _bird._ The second sentence has a plural subject: _birds._ The subject and verb must agree.

TEACH/MODEL Present the general concept and provide examples:

- If the subject is singular, add _-s_ to the verb.
- If the subject is plural, do not add _-s_ to the verb.

Subject	Verb
man	dances
Mom	works
friends	play
both feet	hurt

PRACTICE Encourage students to scour the day's news headlines for examples of subject-verb agreement. For example: _Schools Close; Team Wins; Gas Prices Rise; Dog Saves Girl._

ENGLISH LANGUAGE LEARNERS

Students of various language backgrounds may add _-s_ to both the nouns and verbs in sentences: _The robots walks._ Point out that in English, verbs add _-s_ for singular nouns (A robot walks), not for verbs with plural nouns (The robots walk).

Word Order

INTRODUCE Display these sentences and read them aloud, gesturing: The bird flies. Flies the bird. **Ask:** What is the subject of the first sentence? (*The bird*) The second sentence does not sound right. The words are not in the right order to make a statement. In an English statement, the subject usually comes first. The predicate usually follows.

TEACH/MODEL Present the concept and provide examples:

* Sentences need to have words in the right order.

* In a statement, the subject usually comes first. The predicate usually follows.

In the Right Order:	Pablo is my friend.
Not in the Right Order:	Is friend my Pablo.

PRACTICE Say these groups of words: The food is good. Is good the food. My friend rides a bike. Rides a bike my friend. Plays the dog. The dog plays. **Have students say which sentences are in correct word order.**

ENGLISH LANGUAGE LEARNERS

Help students see that word order strongly affects meaning in English. *Lee thanked Tony* has a different meaning from *Tony thanked Lee.*

Complete Sentences and Sentence Fragments

INTRODUCE Write this sentence and fragment on the board: *Tom went to the library. Went to the library.* **Ask:** Who went to the library? (**Tom**) Which sentence tells you this? The first sentence tells a complete idea. It says who did something. The second set of words (*went to the library*) is called a sentence fragment. It does not tell a complete idea. It does not say who went to the library. How would you make this fragment a complete sentence? (**Add a subject.**)

TEACH/MODEL Present the concept and provide examples:

* A sentence tells a complete idea.

* A fragment is a piece of a sentence. It does not tell a complete idea.

Sentence	Ava eats her lunch.
Fragment	Her lunch in a bag.

PRACTICE Say these groups of words. Have students call out "sentence" or "fragment" after each one: My brother. We walk to school. We ride on the bus. In the car. After school. **Invite students to contribute other sentences.**

ENGLISH LANGUAGE LEARNERS

Spanish- and Chinese-speaking students may omit some pronouns as sentence subjects because in their home languages the pronoun may be unnecessary. For example, the Spanish equivalent of *Am reading* is a complete sentence.

Types of Sentences: Statements

INTRODUCE Display these sentences: *I went to the library. My brother went, too. We both found good books.* Say: Let's look at these sentences. Each one starts with a capital letter and ends with a period. Each one tells something. A sentence that tells something is called a statement.

TEACH/MODEL Present the concept and provide examples:

- A sentence that tells something is called a statement.
- It begins with a capital letter and ends with a period.

Statements

I had a party yesterday.

All of my friends came to my house.

You ate pizza.

PRACTICE Write groups of words such as these on the board, including the mistakes: *my friends are funny. / They tell me jokes / I laugh every day* Have volunteers come up and fix the statements by adding correct punctuation and a capital letter at the beginning.

Types of Sentences: Questions

INTRODUCE Display these sentences: *What is your name? Where do you live? How old are you? Do you have any brothers?* Ask: How are these sentences different from statements? They each ask something, and they end with question marks. A sentence that asks something is called a question. **Model the difference in vocal intonation between these two sentences:** That is your dog. Is that your dog?

TEACH/MODEL Present the general concept and provide examples:

- A sentence that asks something is called a question.
- It starts with a capital letter and ends with a question mark.

Questions

How are you?

Did you go to Sam's party?

Does Ami like pizza?

PRACTICE Have pairs of students ask each other questions about what they did yesterday. For example: *What did you do in school yesterday? What is your favorite subject?*

ENGLISH LANGUAGE LEARNERS

Speakers of Chinese, Vietnamese, and other Asian languages often form questions by adding words to statements, comparable to *The food is hot, no?* or *You see or not see the bird?* Provide model English questions for students to understand and to follow the pattern.

Types of Sentences: Exclamations and Interjections

INTRODUCE Write and say in an excited voice: I am so happy! **Ask:** What feeling does that sentence express? (excitement; happiness) Whenever you say something with strong feeling, you are saying an exclamation. A written exclamation ends with an exclamation mark. **Next, write and say:** Hooray! **Explain:** This word also shows strong feeling and ends in an exclamation mark. However, it is *not* a complete sentence. It is called an interjection.

TEACH/MODEL Present the concept and provide examples:

- An exclamation is a sentence that shows strong feeling. It ends with an exclamation mark.

- An interjection is a word or group of words that shows strong feeling. It ends with an exclamation mark, but it is not a complete sentence.

Exclamation	I have a new baby brother!
Interjection	Wow!

PRACTICE Write these interjections on index cards: *Ouch! Wow! Oh, no! Hooray!* Display them. Have a volunteer secretly choose an interjection and pantomime a scene that would elicit that interjection. Whoever guesses correctly takes the next turn. Then have students share exclamations with the class.

ENGLISH LANGUAGE LEARNERS

Speakers of Russian, Polish, and other languages may need to practice correct word order in exclamations. Have students make and use sentence strips to correct exclamations such as *We enjoy very much movies!*

Types of Sentences: Commands

INTRODUCE Give students various commands such as these: Please stand up. Walk to the front of the class. Say hello. Sit down. **Ask:** How are these sentences the same? (They told us to do something.) Sentences that tell someone to do something are called commands.

TEACH/MODEL Present the concept and provide examples:

- A command is a sentence that tells someone to do something.

- It begins with a capital letter and ends with a period.

Commands

Open the door.

Turn on the light.

Sweep the floor.

PRACTICE As a class, play the game "I Said So" in which a leader says command sentences, such as "Touch your nose," and the rest of the class follows.

ENGLISH LANGUAGE LEARNERS

Vietnamese speakers may recognize commands when they include an adverb or another clue word: *Go to school now. Take this to the office; go now.*

Simple and Compound Sentences

INTRODUCE Display these sentences: *I went to Sal's house. We watched a movie.* Ask students to tell the subject and predicate (verb) of each sentence. Explain: A simple sentence has one subject and one predicate. But we can join the two simple sentences this way: *I went to Sal's house, and we watched a movie.* The new sentence is called a compound sentence. The two simple sentences are joined with the word *and*. Now the sentence has two subjects and two predicates.

TEACH/MODEL Present the concept and provide examples from a reading selection:

- A simple sentence has one subject and one predicate.
- A compound sentence has two simple sentences joined by a comma and one of these words: *and*, *but*, or *or*.

Simple Sentences	**Compound Sentences**
Lena is my sister. I love her.	Lena is my sister, and I love her.
I like peanuts. They make me sick.	I like peanuts, but they make me sick.
You can walk to school. I can drive you.	You can walk to school, or I can drive you.

PRACTICE Provide several pairs of simple sentences from the current reading selection. Have students rewrite them as compound sentences.

ENGLISH LANGUAGE LEARNERS

Students may have difficulty distinguishing the clauses in a compound sentence in English. Give them additional practice finding the subject and verb within each independent clause.

Combining Sentences

INTRODUCE Display these sentences: *I ate a sandwich. I drank some milk.* Ask: What is the subject of both sentences? You can combine two sentences that have the same subject: *I ate a sandwich and drank some milk.* Display these sentences: *Max <u>went to the beach</u>. I <u>went to the beach</u>.* Ask: What is the predicate of both sentences? You can combine two sentences that have the same predicate: Max and I <u>went to the beach</u>.

TEACH/MODEL Present the concept and provide examples from the current reading selection:

- Combine two sentences that have the same subject.
- Combine two sentences that have the same predicate.

Same Subject	**Same Predicate**
<u>Dan</u> sat down. <u>Dan</u> did his homework.	Miguel <u>walked to school</u>. I <u>walked to school</u>.
<u>Dan</u> sat down and did his homework.	Miguel and I <u>walked to school</u>.

PRACTICE Make a set of sentence cards using sentences from the current reading selection. Include sentences with the same subject as well as sentences with the same predicate. Distribute the sentence cards to students. Have volunteers read their sentence. Ask the student with the same subject or predicate to raise his or her hand. Then have those two students combine their sentences.

Complex Sentences

INTRODUCE Review compound sentences. Then present these complex sentences: _When I run, I feel good. I feel good when I run._ Explain: This type of sentence is called a complex sentence. It has two parts, called clauses. The underlined part cannot stand alone as a sentence. If it comes first in the sentence, use a comma. The other part (_I feel good_) can stand alone as a complete sentence.

TEACH/MODEL Present the concept and provide examples from a reading selection:

- A complex sentence contains two clauses.
- The two clauses are joined together with words such as _because_, _when_, _since_, _if_, or _until_.
- Example complex sentences: _When I grow up, I will be a teacher. I will be a teacher when I grow up._

PRACTICE Have students write sentences and tell whether they are complex: _My sister's name is Lupe._ (no) _Since she is little, I help her with homework._ (yes) _I also tie her shoes._ (no) _When I was little, my mom helped me._ (yes)

ENGLISH LANGUAGE LEARNERS

Functional words, such as _if_, _that_, _so_, and _because_, are often used somewhat differently in English than their equivalents in other languages. Help students practice and understand usages of these words.

Independent and Dependent Clauses

INTRODUCE Present this complex sentence: _We cross the street when the light is green._ Explain: The underlined part of the sentence cannot stand alone as a sentence. It is a dependent clause. It depends on another part of the sentence. The other part (_we cross the street_) can stand alone as a sentence. It is an independent clause.

TEACH/MODEL Present the concept and provide examples from a reading selection:

- A complex sentence is made of an independent clause and a dependent clause.
- The dependent clause cannot stand alone.
- The independent clause can stand alone.

Independent Clause	Dependent Clause
I am happy	because I passed the test.

PRACTICE Display the following dependent clauses, and have students add an independent clause to each to form complex sentences: _Since he was little, When I grow up, Because it was raining, If you help me._ Have students write the complex sentences.

ENGLISH LANGUAGE LEARNERS

Provide models of dependent clauses that begin with words such as _after_, _although_, _as_, _because_, _before_, _if_, _since_, _then_, _until_, _when_, and _while_. These words may have uses that are unfamiliar to students of many language backgrounds.

Commas: In a Series and in Direct Address

INTRODUCE Display this sentence: *My favorite colors are red, blue, and yellow.* Point out the commas. Say: Commas help you understand a sentence. They tell you when to pause, or rest. Put commas after items in a series of words such as *red, blue, and yellow.* Display these sentences: *Kim, may I use your pen? Yes, Lucas, you may.* Say: When we write a sentence in which a person is directly addressed by name, we use a comma.

TEACH/MODEL Present the concept and provide examples:

- Use commas to separate items in a series.
- Use commas with direct address.

Commas in a Series	I like baseball, basketball, and soccer. I play Monday, Wednesday, and Friday.
Commas in Direct Address	Lori, would you come here? Yes, Mom, I'm coming. I need your help, Lori.

PRACTICE On the board, write menu items such as *soup, salad, sandwich, milk, tea,* and *juice.* Have pairs play the roles of server and customer at a café. The server says, "May I take your order?" The customer names three items such as: "I want soup, salad, and milk." The server says and writes the order. Next, the customer says and writes a sentence thanking the server by name. Have pairs switch roles.

ENGLISH LANGUAGE LEARNERS

Some students may use commas where periods are used in the United States (1,5 for 1.5). Determine the meaning, and clarify the standard usage in American English.

Commas: With Appositives and Introductory Phrases

INTRODUCE Display these sentences: *Mr. Hays, my teacher, speaks Spanish. Yes, I know.* Explain: The underlined part of the first sentence is called an appositive. It is a noun phrase that describes another noun. Use a comma before and after an appositive. The underlined part of the second sentence is called an introductory word. Put a comma after an introductory word or phrase such as *well, no, oh,* and *in other words.*

TEACH/MODEL Present the concept and provide examples:

- Use a comma before and after an appositive.
- Use a comma after an introductory word or phrase.

Appositives	Mr. Simms, my neighbor, has a dog. The dog, a poodle, barks all night.
Introductory Words or Phrases	Oh, I am very sorry. In other words, you cannot sleep.

PRACTICE Write names and job titles of school staff, such as *Mrs. Olson, the bus driver.* Have students use this information to write sentences with appositives.

Quotation Marks

INTRODUCE Display and read aloud the following dialogue: "Do you have homework?" my mother asked. "Yes, I have to read a book," I said. "What is the name of the book?" my mother wanted to know. Point out the position of the quotation marks in the dialogue.

TEACH/MODEL Present the concept and provide examples:

- A quotation shows the exact words of a speaker.
- Quotation marks enclose a quotation.
- Use a comma to separate the speaker's exact words from the rest of the sentence. Don't add a comma when the quotation ends with a question mark or exclamation mark.
- Quotation marks are also used for poetry titles, song titles, and story titles.

Quotation	Story Title
"Mr. Chung is my favorite teacher," said Joy.	"The Cat Has a Hat"

PRACTICE Display correct and incorrect examples of quotation marks used within a sentence. Write the sentences: *"He plays soccer"* (incorrect) *He said, "I am going to play soccer."* (correct) Offer several examples and ask students to identify correct and incorrect usage.

ENGLISH LANGUAGE LEARNERS

Help students use quotation marks in English by having them complete the following sentence frame in English and their home language: My favorite movie is "___." Model an answer as you make a gesture for quotation marks with your fingers when you say the name of the movie. Have students repeat.

Parentheses

INTRODUCE Write and say the following sentence: Jin has several pets (dog, bird, fish), but he is allergic to cats. Ask: What information is provided in the parentheses of this sentence? Explain: The information in the parentheses tells us more about Jin's pets.

TEACH/MODEL Present the concept and provide examples:

- Words in parentheses give an explanation or a comment in an already complete sentence.
- The information in parentheses is not necessary but adds detail to the sentence.

Sentence without Parentheses	Sentence with Parentheses
Some subjects are very hard for me.	Some subjects (especially math and science) are very hard for me.

PRACTICE Have students give extra details about a friend by completing the following sentence frame: My friend likes to do many things after school (such as ___).

ENGLISH LANGUAGE LEARNERS

The writing systems of students' home languages may have different conventions for parentheses. Have students practice finding parentheses in classroom texts.

Plurals and Possessives

INTRODUCE Write the following pair of sentences on the board, and ask students how they are different: *A chair and a table are in the room. Chairs and tables are in the room.* Students will probably notice that the nouns in the first sentence are in the singular form, whereas the nouns in the second sentence are in the plural form. Next, write these two sentences on the board, again asking students what they notice about them: *The pen of the teacher is red. The teacher's pen is red.* Say: Both sentences mean the same, but they use different ways to show possession, or ownership.

TEACH/MODEL Copy the following chart on the board and use it to teach students how to form plurals and possessives in English.

	Rules	Examples
Plurals	Add -*s* to the singular form of most nouns.	boys, girls, pens, balls, days
	Add -*es* to words that end with *sh, ch, x, s,* and *z*.	brushes, arches, boxes, classes, quizzes
	For words that end with a consonant and *y*, change the *y* to *i* before adding -*es*.	cities, stories, candies
Possessives with an Apostrophe	Add an apostrophe and *s* to most singular nouns.	Trina's idea, Kin's report, Carlos's dog
	Add an apostrophe to plural nouns that end in -*s*.	the girls' uniforms, the boys' team

PRACTICE Have students take turns pointing to an object belonging to a classmate and then saying a sentence using both the name of the object and the classmate, such as "This is Marco's notebook." Have students write sentences about their classmates, using the possessive form.

Tell students to write pairs of sentences about a friend and a family member. The first sentence should introduce the person, and the second sentence should tell about something that person has or owns. Write this example on the board: *My friend's name is Samuel. Samuel's wheelchair can go fast.*

Verb Endings: *-s, -ed, -ing*

INTRODUCE Write these verbs on the board and read them aloud, slowly, for the class, asking students to pay close attention to the sound at the end of each word: *washes, cleans, writes, sleeps, fixes, plays, swims, talks.* Ask students if they noticed a difference in the way the final *-s* was pronounced in certain words. Confirm for them that *writes, sleeps,* and *talks* are pronounced with the sound of /s/ at the end, while *washes, cleans, fixes, plays,* and *swims* are pronounced with the ending sound of /z/. In a similar way, ask students to determine if the following words end with the sound of /d/ or /t/: *walked, enjoyed, liked, talked, played, measured.* Finally, have students practice saying the following gerunds aloud, modeling correct pronunciation as necessary: *playing, cleaning, jogging, talking, washing, swimming.*

TEACH/MODEL The following rules may help students know which pronunciation to use with words that end in *-s* and *-ed*. Remind students that these are general guidelines and that they should listen carefully to native speakers for further guidance.

For words that end in *-s,*

* use the sound of /s/ if the letter before it is *k, p,* or *t.*
* use the sound of /z/ if the letter before it is *b, g, m, n,* or a vowel.

Note: If a word ends in silent *e,* the sound of *-s* depends on the letter before the *e.*

For words that end in *-ed,*

* use the sound of /d/ if the letter before it is *b, l, m, n,* or a vowel.
* use the sound of /t/ if the letter before it is *ch, k, p, s, sh,* or *x.*

To make the *-ing* form of a verb,

* add *-ing* to the simple verb.
* double final *b, g, m, n,* or *p* before adding *-ing.*
* drop silent *e* before adding *-ing.*

PRACTICE Ask students to write *s, z, d,* or *t* after you have said the following verbs aloud to indicate which sound they heard at the end of the word: *asks, plays, calls, runs, helps, walks, writes, sees, called, played, fixed, rubbed, helped, opened, walked, washed.* Then ask students to write the correct *-ing* form of each of the following verbs: *call, hope, play, run.* If needed, write the verbs on the board.

ENGLISH LANGUAGE LEARNERS

Some languages such as Chinese, Hmong, and Vietnamese do not use inflected endings to form verb tenses. Students may need help understanding that adding *-ed* to a verb indicates that the action happened in the past. Spelling changes in inflected verbs may also be difficult for English language learners to master. Provide students with extra practice as needed.

Compound Words

PURPOSE Compound words exist in many languages, including Spanish, Vietnamese, Haitian Creole, German, and Russian. Students may readily understand the concept of compound words but may need additional support determining how to break English compound words into their parts. The following activity provides practice with compound words.

INTRODUCE On two separate index cards, write two words that make up a compound word, such as the words *story* and *teller*. Ask students to define each word. If necessary, define *teller* as "a person who talks or tells something." Then, hold the cards side by side. Based on their previous definitions, ask students what *storyteller* means, and confirm that it means "a person who tells stories." Explain that the new word is a compound word. It is made up of two smaller words.

TEACH/MODEL Tell students: When you make a compound word, you put two words together to make a new word. Usually, there isn't any change to the spellings of the two smaller words. Use examples of compound words from a text, such as *snowbanks, heartberries, driftwood, lakeshore,* or *blueberry*. Discuss the meaning of each separate word, and then show how the words can be combined to create a new word. Point out that neither of the smaller words has a spelling change. The words are simply put together to create a new word. Ask students to share any other compound words that they know, and record their answers.

PRACTICE Give students note cards with small words that can be combined into compound words. Tell students to combine the small words to make logical compound words. Have students record the words they create. Conversely, students can take the compound word and draw a line to separate the two smaller words.

TEACHING TIP Providing visuals of the words can help students understand the meaning of compound words. Sometimes the smaller words have different meanings from the compound word. Point these out to students.

ENGLISH LANGUAGE LEARNERS

There are compound words in Spanish. Examples include *abrelatas* (can opener) and *rascacielos* (skyscraper). Point these out to students to help them make connections.

Related Words

INTRODUCE On the board, write *breath, breathe,* and *breathless.* Ask students: What do these words have in common? Point out that they all have the word *breath* as the base. The endings on the other two words change their part of speech and meaning. *Breathe* is a verb and *breathless* is an adjective. Many other words are closely related in the same way. Tell students that they will expand their vocabularies if they try to learn new words in groups with other related words.

TEACH/MODEL Write the following chart on the board, asking students to provide additional examples for the second column. Once students are familiar with these examples, have them find words that are related to words from the text they are currently reading. Provide students with a list of base words from the current reading selection. Have students fill in a chart with the words that are related to each base word.

Base Word	Related Words
jewel	jeweler, jewelry
planet	planetary, planetarium
paint	painter, painting
act	action, actor, active
sign	signature
compute	computer, computation
horizon	horizontal
pot	potter, pottery
bank	banker, banking
heal	health, healthy
relate	relative, relationship
produce	product, production
please	pleasant, pleasure

EXTEND Ask students to find base words from the selection and make a chart listing the related words. Students can refer to and expand on these charts of word groups.

Homophones

INTRODUCE Tell students this joke in the form of a question and answer: What is black and white and read all over? A newspaper! Explain to students that the question seems to be asking about colors (black, white, and red), but there is a play on the word *red*. The color *red* sounds the same as *read*, a past-tense form of the verb *read*. Explain that this joke is based on a pair of homophones (*red* and *read*), two words that sound the same but are spelled differently and mean completely different things.

TEACH/MODEL Write the following homophone pairs on the board: *pair, pear; flour, flower; made, maid; week, weak*. Explain the meaning of each word and point out the two different spellings. Model the pronunciation, emphasizing that the two words in each pair are pronounced in exactly the same way. Invite students to share any other homophones that they know. Spanish examples include *casa/caza* (house/hunt), *hola/ola* (hello/wave), and *ciento/siento* (one hundred/I feel).

PRACTICE Have students create a T-chart with the headings Same and Different. Write the following pairs of words on the board and have students read them aloud. Have them put a checkmark in the Same column if the words sound the same. Have them put a checkmark in the Different column if the words sound different. Write: *knew/new; flour/flower; meal/ mail; tow/toe; hour/our; through/threw; sun/son; plate/played; best/beast; week/weak.* Invite volunteers to share their answers. Review the meanings of the words. Make corrections as necessary, and tell students to correct their own work as well.

Ask students to write three sentences that include a pair of homophones, such as: *Our English class is an hour long.* Encourage students to make simple jokes with the homophones; they can also write sentences that are fanciful or silly, as in: *On Monday, I was too weak to make it through the whole week.*

ENGLISH LANGUAGE LEARNERS

Homophones are also common in other languages, but English learners may not recognize that English homophone pairs have the same pronunciation despite their different spellings. They may need to learn to use their knowledge of word meanings to choose the correct spelling of homophones.

Prefixes: *un-, re-*

INTRODUCE Write these word pairs on the board: *happy, unhappy; safe, unsafe; lucky, unlucky*. Read the words aloud with students and discuss their meanings. Ask: What do you notice about these words? Guide students to see that each word pair is a set of opposites and that one word in each pair begins with *un-*. Circle the prefix *un-* in each word and say: This syllable, *un-*, is a prefix. A prefix is a word part that is added to the beginning of a word. Adding a prefix changes the meaning of a word. A new word is made.

TEACH/MODEL Present the prefixes *un-* and *re-*. Use these examples to explain how the prefixes can change the meanings of words.

Prefix	Meaning	Examples
un-	not	happy → unhappy safe → unsafe locked → unlocked
re-	again	tell → retell do → redo write → rewrite

PRACTICE Write the following word combinations on the board. Have students write a new word for each pair, using *un-* or *re-*: *read again; appear again; not believable; not familiar; heat again; not interested; not like; start again; use again; not kind*. Invite volunteers to write their new words on the board.

Have students write these prefixes and base words on cards: *un-, re-, afraid, lock, run, unite*. Have students use the cards in different combinations to make words that have prefixes. Have students show you a base word without a prefix, add a prefix, say the new word, and tell what it means.

ENGLISH LANGUAGE LEARNERS

Some English prefixes and suffixes have equivalent forms in the Romance languages. For example, the prefix *dis-* in English *(disapprove)* corresponds to the Spanish *des- (desaprobar),* the French *des- (desapprouver)*, and the Haitian Creole *dis-* or *dez- (dezaprouve).* Students who are literate in these languages may be able to transfer their understanding of prefixes and suffixes by using parallel examples in their home language and in English.

Prefixes: *im-, in-, mis-, over-*

INTRODUCE Write these word pairs on the board: *patient, impatient; polite, impolite; proper, improper; pure, impure*. Read the words aloud with students and discuss their meanings. Ask students what they notice about these words. Guide students to see that each word pair is a set of opposites and that one word in each pair begins with *im-*. Circle the prefix *im-* in each word and explain: This word part, *im-*, is a prefix. It usually changes the meaning of a word to its opposite.

TEACH/MODEL Present the prefixes *im-, in-, mis-,* and *over-*. Use these examples to explain how the prefixes can change the meanings of words.

Prefix	Meaning	Examples
im-	not	impatient, imperfect, impossible
in-	not	insecure, intolerant, indestructible
mis-	wrong	misunderstood, misbehave, mismatch
over-	beyond, more than	overcook, overpay, overweight

PRACTICE Have students write these prefixes and base words on index cards: *im-, in-, mis-, over-, correct, interpret, load, look, mature, take, use*. Tell students to combine the cards to make words with prefixes.

Circulate as the students work, asking them to show you a base word and a prefix that goes with it. Ask advanced students to tell you what the word means and to use it in an oral sentence.

ENGLISH LANGUAGE LEARNERS

Tell Spanish speakers that the Spanish prefixes *im-* and *in-* have similar meanings *(impaciente, intolerante)*. The Spanish prefix *sobre-* is sometimes used like the English prefix *over- (sobrecarga)*.

Prefixes: *pre-, mid-, over-, out-, bi-*

INTRODUCE Write these word pairs on the board: *test, pretest; air, midair; time, overtime; run, outrun; monthly, bimonthly*. Read the words aloud with students and discuss their meanings. Ask: What do you notice about these words? Explain that the second word in each pair has a prefix that changes the meaning of the first word. Circle the prefix *pre-* and say: This syllable, *pre-*, is a prefix. A prefix is a word part that is added to the beginning of a word to change its meaning. When you add a prefix, a new word is made. The prefix *pre-* means "before." So, *prepay* means "to pay before."

TEACH/MODEL Present the prefixes *pre-, mid-, over-, out-,* and *bi-*. Using the chart below, explain how adding prefixes to base words changes the meaning of each word.

Prefix	Meaning	Examples
pre-	before	paid → prepaid view → preview
mid-	in the middle of	day → midday night → midnight
over-	more than normal, too much	grown → overgrown cooked → overcooked
out-	more, to a greater degree	side → outside run → outrun
bi-	two	cycle → bicycle

PRACTICE Have students write these prefixes and base words on index cards: *pre-, mid-, over-, out-, bi-, paid, air, time, field, weekly*. Have them use the cards in different combinations to make words with prefixes. As an additional challenge, have students show a base word without a prefix, add a prefix, say the new word, and tell what it means.

ENGLISH LANGUAGE LEARNERS

Point out to Spanish speakers that the prefix *mid-* is related in meaning to the Spanish word *medio*, which means "half" or "middle." Display cognates such as *midnight/medianoche* and *midday/mediodía* as examples.

Suffixes: *-ly, -ful, -less, -ness*

INTRODUCE Write the following words on the board: *careful, carefully, careless, carelessness.* Ask students what these words have in common and what makes them different from each other. Students should notice that all the words have the same base, *care.* But each successive word also has a different word part at the end. Explain that each of these word parts is a suffix. Say: A suffix is a word part that is added to the end of a word. Adding a suffix changes the meaning of a word.

TEACH/MODEL Present the suffixes *-ly, -ful, -less,* and *-ness.* Write the following chart on the board, asking students to provide additional examples for the last column.

Suffix	How and Why to Use It	Part of Speech	Examples
-ly	Add it to an adjective to tell how an action is done.	adverb	quickly calmly completely
-ful	Add it to a noun to mean "full of" the noun.	adjective	thoughtful colorful helpful
-less	Add it to a noun to mean "without" the noun.	adjective	spotless joyless flawless
-ness	Add it to an adjective to describe a state of being.	noun	darkness happiness carelessness peacefulness

PRACTICE Have students write these suffixes and base words on index cards: *-ly, -ful, -less, -ness, slow, quiet, good, fear, rude.* Tell students to combine the cards to make words with suffixes. Circulate as they work, asking students to show you a base word and a suffix that goes with it. Ask advanced students to tell you what the word means and to use it in an oral sentence.

Suffixes: *-tion, -sion, -able, -ible*

INTRODUCE Write the following words on the board: *perfection, decision, walkable, sensible.* Tell students that each of these words is made up of a base word and a suffix. Circle the suffix *-tion* in the first word and explain: This word part, *-tion,* is a suffix. Ask volunteers to find the suffixes in the other three words. Point out that the base word might need a spelling change before the suffix is added. The word *decide,* for example, drops the final *-de* before adding *-sion.* The reason for these spelling changes has to do with pronunciation, and the rules are hard to generalize, as there are many exceptions to the rules. Students will learn the different spellings with practice.

TEACH/MODEL Present the suffixes *-tion, -sion, -able,* and *-ible.* Explain that *-tion* and *-sion* have the same meaning, as do *-able* and *-ible.* Write the following chart on the board, asking students to provide additional examples for the last column. Spanish examples of these suffixes are *-ción (reacción), -sión (decisión), -able (confortable),* and *-ible (sensible).*

Suffix	How and Why to Use It	Part of Speech	Examples
-tion, -sion	Add it to a verb to describe an action or a state of being.	noun	perfection imagination reaction decision admission confusion
-able, -ible	Add it to a verb to add the meaning "can be."	adjective	workable comfortable dependable sensible reversible flexible

PRACTICE Have students write these suffixes and base words on index cards: *-tion, -sion, -able, -ible, sense, comfort, confuse, react.* Tell students to combine the cards to make words with suffixes. Circulate as they work, asking students to show you a base word and a suffix that goes with it. Ask advanced students to tell you what the word means and to use it in an oral sentence.

Suffixes: *-er, -or, -ess, -ist*

INTRODUCE Write the following words on the board: *swimmer, actor, hostess, tourist.* Tell students that each of these words is made up of a base word and a suffix. Remind students that a suffix is a word part added to the end of a word to change its meaning. Circle the suffix *-er* in the first word and explain: This word part, *-er,* is a suffix. Ask individuals to find suffixes in the other three words. Explain that the base word may require a spelling change before a suffix is added. For example, the word *swimmer* adds an *m* before the suffix. Point out that some spelling changes are related to pronunciation. Explain to students that they will become familiar with different spellings as they practice using the words.

TEACH/MODEL Present this chart to practice the suffixes *-er, -or, -ess,* and *-ist.* Ask students for additional examples of words with these suffixes.

Suffix	What It Means	Examples
-er -or	a person or thing that does something	teacher opener editor
-ess	a female who does something as a job; a female	actress lioness
-ist	a person who has studied something or does something frequently or as a job	artist dentist

PRACTICE Have students write these suffixes and base words or word parts on index cards: *-er, -or, -ess, -ist, act, sell, host, dent, tour, teach, lion.* Have students use the cards in different combinations to make words that have suffixes. As an additional challenge, have students show a base word without a suffix, add a suffix, say the new word, and tell what it means.

Suffixes: *-y, -ish, -hood, -ment*

INTRODUCE Write the following words on the board: *rocky, foolish, parenthood, shipment.* Say each word aloud and tell students that each of these words is made up of a base word and a suffix. Remind students that a suffix is a word part that is added to the end of a word to change its meaning. Circle the suffix *-y* in *rocky* and explain: This word part, *-y,* is a suffix. The base word in *rocky* is *rock.* Ask students to find base words in the other three words. Have them tell you what each base word means.

TEACH/MODEL Present this chart to practice the suffixes *-y, -ish, -hood,* and *-ment.* Have students identify each base word and suffix in the examples. Ask students for additional examples of words with these suffixes.

Suffix	What It Means	Examples
-y	having the quality of	cloudy rainy thirsty
-ish	describing a nationality or language; somewhat	Spanish brownish foolish
-hood	a state or condition of	childhood fatherhood
-ment	a state, action, or quality	excitement movement

PRACTICE Have students write these suffixes and base words on index cards: *-y, -ish, -hood, -ment, smell, mother, excite, wind, green, false, ship.* Have students use the cards in different combinations to make words that have suffixes. As an additional challenge, have students show you a base word without a suffix, add a suffix, say the new word, and tell what it means.

Words with Greek Roots

INTRODUCE Write the following words on the board: *autograph, phonograph, photograph, paragraph.* Say them aloud and then ask students what all these words have in common. Confirm for them that they all have the word part *graph.* Tell students that this word part comes from the Greek language. It means "written." Conclude by saying: Many other words in English have Greek roots, too. Learning these roots can help you learn more words.

TEACH/MODEL Write the following chart on the board, asking students to provide additional examples for the last column.

Greek Root	Meaning	Sample Words
biblio	book	bibliography
bio	life	biography
crac, crat	rule, govern	democrat
demos	people	democracy
geo	earth	geology
graph, gram	written, drawn, describe, record	photograph
log	idea, word, speech, study	biology
meter	measure	perimeter
phono	sound	symphony
scope	to see	telescope

Show students how different word parts can be combined. The root *bio,* for example, can be combined with *graph* to form *biography* (meaning "record of life"), and it can also be combined with *log* to form *biology* (meaning "study of life"). Knowing this, students can conclude that any word with the root *bio* has to do with life. Tell Spanish speakers that many Spanish words have these same Greek roots. Ask these students to provide translations for the sample words in the chart (*bibliografía, biografía, demócrata, democracia, geología, fotografía, biología, perímetro, sinfonía, telescopio*).

PRACTICE Write the following words on the board: *autobiography, phonology, geography,* and *telescope.* Ask students to copy these words and to write their definitions based on what they've learned. When they've finished, have a volunteer write his or her answers on the board, and model corrections as necessary. You can collect students' work for later assessment.

Words with Latin Roots

INTRODUCE Write the following words on the board: *animal, animation, animated.* Ask students what all these words have in common. Confirm for them that they all have the word part *anima.* Tell students that this word part is from Latin, an ancient language that was originally spoken in Italy. *Anima* means "living." Conclude by saying: Many other words in English have Latin roots, too. Learning these roots can help you learn more words.

TEACH/MODEL Write the following chart on the board, asking students to provide additional examples for the last column. Tell Spanish speakers that Spanish comes from Latin, so these roots should be familiar.

Latin Root	Meaning	Sample Words
aqua	water	aquarium
aud	to hear	auditorium
cent	one hundred	century
cert	sure, to trust	certificate, certify
circ	around	circle
computar	to compute	computer, computation
dic, dict	to say, to speak	dictionary, dictate
fin	to end	finish
grad	step, degree	graduate
scrib	to write	scribble

PRACTICE Write the following words on the board: *certain, final, audition,* and *gradual.* Ask students to copy these words and to identify their Latin roots. To check comprehension, ask students to write a sentence with each of these words.

Syllable Patterns: V/CV and VC/V

INTRODUCE Write the word *lemon* on the board and draw or show a small picture of a lemon. Say: This is a lemon, lem/ən. How many vowel sounds do you hear in the word *lemon*? Say it with me, lem/ən, lemon. That's right, there are two vowel sounds. Cover the letters *mon.* Say: If the syllable ended after the *e*, I would pronounce the word with a long *e*: lē/mon. This does not make a word that I know. Cover the letters *on,* then say: I will try it with a short *e*, lem/ən. Now I pronounce the word *lemon*, and I recognize it. The short-vowel sound is correct. Repeat with the words *broken* and *finish*, emphasizing the short- or long-vowel sound in the first syllable.

TEACH/MODEL Write the word *pupil* on the board. Draw a line between the two syllables and tell students: When you hear a word with more than one vowel sound, divide it into parts. Explain that when there is one consonant between two vowels, it is important to figure out if the first vowel has a short or long sound in order to know where to divide the syllable.

Point out that because the first syllable in *pupil* has a long-vowel sound, it ends after the first vowel. Then write *finish* on the board. Draw a line between the *n* and the second *i*, then say: This word also has one consonant between two vowels. The first vowel sound in *finish* is short, so we know that the first syllable ends with a consonant. Say it with me: finish, fin/ish.

PRACTICE Write these words on the board: *music, lemon, frozen, tulip, broken, salad.* Clap as you read each word to emphasize the syllable break in the word. Then have students record the words. Say: I am going to read the words again. This time, circle each word with a long-vowel sound in the first syllable. Underline each word with a short-vowel sound in the first syllable. Review the answers as a class. (circle: *broken, frozen, music, tulip;* underline: *salad, lemon*)

EXTEND Make word cards with these word parts: *bro, ken, si, lent, sev, en, fe, male, rap, id.* Give student pairs the pile of word cards. Have students put the various word parts together to create complete words. If necessary, list the words *broken, silent, seven, female,* and *rapid* on the board.

Syllable Patterns: CV/VC

INTRODUCE Write the word *violin* on the board and draw or show a small picture of a violin. Say: This is a violin, vī/ə/lin. How many vowel sounds do you hear in the word *violin*? Say it with me, vī/ə/lin, violin. That's right, there are three vowel sounds. Explain that if a word in English has three vowel sounds, it must also have three syllables. Repeat with the words *computer* and *calendar*, emphasizing vowel sounds and reviewing what students have learned about breaking words into syllables.

TEACH/MODEL Write the word *create* on the board. Draw a line between the first *e* and *a* and tell students: When you hear a word with more than one vowel sound, divide it into parts. Explain that when there are two vowels side by side, there is a syllable break between the two vowels.

Practice breaking multisyllabic words with the CV/VC syllable pattern into meaningful parts. Write the word *reorganize*. Read the word aloud, then point out the prefix *re-* and say: We know that the prefix *re-* is its own syllable and means "again." Then cover up the prefix so that only *organize* is visible. Say: *Organize* means "to put in order." We know that *organize* has three vowel sounds, so it has three syllables. Uncover the prefix, draw lines between the syllables, and blend the word. Have students repeat the word after you. Have them explain the meaning of *reorganize*. Repeat this exercise with the words *reunite, deactivate,* and *scientists*.

PRACTICE Make word cards with these word parts: *studi-, cre-, ide-, me-, pio-, immedi-, bi-, reli-.* Make another set of cards with these word parts: *-neer, -onic, -o, -ate, -dium, -ance, -a, -ate.* Divide the class into pairs. Give one student the first set of word parts. Give the second student the second set. Once students have pieced the words together, have them write out the words and draw lines between each syllable.

ENGLISH LANGUAGE LEARNERS

Speakers of monosyllabic languages such as Cantonese, Hmong, Khmer, Korean, and Vietnamese may pronounce a two-syllable word as two separate words. Have students practice saying multisyllabic words.

Syllable Patterns: VCCCV

INTRODUCE Write *dolphin* on the board and draw or show a small picture of a dolphin. Say: This is a dolphin, dol/fən. Point out that there are two vowel sounds in *dolphin* and therefore two syllables. Say: How many consonants do you see between the vowels *o* and *i* in the word *dolphin*? Point to the *l, p,* and *h* as you say: That's right, there are three consonants between the vowels. Remind students that when two consonants, such as the *ph* in *dolphin*, make one sound, those letters stay together when you divide the word into syllables. Say: Now let's break the word *dolphin* into syllables: dol/fən, dolphin. Repeat with the words *explode* and *contract*, emphasizing vowel sounds.

TEACH/MODEL Write *surprise* on the board. Underline the three consonants between the vowels *u* and *i* and tell students: There are three consonants between two vowels in this word. Each vowel means that there is a syllable, so we know that there are two syllables in this pattern. Since it is hard to generalize where the syllable break comes in a word with the VCCCV syllable pattern, help students understand that they must look at each word separately to find its syllable breaks.

Practice breaking words with the VCCCV syllable pattern. Distribute several copies of a dictionary and point out how each word is divided into syllables. Write the word *complain* on the board. Ask: How many syllables does this word have? (two) What is the first syllable? (com) What is the second syllable? (plain) Repeat this exercise with the words *explore, sample, enclose,* and *hundred*.

PRACTICE Write the following words on the board: *address, district, substance, complete,* and *control*. Have students write the words on a piece of paper, showing the syllable divisions. Students should use what they know about dividing words into syllables. If they have difficulty with a word, they may use a dictionary to see how a word is divided into syllables.

ENGLISH LANGUAGE LEARNERS

Speakers of monosyllabic languages such as Cantonese, Hmong, Khmer, Korean, and Vietnamese may pronounce a two-syllable word as two separate words. Have students practice saying multisyllabic words.

Syllable Patterns: C + *-le*

INTRODUCE Draw or show a small picture of a candle. Say: This is a candle, kan/dl. How many syllables do you hear in the word *candle*? That's right, there are two syllables. Sound out and blend the following words with C + *-le*: *bubble, puddle, table.* Point out that the first syllable in each word carries more stress than the second syllable.

TEACH/MODEL Write *candle* on the board. Draw a line between the two syllables and tell students: When you hear a word with more than one vowel sound, divide it into parts. Cover the letters *can*. Say: If a word ends with *-le,* then the consonant before the *-le* is part of the last syllable. Show that in the word *candle*, the letter *d* comes right before the *-le* and is part of the second syllable. Now write *double* on the board. Draw a line between the *u* and the *b* and say: In the word *double*, the letter *b* comes before the *-le* and is part of the second syllable. Say it with me: double, dou/ble.

PRACTICE Display the following words for students, and have students record them on paper: *puddle, eagle, marble, middle, double, little, title, handle.* Ask students to write the two syllable parts that make up each word. For example, *mar* + *ble* = *marble*. If needed, write the following frame on the board for students to refer to: ___ + ___ = ___.

EXTEND Tell students: I will say some words. Put your thumb up if you hear a consonant with *-le* at the end of the word. Put your thumb down if you do not: *purple, bubble, puppy, people, softball, broken, noodle.* Then have students repeat the C + *-le* words back to you.

ENGLISH LANGUAGE LEARNERS

Many languages do not have the schwa /ə/ sound, so English learners may have difficulty pronouncing and spelling the unstressed syllable in words such as *table* and *apple*. Provide additional practice pronouncing these words.

PREPARE TO READ

Context Clue Caper

Display the vocabulary words for a particular selection. Explain that you will say each word aloud and use it in a sentence or two that provides effective context. Challenge students to be the first to explain, in their own words, what each word means based on its context clues. For example, for the word *reluctant,* you might provide a context sentence similar to the following: *At first, I was reluctant to drink the bluish-green vegetable smoothie my mom made for a snack.*

Vocabulary in a Flash

Write the vocabulary words for a selection or module on cards. Display each card. Ask students to indicate whether they have heard of the word. If some students have heard of the word, ask them to share the context in which they heard it or explain what they know about it. Once all ideas have been shared, challenge students to use the word in a sentence of their own.

Realia and Visuals

Write the vocabulary words for a selection or module on the board. Point to each in turn and provide a student-friendly definition. Then display items that evoke the words' meanings. For example, for the word *miniature,* you might show a tiny chair from a dollhouse and point out the difference between its size and the size of a classroom chair. Then ask students to name other miniature items.

INTERACT WITH TEXT

Situation Skits

Prepare a set of word cards by writing the vocabulary words from a particular selection, their meanings, examples of situations in which the words are used, and questions. For example, after writing on a card the word *gleeful* and its meaning ("so happy that you feel a little silly"), you might provide the following situation: *You just found out that school is closed because of a big snowstorm the night before. You jump up and down, hurry to put on your hat, coat, mittens, and boots, and then run outside to make snow angels.* Then you might write the following question: *When is the last time you felt gleeful? Describe the situation.* Form groups of students and give one card set to each group. Give the actors time to discuss the word and plan a brief skit using the situation on the card. Before a skit is performed, have one member of the group write the word on the board and pronounce it. After the skit is performed, have another cast member ask the audience the meaning of the word and then ask the question you prepared. The audience response can help you assess understanding and provide feedback.

Word Drawings

Assign each student a word from the reading selections that lends itself to a visual representation. Have students create drawings that evoke or convey meanings. For example, to convey the word *shiver,* a student might write the word in shaky letters. Have students present and explain their drawings to the class. Display students' drawings around the room.

Dictionary Dash

Select words from the reading selections that have multiple meanings. Divide the class into groups and provide each group with a word and the selection and page number where it appears. Have students reread the sentence in the selection and use a dictionary to identify the correct definition of the word in this context. Then have them use the dictionary to identify another definition of the word. Challenge them to write a sentence that uses both meanings of the word correctly. For example, *I put a dash of salt on my boiled egg and then dash off to school!* Have groups read and explain their sentences to the class.

Word Sorts

Provide students with index cards on which vocabulary words are written, one word per card. Ask students to sort the words into categories you provide, such as Words That Show Action, Words That Name Things, Words That Connect to the Unit Theme, and so on. Or have students create the categories and explain the rationale behind their categories.

EXPRESS AND EXTEND

Card Games

Prepare a deck of 40 word cards, using the words students explored in a particular module or unit. Then prepare match cards for each word card, which might include a definition, a synonym, an antonym, a cloze sentence in which the word makes sense, a picture symbolizing the word's meaning, an English translation, or some other appropriate match. For example, a student might pair a word card labeled *desist* with a match card on which its definition appears: "to stop." Students can play a variety of games with these cards. For Fish, all the cards are dealt and players pick one card from the player on their left in turn, placing any pairs they make on the table. The first player to pair all cards wins. For Old Teacher (a variation of Old Maid), an extra card is prepared with a generic drawing of a teacher. The game is played like Fish, except the student who is left with this card is the "old teacher." In all card games, students must read their pairs aloud. Other players can challenge a student's pair, in which case a dictionary would be used to settle the dispute. Either the challenger or the player may get an extra turn, depending upon who is correct.

Memory Game

Prepare a maximum of 25 cards: 12 word cards with vocabulary words from the module; 12 match cards with definitions, synonyms, antonyms, pictures, and so on; and 1 wild card. Shuffle the cards and place them facedown in a 5 x 5 grid. Explain that for each turn, a student will turn over and read two cards. If the cards are a match (for example, the word *immense* and a picture of an elephant), the student will take the cards. If they are not a match, the student will turn the cards back over and leave them in the same place. Play continues in turn until only a single card remains. Students may use the wild card only if they can provide an appropriate match. For example, if a student draws the elephant picture and the wild card, he can say the word *immense* aloud. This can be checked at the end of the game by looking at the remaining card, which should match the answer supplied earlier. The student with the most cards wins.

Bingo

Give students word cards with vocabulary words from a particular unit and ask them to arrange them in a 5 x 5 grid, placing a "free" card in a space of their choice. Assign one student to be the caller. Explain that the caller will select definitions from the definition pile and read them aloud. The players will then place markers on the words in their grids that match the definitions. The first student to mark an entire row, column, or diagonal wins the game. Have students check their work by reading the words and definitions aloud. Reshuffle the cards, ask students to reorganize their grids, and invite the winner of the game to be the caller for the next game.

Off Limits

Write vocabulary words from a module or unit on cards, along with three of the most common words, phrases, or concepts associated with each vocabulary word. Explain that these common synonyms or related words are considered "off-limits." For example, for the vocabulary word *nutritious*, clues listed as "off-limits" might be *food*, *eat*, and *healthy*. Divide the class into two teams. Explain that a player from Team A will have one minute to help Team A guess as many words as possible by giving any kinds of clues—as long as they are not on the "off-limits" list. A player from Team B will look over this player's shoulder to keep the player honest. Team A gains a point for every word correctly guessed based on the player's clues. If the player accidentally uses one of the "off-limits" clues, Team A loses a point. After one minute, points are totaled for Team A, and Team B takes its turn. The team with the most points after a certain number of rounds wins.

Graphic Organizers

Give partners a list of words from a particular module. Explain that they will create a word web using at least 10 of these words. They can use any words from the list they like and design their webs in any way they like, but their webs should demonstrate their knowledge of the relationships between these 10 words. For example, they might connect two vocabulary words from the module that have similar meanings, such as *forlorn* or *melancholy*. In this case, explain that the line that connects these words on the web would be labeled "synonym." Or they might connect two words that have opposite meanings, such as *saunter* and *stroll*, and label the line connecting them "antonym." They might link two words that can be used to describe the same character in a text or two words that apply to the same scientific concept or topic. Encourage students to think in creative ways and make their webs as intricate as they can, with multiple connections between words. Invite them to present and explain their webs to the class when they have finished drawing and labeling.

Password

For this game, you as the teacher will play the game-show host, and two student players will be the contestants. Split the class into two teams, and have one member from each team come up and sit in chairs facing the class. Give the players one-word clues about a vocabulary word explored in the module or unit. For example, for the word *universe*, you might give clues such as *galaxies, planets, moons, stars,* and *infinite.* The first student to correctly guess the vocabulary word wins the round. If students have difficulty guessing the correct vocabulary word, give more obvious clues in the form of phrases, such as *even bigger than our solar system.*

Yes/No and True/False

Prepare a list of yes/no questions and true/false statements for the vocabulary words in a particular selection or module. For example, for the words *vital, burrow, extreme, spine,* and *disguise,* you might prepare the following questions or statements: *Yes or no: Is sunlight vital to plants and animals? Yes or no: Is a rain shower an example of extreme weather? True or false: No plant or animal can have a disguise. True or false: Generally, animals that burrow are small in size.* As in these examples, questions or statements should be designed so that answers require full knowledge of the words. Divide the class into two teams. Have one player from each team come up and sit in chairs in front of the class. Say each question or statement aloud, and the first student to correctly answer yes or no or true or false has 10 seconds to explain the answer. If the player successfully explains, that player's team gains a point. If the player answers incorrectly or cannot provide an adequate explanation within the time limit, that team loses a point. The team with the most points at the end wins the game.

Category Challenge

Have students draw a 5 x 5 grid and label each vertical row with a category: word; synonym/similar; antonym/different; example; and related word. Choose four challenging vocabulary words from a particular selection or module, and have students write the words in the first column. Give the players a designated time frame to fill in as many squares in each row as they can. For example, for the word *despise,* the remaining four columns might read: *dislike, adore, I despise bullying behavior; scorn.* At the end of the time limit, points are totaled: 5 points for every category square a player filled in that no other player has filled; 2 points for every category square that others have filled in, but with different words; and 1 point for every category square filled in where someone else has the same term.

Either/Or

Divide the class into two teams. Have the members of each team work together to create 10 either/or questions using the vocabulary words for a particular selection or module. For example, for the words *spine, vital,* and *nutrient,* students might create the following either/or questions: *Which animal has spines on its skin—a porcupine or a crocodile? If something is vital, is it very important or not important at all? When you hear the word nutrient, do you think of something that's bad for you or good for you?* Review student questions before the start of the game and provide feedback as necessary. Then have a player from Team A ask a player from Team B a question. If the player from Team B answers correctly and provides an adequate explanation for the response, Team B gets a point. If not, Team A gets a point. Make sure every member of each team participates. When Team A has asked all of its questions, the teams switch roles. The team with the most points at the end wins the game.

COGNATE ACTIVITIES

Cognate Sort

Create word/picture cards for words in English that have numerous cognates, such as *music, computer, park,* and *family*. Then create word cards with cognates for these words, such as *música, musique; computador, komputer; parque, parc; familia, famiglia*. Have students sort the cognates under the correct word/picture cards. Be sure to ask students if they know of other cognates you might add to the list. Afterward, conduct a discussion with students about what similarities and differences they notice between the words and how cognates can be helpful to them as they explore new languages.

Cognate Match

Make a list of words in English and their Spanish cognates, such as *bank, banco; university, universidad; museum, museo*. Give each student in the class either a word in English or a Spanish cognate. If there are an odd number of students, take one of the cards yourself. Challenge the students to move about the room until they find the person who has a match for their card. Then invite each matched pair to write the word and its Spanish cognate on the board and circle letters that are different. Repeat the activity with cognates from other languages.

Cognate Find

Create picture cards for words in English that have numerous cognates, such as *bank, train,* and *telephone*. Give pairs of students one of the picture cards and have them identify as many cognates for the word as they can, by either conducting research on the Internet or consulting multilingual speakers in the classroom or community. Have them share their findings with the class.

True or False?

Organize students in groups and give each group a different list of pairs between English words and true or false Spanish cognates for these words. Have students identify whether the words in each pair are true cognates or false cognates. For example, *class* and *clase* are true cognates, but *rope* and *ropa* are false cognates. Suggest that students consult multilingual speakers in their group or in other groups, use dictionaries, or conduct research on the Internet in order to identify whether each pair is true or false. Have groups share with the class and explain their answers. Repeat with cognates from other languages.

Unlock Language Learning

Part 4 Unlock Language Learning

English Language Learners Support

Unit 1 Becoming Researchers
Module A Anchor Text 367
    Supporting Text 370
    Supporting Text 372
Module B Anchor Text 374
    Supporting Text 377
    Supporting Text 379
Module A and B Writing 381

Unit 2 Interactions in Nature and Culture
Module A Anchor Text 384
    Supporting Text 387
    Supporting Text 389
    Supporting Text 391
Module B Anchor Text 393
    Supporting Text 396
    Supporting Text 398
Module A and B Writing 400

Unit 3 Exploring Impact and Effect
Module A Anchor Text 403
    Supporting Text 406
    Supporting Text 408
    Supporting Text 410
Module B Anchor Text 412
    Supporting Text 415
    Supporting Text 417
Module A and B Writing 419

Unit 4 Creating Innovative Solutions
Module A Anchor Text 422
    Supporting Text 425
    Supporting Text 427
Module B Anchor Text 429
    Supporting Text 432
    Supporting Text 434
Module A and B Writing 436

Language Routines and Resources

Language Routines 439

Language Resources 453

Porpoises in Peril

Reproduce and distribute copies of the *Finless Porpoises* student page on page 369. Explain that to understand the information in *Porpoises in Peril* it helps to know more about porpoises and how they live. Tell students that finless porpoises are mammals that live in the water. Point to each of the four boxes and explain that they will learn about the porpoise's body, habitat, food, and behavior.

Begin by directing students' attention to the box that describes the appearance of the finless porpoise. Who can share a word that describes what a finless porpoise looks like? *The finless porpoise is _____.*

Have students follow along as you read aloud the information in each section of the organizer. Scaffold with sentence frames such as: *Finless porpoises like to eat _____. They use their hearing to _____.* Discuss how the information in each section helps students learn more about finless porpoises.

TALK ABOUT SENTENCES

For students who need support in accessing key ideas and key language in *Porpoises in Peril*, use the Sentence Talk Routine on pages 441–442 to draw students' attention to the relationship between meaning and the words, phrases, and clauses in the text.

Lesson	Sentence(s) to Deconstruct
1	(p 6) Local officials spotted several porpoises near an island off the northern coast of Taiwan, exhibiting uncharacteristic behavior.
2	(p 12) "Okay, it's time to formulate a plan," Jada announced, putting down her knife and fork.
3	(p 18) "Well, about two weeks ago, we started getting reports from fishermen down on the beach about the porpoises acting peculiarly," he said.
4	(p 23) With a marker, he labeled it "Surface Beach Water" and added the date and time.
5	(p 30) Looking down, she realized the water below her looked murky and muddy, and there were no fish.
6	(p 36) I found ocean bed sediment in water hundreds of feet above the seabed, which would fit with mining activity.
7	(p 42) To reach the enclosed, tunnel-like piece of equipment, she had to hold onto the bars of what had seemed like the jungle gym and slowly, bar by bar, center herself over a tunnel-like enclosure.
8	(p 46) After seeing the evidence, Dr. Vloodman told the officers to arrest Drake Darkly as soon as he reached the mainland.

Use the Text-based Writing Routine on pages 443–444 to model how to speak and write about key ideas and details in *Porpoises in Peril.*

Lesson	Text-based Writing	Scaffolded Frames
1	On page 6, what type of "uncharacteristic behavior" is Professor Q talking about?	• She said the porpoises _____. • One cause for this might be _____.
2	What details on page 12 explain how the squad is going to work together?	• Some tools the squad will use to solve the mystery are _____. • After reading the report, they learned _____.
3	On page 18, what information did Dr. Vloodman share with the squad?	• The porpoises have been acting differently for _____. • The first people to notice the change in the animals were _____.
4	What do you learn about Reggie on p. 23?	• Reggie has a _____ with him. • The first thing he does with the water sample is _____.
5	What details on page 30 describe what Kate saw on her dive?	• There were no _____ in the water with her. • The water was _____ and _____.
6	On page 36, what do the results of the squad's experiments explain?	• Ocean bed sediment was _____ the seabed. • The _____ also causes the fish to leave.
7	How does the illustration on p. 42 help you understand the mining equipment?	• The illustration shows how the equipment looks like a _____ _____. • The opening for the tunnel is _____.
8	Use information from p. 46 to explain the ending of the story.	• Kate got _____ _____ from the mine. • This proves that Drake Darkly _____.

Use the Dig Deeper Vocabulary Routine on pages 439–440 to continue to develop conceptual understanding of the following past tense verbs: *contaminated, emerged, dredged, conducted, focused, uploaded,* and *mouthed.* Begin by explaining that past tense verbs often end in *–ed* and refer to actions or states of being that have taken place in the past. Display and read aloud the following sentences.

*Reggie and Kate **rented** a boat.*
*Kate **swims** near the coral reef.*

When does the action take place in each sentence? Explain that in the first sentence, the action has already taken place, but in the second sentence, the action takes place in the present.

Unit 1 Module A

Name _____

Finless Porpoises

What is a finless porpoise?
How do finless porpoises live?

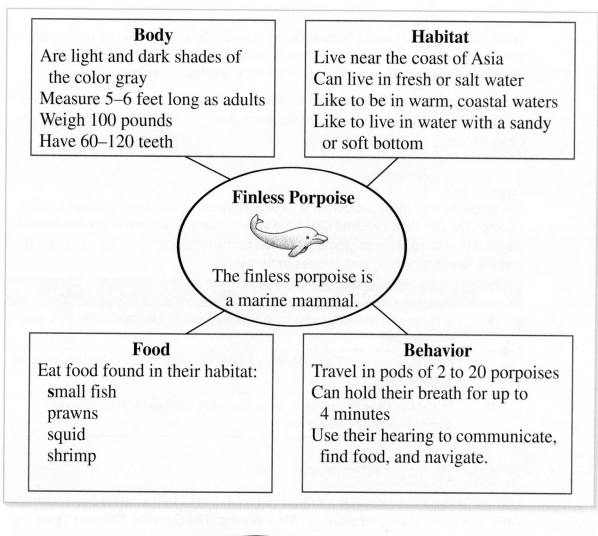

Body
Are light and dark shades of
  the color gray
Measure 5–6 feet long as adults
Weigh 100 pounds
Have 60–120 teeth

Habitat
Live near the coast of Asia
Can live in fresh or salt water
Like to be in warm, coastal waters
Like to live in water with a sandy
  or soft bottom

Finless Porpoise

The finless porpoise is
a marine mammal.

Food
Eat food found in their habitat:
  small fish
  prawns
  squid
  shrimp

Behavior
Travel in pods of 2 to 20 porpoises
Can hold their breath for up to
  4 minutes
Use their hearing to communicate,
  find food, and navigate.

Team Talk

What did you learn about the finless porpoise?
The finless porpoise _____.
The finless porpoise likes to live _____.

Mary Anning: The Girl Who Cracked Open the World

Reproduce and distribute copies of the *Fossils* student page on page 371. Explain that to understand the story events in *Mary Anning: The Girl Who Cracked Open the World,* it helps to understand fossils.

Read aloud the facts about fossils. Confirm students' understanding by explaining what sedimentary rock is and how the earth is made up of layers. Over time the plant or animal becomes preserved in the rock and leaves an impression.

Have students work with a partner to share what they have learned about fossils. Scaffold with sentence frames such as: *A fossil is _____. Fossils are important because _____.*

TALK ABOUT SENTENCES

For students who need support in accessing key ideas and key language in *Mary Anning: The Girl Who Cracked Open the World,* use the Sentence Talk Routine on pages 441–442 to draw students' attention to the relationship between meaning and the words, phrases, and clauses in the text.

Lesson	Sentence(s) to Deconstruct
9	(p 7) The wind and water broke the cliffs open, and fossils that had been buried were now exposed.
11	(p 19) His drawing was so real-looking that Mary felt as if she could step into the world he had created.
12	(p 31) Mary's love of fossils and her curious nature changed her life—and helped change the world of science too.

SPEAK AND WRITE ABOUT THE TEXT

Use the Text-based Writing Routine on pages 443–444 to model how to speak and write about key ideas and details in *Mary Anning: The Girl Who Cracked Open the World.*

Lesson	Text-based Writing	Scaffolded Frames
9	On page 7, why did Mary go to the beach?	• Mary was looking for _____. • She hoped she could find them in _____.
11	How do the illustrations on page 19 help you understand Henry's paintings?	• Henry painted pictures of _____. • The paintings were _____.
12	On page 31, how do you know fossils were important to Mary?	• Mary first found fossils _____. • Fossils were important to Mary because _____.

Unit I Module A

Name _____

Fossils

What are fossils?

- Evidence of ancient life forms or habitats
- Remains, molds, or traces of things once living
- Preserved in rock
- Varied in size and shape
- Entire organisms or parts of organisms
- Information and insight about the past

Share one fact about fossils.

A fossil _____.

Fragile Frogs

Reproduce and distribute copies of the *We Are All Connected* student page on page 373. Explain that to understand the events in *Fragile Frogs*, it helps to know that we are all connected—one small change to a plant or animal species can have broad effects. Help students understand how to read the chart. Point to the three circles and explain that they represent events that affect each other.

Read aloud each circle in the chart. If necessary, confirm students' understanding by discussing small things they can do to affect others in big ways. For example, discuss recycling. If one person recycles, he or she might inspire other people to recycle, and then lots of people might recycle. This one change can have a huge impact on our environment.

After discussing the information in the chart, have students share with a partner how one change to the environment can have many effects. Scaffold with sentence frames such as: *When human beings enter an ecosystem, they can cause _____. When this happens, plant and animal species can _____.*

TALK ABOUT SENTENCES

For students who need support in accessing key ideas and key language in *Fragile Frogs*, use the Sentence Talk Routine on pages 441–442 to draw students' attention to the relationship between meaning and the words, phrases, and clauses in the text.

Lesson	Sentence(s) to Deconstruct
14	(p 5) Concerned scientists surveyed amphibian populations all over the world.
15	(p 9) Often a frog species faces not just one threat but many.

SPEAK AND WRITE ABOUT THE TEXT

Use the Text-based Writing Routine on pages 443–444 to model how to speak and write about key ideas and details in *Fragile Frogs*.

Lesson	Text-based Writing	Scaffolded Frames
14	What details on page 5 explain what the scientists were studying?	The scientists were studying the _____ population. They studied amphibians all over the _____. They wanted to learn _____.
15	Use information on page 9 to explain the threats the frogs are facing.	The frogs are facing _____ threats. One threat is _____. This threatens the frogs because _____.

Unit I Module A

Name _____

We Are All Connected

How can one change to the environment have a large effect on many species?

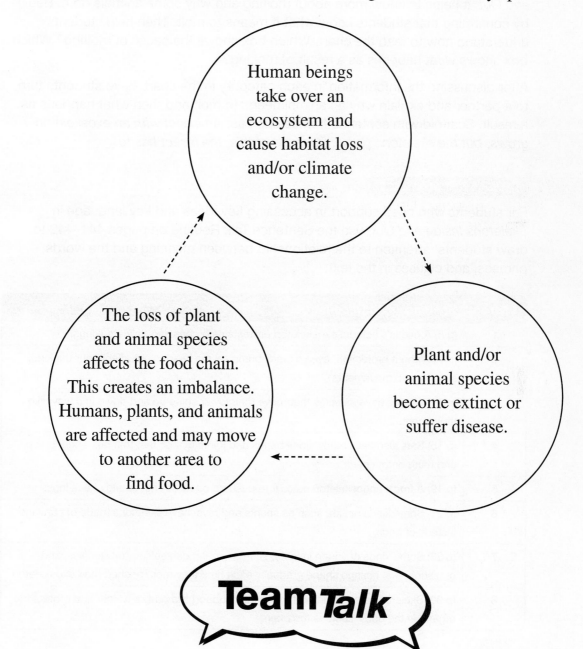

Human beings take over an ecosystem and cause habitat loss and/or climate change.

Plant and/or animal species become extinct or suffer disease.

The loss of plant and animal species affects the food chain. This creates an imbalance. Humans, plants, and animals are affected and may move to another area to find food.

Team Talk

Share one change to the environment that can cause changes to the whole environment.

Human beings cause _____.

Skeletons Inside and Out

Reproduce and distribute copies of the *Why Some Animals Molt* student page on page 376. Explain that to better understand the information in *Skeletons Inside and Out,* it helps to know more about molting and why some animals do it. Begin by confirming that students know what it means to molt. Then help students understand how to read the chart. Which box shows the cause of molting? Which box shows what happens as a result of molting?

After discussing the information in each category in the chart, have students turn to a partner and explain why an animal needs to molt and then what happens as a result. Scaffold with sentence frames such as: *An insect with an exoskeleton grows, but the skeleton _____. Because of this, the insect has to _____.*

TALK ABOUT SENTENCES

For students who need support in accessing key ideas and key language in *Skeletons Inside and Out,* use the Sentence Talk Routine on pages 441–442 to draw students' attention to the relationship between meaning and the words, phrases, and clauses in the text.

Lesson	Sentence(s) to Deconstruct
1	(p 5) A beetle's colorful exoskeleton protects its organs and delicate wings.
2	(p 7) Without protection, even a small bump on the head might affect your thinking, senses, and movements.
3	(p 11) Whales have muscles that move their lower spine up and down in a wavelike movement.
4	(p 15) Bats also have many small bones and joints in their feet that help them grasp and hang onto a perch.
5	(p 19) A frog's endoskeleton helps it to push up off its strong, springy back legs.
6	(p 21) Some kinds of fish, such as sharks and rays, have skeletons made of cartilage instead of bone.
7	(p 28) Some kinds of young insects, such as young damselflies, dragonflies, and grasshoppers, change shape gradually each time they molt, or shed their exoskeleton.
8	(p 30) Skeletons are very important as they support the body's weight and protect the organs of the body, such as the brain.

SPEAK AND WRITE ABOUT THE TEXT

Use the Text-based Writing Routine on pages 443–444 to model how to speak and write about key ideas and details in *Skeletons Inside and Out*.

Lesson	Text-based Writing	Scaffolded Frames
1	On page 5, why does a beetle need an exoskeleton?	• The beetle's exoskeleton _____ its soft _____ and delicate _____.
2	What facts on page 7 tell what could happen if you didn't have a bony skull?	• Without a skull, bumps on the head could _____. • The _____ is useful because _____.
3	Use information on page 11 to explain how the skeleton of a whale allows movement.	• Whales use _____ to move their lower spine in a wavelike _____. • The spine is moved up and down by _____.
4	What details on page 15 describe how bats use the bones in their feet?	• The bones and joints in bats' feet help them _____ and _____. • Two reasons for the many small bones are _____.
5	What facts on page 19 explain the frog's ability to jump?	• The frog's endoskeleton helps it _____ up from its springy _____. • Without the _____, the frog wouldn't be able to _____.
6	What details on page 21 describe a different kind of skeleton found in some fish?	• Sharks and rays have _____ skeletons instead of _____. • Some fish _____.
7	How does information on page 28 help you understand how insects can change shape?	• Young insects change _____ a little bit each time they _____, or shed their _____. • Scientists call the gradual change of shape of some insects _____, but it happens when _____.
8	Why are skeletons important? Use information on page 30 to respond.	• Skeletons support the weight of the _____, and protect the _____. • The skeleton is important to _____ the body and _____.

EXPAND UNDERSTANDING OF VOCABULARY

Use the Dig Deeper Vocabulary Routine on pages 439–440 to continue to develop understanding of the following action verbs: *supports, expand, affect, vary, detach, survive*. Display and read aloud the following sentences: *The human skeleton **supports** the body. Some exoskeletons cannot **expand**.*

Ask students if they know who or what is performing an action in each sentence. Remind students that action verbs are words that show what the subjects in the sentences do. What is it that the skeleton can do? Explain that the next sentence tells what the exoskeleton can or cannot do. What is the verb that shows the action that the exoskeleton cannot do?

Name _____

Why Some Animals Molt

An exoskeleton is a hard covering outside of the body. What happens when the insect grows?

Cause	Effect
The insect grew inside its exoskeleton. The skeleton could not expand.	The insect had to shed, or leave behind, its old exoskeleton. It grew a new one that is larger.

Discuss the reason molting happens to insects with exoskeletons.

The _____ cannot expand when the insect grows.

It has to _____ its old exoskeleton, and _____ a bigger one.

Movers and Shapers

Reproduce and distribute copies of *Muscles and Bones* student page 378. Explain that to understand information in *Movers and Shapers,* it helps to know what muscles and bones are and what they do. Begin by explaining that everyone has muscles and bones. Then help students understand how to read the chart. Point to the box where you will learn about muscles. Now point to where you will learn about bones.

Read aloud the chart categories. Confirm students' understanding by having them discuss the main functions of bones and muscles. Scaffold with frames such as: *Bones ____ the organs in your body. Muscles ____ the bones so you can move.*

TALK ABOUT SENTENCES

For students who need support in accessing key ideas and key language in *Movers and Shapers,* use the Sentence Talk Routine on pages 441–442 to draw students' attention to the relationship between meaning and the words, phrases, and clauses in the text.

Lesson	Sentence(s) to Deconstruct
9	(p 19) Your spine is often called the backbone, but if it was just one stiff bone, you would be unable to bend over.
10	(p 20) The elbow also contains a pivot joint, which lets you turn your hand over and then back again.
11	(p 26) The bones of the cranium fit together very tightly and cannot move or slip unless the skull is hit with great force.

SPEAK AND WRITE ABOUT THE TEXT

Use the Text-based Writing Routine on pages 443–444 to model how to speak and write about key ideas and details in *Movers and Shapers.*

Lesson	Text-based Writing	Scaffolded Frames
9	On page 19, what would happen if your spine was made up of one bone?	• If your spine were a solid ____, you would not be able to ____ over. • The backbone or spine would not be ____.
10	What facts on page 20 explain what helps you turn your hands over and around?	• The elbow has a ____ joint that allows you to ____. • Without the elbow joint, you ____.
11	What details on page 26 describe how the bones of the cranium (head) protect it?	• The bones ____ together very ____ so they don't move unless ____ very hard.

Name _____

Muscles and Bones

What are muscles and bones? How do they help the body function?

MUSCLES

Allow movement
Pull the bones
Never stop working
Are covered with blood vessels and
  nerves

BONES

Protect the organs
Work together as a team with muscles
Support the body
Allow movement

Share one detail about how muscles work.
Muscles _____ the bones _____.
Share one detail about how bones work.
Bones _____ the soft organs inside.

King of the Parking Lot

BUILD BACKGROUND

Reproduce and distribute copies of the *Very Old Bones* student page on page 380. Explain that to better understand *King of the Parking Lot* it helps to know that old bones can provide information about the animal or person they came from.

Read aloud the five outer circles. Have students turn to a partner and explain the kinds of things that old bones can reveal. Scaffold with a sentence frame such as: *By finding old bones, scientists can discover _____.*

TALK ABOUT SENTENCES

For students who need support in accessing key ideas and key language in *King of the Parking Lot,* use the Sentence Talk Routine on pages 441–442 to draw students' attention to the relationship between meaning and the words, phrases, and clauses in the text.

Lesson	Sentence(s) to Deconstruct
13	(p 34) Paintings created after his death portray him with narrowed eyes, a hunched back, and even clawed fingers.
14	(p 38) This was exciting, since it was said that when Richard III died in battle, monks took his body away on a horse.
15	(p 41) Secondly, closer study of the curved spine showed them that the man didn't actually have a hunched back—he had suffered from scoliosis, a condition that causes a curved spine.
16	(p 42–43) Scientists were able to match cell samples taken from the skeleton with cell samples from the two family members.

SPEAK AND WRITE ABOUT THE TEXT

Use the Text-based Writing Routing on pages 443–444 to model how to speak and write about key ideas and details in *King of the Parking Lot*.

Lesson	Text-based Writing	Scaffolded Frames
13	Use information on page 34 to find out how the king looked in the paintings done after he died.	• The paintings showed _____. • The painters of the king must have thought _____.
14	What details on page 38 show what people thought had happened to the king?	• When King Richard III _____ in battle, _____ took his body away on a _____. • It was said that monks _____.
15	According to the text on page 41, what did the spine show?	• The skeleton's curved spine showed _____. • Researchers know that King Richard _____.
16	What details on pages 42–43 prove that the skeleton really belonged to King Richard?	• Scientists proved the cells came from the king by _____. • Scientists knew because _____.

Name _____

Very Old Bones

What can we learn by studying old bones?

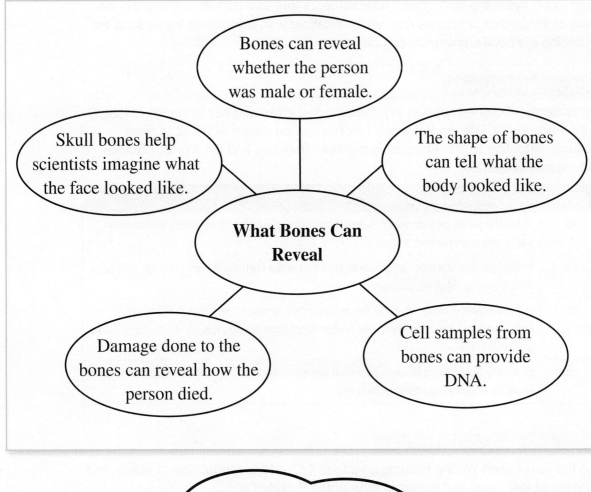

Bones can reveal whether the person was male or female.

Skull bones help scientists imagine what the face looked like.

The shape of bones can tell what the body looked like.

What Bones Can Reveal

Damage done to the bones can reveal how the person died.

Cell samples from bones can provide DNA.

TeamTalk

Share one fact about what bones can reveal.

Bones can teach us _____.

Name _____

Studying the Sky

Caroline Herschel was an astronomer who lived in the 1700s. She was the first woman astronomer to discover a comet.

Herschel was born in Germany in 1750. When she was 22, she moved to England to live with her brother and teach music. Her brother William worked on telescopes and studied astronomy. She began helping him at work. They would stay up all night studying the stars. Soon Caroline learned how to use a telescope and was making her own observations. In 1786, she discovered her first comet. During the next 11 years, she found 8 more comets.

Caroline Herschel was the first woman ever to earn money for doing scientific work. She received many awards for her hard work, including having a crater on the moon named after her.

Name _____

A Surprising, Stretchy, Springy Mammal

Cats can bend and move in amazing ways. We can learn about cats by studying how their body parts work.

A cat's spine is able to bend easily.

The back knee and ankle joints allow cats to spring forward with quick bursts of speed.

Cats' claws are good for hunting, climbing, and defending themselves.

To learn more about cats and how they move in such amazing ways, it helps to study how their body parts work.

Performance-Based Assessment
Unit 1 Module A

Reproduce and distribute copies of the student model on page 381. After completing the Prepare to Write activities on pages 181–186 in Unlock the Writing in Part 2, use the student model to illustrate the elements of a biographical spotlight.

Discuss the student model. Read the first two sentences aloud, and ask: What information does this paragraph provide? *The writer tells the reader who the biography _____.* (will be about)

Read the second paragraph aloud. What information does the writer provide in the second paragraph? *The writer gives _____ and _____ about Caroline Herschel's life.* (facts and details) Continue by asking: How did the writer organize this information? *The writer organized the information in _____.* (chronological order, or the order in which the events took place)

Finally, point out the last paragraph. Explain that this paragraph is the conclusion. How did the writer end this biography? (by explaining the awards Caroline Herschel won)

Unit 1 Module B

Reproduce and distribute copies of the student model on page 382. After completing the Prepare to Write activities on pages 181–186 in Unlock the Writing in Part 2, use the student model to illustrate the features of an infographic.

Examine the student model. Point out how the writer opened with an interesting title followed by an introductory paragraph. Read aloud the introduction, and ask, Did the writer make the purpose clear? *The writer ends the introduction by saying we can _____ a lot about _____ by _____ how their body parts work.*

Read aloud the information about the back knees and ankles of cats. Why does the writer include this information? *The writer tells about the back knees and ankles so the reader can learn how cats can ____.* Read aloud the fact about a cat's spine. What does this fact help you know about the topic? Read aloud the details about cat claws. What was learned about cats from this information? *Learning about claws teaches how cats ____.*

Read aloud the conclusion of the model. How did the writer end the article? (with a summary of how to learn more about cats.)

Why the Sea Is Salty

Reproduce and distribute the *The Philippines* student page on page 386. Explain to students that the events in *Why the Sea Is Salty* will be easier to understand if they know about the Philippine Islands.

Help students understand how to read the chart. Have students locate the Philippines on the world map. Point out the location of Vietnam and explain that the surrounding water is the western Pacific Ocean.

Then read aloud the first description, as students follow along. Discuss the facts. Scaffold with sentence frames such as: *The Philippines is located _____. Many islands are _____ that they _____.*

Follow the same process for the geography and climate information. For geography, scaffold with sentence frames such as: *The Philippines has _____ and _____. Tropical rainforests once _____. Many rainforests are _____.* For climate, scaffold with sentence frames such as: *The Philippines has both _____ and _____ seasons.*

Then have students share with a partner what they have learned about the Philippines.

TALK ABOUT SENTENCES

For students who need support in accessing key ideas and key language in *Why the Sea Is Salty,* use the Sentence Talk Routine on pages 441–442 to draw students' attention to the relationship between meaning and the words, phrases, and clauses in the text.

Lesson	Sentence(s) to Deconstruct
1	(p 7) They would cut the fish down the middle and open them up. Then they would rub salt into the raw flesh and hang them up in the sun to dry.
2	(p 15) "I know we need salt, but it's too dangerous to take the boats out yet," said the man, shaking his head.
3	(p 31) Suddenly, the boy remembered they needed to take food for the giant.
4	(p 33) He wanted to shake the ants off, but he wasn't able to move because the villagers were walking along his legs.

Use the Text-based Writing Routine on pages 443–444 to model how to speak and write about key ideas and details in *Why the Sea Is Salty.*

Lesson	Text-based Writing	Scaffolded Frames
1	Use information from page 7 to explain how the villagers preserved fish.	• Villagers preserved fish by cutting _____ and rubbing _____. • Villagers preserved fish by _____.
2	Look back at page 15 to determine what the man knows the villagers need. What reason does he give for not being able to get what they need?	• The man knows the villagers need _____. He says it is too _____ to take the _____ out. • The villagers need _____, but the storm has made it too _____.
3	Use information on page 31 to explain why the boy wants the villagers to take food to the giant.	• The giant had been _____ when the villagers had no _____ last time. • The giant had been _____. • The boy remembered _____.
4	Reread page 33 to determine what problem the giant faces. Why is he not able to solve his problem?	• The giant wants to shake _____. He cannot do this because the villagers are _____. • The giant wants _____. He cannot do this because _____. • The giant cannot _____ because _____.

Use the Dig Deeper Vocabulary Routine on pages 439–440 to continue to develop conceptual understanding of the following action verbs: *preserve, mined, crouching, measuring, puzzled, wriggled, chuckled,* and *plucked.* Begin by reviewing the role of action verbs in a sentence. Display and read aloud the following sentence: *The salt **killed** germs.*

Point out that the verb *killed* is preceded by the name of who or what is doing the action—*the salt.* Also point out that the word *germs* gives information about the action by indicating what is being killed.

Name _____

The Philippines

What are some facts about the Philippines?

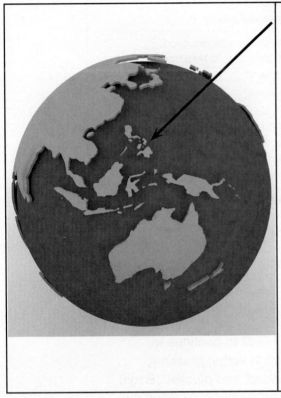

Location and Size The Philippines is located in the western Pacific Ocean about 500 miles off the coast of Vietnam. The country has 7,107 islands. Many of the islands are so small that they are not even named.

Geography The Philippines has many mountains. It also has lowlands along the coast. Tropical rainforests once covered most of the islands. Many of the rainforests are gone today.

Climate The Philippines has wet and dry seasons. During the wet season, tropical storms and typhoons often hit the islands. Typhoons are tropical storms with very high winds and heavy rain.

Share facts about the Philippines.

Tropical storms and typhoons hit during the _____.

The Philippines is located _____. The Philippines was once covered by

_____.

How the Stars Fell into the Sky

BUILD BACKGROUND

Reproduce and distribute the *Navajo Beliefs* student page on page 388. Explain that to understand the story events in *How the Stars Fell into the Sky,* it helps to know about some things early Navajo people believed. Help students understand how to read the chart. What parts of the chart will show early beliefs of the Navajo people?

After discussing the information about the early Navajo people and their beliefs, have students talk with a partner. Scaffold with sentence frames such as: *The Navajo people received medical care from _____. They practiced dancing and singing during _____.*

TALK ABOUT SENTENCES

For students who need support in accessing key ideas and key language in the legend, use the Sentence Talk Routine on pages 441–442 to draw students' attention to the relationship between meaning and the words, phrases, and clauses in the text.

Lesson	Sentence(s) to Deconstruct
5	(p 79) "Write them on the water then," he said and turned to go, having more important matters on his mind.
6	(p 82) And so she began, slowly, first one and then the next, placing her jewels across the dome of night, carefully designing her pattern so all could read it.
7	(p 94) "The young mother will sing of them to her child."
8	(p 97) . . . he flung the remaining stars out into the night, spilling them in wild disarray, shattering First Woman's careful patterns.

SPEAK AND WRITE ABOUT THE TEXT

Use the Text-based Writing Routine on pages 443–444 to model how to speak and write about key ideas and details in *How the Stars Fell into the Sky.*

Lesson	Text-based Writing	Scaffolded Frames
5	Use page 79 to explain how First Man is not really interested in the laws.	• The text says he had _____ on this mind. • I know this because the text says he _____.
6	What details on page 82 show that First Woman is being careful?	• She placed _____ and designed _____. • First woman _____.
7	What detail on page 94 tells you that First Woman thinks the laws will last a long time?	• Mothers will sing the _____ to their _____. • Young mothers will sing _____.
8	What details on page 97 tell you why First Woman calls Coyote foolish?	• Coyote flung _____, shattering _____. • Coyote _____.

Name _____

Navajo Beliefs

What were some of the early Navajo beliefs?

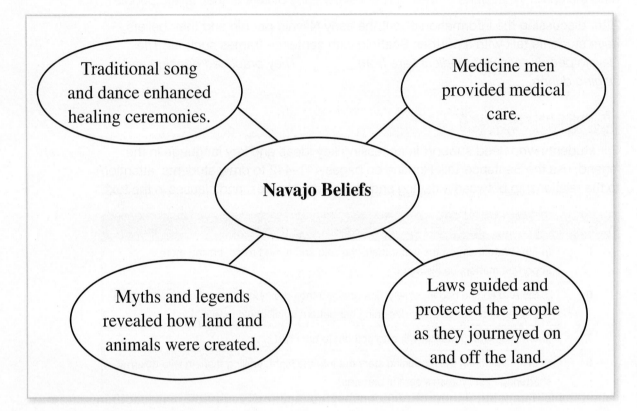

- Traditional song and dance enhanced healing ceremonies.
- Medicine men provided medical care.
- **Navajo Beliefs**
- Myths and legends revealed how land and animals were created.
- Laws guided and protected the people as they journeyed on and off the land.

Share facts about the early Navajo beliefs.
One thing I learned about early Navajo beliefs is _____.

Pecos Bill

BUILD BACKGROUND

Reproduce and distribute copies of the *Wild West Words* student page on page 390. Explain that knowing some of the words cowboys used will help students understand *Pecos Bill*. Read aloud the information in the chart.

Discuss each word in the chart. Scaffold with sentence frames such as: *A varmint (cyclone, lariat, bronco) is _____.* Then have students work with a partner to use the words they have learned in sentences.

TALK ABOUT SENTENCES

For students who need support in accessing key ideas and key language in *Pecos Bill,* use the Sentence Talk Routine on pages 441–442 to draw students' attention to the relationship between meaning and the words, phrases, and clauses in the text.

Lesson	Sentence(s) to Deconstruct
9	(p 54) "Varmint," said Bill hoarsely, for he hadn't used his human voice in seventeen years.
10	(p 57) "Don't jump, you mangy bobtailed fleabag!" Bill said.
11	(p 61) The mighty cyclone bucked, arched, and screamed like a wild bronco.
12	(p 62) He sat on his haunches in the moonlight and began a-howling and ah-hooing.

SPEAK AND WRITE ABOUT THE TEXT

Use the Text-based Writing Routine on pages 443–444 to model how to speak and write about key ideas and details in *Pecos Bill*.

Lesson	Text-based Writing	Scaffolded Frames
9	Based on information on page 54, why is Bill's voice hoarse?	• When Bill was with the coyotes, he _____. • Bill is hoarse because _____.
10	On page 57, what does Bill say to make the mountain lion jump on his back?	• Bill calls the mountain lion _____, _____, and ____. • Bill calls the mountain lion _____.
11	On page 61, what human qualities does the author give the cyclone?	• The author says the cyclone _____, _____, and ____ like a _____. • The author says _____.
12	What detail on page 62 shows that Bill was love-struck?	• Bill sat on _____ and began _____. • Bill reverted to his coyote ways by _____.

Name _____

Wild West Words

	varmint: Any animal that is a pest or problem is called a varmint. Coyotes are varmints because they kill cattle and sheep. Bad people can also be called varmints.
	cyclone: A cyclone is another name for a tornado. The winds in a cyclone spin tightly in a cone shape as they race across the land.
	lariat: A lariat is a rope used to catch cattle, horses, or other animals. The rope is tied in a loop that tightens when the animal is caught. A lariat is also called a lasso.
	bronco: A bronco is a wild horse. The name comes from the Spanish word *broncos,* meaning "rough." It is a fitting name because broncos are untrained horses. They buck—or kick up their back feet—to try to throw riders.

Share what you know about Wild West words.

A varmint is _____.

A cyclone is _____.

A lariat is _____.

A bronco is _____.

John Henry

Reproduce and distribute copies of the *Muscle or Machine?* student page on page 392. Explain that knowing the roles of people and machines in building railroads will help students understand *John Henry*. Help students understand how to read the chart. Point to the column that shows how muscle power built railroads. Now point to the column that shows how machine power built railroads.

Read aloud the information in the chart. Discuss the two processes. Scaffold with sentence frames such as: *The steel driver used a_____ to_____. The shaker or turner held _____ and _____ after each strike. The steam drill copied _____ by _____.* Then have students work with a partner to discuss what they learned.

For students who need support in accessing key ideas and key language in *John Henry,* use the Sentence Talk Routine on pages 441–442 to draw students' attention to the relationship between meaning and the words, phrases, and clauses in the text.

Lesson	Sentence(s) to Deconstruct
13	(p 67) When John Henry raised his arm, folks gasped and brought their hands to their faces, for they saw that the mighty baby had been born with a hammer in his hand.
14	(p 69) He saw men robbed of their dignity and robbed of their families.
15	(p 71) But John Henry kept hammering, hammering faster than any man had ever hammered before, hammering against all the machines of the future.
16	(p 73) Lucy stood still as stone, for she knew what had happened.

Use the Text-based Writing Routine on pages 443–444 to model how to speak and write about key ideas and details in *John Henry*.

Lesson	Text-based Writing	Scaffolded Frames
13	What clues on page 67 tell you why John Henry is described as a "mighty baby?"	• One reason is that he was born _____. • He had _____ and was born with a _____. • John Henry was mighty because _____.
14	What details on page 69 tell you what it means to be robbed of dignity?	• John Henry saw machines _____. • John Henry saw _____, _____, and _____.
15	Using the text on page 71, explain what John Henry does after the steam drill breaks down.	• He keeps _____, faster than _____. • He keeps _____ because _____.
16	The text on page 73 states that Lucy stands still as stone. What does this tell you?	• It tells me that Lucy is _____. • Lucy stands still as stone because _____.

Name _____

Muscle or Machine?

In the 1870s, machines were introduced to do difficult jobs. People still did most of the work of building railroads. Tunneling through mountains was one of the biggest challenges. People hoped machines would make the job easier and faster.

Muscle Power	Machine Power
• The men who tunneled through rock worked in two-person teams. • One man, called the **Steel Driver**, used a hammer to strike a spike deep into the rock. • The **Shaker** or **Turner** was the man who held the spike. After each strike he turned the spike for the Steel Driver. • Once the hole was deep enough, the spike was removed. Workers packed the hole with explosives to blow the big rock apart. Then the team began again. The job was dangerous, dirty, and slow.	• The **Steam Drill** machine copied the movement of the men. The machine pounded the drill into the rock with great force. It also turned the drill between strikes. This process cleared the broken rock. These early drills often broke. Because of this problem, men often worked with the machines.

Share what you learned about digging railroad tunnels.

The steel driver used a _____ to _____.

The shaker or turner held _____ and _____ after each strike.

The Longest Night

BUILD BACKGROUND

Reproduce and distribute copies of *What is a Quest?* student page on page 395. Explain that to understand the story events in *The Longest Night,* it helps to know what a quest is. Start by clarifying for students that the word *characteristics* refers to features that are typical of something or someone—in this case, those of a quest. Then help students understand how to read the chart. Point to the circles that explain the different characteristics, or parts, of a quest.

Read aloud the contents of each circle. If necessary, confirm students' understanding by having them discuss the meanings of certain words featured in the circles. Scaffold with sentence frames such as the following: *A journey is _____. Challenges are _____.*

After discussing the information in the circles, have students turn to a partner and explain the characteristics of a quest. Scaffold with sentence frames such as the following: *During a quest a person _____. The person also _____.*

Then have students share with a partner the remaining features of a quest. Scaffold with an additional sentence frame such as the following: *In addition, a person on a quest _____ and _____.*

TALK ABOUT SENTENCES

For students who need support in accessing key ideas and key language in *The Longest Night,* use the Sentence Talk Routine on pages 441–442 to draw students' attention to the relationship between meaning and the words, phrases, and clauses in the text.

Lesson	Sentence(s) to Deconstruct
1	(p 4) Tomorrow, I would start the most important journey of my life, my Vision Quest, and when I returned home from three nights in the wilderness alone, I would be a warrior.
2	(p 10) "You, Wind Runner, do not tell Creator what Spirit Helper you want. If you deserve one at all, he will send what he thinks you need most for your life journey."
3	(p 22) I hadn't earned the song, which was a tribute to a warrior's courage and bravery, but figured it wouldn't be long before I had.
4	(p 27) The mutt must have sensed something, because it yawned lazily, as though coming out of a deep slumber.
5	(p 36) As I watched, the old dog padded up beside the circle, raised its hackles, and began to howl.
6	(p 40) Trying not to startle the huge monster, I prepared to leap up and run.

Use the Text-based Writing Routine on pages 443–444 to model how to speak and write about key ideas and details in *The Longest Night*.

Lesson	Text-based Writing	Scaffolded Frames
1	Why was spending three nights in the wilderness so important to Wind Runner, according to page 4?	After three nights Wind Runner would _____. Wind Runner wanted to _____ so that _____.
2	On page 10, what details tell you the Elder is angry with Wind Runner?	The Elder says that Wind Runner does not tell _____. The Elder says _____ because Creator will send _____.
3	On page 22, what does Wind Runner's excuse for singing the song before he's earned it tell you about him?	Wind Runner is _____. Wind Runner thinks he is _____. Wind Runner is _____ because he _____.
4	On page 27, how is the dog's reaction to the rattlesnake different from Wind Runner's?	The dog _____ like Wind Runner is. The dog _____, while Wind Runner is _____. Wind Runner _____, but the dog _____.
5	According to the text on pages 36 and 37, what effect does the dog's behavior have on the wolf?	The dog makes the wolf _____. The dog _____ the wolf and makes it _____. By _____, the dog _____.
6	Given his reaction on pages 39 and 40, how do you think Wind Runner feels about the bear?	Wind Runner is _____ of the bear. Wind Runner is _____. He thinks the bear _____.

Use the Dig Deeper Vocabulary Routine on pages 439–440 to continue to develop conceptual understanding of the following action verbs: *chanted, raked, endured, retrieved, recoiled, lumbered, gazed,* and *foraged*. Begin by reviewing the purpose of action verbs in a sentence. Then display and read aloud the following sentence: *Wind Runner **climbed** up the mountain.*

Point out that *Wind Runner* tells who climbed and *up the mountain* tells where he climbed. Discuss with a partner how action verbs help you understand what someone or something is doing.

Unit 2 Module B

Name _____

What is a Quest?

What are the characteristics of a quest?

```
   ┌─────────────┐              ┌─────────────┐
   │ a person    │              │ a person    │
   │ goes on a   │              │ faces       │
   │ journey     │              │ challenges  │
   └─────────────┘   ┌───────┐  └─────────────┘
                     │ Quest │
                     └───────┘
   ┌─────────────┐              ┌─────────────┐
   │ a person    │              │ a person    │
   │ searches    │              │ changes     │
   │ for         │              │ in some way │
   │ something   │              │             │
   └─────────────┘              └─────────────┘
```

What happens to a person on a quest?

A person on a quest goes on a _____.
The a person also faces _____.

Northwest Coast Peoples

Reproduce and distribute copies of the *Natural Resources* student page on page 397. Explain that to understand the information in *Northwest Coast Peoples,* it helps to know about natural resources. Help students understand how to read the chart. Point to each circle that tells something about natural resources.

Read aloud the information in the chart. If necessary, confirm students' understanding by having them discuss what a natural resource is. Scaffold with a sentence frame: *People can find natural resources _____.*

After discussing the information in each circle in the chart, have students work with a partner to find examples of how people use natural resources. Scaffold with sentence frames such as: *People use natural resources for _____, _____, and _____.*

TALK ABOUT SENTENCES

For students who need support in accessing key ideas and key language in *Northwest Coast Peoples*, use the Sentence Talk Routine on pages 441–442 to draw students' attention to the relationship between meaning and the words, phrases, and clauses in the text.

Lesson	Sentence(s) to Deconstruct
7	(p 108) The members of a clan considered themselves related because they shared the same spirit ancestor.
8	(p 115) Some children were sent to boarding schools, where they were punished if they spoke their language.

SPEAK AND WRITE ABOUT THE TEXT

Use the Text-based Writing Routine on pages 443–444 to model how to speak and write about key ideas and details in *Northwest Coast Peoples.*

Lesson	Text-based Writing	Scaffolded Frames
7	Using information on page 108, tell why a person's rank was important.	Rank was important because it indicated a person's _____. Rank was based on a person's _____, so _____ were considered nobles.
8	Why were children punished for speaking their language, according to page 115?	Government agents and missionaries wanted the children to live _____. They wanted the children to behave more like _____, so they made them _____.

Unit 2 Module B

Name _____

Natural Resources

What are natural resources?

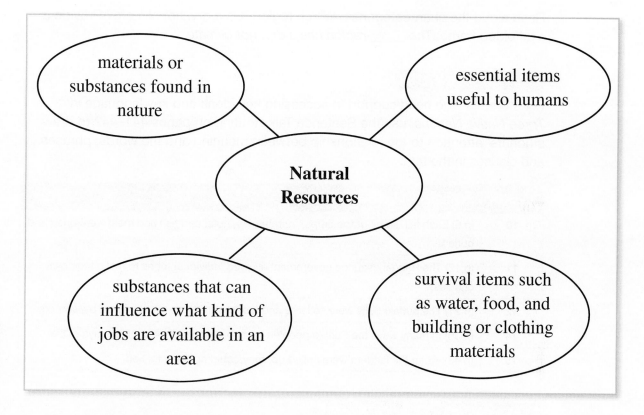

materials or substances found in nature

essential items useful to humans

Natural Resources

substances that can influence what kind of jobs are available in an area

survival items such as water, food, and building or clothing materials

Share two facts about natural resources.

Natural resources are things found in nature that people _____.

Two examples of natural resources are _____ and _____.

Three Native Nations

Reproduce and distribute copies of the *Features of the Land* student page on page 399. Explain that to understand the information in *Three Native Nations,* it helps to know something about the climate and geography of the land.

Read aloud the chart categories. Which region has a dry, hot climate? Provide a scaffolded frame: *The _____ region has a dry, hot climate.*

TALK ABOUT SENTENCES

For students who need support in accessing key ideas and key language in *Three Native Nations*, use the Sentence Talk Routine on pages 441–442 to draw students' attention to the relationship between meaning and the words, phrases, and clauses in the text.

Lesson	Sentence(s) to Deconstruct
10	(p 6) Each fall, some of the crops, fruit, berries, nuts, and fish and meat were dried and buried.
11	(p 12) The Haudenosaunee government allowed individual tribes to make their own choices.
12	(p 21) The buffalo bulls were so large and fearless that they were revered by warriors.
14	(p 36) In many ways the Pueblo peoples have maintained their ancient ways of life.
15	(p 43) When the ladders were pulled up, they could not be attacked.

SPEAK AND WRITE ABOUT THE TEXT

Use the Text-based Writing Routine on pages 443–444 to model how to speak and write about key ideas and details in *Three Native Nations*.

Lesson	Text-based Writing	Scaffolded Frames
10	Why was it useful to dry and bury food, according to information on page 6?	By drying and burying the food, the women could _____. The women wanted _____ so they would _____.
11	How do the maps starting on page 12 show land ownership?	The maps show how the nations' land got _____. Before the war _____. But now _____.
12	What do the details on page 21 tell you about the Sioux's feelings for the buffalo?	The Sioux thought the buffalo was a _____ gift from _____. The Sioux _____ the buffalo because _____.
14	Use information on page 36 to describe Pueblo ways of life.	The Pueblo still make ___ jewelry using ____. The Pueblo still fashion ____ and form ____.
15	Use the text and illustration on page 43 to explain safety.	The Pueblo would use ladders to climb to the second level and then would _____.

Unit 2 Module B

Name _____

Features of the Land

What important features of the different regions make them different?

Region	Woodlands	Plains	Deserts
Climate	hot in the summer and cold in the winter	hot in the summer and very cold in the winter	dry and hot
Geography	many trees and lakes	open land; few trees; grassy	sandy soil and soil of clay; few trees

Share facts about the climate and geography of the different regions.

The climate in the woodlands region is _____.

Neither the plains nor the desert has many _____.

Name _____

Big Jack and the Hoppers

Big Jack was born on the plains in Kansas in the 1860s. He wasn't like other babies right from the start. When he let out a cry, a gust of air blew the curtains sideways and the dishes flew off the table! A good sneeze could blow the farmhouse to the next county! Troublesome as it was, Jack's big breath came in real handy in the summer of 1875.

Jack and his father were working in their wheat field. All of a sudden, the sky darkened. A terrible buzzing and crunching sound filled the air. It got louder by the minute.

"Jack, look," Pa said, pointing to the western sky. A huge dark cloud was coming toward them. "That is a powerful storm! We'd better run!"

Jack stared at the cloud and the sound got louder. "That's no rainstorm, Pa," Jack shouted over the roar. "Those are Rocky Mountain hoppers!"

Now every farmer on the plains feared these grasshoppers. These grasshoppers could eat the clothes off your back. "Save the farm, Jack!" Pa screamed, as he ran toward the barn to escape the hungry grasshoppers.

Jack turned calmly toward the west. He took in the deepest breath he had ever breathed. Then he reached for some wheat to tickle his nose. In one mighty sneeze, he blew every single grasshopper over the Rocky Mountains and far out to sea. To this day, nobody has seen a single Rocky Mountain hopper on the plains!

Name _____

The Peaceful Haudenosaunee People

If I had to choose a Native American group to grow up in, I would pick the Haudenosaunee. I like how peaceful they were and how they had cooperative communities.

Haudenosaunee society was divided into clans named after animals. They had a turtle clan and a bear clan, for example. Haudenosaunee families that belonged to the same clan lived together in longhouses. These longhouses displayed the clan symbols above the door. Women owned the longhouses. A man would join whichever longhouse his new wife's family lived in. Besides living together in longhouses, the Haudenosaunee also played games like lacrosse. Lacrosse games helped the clans have fun together and avoid conflict.

The Haudenosaunee had a very peaceful life that was based around cooperation. This is why I would choose to grow up with the Haudenosaunee.

Performance-Based Assessment
Unit 2 Module A

Reproduce and distribute copies of the student model on page 400. After completing the Prepare to Write activities on pages 188–189 in Unlock the Writing in Part 2, use the student model to illustrate the features of a legend.

Discuss the student model. Read the title aloud and ask students what they think the tall tale might be about. If necessary, use a sentence frame such as: *I think this tall tale will be about _____.* (someone named Jack) Explain that a hopper means a grasshopper. *Next,* read the first paragraph aloud, and ask: What is important about the first paragraph? Provide sentence frames: *The writer introduces _____. The writer explains that the character is special because _____.* Read aloud the body of the story. Discuss how the writer uses dialogue to describe the setting, set up the story problem, and help readers get to know the characters. Point out concrete words and phrases. Also point out how the writer uses sensory words to set the scene. Help students understand the sequence of events by pointing out transition words. Read aloud the last paragraph, and ask: How does the writer provide a conclusion to the story? *The writer provides a conclusion by having Jack use his _____ to blow the _____.*

Unit 2 Module B

Reproduce and distribute copies of the student model on page 401. After completing the Prepare to Write activities on pages 188–189 in Unlock the Writing in Part 2, use the student model to illustrate the features of an opinion essay.

Discuss the student model. Read the first paragraph to students. Ask: What information does the writer give in the first paragraph of the opinion essay? *The writer tells which Native American group he or she _____.* (would have liked to grow up in and why) How do you know this is an opinion? *I know that this is an opinion essay because _____.* (it tells how the writer feels)

Read aloud the second paragraph. What information does the writer provide in the second paragraph? If necessary, provide a sentence frame such as: *The writer gives information about how the Haudenosaunee _____.* (lived and played together) Ask students why this information helps support the writer's opinion. *This information helps support the idea that the Haudenosaunee were _____.* (peaceful and cooperative)

Finally, read aloud the third paragraph. How does the writer end the essay? (by saying again why he or she chose the Haudenosaunee) Why is this important? *It summarizes the writer's _____.* (point of view/opinion)

Earthquakes

Reproduce and distribute copies of the *Earth's Layers* student page on page 405. Explain that to understand the information in *Earthquakes,* it helps to know the word *layers.* Turn and talk to a partner about the meaning of *layer.* What is an example of a thing with layers?

Have students count the layers in the Earth. Which layer is on the surface of the Earth? *The _____ is on the Earth's surface.* Which layer is in the center of the Earth? *The _____ is in the center of the Earth.*

Read aloud the descriptions of each layer, as students follow along. Discuss what each layer is made of and how deep the layer is. Scaffold with sentence frames such as: *The _____ is made of _____. It is _____ deep.*

Then have students work with a partner to report what they learned about each layer.

TALK ABOUT SENTENCES

For students who need support in accessing key ideas and key language in *Earthquakes,* use the Sentence Talk Routine on pages 441–442 to draw students' attention to the relationship between meaning and the words, phrases, and clauses in the text.

Lesson	Sentence(s) to Deconstruct
1	(p 8) In one type of fault, called a strike-slip fault, the rocks on one side of the fault try to move past the rocks on the other side, causing energy to build up.
2	(p 13) The slowly moving mantle carries along the solid crust, which is cracked like an eggshell into a number of huge pieces called plates.
3	(p 14) Scientists think that a huge, deadly earthquake will strike along the San Andreas Fault in the near future.
4	(p 18) Modern seismographs record their data to a computer and are able to detect a tiny earth tremor thousands of miles away.
5	(p 26) On the afternoon of Good Friday, March 27, 1964, Anchorage, Alaska was shaken apart by the most violent earthquake ever recorded in the United States.
6	(p 30) But we need to know much more about earthquakes before we can predict weeks or even days in advance when a big one will hit.

Use the Text-based Writing Routine on pages 443–444 to model how to speak and write about key ideas and details in *Earthquakes*.

Lesson	Text-based Writing	Scaffolded Frames
1	On page 8, why might an earthquake happen at a strike-slip fault?	• In a strike-slip fault, rocks _____ try to _____. • This causes _____. • The energy can _____.
2	According to page 13, how does the movement of plates cause an earthquake?	• The plates _____ each other. • The plates _____ each other and cause _____.
3	What facts on page 14 explain why the San Andreas fault is dangerous?	• One reason that the San Andreas fault is dangerous is _____. • The San Andreas fault is dangerous because _____, _____, and _____. • The San Andreas fault is _____ because _____.
4	Use information on page 18 to explain what a seismograph is and to tell why it is important.	• A seismograph is _____. • It _____. • One reason that a seismograph is important is _____. • Another reason is _____.
5	What details on page 26 describe the earthquake that happened in Anchorage, Alaska?	• I learned that _____. • Another thing I learned was _____. • One reason the earthquake was the most violent ever recorded in the United States is _____.
6	Why is it important to build earthquake-resistant homes? Use information on page 30 to respond.	• It is important to _____ because _____. • Scientists can _____. However, they can't _____. That is why it is important to _____.

Use the Dig Deeper Vocabulary Routine on pages 439–440 to continue to develop conceptual understanding of the following adjectives: *populated, dense, violent, vertical, immense, miniature, slightest*. Begin by reviewing what adjectives do in sentences. Display and read aloud the following sentences. *There was a **violent** earthquake. It happened in a **populated** area.* Discuss the sentences. What is each sentence about? Explain that *earthquake* is a noun because it names something. Explain that *violent* is an adjective that proceeds the noun *earthquake* and gives information that tells more about the earthquake. Then explain that *populated* is an adjective that proceeds the noun *area* and gives more information about it. Turn and talk to a partner about why it is important to pay attention to adjectives when you read.

Name _____

Earth's Layers

The Earth is round and made up of several layers.

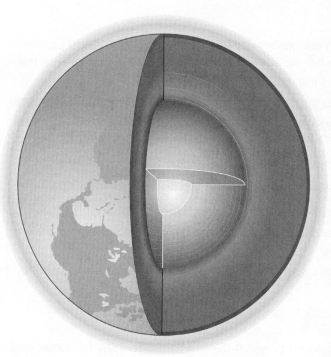

Crust The top layer is the Earth's crust. This is the layer that begins under the land and the oceans. It is made of rock and other materials. The crust is about ten miles thick.

Mantle The mantle is under the crust. It is made of chunks of thick, hard rocky material that move around. The mantle layer is about 1,800 miles thick.

Outer Core Below the mantle is the outer core. This layer is made of super-hot molten lava. The outer core reaches a depth of about 1,000 miles.

Inner Core The inner core is the very center of the Earth. Scientists think it is a hard ball of iron. They think the inner core is about 900 miles thick.

Share facts about one of Earth's layers.

The _____ is made of _____.

It is _____ deep.

Quake!

Reproduce and distribute copies of the *Foreshocks and Aftershocks* student page on page 407. Explain that to understand the story events in *Quake!*, it helps to understand that earthquakes happen in groups.

Provide a sentence frame: *Small earthquakes that come before the mainshock are called _____. The _____ comes last.*

TALK ABOUT SENTENCES

For students who need support in accessing key ideas and key language in *Quake!*, use the Sentence Talk Routine on pages 441–442 to draw students' attention to the relationship between meaning and the words, phrases, and clauses in the text.

Lesson	Sentence(s) to Deconstruct
7	(p 8) The dog ran a few yards toward the docks, then turned and barked again.
8	(p 9) He whirled in time to see the front wall of the building collapse in a heap.
9	(p 12) Jacob fell to his knees and covered his head with his arms.
10	(p 16) He pictured Sophie trapped in the rubble and Papa frantically digging to reach her.
11	(p 17) Two of the men kneeled to look at something, and one cupped his hands over his mouth and began to yell.
12	(p 23) Jacob thanked him and went from person to person, asking the same questions.

SPEAK AND WRITE ABOUT THE TEXT

Use the Text-based Writing Routine on pages 443–444 to model how to speak and write about key ideas and details in *Quake!*

Lesson	Text-based Writing	Scaffolded Frames
7	Use information on page 8 to explain how Jacob and the dog communicate with each other.	• The dog _____ to check on Jacob. • The dog wants Jacob to walk toward _____ because _____.
8	What details on page 9 describe the damage?	• The front wall of the building _____. • The loud noises were _____.
9	On page 12, how does Jacob protect himself?	• Jacob gets down on his _____. • He protects his head with _____.
10	On page 16, what does Jacob imagine has happened to his family?	• Jacob thinks Sophie _____. • He imagines Papa is _____.
11	Using details on page 17, describe how some people began working again.	• To talk to each other, the men have to _____. • The men kneel down so they can _____.
12	What details on page 23 tell how Jacob continues his search for his family?	• Jacob asked each person whether _____. • He explains that his sister _____.

Unit 3 Module A

Name _____

Foreshocks and Aftershocks

Earthquakes usually occur in groups. Often several earthquakes occur in a row.

Foreshocks	**Mainshocks**	**Aftershocks**
occur before the mainshock	represent the largest earthquake in a series	occur shortly after the mainshock
usually take place within a day of the mainshock	are caused by a stress on both sides of a fault	can take place on the same fault as the mainshock or another smaller fault nearby
occur in the same area as the mainshock	cause the most damage	take place before the activity in the ground returns to normal
do not always occur before earthquakes		can occur repeatedly after large earthquakes
		are generally expected after earthquakes

Share facts about the three categories of earthquakes.

I learned that foreshocks and aftershocks _____.

The mainshock _____.

Aftershocks _____.

Earthshaker's Bad Day

BUILD BACKGROUND

Reproduce and distribute copies of the *Meet the Greeks* student page on page 409. Explain that to understand the story events in *Earthshaker's Bad Day*, it helps to know more about the Greek gods and goddesses in the story. Begin by helping students understand the captions. Point to where you can learn about each of the gods and goddesses. By looking at the pictures and reading the captions, you can get a better idea of what each god or goddess was like.

Remind students that captions often give important information about pictures. Ask students to follow along as you read aloud the information about Zeus. What words would you use to describe Zeus? If necessary, provide sentence frames: *Zeus is the supreme leader of all the _____ .*

Encourage students to look at the pictures and listen carefully as you read aloud the captions about Poseidon and Athena. Discuss each one and conclude by scaffolding with sentence frames: *When Poseidon is _____, he often causes _____. Athena is the goddess of _____ and _____. The city of _____ is named after her.*

Ask students to discuss with a partner what they have learned about these three Greek gods.

TALK ABOUT SENTENCES

For students who need support in accessing key ideas and key language in *Earthshaker's Bad Day,* use the Sentence Talk Routine on pages 441–442 to draw students' attention to the relationship between meaning and the words, phrases, and clauses in the text.

Lesson	Sentence(s) to Deconstruct
14	(p 25) If the king chose him, then he could be near humans *all* the time, instead of alone in the sea.

SPEAK AND WRITE ABOUT THE TEXT

Use the Text-based Writing Routine on pages 443–444 to model how to speak write about key ideas and details in *Earthshaker's Bad Day*.

Lesson	Text-based Writing	Scaffolded Frames
14	Use the details on page 25 to explain why Poseidon wanted to be the patron god of the new city.	Poseidon wanted to be near _____. He was _____ living in the sea. If he were chosen, he could _____.

Name _____

Meet the Greeks

The ancient Greeks told stories to explain their beliefs about the world. These stories told of many different gods. Who are these gods?

ZEUS

Zeus is the supreme ruler of all the Greek gods. He is the God of Lightning and Thunder. He lives on Mount Olympus and rules the land and the air. He is very powerful.

POSEIDON

Poseidon is the god of the sea and water. He lives in a palace under the sea. When he is angry or upset, he can create huge waves, storms, and earthquakes.

ATHENA

Athena is the goddess of wisdom and military victory. She is brave in battle. She is well known for helping heroes. The city of Athens is named for her.

Share something you learned about one of the Greek gods or goddesses.

I learned _____ about _____.

The Monster Beneath the Sea

BUILD BACKGROUND

Reproduce and distribute copies of the *Personification* student page on page 411. Explain that to understand the story events in *The Monster Beneath the Sea,* it helps to know what personification is. Help students understand how to read the chart. Which circle tells what the chart is about? Now point to the circles that show pieces of information.

Read aloud the information in the chart. Explain that the subjects in the circles are all nonliving things with human qualities. Scaffold with frames such as: *Video games cannot really _____ off of shelves. People must have bought them _____.*

After discussing all of the examples of personification in the chart, have students share something they learned about personification.

TALK ABOUT SENTENCES

For students who need support in accessing key ideas and key language in *The Monster Beneath the Sea,* use the Sentence Talk Routine on pages 441–442 to draw students' attention to the relationship between meaning and the words, phrases, and clauses in the text.

Lesson	Sentence(s) to Deconstruct
15	(p 31) When Namazu wiggled, even just a tiny bit, the buildings in Japan rattled.

SPEAK AND WRITE ABOUT THE TEXT

Use the Text-based Writing Routine on pages 443–444 to model how to speak and write about key ideas and details in *The Monster Beneath the Sea.*

Lesson	Text-based Writing	Scaffolded Frames
15	Use information on page 31 to explain why Namazu caused problems on land.	When Namazu wiggled _____. He caused _____ on the land. Namazu was able to create large waves and rattle buildings because _____.

Name _____

Personification

Personification is when an author gives qualities of a person to something that is not human or something that is not even living.

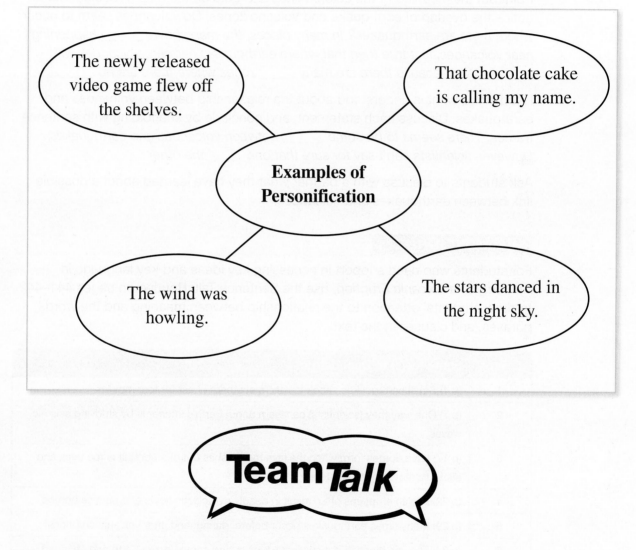

The newly released video game flew off the shelves.

That chocolate cake is calling my name.

Examples of Personification

The wind was howling.

The stars danced in the night sky.

Team Talk

Share something you learned about personification.
I learned that _____.

Anatomy of a Volcanic Eruption

Reproduce and distribute copies of the *What's the Connection?* student page on page 414. Explain that to understand the information in *Anatomy of a Volcanic Eruption,* it helps to think about the relationship between volcanoes and earthquakes. Discuss with a partner whether or not you think there are connections between volcanoes and earthquakes. If helpful, review how to read a map legend. Point out the meaning of the colored lines and dots on the map. Ask students to notice the overlap of earthquake and volcano zones. Do volcanoes seem to occur where there are earthquakes? *In many places, the map shows _____ happening near volcanoes. Is it true then that where earthquakes happen, volcanoes will happen? No, because there are many _____ zones where there are no _____.*

Read aloud what is understood about the relationship between volcanoes and earthquakes. Discuss each statement, and conclude by scaffolding with sentence frames: *There seems to be some _____ between volcanoes and earthquakes. However, scientists can't say for sure that one _____ the other.*

Ask students to discuss with a partner what they have learned about a possible link between earthquakes and volcanoes.

TALK ABOUT SENTENCES

For students who need support in accessing key ideas and key language in *Anatomy of a Volcanic Eruption,* use the Sentence Talk Routine on pages 441–442 to draw students' attention to the relationship between meaning and the words, phrases, and clauses in the text.

Lesson	Sentence(s) to Deconstruct
1	(p 4) Small earthquakes shook Iceland's southern coast for four months.
2	(p 7) One way they (scientists) can learn about Earth's interior is by studying seismic waves.
3	(p 17) Lava domes form when the lava that pushes out of a conduit is too thick and sticky to move a great distance.
4	(p 22) Plinian eruptions often result in deadly pyroclastic flows and pumice bombs.
5	(p 29) Many times earthquakes occur before, during, and after volcanic eruptions.
6	(p 34) The ash blocked out sunlight which in turn cooled down Earth and changed weather patterns.
7	(p 37) If Vesuvius erupted today at the same magnitude as the AD 79 eruption, the results would be catastrophic.
8	(p 42) More than 10,000 small earthquakes have occurred near the volcano since March 16.

Use the Text-based Writing Routine on pages 443–444 to model how to speak and write about key ideas and details in *Anatomy of a Volcanic Eruption.*

Lesson	Text-based Writing	Scaffolded Frames
1	On page 4, why did the writer give details about small earthquakes first?	• Before the _____ there were small earthquakes.
2	Use information from page 7 to explain what scientists do to learn about the inside of Earth.	• Scientists can study _____ waves that take place during _____. • Scientists can study _____ waves.
3	How does page 17 help you know how lava domes form?	• The lava domes form when lava pushes up but is too _____ to travel.
4	Which details on page 22 explain why Plinian eruptions are so deadly?	• The pyroclastic flows are _____ and they throw _____ gas and rocks out.
5	Why is it important to know about earthquakes when studying volcanoes? Use information from page 29.	• It is important because we learn that _____ often happen _____, during, and _____ volcanic eruptions.
6	Which details on page 34 explain how volcanic eruptions have changed the weather?	• The ash _____ the sunlight and so Earth _____ down. • Scientists believe it was the volcanic _____ that caused _____.
7	Using facts from page 37, describe why Vesuvius poses a great risk of danger today?	• More than _____ people now live _____. • A Vesuvious eruption today would pose a great risk because _____.
8	Explain what happened at Mount St. Helens using facts from page 42.	• More than ten _____ small _____ took place before Mount St. Helens blew. • Thousands of _____ before the May _____.

Use the Dig Deeper Vocabulary Routine on pages 439–440 to continue to develop conceptual understanding of the following nouns: *atmosphere, disruption, structure, investigations, benefits, resources, nutrients, residents, survivors, tremors.* Review what nouns do in sentences and display and read aloud the following sentences.

> *Gas shot up high into the* **atmosphere.**
> *There were no* **survivors.**
> **Tremors** *are often felt on the island of Hawaii.*

Discuss the function each of these three nouns has in the sentences. Is the noun, *survivors* referring to a person, place, or thing? Explain that *survivors* are people who make it through a tragedy. If necessary, discuss the word *atmosphere,* explaining that it refers to a place. Are *tremors* people, places, or things?

Name _____

What's the Connection?

Some people think that there is a connection between earthquakes and volcanoes. Do earthquakes cause volcanoes? Why do people think that earthquakes and volcanoes are connected?

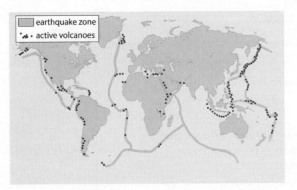

- Notice on the map that where there are active volcanoes, there is almost always an earthquake zone. However, there are earthquake locations where there are no active volcanoes.
- When Earth's plates bump into each other, the force often causes earthquakes. Melting rock below the surface gets pushed up. This can form a volcano.
- Large earthquake tremors can affect pockets of magma below the surface. If a volcano is ready to erupt, underground stress may make that eruption more likely.

Share something you learned about the connection between earthquakes and volcanoes.

I learned that earthquakes and volcanoes are connected because _____.

Escape From Pompeii

Reproduce and distribute copies of the *Life in Pompeii* student page on page 416. Explain that to understand the story events in *Escape from Pompeii*, it helps to know what Pompeii was like before the eruption of Mount Vesuvius destroyed the city. Help students understand how to read the chart. Point to where you will learn about life in Pompeii.

Read aloud and discuss the information in the chart. Have students discuss with a partner what it must have been like to live in Pompeii before the volcano destroyed the city. Scaffold with sentence frames such as: *Pompeii was a place to vacation and _____. Rome's most distinguished citizens lived in Pompeii in beautiful _____.*

TALK ABOUT SENTENCES

For students who need support in accessing key ideas and key language in *Escape from Pompeii* use the Sentence Talk Routine on pages 441–442 to draw students' attention to the relationship between meaning and the words, phrases, and clauses in the text.

Lesson	Sentence(s) to Deconstruct
9	(p 43) A few years before Tranio was born, there had been a big earthquake in Pompeii, and parts of the town had still not been fully repaired.
10	(p 52) At first its slopes were burnt and barren, but in time plants began to grow as the volcanic soil brought forth its riches once more.

SPEAK AND WRITE ABOUT THE TEXT

Use the Text-based Writing Routine on pages 443–444 to model how to speak and write about key ideas and details in *Escape from Pompeii*.

Lesson	Text-based Writing	Scaffolded Frames
9	According to page 43, why did Tranio not worry about the earthquake tremors?	• He wasn't _____ when the big _____ happened. • The earthquake was past _____. • The people in Pompeii _____.
10	What information on page 52 helps you understand the good things about living near a volcano?	• The volcanic _____ was rich and good for _____. • After a volcano _____. • Crops can grow well because _____.

Name _____

Life in Pompeii

Before the eruption of Mount Vesuvius destroyed the city, life in Pompeii was good. What was it like to live in Pompeii?

Life in Pompeii
• Wealthy people came to vacation and enjoy life in the beautiful Bay of Naples.
• Rome's most distinguished citizens lived in beautiful homes and villas that lined the streets of Pompeii.
• People enjoyed the many shops and cafes.
• An estimated 20,000 people lived in Pompeii. They likely gathered for entertainment in the arena or the city's marketplace.

Share two things you learned about life in the ancient city of Pompeii.

I learned _____ and _____ about life in the ancient city of Pompeii.

A Tsunami Unfolds

BUILD BACKGROUND

Reproduce and distribute copies of the *Risky Radiation* student page on page 418. Explain that to understand the information in *A Tsunami Unfolds,* it helps to understand the effects of radiation.

Read aloud the information in the chart. Confirm students understanding by scaffolding with sentence frames such as: *Radiation can leak into the ground and get into the* _____ *supply.*

TALK ABOUT SENTENCES

For students who need support in accessing key ideas and key language in *A Tsunami Unfolds,* use the Sentence Talk Routine on pages 441–442 to draw students' attention to the relationship between meaning and the words, phrases, and clauses in the text.

Lesson	Sentence(s) to Deconstruct
12	(p 7) The powerful vibrations shook the building hard and collapsed the ceiling inside the airport's central hall.
13	(p 17) Workers were busy monitoring damage from the quake when the giant tsunami surprised them, crashing right over the plant's sea wall.
14	(p 20) Worst of all, many people were separated from their families with no way to find out who had survived and who had died.
15	(p 26) Officials had begun scanning people and pets with radiation detectors to check radiation levels.

SPEAK AND WRITE ABOUT THE TEXT

Use the Text-based Writing Routine on pages 443–444 to model how to speak and write about key ideas and details in *A Tsunami Unfolds.*

Lesson	Text-based Writing	Scaffolded Frames
12	How do details on page 7 help you understand the earthquake?	• Yumi told how the _____ shook the building making the _____ collapse.
13	Using page 17, why might the nuclear plant workers have been surprised?	• The workers were caught off-guard because _____. • The quake damage _____.
14	What details on page 20 describe how the tsunami affected people?	• Families were _____ and they couldn't _____ each other. • Families couldn't find out _____.
15	According to page 26, why did officials check radiation levels?	• Two reactors had hydrogen _____ releasing unsafe radiation.

Name _____

Risky Radiation

Why are nuclear power plants risky to humans?

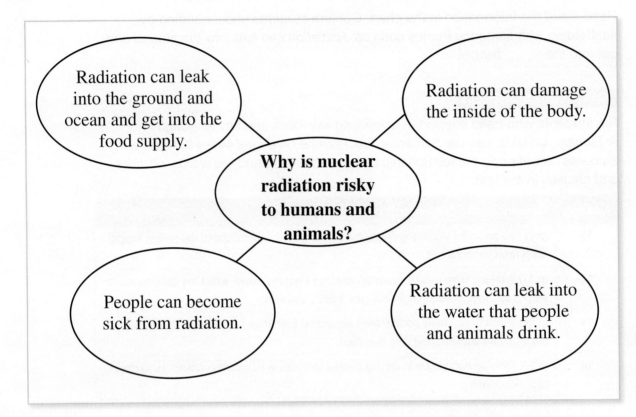

Radiation can leak into the ground and ocean and get into the food supply.

Radiation can damage the inside of the body.

Why is nuclear radiation risky to humans and animals?

People can become sick from radiation.

Radiation can leak into the water that people and animals drink.

Share facts about the risk that comes with nuclear power plants.

Radiation can leak into the water supply and then animals and people _____.

Radiation can damage _____.

Name _____

Earthquakes

In my opinion, the book *Quake!* tells more about the impact of earthquakes on humans. One reason is that this book is a story that tells about people who live through an earthquake.

At the beginning of the story, Jacob's dog was nervous. Then the earthquake hit and Jacob tried to make sense of what was happening. After the earthquake, he was very scared because there was danger everywhere. For example, he saw buildings weaving in and out. Some buildings collapsed. Bricks were raining all over the street. In addition, when horses were stampeding, the dog saved Jacob's life. The destruction caused Jacob to get a cut on his wrist. A picture in the story also shows the destruction the earthquake caused.

The story does more than give facts about earthquakes. Readers can understand what Jacob thought and how he felt. The story also shows the destruction. For these reasons I think *Quake!* does a better job of teaching about the impact of earthquakes on human beings.

Name _____

The Terror of Tornadoes

Tornadoes have created some of the worst storm disasters in history. They may carry winds up to 300 miles per hour. Tornadoes can cause loss of life and property.

To be prepared, it is helpful to understand tornadoes. A strong tornado can leave damage a mile wide. It can wreck buildings and hurt people along a 50-mile long path. People should know the signs of tornado weather. For example, tornadoes often take place near the edge of strong thunderstorms. Skies often become a very dark, greenish color. Before a tornado hits, the air may become still and quiet. A funnel-shaped cloud might be seen twisting down from a thunderstorm. If it moves toward the ground, take cover!

Respect tornadoes for the danger they can cause. Be sure to listen to warnings so you don't get caught in a storm. Also, prepare a safe place. You don't want to come face to face with a tornado!

Performance-Based Assessment
Unit 3 Module A

DISCUSS THE STUDENT MODEL

Reproduce and distribute copies of the student model on page 419. After completing the Prepare to Write activities on pages 206–207 in Unlock the Writing in Part 2, use the student model to illustrate the features of an opinion essay.

Discuss the student model. Point out that the writer has divided the model into three parts or paragraphs. Read aloud the first paragraph, and ask: How does the writer begin the opinion essay? Use a sentence frame if students need help answering. *The writer begins by clearly stating an _____. (opinion)* Why do you think the writer used some of the words from the writing assignment? (so readers would clearly understand what the essay would be about) Read aloud the second paragraph. What does the writer include in this paragraph? If necessary, provide a frame for students to answer. *The writer gives ____ for the opinion. (reasons)* Point out that each reason is a detail from the story. Ask students if they can think of any other details that would make good reasons for this opinion. If needed, scaffold with a sentence frame: *I think another good reason is _____.*

Read aloud the third paragraph of the model. Check to make sure that students understand what a summary is and its purpose. How did the writer end the essay? (ended with a summary) What does a summary do? *The summary summarizes the writer's _____ and restates the writer's ____.*

Unit 3 Module B

DISCUSS THE STUDENT MODEL

Reproduce and distribute copies of the student model on page 420. After completing the Prepare to Write activities on pages 206–207 in Unlock the Writing in Part 2, use the student model to illustrate the features of a news report.

Discuss the student model. Read aloud the first paragraph and ask: Does the writer include important information in the first paragraph so the reader knows what it is about? Is the purpose of the article clear? Use sentence frames if students need help answering. *The writer begins by clearly ____ the topic of the ____ of tornadoes. The purpose of the news article includes a ____ that tornadoes should not be ____.*

Read aloud the second paragraph. Ask: What details does the writer give to help the reader understand more about tornadoes? Use sentence frames to help clarify the answer. *The writer tells how ____ a tornado can be. The reader ____ how to identify the signs of a ____.*

Read aloud the conclusion. What does the conclusion do? *The conclusion summarizes the writer's ____ and reminds the reader to listen to the ____.*

Lunch Money

Reproduce and distribute copies of the *Let's Work Together* student page on page 424. Explain to students that to better understand the story events in *Lunch Money,* it is important to understand the word *compromise.* Begin by telling students the definition of *compromise*: A compromise is an agreement made when people adjust the way they think or act in order to work well together.

Read aloud the examples of compromise. If necessary, confirm students' understanding by having them discuss a time that they were able to work through differences by making a compromise. Scaffold with frames such as: *We disagreed about _____, so we compromised by _____.*

After discussing examples of compromise, have students work with a partner to share times when they needed to compromise with friends or family.

TALK ABOUT SENTENCES

For students who need support in accessing key ideas and key language in *Lunch Money,* use the Sentence Talk Routine on pages 441–442 to draw students' attention to the relationship between meaning and the words, phrases, and clauses in the text.

Lesson	Sentence(s) to Deconstruct
1	(p 8) He had eight customers within two blocks of his house, and every time it snowed, he shoveled the front walks for a flat rate: ten dollars.
2	(p 40) And when Greg went speeding out of his driveway and zipped along the sidewalk, she did the same thing, a mirror image.
3	(p 59) Mr. Z believed that even the smile of the Mona Lisa, like the spiral of the chambered Nautilus, could be expressed as a ratio, a set of elegant numbers.
4	(p 88) "Mass production, economies of scale, increased profits, and market dominance, right?"
5	(p 112) With a little work, and if they were inked and shaded just right, they would be fabulous, they would be . . . dangerous.
6	(p 155) Greg felt the urge to lash out, like he'd done with Eileen and Brittany at school on Friday morning. But this time he didn't take the bait.
7	(p 180) "Oh, *right,*" Greg said, "because everybody knows you're such a great—"
8	(p 200) Mr. Z made a note, a quick scribble, and said, "That's eighty-five percent of us."
9	(p 205) And here's my confession: I enjoyed myself.

SPEAK AND WRITE ABOUT THE TEXT

Use the Text-based Writing Routine on pages 443–444 to model how to speak and write about key ideas and details in *Lunch Money*.

Lesson	Text-based Writing	Scaffolded Frames
1	According to page 8, how does Greg make money shoveling snow?	• He shovels walks at a flat rate of _____. • He _____ at a flat rate of _____.
2	How does the story of the Big Wheels on page 40 show that Maura is competitive with Greg?	• Maura _____ everything that Greg does. • When Greg does _____, Maura _____. • Maura _____.
3	What details on page 59 show that Mr. Z thinks math is the source of all that is beautiful?	• He thinks Mona Lisa's smile can be expressed as a _____. • He thought Mona Lisa's _____ could _____.
4	What detail on page 88 shows that Greg understands mass production?	• He can make _____ copies in an hour. • He can make _____.
5	Based on page 112, what does Greg mean when he says Maura's drawings would be dangerous?	• Maura's comics might _____ more than his. • Maura's comics might _____. • Maura's comics might _____ because _____.
6	Based on page 155, how does Greg react differently to his brother than he does to Eileen's and Brittany's teasing?	• He does not _____ at his brother. • He does not _____ or _____.
7	According to page 180, how can you tell that Greg and Maura are snapping at each other?	• The author puts some words in _____. • The author uses _____ to _____. • The author uses _____.
8	What evidence is there on page 200 that Mr. Z thinks mathematically?	• He surveys the audience and gives _____. • He _____ the audience and gives _____.
9	What does Mrs. Davenport confess on page 205?	• She confesses that she _____ the _____. • She confesses that _____.

EXPAND UNDERSTANDING OF VOCABULARY

Use the Dig Deeper Vocabulary Routine on pages 439–440 to continue to develop conceptual understanding of the following nouns: *profit, initiative, operation, bargain, production, imitation, empire, agenda,* and *negotiations*. Begin by reviewing the purpose of nouns in sentences. Then point out that all of the words are related to making and selling products.

Name _____

Let's Work Together

Sometimes we must adjust the way we think and act in order to get along with others. This is called a compromise. What are some examples of ways people compromise?

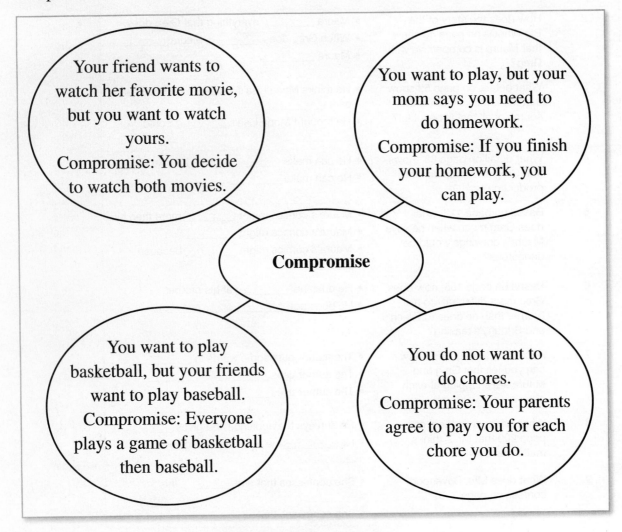

Your friend wants to watch her favorite movie, but you want to watch yours.
Compromise: You decide to watch both movies.

You want to play, but your mom says you need to do homework.
Compromise: If you finish your homework, you can play.

Compromise

You want to play basketball, but your friends want to play baseball.
Compromise: Everyone plays a game of basketball then baseball.

You do not want to do chores.
Compromise: Your parents agree to pay you for each chore you do.

Team Talk

Share one thing you learned about making a compromise.
I learned that in order to compromise, _____.

Max Malone Makes a Million

BUILD BACKGROUND

Reproduce and distribute copies of the *Ingredients Matter* student page on page 426. Explain that to better understand the story events in *Max Malone Makes a Million,* it helps to know about ingredients that go into making a cookie. Help students understand how to read the chart. Point to the details about the ingredients in cookies.

Discuss each ingredient in the chart. Have students work with a partner to explain how each ingredient is important to making a good cookie. Scaffold with sentence frames such as: _____ *makes cookies* _____. *By adding* _____, *cookies become* _____.

TALK ABOUT SENTENCES

For students who need support in accessing key ideas and key language in *Max Malone Makes a Million* use the Sentence Talk Routine on pages 441–442 to draw students' attention to the relationship between meaning and the words, phrases, and clauses in the text.

Lesson	Sentence(s) to Deconstruct
10	(p 79) "Twenty years from now I don't want you to come to me and tell me that I kept you from becoming a millionaire."
11	(p 85) Max turned off the mixer and added two eggs according to the recipe, and one more because of all the extra ingredients.
12	(p 89) "We weren't running a real business before," said Max. "We were just fooling around. Besides, do you have any better ideas?"

SPEAK AND WRITE ABOUT THE TEXT

Use the Text-based Writing Routine on pages 443–444 to model how to speak and write about key ideas and details in *Max Malone Makes a Million.*

Lesson	Text-based Writing	Scaffolded Frames
10	Based on page 79, what does Mrs. Malone want to keep Max from doing in the future?	• She does not want him to tell her that she kept him from becoming a _____. • She does not want him to tell her _____.
11	According to page 85, why does Max not follow the recipe when he adds the eggs?	• He adds an extra egg to make up for the extra _____. • He adds _____ because _____.
12	What excuse does Max give on page 89 for past failures at selling lemonade?	• In the past, they were not running a _____. • They were just _____, not running a _____.

Name _____ .

Ingredients Matter

When baking cookies, it really matters what is in the dough. What is the importance of each of the main ingredients of most cookies?

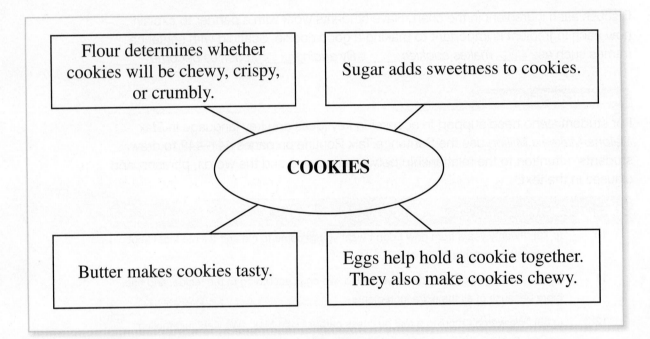

Share two facts you learned about making cookies.

I learned _____ .

I also learned _____ .

Coyote School News

BUILD BACKGROUND

Reproduce and distribute *The Little Cowpuncher Schools* student page on page 428. Explain that to better understand the story events in *Coyote School News*, it helps to know about the real cowpuncher schools and their newspapers.

Discuss details about the *Little Cowpuncher* newspapers and schools and explain that the author of *Coyote School News* wrote the book because she was inspired by the culture of the schools in rural southern Arizona at that time. Scaffold with sentence frames such as: *The schools were located in _____. They had _____ or _____ classrooms. The students _____ and _____ the Little Cowpuncher newspapers.*

TALK ABOUT SENTENCES

For students who need support in accessing key ideas and key language in *Coyote School News*, use the Sentence Talk Routine on pages 441–442 to draw students' attention to the relationship between meaning and the words, phrases, and clauses in the text.

Lesson	Sentence(s) to Deconstruct
14	(p 61) He says my great-grandfather was an *americano*, not because he crossed the line, but because the line crossed him.
15	(p 68) It doesn't have a dollar yet, only a hole, but when I win the Perfect Attendance I will put my silver dollar in that hole.
16	(p 70) "Monchi, you are crazier than a goat. You are a Ramírez. We are a family of vaqueros. Roundup is more important than the Perfect Attendance."

SPEAK AND WRITE ABOUT THE TEXT

Use the Text-based Writing Routine on pages 443–444 to model how to speak and write about key ideas and details in *Coyote School News*.

Lesson	Text-based Writing	Scaffolded Frames
14	According to page 61, how did Monchi's great-grandfather become an *americano*?	• The United States purchased the land _____. • He became an *americano* because _____.
15	What detail on page 68 tells you why Monchi wants to win Perfect Attendance?	• He wants to win the _____ for his buckle. • He wants to win because _____.
16	Use the details on page 70 to explain why Junior says that Monchi is "crazier than a goat."	• Junior thinks the most important thing is _____. • Junior thinks _____ is more important than _____ because _____.

Name _____

The *Little Cowpuncher* Schools

Author Joan Sandin based *Coyote School News* on real life. Sandin's best friend lived on a ranch in southern Arizona. She went to a cowpuncher school. "Cowpuncher" is another name for a cowboy or cowgirl.

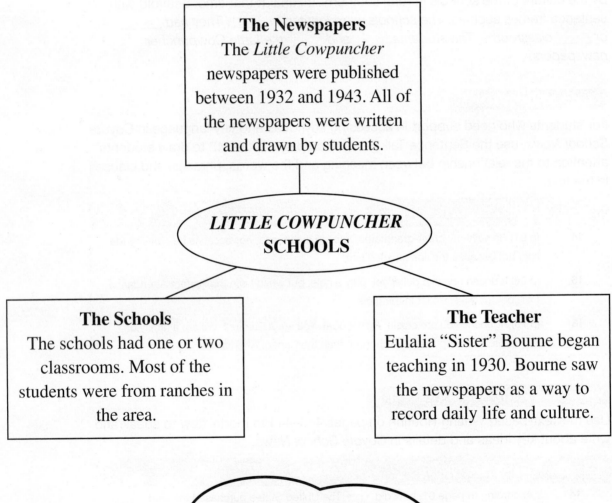

The Newspapers
The *Little Cowpuncher* newspapers were published between 1932 and 1943. All of the newspapers were written and drawn by students.

LITTLE COWPUNCHER SCHOOLS

The Schools
The schools had one or two classrooms. Most of the students were from ranches in the area.

The Teacher
Eulalia "Sister" Bourne began teaching in 1930. Bourne saw the newspapers as a way to record daily life and culture.

Team Talk

What did you learn about *Little Cowpuncher* schools and newspapers?

Little Cowpuncher schools were located _____.

Little Cowpuncher newspapers were _____.

Using Money

BUILD BACKGROUND

Reproduce and distribute copies of the *Where Does All the Money Go?* student page on page 431. Explain that to understand the information in *Using Money*, it helps to know what kinds of things people need to spend money on.

Point out that the first column lists common types of expenses and the other three columns show how costly these items are. Is a car a high-, medium-, or low-cost item? Scaffold with a sentence frame: *A car is a _____ item.*

Discuss some of the differences in costs. In this chart, is entertainment considered a high-, medium-, or low-cost item? Provide a sentence frame, if necessary: *Entertainment is considered a _____ item.* Why do you think entertainment might cost less than a car does? Scaffold with a frame: *I think entertainment costs less than a car because _____.*

Have students work with a partner to discuss the differences in costs between items people buy.

TALK ABOUT SENTENCES

For students who need support in accessing key ideas and key language in *Using Money*, use the Sentence Talk Routine on pages 441–442 to draw students' attention to the relationship between meaning and the words, phrases, and clauses in the text.

Lesson	Sentence(s) to Deconstruct
1	(p 6) When you are young, gifts might be one of your main sources of money.
2	(p 8) People use banks to keep their money safe or to borrow money to buy things such as homes and cars.
3	(p 16) You cannot get a checking account until you are older, but you should know how they work.
4	(p 27) Having good credit means you can be trusted to pay back what you borrow.
5	(p 30) A budget is a plan that lists income, or money earned, and expenses, or money spent.
6	(p 37) Millions of people jumped at the chance to own a home, but many did not figure out what they would have to pay once the rate increased.
7	(p 40) If the company loses sales or has other problems, its stock price goes down and you could lose money.
8	(p 44) The chart on page 44 shows how important it is to start saving when you are young.

Use the Text-based Writing Routine on pages 443–444 to model how to speak and write about key ideas and details in *Using Money*.

Lesson	Text-based Writing	Scaffolded Frames
1	Using information on page 6, explain why gifts might be a good source of money for young people.	Young people often get money for _____. Young people often receive money as _____ for events like _____.
2	Based on information on page 8, why do you think people might need to borrow money to buy homes or cars?	People might need to borrow money to buy those things because _____. Because homes and cars _____, people don't always _____.
3	Using information on page 16, explain why it's important for you to know how a checking account works.	Checks are useful for paying for items such as _____. When I'm older, I'll need to use checks _____.
4	What details on page 27 tell you why having good credit is important?	The page says that having good credit lets people know that _____. Having good credit means you're more likely to _____.
5	Use information on page 30 to explain why having a budget can help you be smart with money.	A budget helps you know how much _____ and what you can afford _____. A budget helps you know _____ and _____.
6	According to page 37, why should a person be careful when taking out a loan?	If a person cannot pay a loan back, then _____. It is important to _____ because _____.
7	How does the graph on page 40 show that investing in the stock market can be risky?	The graph shows how stock prices can go _____, and you _____ when that happens. The graph shows how stock prices can go _____. When stock prices are low, _____.
8	How does the chart on page 44 help show why you should start saving money at a young age?	The chart shows how you can make _____ if you start saving at an early age. The chart shows how you can _____ if you _____.

Use the Dig Deeper Vocabulary Routine on pages 439–440 to continue to develop conceptual understanding of the following nouns: *value, allowance, charges, convenience, security, income, expenses, purchases, organizations,* and *scholarships.* Begin by reviewing the role nouns play in a sentence. Then display and read aloud the following sentence. *A person uses money to make **purchases**.*

Point out that *purchases* names something a person uses money to make. Mention that the words *person* and *money* are also nouns in the sentence. Discuss with a partner how nouns provide necessary information in the sentence by telling who and what the sentence is about. Imagine how confusing the sentence would be without nouns.

Name _____

Where Does All the Money Go?

An expense is the amount of money that it costs to buy something. What are some items people need money for?

Expense	High Cost	Medium Cost	Low Cost
Home	X		
Food		X	
Car	X		
Entertainment			X
Clothing		X	
Healthcare	X		
School	X		

Share details about expenses people have.

People spend _____ of money on homes.

People spend _____ money on clothing.

A Tale of Two Poggles

Reproduce and distribute copies of the *Factories and Amusement Parks* student page on page 433. Explain that to understand the story events in *A Tale of Two Poggles,* it helps to know how factories and amusement parks are alike and different.

Explain that the chart lists details about factories and amusement parks. Which place is mostly indoors? Scaffold with a sentence frame: _____ *is mostly indoors.* Are factories and amusement parks mostly alike or different? *Factories and amusement parks are mostly _____.*

TALK ABOUT SENTENCES

For students who need support in accessing key ideas and key language in *A Tale of Two Poggles,* use the Sentence Talk Routine on pages 441–442 to draw students' attention to the relationship between meaning and the words, phrases, and clauses in the text.

Lesson	Sentence(s) to Deconstruct
9	(p 4) The factory was long and gray and looked a bit like an envelope itself.
12	(p 34) Already she was picturing a bright, lively place, full of people whirling on carousels and children rolling around in a ball pit.
13	(p 44) The amusement park became so popular that busloads of people came to visit it every day.

SPEAK AND WRITE ABOUT THE TEXT

Use the Text-based Writing Routine on pages 443–444 to model how to speak and write about key ideas and details in *A Tale of Two Poggles.*

Lesson	Text-based Writing	Scaffolded Frames
9	Look at the illustration on pages 4–5. How does it reflect the text's description of the factory?	The illustration shows how the factory is _____ and looks _____. The illustration shows how the factory _____.
12	What statements does Nina make on pages 34 and 36 that let you know she thinks the plan for an amusement park could work?	On page 34, Nina says that the plan could work if _____. On page 36, she says that Gloria Grabber _____. Nina says on page 34 that the plan_____, and on page 36 she says that _____.
13	On page 44, what details let you know that the amusement park is a success?	The story talks about how the park is so popular that _____ open up in the town. The story says that the town gets _____, _____, and _____.

Name _____

Factories and Amusement Parks

How are factories and amusements parks alike and different?

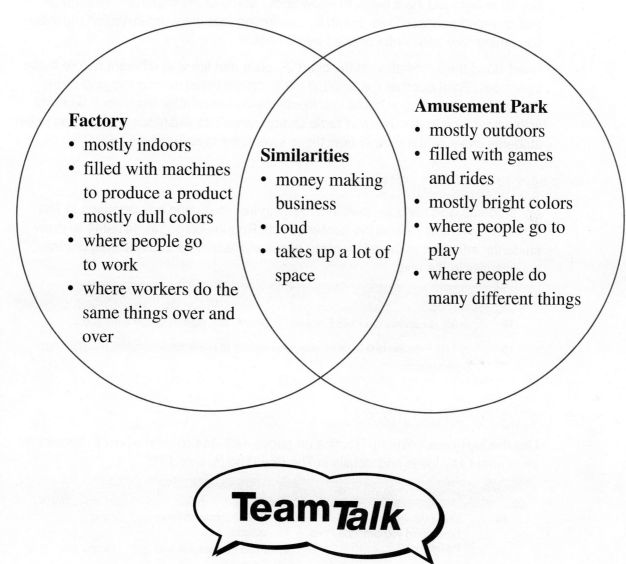

Factory
- mostly indoors
- filled with machines to produce a product
- mostly dull colors
- where people go to work
- where workers do the same things over and over

Similarities
- money making business
- loud
- takes up a lot of space

Amusement Park
- mostly outdoors
- filled with games and rides
- mostly bright colors
- where people go to play
- where people do many different things

TeamTalk

Share details about factories and amusement parks.

Both factories and amusement parks _____.

The colors of factories are _____, but the colors of amusement parks are _____.

People _____ at a factory. People _____ at an amusement park

The Boy Who Invented TV

Reproduce and distribute copies of the *Inventions That Changed Everything* student page on page 435. Explain that to understand the information in *The Boy Who Invented TV,* it helps to know about some of the important inventions that changed people's lives. Begin by confirming that the word *invention* means something new and useful created by someone.

Read aloud the information in the chart. Explain that life was different before these inventions. Point out that the dates in the chart are listed in chronological order. Did the first radio station come into existence before or after television? Scaffold with a sentence frame: *The first radio station came into existence _____.* Then have students share with a partner how these inventions changed lives.

TALK ABOUT SENTENCES

For students who need support in accessing key ideas and key language in *The Boy Who Invented TV,* use the Sentence Talk Routine on pages 441–442 to draw students' attention to the relationship between meaning and the words, phrases, and clauses in the text.

Lesson	Sentence(s) to Deconstruct
14	(p 95) No sooner did Philo Farnsworth learn to talk than he asked a question.
15	(p 116) Pem learned to use a precision welder to make tube elements—everything from scratch.

SPEAK AND WRITE ABOUT THE TEXT

Use the Text-based Writing Routine on pages 443–444 to model how to speak and write about key ideas and details in *The Boy Who Invented TV.*

Lesson	Text-based Writing	Scaffolded Frames
14	Using details on page 95, how would you describe Philo Farnsworth?	• Philo Farnsworth was a _____ and _____ person. • Philo Farnsworth was _____. I know this because _____.
15	Use information on page 116 to explain how Pem showed her support of Philo.	• Pem would use a precision welder to _____, and she would _____ about the experiments. • Pem helped by _____ and _____.

Unit 4 Module B

Name _____

Inventions That Changed Everything

An invention is something new and useful that a person creates. When did some of the most important inventions happen?

Invention	Date
telephone	1876
incandescent light bulb	1879
electric fan	1882
air conditioning	1902
Model T car	1908
radio station	1920
television	1927

Share details about some of the most important inventions.

The incandescent light bulb was invented _____ television.

Television was invented _____ the telephone.

Name _____

The Toss and Fetch Machine

"I love my dog Abby, but she *always* wants to play!" Sam complained to his friend Andy. "She carries a ball around in her mouth *all day long*. She only drops it long enough to eat. She even sleeps with it at night!"

Sam didn't usually mind Abby's attachment to her ball. But the boys were busy and couldn't be bothered today. They had to study for the big science test.

Abby kept bothering them to play with her, so Sam stood up. He was frustrated. "Come on, Andy. We're going to solve this problem, once and for all!" Without waiting for an answer, Sam marched to the garage.

Sam liked to build things, so Andy wasn't surprised when Sam started to think of a plan. Soon he had a simple drawing of a flat box with a metal arm inside attached to a small motor. A spring connected the arm to the inside of the box. Andy was confused until Sam drew a ball flying out of the end of the box. A ball launcher! Sam wanted to build a ball launcher!

The boys gathered the supplies. They then built the box out of wood and attached the parts. The finished product was about the size of a large pizza box, only taller.

The machine was a big success! Abby chased the ball around all day long. Sam and Andy were able to study for their big test!

Name _____

The Internet's Impact

I think the Internet, of all recent innovations, has had the biggest impact on the way people live. The Internet has forever changed schoolwork, jobs, and daily life.

Before the Internet, students had to go to the library to use books for research. Now, it's easy to use the Internet to find any types of information needed. The Internet has also changed how people communicate at work. People used to have to gather in a meeting if they wanted to share information with each other. Now, people can send emails. The Internet also affects daily life in a variety of ways. For example, people can look up directions and maps on the Internet. They can order most products from the Internet instead of having to go to stores. People can also use the Internet to watch movies and television, read newspapers, and connect with friends.

Because the Internet affects most people in so many ways, I think it is the innovation that has had the biggest impact on people's lives.

Performance-Based Assessment
Unit 4 Module A

DISCUSS THE STUDENT MODEL

Reproduce and distribute copies of the student model on page 436. After completing the Prepare to Write activities on pages 212–213 in Unlock the Writing in Part 2, use the student model to illustrate the features of a short story.

Discuss the student model. Read the first paragraph aloud, and ask: What is the problem that the writer introduces in the first paragraph? Provide sentence frames if students need help answering: *Sam's dog loves to _____, but she wants to do it _____.* Point out concrete words and phrases that describe the sequence of events and characters. Read aloud the last paragraph, and ask: How does the writer provide a conclusion to the story that follows from the narrated events? Provide a sentence frame if students need help answering: *The boys solve their problem by building a _____. Then they are able to _____.*

Unit 4 Module B

DISCUSS THE STUDENT MODEL

Reproduce and distribute copies of the student model on page 437. After completing the Prepare to Write activities on pages 212–213 in Unlock the Writing in Part 2, use the student model to illustrate the features of an opinion essay.

Discuss the student model. Point out that the essay is made up of three paragraphs. Read the first paragraph to students. Then ask: How does the writer begin the opinion essay? Provide a sentence frame if students need help responding. *The writer begins by explaining which innovation he or she _____.* (thinks had the greatest impact) What words help you know that this is the writer's opinion, and not a fact? ("I think")

Read aloud the second paragraph. What does the writer talk about in the second paragraph? Provide a sentence frame if needed. *The writer talks about the different ways _____.* (the Internet has an impact on people's lives) Ask students how these details help support the writer's opinion. Supply a sentence frame. *The details support the idea that the Internet affects how people _____.* (study, work, and function in their daily lives)

Next, read aloud the third paragraph of the student model. Check to make sure students understand what a conclusion is. How does the writer end the essay? (by again stating that he or she thinks the Internet has had the greatest impact and telling why) What is the purpose of restating this information? Provide a sentence frame. *It summarizes the writer's _____.* (point of view/opinion)

Dig Deeper Vocabulary

PURPOSE

Use this routine to help students acquire a more in-depth understanding for select academic vocabulary. Through discussion using multimodal methods, students will unlock the meaning of vocabulary so they can use the words and learn elements of syntax.

PROCEDURE

1. Display the words listed in the Expand Understanding of Vocabulary section. Explain to students that these words appear in the text they are reading and that they are all similar in some way.

2. Model reading the words. Then have students practice saying the words aloud with you. Poll students about their familiarity with each word in order to gauge understanding.

3. Convey the meaning of the words using different modalities such as showing a picture from a magazine or the Internet, drawing a picture, acting out or gesturing, or using realia. Describe each word in context to guide students to associate the new words with familiar vocabulary. For example, for the word *miniature,* show students a pencil and then draw one that is much smaller than in real life. This pencil is normal size. The picture I've drawn shows a *miniature* pencil. Ask students how big something that is miniature is? (much smaller than it is in real life)

4. Enrich students with a deeper understanding of each word by creating a list of synonyms. Provide students with one or two examples of synonyms for each word, then proceed to generate a list of additional synonyms with students.

5. Have students turn to a partner and take turns telling a sentence for each word. Use sentence frames as needed. For example: *I have seen _____ that is miniature. A _____ is a miniature _____ of _____.*

6. Help students understand how different types of words function in a sentence. For example, share a sentence in which you signal out a specific kind of word or phrase using different colors to write each part of the sentence. Then explain the parts of the sentence and ask students to identify specific words or phrases in the sentence. Look at this example for using describing words:

The *miniature* house was very small.

What person, place, or thing is being described? *(house)* What word describes the house? *(miniature)* The last part of the sentence gives more details about the house. What is the detail? **(was very small)** Notice that the describing word comes before the noun it describes.

TEACHING TIPS

- Have students use different modalities to figure out the meaning of words. Doing this aids their understanding, since they are using different formats to gain meaning.

- Have students write each vocabulary word on separate index cards and add a simple drawing or photograph from the Internet or a magazine that exemplifies the word on the back. Students can work in pairs to look at the picture and then name the word.

EXTEND

Have students create a word web relating the vocabulary words to other words they know. For example, words can be the same part of speech or have similar affixes, sounds, or meanings. Have students discuss how understanding word meanings helps them better understand the meaning of texts they read.

Sentence Talk

PURPOSE

Use this routine to deconstruct complex sentences from the texts that students are reading. Through instructional conversations students analyze key ideas, vocabulary, and sentence structures.

PROCEDURE

1. Identify a complex sentence from the current text. Recommended sentences can be found in the **Talk About Sentences** section of the Part 4 Unlock Language Learning lessons for each Unit/Module. Sentences should include key details or explain a key concept, important vocabulary, and phrases and clauses that merit attention. They may also include figurative language.

2. Decide how to break up the sentence for discussion, focusing on identifying meaning-based phrases and clauses. For example, you could break the sentence below into three parts.

   The slowly moving mantle carries along the solid crust, which is cracked like an eggshell into a number of huge pieces called plates.

3. Display the sentence, writing each sentence part in a different color. Prepare conversation starters to focus students' attention on each sentence part. As you discuss each part of the sentence, record students' comments.

   - Why are the words *mantle* and *crust* important words? Turn and talk to a partner about what you know about the layers of Earth.
   - What do the words *cracked like an eggshell* tell us about Earth's crust?
   - What are the pieces of Earth's crust called?

4. Identify key words that may need to be defined in context or have structural significance.

   - What two words does the author use to tell about how Earth's mantle and crust move? Yes, *slowly* and *carries.* When someone or something moves slowly, it takes a long time to get from one place to another. Who would like to stand up and show what it looks like to move slowly?
   - Now let's read the entire sentence together. The word *carries* tells me that the *crust* is on top of the *mantle* and it is cracked into pieces called *plates.*

5. Initiate the activity with students by reading together the page or paragraph in which the sentence appears. Have students turn and talk to a partner about key ideas and details in the text.

6. Then draw attention to the color-coded sentence on display. Use the conversation starters you prepared to focus students' attention on each part of the sentence. Students should take an active role and should be speaking as much or more than you do in this conversation. Periodically, also have students turn and talk to a partner or a small group of peers. Record students' responses during the conversation and reread them at the end of the conversation.

7. Reread the entire sentence and have students discuss or write about what it means. Provide scaffolds as necessary.

- The mantle moves _____ and _____ Earth's solid crust.
- The Earth's crust is _____ like an eggshell. These pieces are called _____.
- This means that as the mantle carries Earth's crust, the plates might _____, causing _____.

TEACHING TIPS

- When recording students' comments, write each comment in the same color as the sentence part it refers to.
- Create and display a list of key words and phrases from the Sentence Talk instructional conversations and encourage students to use the vocabulary when they speak and write about the text.

EXTEND

Have students discuss how understanding the meaning of the sentence helps them better understand the overall meaning of the text. Ask: What was the most important thing you learned? What will you keep in mind as you continue to read?

Text-Based Writing

PURPOSE

Use this routine to explore linguistic and rhetorical patterns and registers in writing. Model how to include evidence from text in a written response.

From the section of the text that was read closely that day, present students with a question for guided/shared writing. See the **Text-Based Writing** column in the Speak and Write About the Text section of the English Language Learners Support lesson for recommended questions.

PROCEDURE

1. Write the question on the board and read it aloud with students. For example: *Use information on page 18 to explain what a seismograph is and to tell why it is important.* Identify key words in the question and check understanding. Help students determine what the question is asking and what information they need to respond to it. The question asks what a seismograph is and why it is important. According to the text, what is a seismograph? A seismograph is an instrument that measures an earthquake shock. I can tell from the question that a seismograph is an important tool. How can we find out why a seismograph is so important? *We can _____ to find evidence in the text about _____.*

2. Locate and read aloud the sentence/sentences in the text that the question refers to. If appropriate, also read the text that comes before/after the sentence. Lead students in a discussion of the text, checking comprehension and explaining key vocabulary and concepts as needed.

   What is a seismograph? A seismograph is a tool that measures earthquake shocks. Why is this tool important? It can help us know more about an earthquake, including when it will take place, where it is located, and how big it is. Which words show **why** a seismograph is important? *The words, "Scientists use ____."* Why is it so important to know this information? *Scientists can study how _____ and better understand _____.*

3. Guide students to answer the question orally, using the scaffolded sentence frames as needed. Check that students use a rhetorical pattern appropriate to the question. For example, a question that asks *why* something occurred should elicit a response that identifies a cause and effect.

4. Restate the question for students: Use information on page 18 to explain what a seismograph is and to tell why it is important. Model writing a response, talking through the process as you write.

   A seismograph measures earthquake shocks, and is important because it helps scientists better understand the size of an earthquake and the damage it causes.

   I will start my sentence with a capital letter. The verb *measures* tells what a seismograph **does**. **Who** does it help? It helps _____. Now I will use text evidence to tell **how** it helps. A seismograph is a tool to measure earthquakes. It helps scientists better understand the size and damage. I will add those words to my sentence. I will put a period here to show that this is the end of the sentence.

5. Have students write their answers. For shared writing, have students work with a partner.

6. Give students the opportunity to share their writing with the group. Have students read their answers aloud or write them on the board. Check that students have used appropriate linguistic and rhetorical patterns and included text evidence as needed.

TEACHING TIPS

- Use graphic organizers, such as idea webs and cause/effect charts, to help students organize the text evidence needed to answer the questions.

- As you evaluate students' writing, identify sentences that can be expanded by adding details.

- Encourage students to write in complete sentences to reflect the more formal register of written English.

EXTEND

Ask a second question about the day's close read section and have students work with a partner or independently to discuss and write a response.

Clarifying Key Details

PURPOSE

Use this routine to provide frames for conducting accountable conversations that require clarification.

PROCEDURE

1. **Explain:** Sometimes in a discussion, I don't understand what someone has said. Maybe the speaker talks very softly or uses words I have not heard before. Maybe the speaker needs to give key details to explain an idea. When this happens, I need to ask questions to help me understand what the speaker means. This is called clarifying.

2. Explain that sometimes others might have questions about what students say. Remind them that they should answer other students' questions and help them understand.

3. Remind students that when they ask questions in a group, they should be polite and not interrupt. Wait until the person finishes speaking. Then raise your hand or say, "excuse me." Wait for the person to look at you or say your name. Then you can ask your question.

4. Share the worksheet on the following page with students. Talk about situations in which they might use the questions. Model completing the sentence frames using a topic that is familiar to students.

5. Have students use the questions and frames in a discussion about a selection you have recently read.

TEACHING TIPS

- Have students role-play discussions in which they ask questions for clarification.
- Create a classroom poster listing useful clarifying questions for students to refer to as needed.

EXTEND

Have students think of more clarifying questions and add them to the worksheet. Have them practice asking the questions with a partner or in a group.

Clarifying Key Details

Look at the examples of questions.
Use them when you do not understand.

When you did not hear what the speaker said:
I did not hear you. What did you say?

When you do not understand what the speaker means:
You said _____. What does that mean?
I do not understand _____. Can you please explain?
Can you give me more details?

When someone says something you think is wrong:
I think you made a mistake. Can you show me in the book?

When you answer someone's question:
I said _____.
I mean _____.

Look at the picture.
Say questions the people can ask.

Clarifying Information

PURPOSE

Use this routine to provide frames for conducting accountable conversations that require elaboration.

PROCEDURE

1. **Explain:** Sometimes I need more information to understand what a speaker means. I can ask the speaker to explain his or her ideas. I can ask the speaker for more details and information. This is called elaborating.

2. **Point out that sometimes students might want to add ideas to a group discussion.** I can give more information, too. I can explain my ideas and give information from the text. I can give reasons for my opinions. I can give evidence to support my ideas.

3. **Remind students that when they add to a group discussion, they should be polite and not interrupt.** Wait until the person finishes speaking. Then raise your hand or say, "excuse me." Wait for the person to look at you or say your name. Then, you can speak.

4. **Share the worksheet on the following page with students. Talk about situations in which they might use the questions and statements. Model completing the sentence frames using a topic that is familiar to students.**

5. **Have students work with a partner to write an elaborating question and answer in the conversation at the bottom of the worksheet.**

TEACHING TIPS

- Have students role-play discussions in which they ask for more information and elaborate on their ideas.
- Create a classroom poster listing useful elaboration frames for students to refer to as needed.

EXTEND

Have students write another conversation between Pat and Jan, using the frames to ask for and give more information about another topic, such as a favorite story.

Clarifying Information

Look at the examples of questions and statements.

Use the questions when you need more information from the speaker.

Use the statements when you give more information.

When you want more information from the speaker:

I want to know more about _____.

Can you please explain _____?

Can you give me more information about _____?

What details support your idea?

When you want to give more information:

This makes me think _____.

Now I am wondering _____.

This reminds me of _____ because _____.

I believe this is true because _____.

I want to add to what [speaker's name] said about _____.

Pat and Dan are talking. Dan needs to ask for more information.

Pat needs to give more information. Write a question and an answer.

Pat: I think playing sports is important.

Dan: Why do you think _____?

Pat: _____.

Reach a Consensus

PURPOSE

Use this routine to provide frames for conducting accountable conversations that require achieving consensus.

PROCEDURE

1. Explain: Sometimes when I work with a group, my group has to decide something together. We all have to agree about something. This is called reaching a consensus.

2. Explain that sometimes when they are in a group, students will need to tell what they think. When you tell others what you think, give reasons and evidence to explain your ideas and feelings.

3. Point out that all the members of the group should have a chance to tell what they think. When others tell what they think, listen carefully. If you need more information, ask clarifying and elaborating questions. Remind students to use the frames they practiced on the other worksheets.

4. Explain that group members may agree or disagree. When you have the same idea as someone else, you agree. When you have a different idea, or when you think the person is incorrect, you disagree. Say if you agree or disagree. Give reasons and evidence.

5. Remind students that it is important to be polite when they disagree. If you disagree, explain why in a friendly way.

6. Explain that to achieve consensus, most of the group members must agree. This is called reaching a consensus. When everyone agrees, you have a consensus. If some group members do not agree, you can vote. Count how many people agree and how many disagree.

7. Read the worksheet on the following page aloud to students. Talk about situations in which they might use the questions and statements. Model completing the sentence frames using a topic that is familiar to students.

TEACHING TIPS

- Have students role-play discussions in which they reach a consensus.
- Create a classroom poster listing useful consensus frames for students to refer to as needed.

EXTEND

Have students work with a group to choose the best activity for a rainy day. Remind them to use the frames on the worksheet to express ideas and agree or disagree. Encourage them to reach a consensus and present their conclusions.

Reach a Consensus

Look at the examples of questions and statements.
Use them when your group must decide something.

When you say what you think:

I think _____.

I believe _____.

When you ask what others think:

What do you think, [name]?

Do you agree, [name]?

When you agree:

I agree with [name] because _____.

I like what [name] said because _____.

When you disagree:

I disagree with _____ because _____.

When you both disagree and agree:

I think you are right about _____, but I do not agree that

_____.

When you want to reach a consensus:

Do we all agree that _____?

How many think that _____?

Raise your hand if you think _____.

Have a Discussion

PURPOSE

Use this routine to provide a frame for conducting accountable discussions.

PROCEDURE

1. **Explain:** Sometimes we talk about things in a group. Three or more people can be a group. When the people in the group talk about a topic, they are having a discussion.

2. **Point out that students can contribute to a good discussion.** How can you help the group have a good discussion? You can listen carefully to each speaker. When you listen, look at the speaker and pay attention.

3. **Explain that students should think before speaking, and stay on the topic.** Remember to explain your ideas. Ask questions if you need more information to understand a speaker's ideas.

4. Share the worksheet on the following page with students. Review the rules it lists. Have students use the worksheet to rate their behavior during group discussions.

5. Have students write the sentences at the bottom of the worksheet. Then, ask students to share their sentences with a partner.

TEACHING TIPS

- Have students role-play discussions in which they follow the rules listed on the worksheet.
- Model examples of nonverbal communication skills listeners can use, such as nodding and making eye contact.
- Create a classroom poster listing tips for successful group discussions for students to refer to as needed.

EXTEND

Have a group of volunteers model a discussion while the rest of the class listens. Have listeners rate the group members' behavior during the discussion using the worksheet.

Have a Discussion

Rate what you do during a discussion with a group.

1 I need to practice this skill.
2 I do this sometimes.
3 I almost always do this.

I listen carefully.	1	2	3
I look at the speaker.	1	2	3
I am polite.	1	2	3
I explain and give evidence.	1	2	3
I ask for clarification.	1	2	3
I ask for elaboration.	1	2	3
I build on others' ideas.	1	2	3
I stay on the topic.	1	2	3
I think before speaking.	1	2	3

Write sentences that you can use in discussions during the situations below.

When you disagree with the speaker: _____

When you tell your ideas about a topic to the group: _____

When you ask for more information: _____

Scaffolded Reading/Writing Goals

UNIT 1: MODULE A

Reading Goal: Readers find text evidence and discuss events and details in the text.

Emerging	Expanding	Bridging
Readers use simple language frames to find text evidence and discuss events and details.	Readers use language frames to find evidence and discuss events and details.	Readers used advanced frames to find evidence and discuss events and details.

Writing Goal: Writers write a biography, employing simple sentence structure.

Emerging	Expanding	Bridging
Writers use sentence frames to write ideas for a biography.	Writers use facts and details to write a biography, employing simple transitional words and phrases.	Writers use facts and details to write a biography, employing advanced sentence structures and more complex transitional words and phrases.

UNIT 1: MODULE B

Reading Goal: Readers retell parts of informational text.

Emerging	Expanding	Bridging
Readers use illustrations and language frames to retell parts of informational text. Students use academic and domain specific vocabulary.	Readers can apply domain specific vocabulary in more contexts and can use a variety of linguistic structures in informational text.	Readers can apply a range of high-level English language skills in a variety of contexts, including comprehension of informational and technical texts.

Writing Goal: Writers retell parts of an informational text.

Emerging	Expanding	Bridging
Writers retell parts of informational text. Students use academic and domain specific vocabulary.	Writers can apply domain specific vocabulary in more contexts and can use a variety of linguistic structures in informational text.	Writers can apply a range of high-level skills in a variety of contexts, including comprehension of informational and technical texts.

UNIT 2: MODULE A

Reading Goal: Readers retell legends, tall tales, and folktales, including key details.

Emerging	Expanding	Bridging
Readers use illustrations and simple language frames to retell parts of a legend, tall tale, and folktale.	Readers use frames to retell what happens in the beginning, middle, and end of a legend, tall tale, and folktale.	Readers retell what happens in the beginning, middle, and end of a legend, tall tale, and folktale.

Writing Goal: Writers write a legend or tall tale that includes an element of nature, larger-than-life characters, a problem that is solved in a humorous way, and exaggeration of characters and events.

Emerging	Expanding	Bridging
Writers use simple sentence structures to write a legend or tall tale.	Writers use sentence structures to write a legend or tall tale that explains an element of nature in a humorous way.	Writers write a legend or tall tale that explains an element of nature in a humorous way.

UNIT 2: MODULE B

Reading Goal: Readers state and support opinions to demonstrate their understanding of both literary and informational texts.

Emerging	Expanding	Bridging
Readers use simple language frames to state their opinions about a story or an informational text.	Readers use more complicated language frames to state and support their opinions about a story or an informational text.	Readers state and support their opinions about a story or an informational text.

Writing Goal: Writers use text-based evidence to state and support opinions.

Emerging	Expanding	Bridging
Writers state and support their opinions using simple sentence frames.	Writers use text-based evidence to write an opinion essay.	Writers use text-based evidence to write an opinion essay, employing advanced sentence structures to state and support their opinions.

UNIT 3: MODULE A

Reading Goal: Readers analyze both literary and informational texts on the same topic.

Emerging	Expanding	Bridging
Readers read literary and informational texts on the same topic.	Readers compare and contrast literary and informational texts on the same topic.	Readers carefully analyze literary and informational texts on the same topic.

Writing Goal: Writers use evidence from both literary and informational texts to write an opinion essay.

Emerging	Expanding	Bridging
Writers gather information from a literary and an informational text to form an opinion.	Writers use evidence from a literary and an informational text to write an opinion.	Writers use evidence from a literary and an informational text to write an opinion essay.

UNIT 3: MODULE B

Reading Goal: Readers understand story structure in order to retell the characters, plot, and resolution. Readers summarize important ideas and supporting details in informational text.

Emerging	Expanding	Bridging
Readers retell parts of a story or informational text. Students begin to understand how to use academic and domain specific vocabulary.	Readers can apply vocabulary in more contexts and can linguistic structures to describe factual information or story narratives.	Readers can apply language skills in a variety of contexts, including comprehension of informational and technical texts or fictional narratives.

Writing Goal: Writers be able to identify and create the elements of a news report, including headline, introduction, body, and conclusion.

Emerging	Expanding	Bridging
Writers use illustrations and writing frames to communicate a headline and the main idea of a news report.	Writers can use illustrations, sentence frames, and simple sentences to create a headline, introduction, body details and at least one concluding sentence.	Writers can write simple sentences using the elements of a news report to express their ideas. Writers should include visuals or illustrations to help explain their ideas.

UNIT 4: MODULE A

Reading Goal: Readers retell chapter and short stories, including key details.

Emerging	Expanding	Bridging
Readers use illustrations and simple language frames to retell parts of stories.	Readers use more complicated language frames to retell what happens in the beginning, middle, and end of a stories.	Readers use advanced language frames to retell what happens in the beginning, middle, and end of stories.

Writing Goal: Writers write a short story that establishes a situation in which characters overcome a challenge with an innovative solution.

Emerging	Expanding	Bridging
Writers use simple sentence structures to write a short story that establishes a situation that characters overcome by using an innovative solution.	Writers use more complicated sentence structures to write a short story that establishes a situation that characters overcome by using an innovative solution.	Writers use advanced sentence structures to write a short story that establishes a situation that characters overcome by using an innovative solution.

UNIT 4: MODULE B

Reading Goal: Readers use evidence from texts to state and support opinions, ideas, and information.

Emerging	Expanding	Bridging
Readers use simple language frames to state and support opinions, ideas, and information about texts.	Readers use more complicated language frames to state and support opinions, ideas, and information about texts.	Readers state and support opinions, ideas, and information about texts.

Writing Goal: Writers state and support an opinion with reasons and evidence.

Emerging	Expanding	Bridging
Writers state and support their opinions.	Writers write an opinion essay, employing complicated sentence structures to state and support opinions.	Writers write an opinion essay, employing advanced sentence structures to state and support their opinions.

Linguistic Contrastive Analysis Chart

THE CONSONANTS OF ENGLISH				
IPA*	English	Spanish	Vietnamese	Cantonese
p	*p*it Aspirated at the start of a word or stressed syllable	*pato* (duck) Never aspirated	*p*in (battery)	*p*ʰa *(to lie prone)* Always aspirated
b	*b*it	*b*arco (boat) Substitute voiced bilabial fricative /ə/ in between vowels	*b*a (three) Implosive (air moves into the mouth during articulation)	**NO EQUIVALENT** Substitute /p/
m	*m*an	*m*undo (world)	*m*ot (one)	*m*a (mother)
w	*w*in	a*gu*a (water)	**NO EQUIVALENT** Substitute word-initial /u/	*w*a (frog)
f	*f*un	*f*lor (flower)	*ph*uʼoʼ*ng* (phoenix) Substitute sound made with both lips, rather than with the lower lip and the teeth like English /f/	*f*a (flower) Only occurs at the beginning of syllables
v	*v*ery	**NO EQUIVALENT** Learners can use correct sound	*V*iệt Nam (Vietnam)	**NO EQUIVALENT** Substitute /f/
θ	*th*ing Rare in other languages. When done correctly, the tongue will stick out between the teeth.	**NO EQUIVALENT** Learners can use correct sound	**NO EQUIVALENT** Substitute /tʰ/ or /f/	**NO EQUIVALENT** Substitute /tʰ/ or /f/
ð	*th*ere Rare in other languages. When done correctly, the tongue will stick out between the teeth.	ca*d*a (every) Sound exists in Spanish only between vowels; sometimes substitute voiceless θ.	**NO EQUIVALENT** Substitute /d/	**NO EQUIVALENT** Substitute /t/ or /f/
t	*t*ime Aspirated at the start of a word or stressed syllable English tongue-touch. Is a little farther back in the mouth than the other languages.	*t*ocar (touch) Never aspirated	*t*ám (eight) Distinguishes aspirated and non-aspirated	*t*ʰa (he/she) Distinguishes aspirated and non-aspirated
d	*d*ime English tongue-touch is a little farther back in the mouth than the other languages.	*d*os (two)	Đ*ō*ng (Dong = unit of currency) Vietnamese /d/ is implosive (air moves into the mouth during articulation)	**NO EQUIVALENT** Substitute /t/
n	*n*ame English tongue-touch is a little farther back in the mouth than the other languages.	*n*ube (cloud)	*n*am (south)	*n*a (take)
s	*s*oy	*s*eco (dry)	*x*em (to see)	*s*a (sand) Substitute *sh*– sound before /u/ Difficult at ends of syllables and words
z	*z*eal	**NO EQUIVALENT** Learners can use correct sound	*r*òi (already) In northern dialect only Southern dialect, substitute /y/	**NO EQUIVALENT** Substitute /s/
ɾ	but*t*er Written 't' and 'd' are pronounced with a quick tongue-tip tap.	*r*ana (toad) Written as single *r* and thought of as an /r/ sound.	**NO EQUIVALENT** Substitute /t/	**NO EQUIVALENT** Substitute /t/
l	*l*oop English tongue-touch is a little farther back in the mouth than the other languages. At the ends of syllables, the /l/ bunches up the back of the tongue, becoming velarized /ɫ/ or dark-l as in the word *ball*.	*l*ibro (book)	cú *l*ao (island) /l/ does not occur at the ends of syllables	*l*au (angry) /l/ does not occur at the ends of syllables

* International Phonetic Alphabet

THE CONSONANTS OF ENGLISH

IPA*	Hmong	Filipino	Korean	Mandarin
p	*peb* (we/us/our) Distinguishes aspirated and non-aspirated	*paalam* (goodbye) Never aspirated	*pal* (sucking)	*pʰei* (cape) Always aspirated
b	**NO EQUIVALENT** Substitute /p/	*baka* (beef)	**NO EQUIVALENT** /b/ said between vowels Substitute /p/ elsewhere	**NO EQUIVALENT**
m	*mus* (to go)	*mabuti* (good)	*mal* (horse)	*mei* (rose)
w	**NO EQUIVALENT** Substitute word-initial /u/	*walo* (eight)	*gwe* (box)	*wen* (mosquito)
f	*faib* (to divide)	**NO EQUIVALENT** Substitute /p/	**NO EQUIVALENT** Substitute /p/	*fa* (issue)
v	*Vaj* ('Vang' clan name)	**NO EQUIVALENT** Substitute /b/	**NO EQUIVALENT** Substitute /b/	**NO EQUIVALENT** Substitute /w/ or /f/
θ	**NO EQUIVALENT** Substitute /tʰ/ or /f/	**NO EQUIVALENT** Learners can use correct sound, but sometimes mispronounce voiced /ð/.	**NO EQUIVALENT** Substitute /t/	**NO EQUIVALENT** Substitute /t/ or /s/
ð	**NO EQUIVALENT** Substitute /d/	**NO EQUIVALENT** Learners can use correct sound	**NO EQUIVALENT** Substitute /d/	**NO EQUIVALENT** Substitute /t/ or /s/
t	*them* (to pay) Distinguishes aspirated and non-aspirated	*takbo* (run) Never aspirated	*tal* (daughter)	*ta* (wet) Distinguishes aspirated and non-aspirated
d	*dev* (dog)	*deretso* (straight)	**NO EQUIVALENT** Substitute /d/ when said between vowels and /t/ elsewhere.	**NO EQUIVALENT** Substitute /t/
n	*noj* (to eat)	*naman* (too)	*nal* (day)	*ni* (you) May be confused with /l/
s	*xa* (to send)	*sila* (they)	*sal* (rice) Substitute *shi*– sound before /i/ and /z/ after a nasal consonant	*san* (three)
z	**NO EQUIVALENT** Learners can use correct sound	**NO EQUIVALENT** Learners can use correct sound	**NO EQUIVALENT** Learners can use correct sound	**NO EQUIVALENT** Substitute /ts/ or /tsʰ/
ɾ	**NO EQUIVALENT** Substitute /t/	*rin/din* (too) Variant of the /d/ sound	Only occurs between two vowels Considered an /l/ sound	**NO EQUIVALENT**
l	*los* (to come) /l/ does not occur at the ends of syllables	*salamat* (thank you)	*balam* (wind)	*lan* (blue) Can be confused and substituted with /r/

* International Phonetic Alphabet

THE CONSONANTS OF ENGLISH

IPA*	English	Spanish	Vietnamese	Cantonese
ɹ	*red* Rare sound in the world Includes lip-rounding	**NO EQUIVALENT** Substitute /r/ sound such as the tap /ɾ/ or the trilled /r/	**NO EQUIVALENT** Substitute /l/	**NO EQUIVALENT** Substitute /l/
ʃ	*sh*allow Often said with lip-rounding	**NO EQUIVALENT** Substitute /s/ or /tʃ/	*si*eu *th*ị (supermarket) Southern dialect only	**NO EQUIVALENT** Substitute /s/
ʒ	*vi*sion Rare sound in English	**NO EQUIVALENT** Substitute /z/ or /dʒ/	**NO EQUIVALENT** Substitute /s/	**NO EQUIVALENT** Substitute /s/
tʃ	*ch*irp	*ch*ico (boy)	*ch*ính *ph*ủ (government) Pronounced harder than English *ch*	**NO EQUIVALENT** Substitute /ts/
dʒ	*j*oy	**NO EQUIVALENT** Sometimes substituted with /ʃ/ sound Some dialects have this sound for the *ll* spelling as in *llamar*	**NO EQUIVALENT** Substitute /c/, the equivalent sound, but voiceless	**NO EQUIVALENT** Substitute /ts/ Only occurs at beginnings of syllables
j	*y*ou	*c*ielo (sky) Often substitute /dʒ/	*y*eu (to love)	*j*au (worry)
k	*k*ite Aspirated at the start of a word or stressed syllable	*c*asa (house) Never aspirated	*c*om (rice) Never aspirated	*kʰ*a (family) Distinguishes aspirated and non-aspirated
g	*g*oat	*g*ato (cat)	**NO EQUIVALENT** Substitute /k/	**NO EQUIVALENT** Substitute /k/
ŋ	*ki*ng	*ma*ng*o (mango)	*Ng*ūyen (proper last name)	*pha*ŋ (to cook)
h	*h*ope	*g*ente (people) Sometimes substitute sound with friction higher in the vocal tract as velar /x/ or uvular /χ/	*h*oa (flower)	*h*a (shrimp)

* International Phonetic Alphabet

	THE CONSONANTS OF ENGLISH			
IPA*	Hmong	Filipino	Korean	Mandarin
ɹ	**NO EQUIVALENT** Substitute /l/	**NO EQUIVALENT** Substitute the tap /ɾ/	**NO EQUIVALENT** Substitute the tap or /l/ confused with /l/	*ran* (caterpillar) Tongue tip curled further backward than for English /r/
ʃ	*sau* (to write)	*siya* (s/he)	Only occurs before /i/; Considered an /s/ sound	*shi* (wet)
ʒ	*zos* village)	**NO EQUIVALENT** Learners can use correct sound	**NO EQUIVALENT**	**NO EQUIVALENT** Substitute palatal affricate /tɕ/
tʃ	*cheb* (to sweep)	*tsa* (tea)	*cʰal* (kicking)	*cheng* (red)
dʒ	**NO EQUIVALENT** Substitute *ch* sound	*Dios* (God)	**NO EQUIVALENT** Substitute *ch* sound	**NO EQUIVALENT** Substitute /ts/
j	*Yaj* (Yang, clan name)	*tayo* (we)	*je:zan* (budget)	*yan* (eye)
k	*Koo* (Kong, clan name) Distinguishes aspirated and non-aspirated	*kalian* (when) Never aspirated	*kal* (spreading)	*ke* (nest) Distinguishes aspirated and non-aspirated
g	**NO EQUIVALENT** Substitute /k/	*gulay* (vegetable)	**NO EQUIVALENT** Substitute /k/ Learners use correct sound between two vowels	**NO EQUIVALENT** Substitute /k/
ŋ	*gus* (goose)	*angaw* (one million)	*baŋ* (room)	*tang* (gong) Sometimes add /k/ sound to the end
h	*hais* (to speak)	*hindi* (no)	*hal* (doing)	**NO EQUIVALENT** Substitute velar fricative /x/

International Phonetic Alphabet

	THE VOWELS OF ENGLISH			
IPA*	English	Spanish	Vietnamese	Cantonese
i	*beat*	*hijo* (son)	*di* (to go)	*si* (silk)
ɪ	*bit* Rare in other languages Usually confused with /i/ (*meat* vs. *mit*)	**NO EQUIVALENT** Substitute /ē/	**NO EQUIVALENT** Substitute /ē/	*sik* (color) Only occurs before velars Substitute /ē/
e	*bait* End of vowel diphthongized—tongue moves up to /ē/ or short *e* position	*eco* (echo)	*kê* (millet)	*se* (to lend)
ɛ	*bet* Rare in other languages Learners may have difficulty distinguishing /ā/ and /e/ (short *e*): *pain* vs. *pen*	**NO EQUIVALENT** Substitute /ā/	**NO EQUIVALENT** Substitute /ā/	*seŋ* (sound) Only occurs before velars; difficult to distinguish from /ā/ in all positions
æ	*bat* Rare in other languages Learners may have trouble getting the tongue farther forward in the mouth	**NO EQUIVALENT** Substitute mid central /u/ (short *u*) or low front tense /o/ (short *o*)	*ghe* (boat)	**NO EQUIVALENT** Hard to distinguish between /æ/ and /ā/
u	*boot*	*uva* (grape)	*mua* (to buy)	*fu* (husband)
ʊ	*could* Rare in other languages Learners may have difficulty distinguishing the vowel sounds in *wooed* vs. *wood*	**NO EQUIVALENT** Substitute long *u*	**NO EQUIVALENT** Substitute long *u* (high back unrounded)	*suk* (uncle) Only occurs before velars Difficult to distinguish from long *u* in all positions
o	*boat* End of vowel diphthongized—tongue moves up to long *u* or ʊ position	*ojo* (eye)	*cô* (aunt)	*so* (comb)
ɔ	*law*	**NO EQUIVALENT** Substitute long *o* or short *o* Substituting long *o* will cause confusion (*low* vs. *law*); substituting short *o* will not	*cá* (fish)	*hok* (shell) Only occurs before velars Difficult to distinguish from long *o* in all positions
ɑ	*hot*	*mal* (bad)	*con* (child)	*sa* (sand)
ɑʊ	*house* Diphthong	*pauta*	*dao* (knife)	*sau* (basket)
ɔɪ	*boy* Diphthong	*hoy* (today)	*ròi* (already)	*soi* (grill)
ɑɪ	*bite* Diphthong	*baile* (dance)	*hai* (two)	*sai* (to waste)
ə	*about* Most common vowel in English; only in unstressed syllables Learners may have difficulty keeping it very short	**NO EQUIVALENT** Substitute short *u* or the full vowel from the word's spelling	*mua* (to buy)	**NO EQUIVALENT**
ʌ	*cut* Similar to schwa /ə/	**NO EQUIVALENT** Substitute short *o*	*giờ* (time)	*san* (new)
ɝ	*bird* Difficult articulation, unusual in the world but common in American English Learners must bunch the tongue and constrict the throat	**NO EQUIVALENT** Substitute short *u* or /er/ with trill	**NO EQUIVALENT** Substitute /ɨ/	*hæ* (boot)

* *International Phonetic Alphabet*

THE VOWELS OF ENGLISH

IPA*	Hmong	Filipino	Korean	Mandarin
i	*ib* (one)	*ikaw* (you) This vowel is interchangeable with /ɪ/; hard for speakers to distinguish these	zɪːʃaŋ (market)	*ti* (ladder) Sometimes English /i/ can be produced shorter
ɪ	**NO EQUIVALENT** Substitute /ē/	*li*mampu (fifty) This vowel is interchangeable with /ē/; hard for speakers to distinguish these	**NO EQUIVALENT** Substitute /ē/	**NO EQUIVALENT**
e	*tes* (hand)	*sero* (zero)	be:da (to cut)	*te* (nervous) Sometimes substitute English schwa /ə/
ɛ	**NO EQUIVALENT** Substitute /ā/	*sero* (zero) This vowel interchanges with /ā/ like *bait*; not difficult for speakers to learn	thɛ:do (attitude)	**NO EQUIVALENT**
æ	**NO EQUIVALENT** Substitute short *e*	**NO EQUIVALENT** Substitute short *o* as in *hot*	**NO EQUIVALENT**	**NO EQUIVALENT** Substitute /ə/ or short *u*
u	*kub* (hot or gold)	*tunay* (actual) This vowel interchanges with vowel in *could*; not difficult for speakers to learn	zu:bag (watermelon)	*lu* (hut) Sometimes English long *u* can be produced shorter
ʊ	**NO EQUIVALENT** Substitute a sound like long *e* (mid central with lips slightly rounded)	*gu*mawa (act) This vowel interchanges with long *u* like *boot*; not difficult for speakers to learn	**NO EQUIVALENT**	**NO EQUIVALENT**
o	**NO EQUIVALENT**	*ubo* (cough)	bo:zu (salary)	*mo* (sword) This vowel is a little lower than English vowel
ɔ	*Yaj* (Yang clan name)	**NO EQUIVALENT** Spoken as short *o*, as in *hot*	**NO EQUIVALENT**	**NO EQUIVALENT** Substitute long *o*
ɑ	*mov* (cooked rice)	*talim* (blade)	ma:l (speech)	*ta* (he/she) Sometimes substitute back long *o* or *u*
ɑ ʊ	*plaub* (four)	*ikaw* (you)	**NO EQUIVALENT**	**NO EQUIVALENT**
ɔ ɪ	**NO EQUIVALENT**	*apoy* (fire)	**NO EQUIVALENT**	**NO EQUIVALENT**
ɑ ɪ	*qaib* (chicken)	*himatay* (faint)	**NO EQUIVALENT**	**NO EQUIVALENT**
ə	**NO EQUIVALENT**	**NO EQUIVALENT** Spoken as short *o*, as in *hot*	**NO EQUIVALENT** Difficult sound for learners	**NO EQUIVALENT**
ʌ	**NO EQUIVALENT**	**NO EQUIVALENT** Spoken as short *o*, as in *hot*	**NO EQUIVALENT**	**NO EQUIVALENT**
ɝ	**NO EQUIVALENT** Substitute diphthong /əɨ/	**NO EQUIVALENT** Spoken as many different vowels (depending on English spelling) plus tongue tap /ɾ/	**NO EQUIVALENT**	**NO EQUIVALENT**

* International Phonetic Alphabet

RESOURCES

Acknowledgments

Photographs

Photo locators denoted as follows: Top (T), Center (C), Bottom (B), Left (L), Right (R), Background (Bkgd)

4 blickwinkel/Alamy Images; **5(BL), 28, 30, 32** Celebration Press/Pearson Learning Group; **46** ©LOOK Die Bildagentur der Fotografen GmbH/Alamy; **88** Chris Wilson/Alamy; **89(TL), 92, 94, 96** HarperCollins Publishers; **89(BL), 112, 114, 116** Capstone Press; **130** Richard Cummins/Getty Images; **131(TL), 134, 136, 138** Simon & Schuster; **131(BL), 154, 156, 158** Heinemann.